EVERYMAN, I will go with thee,

and be thy guide,

In thy most need to go by thy side

Hindu Scriptures

SELECTED, TRANSLATED
AND INTRODUCED BY

R. C. ZAEHNER

*Spalding Professor of Eastern Religions
and Ethics at the University of Oxford,
Fellow of All Souls College*

DENT: LONDON
EVERYMAN'S LIBRARY
DUTTON: NEW YORK

NO. *944*

SBN: 460 00944 3

INTRODUCTION

SINCE 1938 Everyman's Library has included a volume entitled *Hindu Scriptures*, and when the present author was invited to produce a new edition of this volume he was faced with the alternatives of either retaining the previous selection from the vast corpus of Hindu sacred texts in the translations selected by the former editor, or of making a new selection and using already existing translations, or of making his own selection and translation. In the event it was the last alternative he chose.

There seemed to be good reasons for this, for although the 'canon' of Hindu Scripture known collectively as the *Veda* is vast, it is generally agreed that only a relatively small portion of it is of abiding importance and interest; and this portion is the latest in time,—what is called the *Vedānta* or 'End of the Veda', which means those speculative treatises in prose and verse known as the *Upanishads*. In addition there is the *Bhagavad-Gītā*, which actually falls outside the canon but which has from the earliest times been held to rank equally with it in authority. Obviously, then, the Upanishads and the Gītā would have to take pride of place in any new edition of the volume.

The earlier edition contained thirty hymns from the *Rig-Veda*, the two long prose Upanishads almost *in toto*, three shorter verse ones and the Bhagavad-Gītā. This meant that eight of the 'classical' Upanishads were totally unrepresented, though both in matter and in quality some of them at least are of the greatest importance and of striking beauty.

The balance of this selection seemed to be wrong, as the previous edition contained much matter (particularly in the two long prose Upanishads) that is frankly incomprehensible to modern readers. Indeed the former editor, Nicol Macnicol, went so far as to say that 'the Upanishads are themselves witnesses how foolish and how futile their thinking often was as well as sometimes so wise and so discerning' (pp. xviii–xix). Or, in the late Professor Edgerton's words, 'the dry bones of the Vedic ritual cult frequently rattle about in them in quite a noisy fashion and seriously strain our patience and our charity'.[1] It is these passages which even the most ardent admirers of the Upanishads (among whom I count myself) find embarrassing, and I have not hesitated to eliminate them. To compensate I have included all

---

[1] Franklin Edgerton, *The Beginnings of Indian Philosophy*, p. 28.

the shorter Upanishads *in toto* and all (perhaps more than all) that is essential and of abiding value from the rest.

The 'canon' of Hindu Scripture, as we have seen, is called the *Veda*, a Sanskrit word which means 'knowledge' or 'wisdom'. There are in fact four Vedas—the *Rig-Veda* or 'Veda of hymns', the *Sāma-Veda* or 'Veda of chants', the *Yajur-Veda* or 'Veda of sacrifice' and the *Atharva-Veda*, the 'Veda of Atharvan', which is in fact largely composed of magic charms. The Atharva-Veda is later in date than the other three, since even in later times *three* Vedas are usually spoken of, not four.

Each Veda again is divided into three strata—*saṁhitā*, 'collections' of hymns, chants and sacrificial formulas as the case may be; *brāhmana*, expository texts dealing with the minutiae of the sacrifice; and *upanishad*, speculative treatises which began to turn their back on ritual and to speculate on the nature of the universe, on the nature of the inner 'self' of man, and the relationship between the two. It is these Upanishads, or parts of them, that compose the bulk of this book.

The religion of the Rig-Veda is related and comparable to the religions of the other Indo-European peoples—those of Greece and Rome, for example. It starts by being polytheistic, but it does not develop into the modified monotheism that we find in Greece and Rome, with one god—Zeus or Jupiter—emerging as the undisputed ruler of the rest; it takes a very different turning and develops into something wholly Indian, something quite different from the religion of any of the other Indo-European peoples. None of the gods—not even Indra, to whom nearly a quarter of the hymns of the Rig-Veda are dedicated—ever reaches the supreme distinction of being the undisputed king of gods and men. Rather they tend to coalesce the one into the other, and in so doing they lose their identity and indeed their relevance. The supreme principle is felt to be one, and it does not matter very much what you call it: 'They call it Indra, Mitra, Varuna, Fire; or again it is the celestial bird Garutmat. What is but one the wise call [by] manifold [names]. They call it Fire, Yama, Mātariśvan' (*Rig-Veda*, I. clxiv. 46).

At the end of the Rig-Vedic period, then, the gods lose their importance, and new functional deities appear whose names describe the creative functions they had to perform. Thus we have Prajāpati, 'Lord of creatures', who becomes the creator-god *par excellence*; Viśvakarman, the 'Maker of all'; Brihaspati or Brahmanaspati, the 'Lord of *brahman*, the sacred word and power'; and finally Purusha, 'Primal Man', whose sacrificial death gives rise to creation in all its multiplicity. It is these new gods and the hymns dedicated to them which appear in the tenth and last book of the Rig-Veda that point forward to the pantheistic monism that is so characteristic of the Upanishads; and

Hinduism right up to the present day is pervaded by their spirit.

The latest of the four Vedas, the Atharva-Veda, is, as we have seen, largely composed of magical texts and charms, but here and there we find cosmological hymns which anticipate the Upanishads,—hymns to Skambha, the 'Support', who is seen as the first principle which is both the material and efficient cause of the universe, to Prāna, the 'Breath of Life', to Vāc, the 'Word', and so on. Four of these, though thoroughly obscure in places, we have included in this collection.

From the Rig-Veda itself, apart from the 'seminal' hymns devoted to the new functional gods, we have included only three —and these again because they look forward to the 'Hindu' future rather than back to the Indo-European past. The first, a hymn to the sky-god, Varuna, is included because it anticipates two ideas that were later to become important—the cosmic tree with its roots in heaven, and the 'fetters' of sin from which the god is implored to release his devotee. These 'fetters' reappear in the Śvetāśvatara Upanishad (pp. 203-17), but there they are no longer the fetters of sin but the fetters of human life itself from which the suppliant seeks to be freed; and the god is no longer Varuna, but Rudra-Śiva, who, by this time and by a process that is anything but clear, had risen from the status of a quite minor deity to that of supreme pre-eminence: he had become the supreme Being, creator and sustainer of the universe. And it is for this reason that we have included one of the hymns addressed to him in the Rig-Veda, as well as a hymn to Vishnu, who also rose to the rank of supreme Being among his devotees and appears as such in his incarnation as Krishna in the Bhagavad-Gītā.

By the time of the Brāhmanas the emphasis has shifted from the gods to the sacrifice. Sacrifice (which was immensely elaborate) had by now become all-important, for the sacrifice represented the creative process—in a sense it *was* the creative process—and were it to cease the world itself would come to an end; for the sacrifice and the world are one, and the rapport between the two is so close that one can speak of elements of the sacrifice as being identical with natural phenomena in the cosmos. As Edgerton rightly emphasizes, 'a very striking feature of these works is their passion for identification of one thing with another, on the slenderest possible basis; indeed, often on no basis at all that we can discover'.[1] Characteristic is the opening chapter of the *Brihadāranyaka* Upanishad which, like so much similar material that is more characteristic of the Brāhmanas than of the Upanishads proper, we have omitted from our present selection:

---

[1] Ibid., p. 21.

The dawn (it says) is the head of the sacrificial horse; the sun its eye, the wind its breath, universal fire its mouth. The year is the self of the sacrificial horse, the sky its back, the atmosphere its belly,

and so on.

These identifications, endlessly repeated and endlessly varied, though they seem grotesque to us, are nevertheless the background against which the pantheistic monism of the Upanishads must be seen.

THE UPANISHADS

It has been pointed out time and again that the basic doctrine of the Upanishads is the identification of *Brahman* with *Ātman*, that is to say, of the changeless essence that upholds the universe (for *Brahman*, the 'sacred word and power', had by now come to mean this) with the same changeless essence that indwells the human spirit. This identification is rarely complete, and it would be quite false to ascribe to the Upanishads as a whole the later absolute monism of Śankara and his school according to which Brahman-Ātman alone exists and the phenomenal world and empirical lives as ordinarily lived by men and women are, from the absolute point of view, illusory (*māyā*). In point of fact the word *māyā* occurs very rarely in the Upanishads, and when it does so it is best translated as 'uncanny power' (exercised by a god) or 'creative power'. Indeed, in one passage (p. 211) it is roundly identified with 'Nature', which is real enough, though eternally changing, as against Brahman which, being absolutely real, is changeless Being.

There are, it is true, passages which are wholly monist, like the following (p. 121):

This Infinite is below, it is above, it is to the west, to the east, to the south, to the north. Truly it is this whole universe.
Next the teaching concerning the ego.
I am below, I am above, I am to the west, to the east, to the south, to the north. Truly I am this whole universe.
Next the teaching concerning the Self.
The Self is below, the Self is above, the Self is to the west, to the east, to the south, to the north. Truly the Self is this whole universe.

Now this may not sound particularly sensible to the modern mind, but it does express what so-called 'nature mystics' experience and try to describe. The barrier between subject and object seems magically to melt away, and experiencer, experience and the thing experienced seem to merge into one single whole: the One indwelling the human spirit realizes its own identity with the same One which is the unchanging ground of the phenomenal world outside. This is the lesson tirelessly rammed home in the Upanishads: it is an expression of something that cannot be logically formulated, but can only be hinted at in paradox:

> Unmoving—One—swifter than thought—
> The gods could not seize hold of it as it sped before them:
> Standing, It overtakes all others as they run;
> In It the wind incites activity.
>
> It moves. It moves not.
> It is far, yet It is near:
> It is within this whole universe,
> And yet It is without it.   (p. 165.)

This indescribable reality, the 'Real of the real' (p. 44) reveals itself in a flash; the astonished mortal realizes himself as immortal, unconditioned, beyond space and time and causation; and so 'whoso knows that he is Brahman, becomes this whole [universe]. Even the gods have not the power to cause him to un-Be, for he becomes their own self' (p. 37).

To 'become Brahman' is to merge into infinite Being in which all sense of 'ego', all sense of separate individuality is lost:

> As rivers flowing [downwards] find their home
> In the ocean, leaving name and form behind,
> So does the man who knows, from name and form released,
> Draw near to the divine Person who is beyond the beyond.
>   (p. 192.)

Who is this divine 'Person'? The idea first appears in a late hymn of the Rig-Veda (p. 8) where creation is depicted as the dismemberment of Primal Man (or 'male Person', Sanskrit *purusha*): he is the One and the All, but he is not just the sum total of the universe together with the spirit that pervades it, for—

> All beings form a quarter of him,
> Three-quarters are the immortal in heaven.   (p. 9.)

'Person', Brahman (which I have nearly always left untranslated) and Ātman ('Self') are, then, the three terms used more or less indiscriminately to represent the highest principle whether conceived of as the spirit which indwells and controls the world or as that same spirit indwelling the heart of man. Is this spirit a personal God or an impersonal Absolute?

In the Upanishads it is both. It is an ocean into which the soul merges when it is released from the bondage of this life, a fire from which the phenomenal world emerges like sparks, but it is also the 'Inner Controller', Lord, King and God. As the 'Imperishable' it can only be described by negatives, but it is at the behest of this same Imperishable that 'sky and earth are held apart and so abide' (p. 56). It is, in fact, what we in the West understand by God both in his unfathomable timelessness from which all words must recoil and in his creative activity.

There is, however, one fundamental difference between the Brahman, Self and Person of the Upanishads and the Judaeo-Christian God: in Hinduism there is no creation *ex nihilo*. God or Brahman is always the material as well as the efficient cause of creation. He emanates the universe out of his own substance and then re-enters it as its indwelling Spirit. Hence I have, as far as possible, avoided the words 'create' and 'creator' as these might make a false impression.

One of the things in the Upanishads that might strike the reader as odd is their constant preoccupation with dream and dreamless sleep. Contrary to the western way of thinking, dream is regarded as more real than waking life, and dreamless sleep than dream; for although in dreamless sleep there can scarcely be consciousness, it is nevertheless considered to be a form of bliss which itself is a form of the absolute Brahman and the nearest approach to release from empirical life obtainable on earth.

Why, one might ask, this obsession with escaping from this world of space and time? The answer is that the authors of the Upanishads, along with the Buddhists, came to regard human life as being basically miserable, and this was due to the fact that in the Upanishadic period itself the theory of *karma*, and the transmigration of souls that goes with it, had gradually come to be accepted as a self-evident fact of existence. *Karma(n)* is a Sanskrit word meaning simply 'act', 'deed', or 'work'. The 'theory' of *karma*, if we may call it such, is that every action must produce its inevitable 'fruit'; good actions produce good fruit, evil actions evil fruit. Good actions may win you a blissful existence in one of the heavens, evil actions will land you in one of the hells. Ultimately, however, you will return to this world. If you have been good, you will be reborn in a family of Brāhmans, maybe; if you have been bad, you may be unlucky enough to be reborn as a pig or a worm. There is no escaping this 'bondage' of 'works'. Hence the necessity for 'release' (*moksha, mukti*), and hence the speculations on the states of sleep, for in deep dreamless sleep action of any sort is at its lowest ebb and the sleeper is as near as he can be to an eternal state of being—to Brahman—as in ordinary circumstances it is possible to be. Yet the state of dreamless sleep can scarcely be the same as the felt identity of what is most inward in the individual human being, the Ātman or Self, with the power that, though unchanging itself, supports the entire universe—that power which, because it is eternal and changeless, brings release from all 'works' and

from all that takes place in the phenomenal world: for in dreamless sleep one is conscious of nothing. The man in this condition,
the *Chāndogya* Upanishad says, 'has no present knowledge of
[him]self, so that he could say, "This I am", nor, for that matter,
[has he any knowledge] of these creatures [here]. Surely he
might as well be a man annihilated. I see nothing enjoyable in
this' (p. 130). So, one of the latest Upanishads, the *Māndūkya*,
says, there must be a fourth state beyond the waking, dreaming
and dreamless states in which the absolute oneness of Brahman-
Ātman is consciously realized:

> [This is] conscious of neither within nor without, nor of both
> together, not a mass of wisdom, neither wise nor unwise, unseen, one
> with whom there is no commerce, impalpable, devoid of distinguishing
> mark, unthinkable, indescribable, its essence the firm conviction of the
> oneness of itself, bringing all development to an end, tranquil and mild,
> devoid of duality, such do they deem this fourth to be. That is the Self:
> that is what should be known.   (p. 201.)

This state is beyond all dualities and therefore beyond the
creator-God by whatever name he is known. Indeed in the
macrocosm the creator-God corresponds to the state of dreamless sleep which, in the microcosm, man, is seen as both the
material and the efficient cause of both dream and the waking
state, just as 'God' is both the material and the efficient cause of
the phenomenal world. Hence, according to the *Māndūkya*
Upanishad, 'God' is ultimately irrelevant because from the
absolute point of view he does not exist.

This statement of an *absolutely* monist position, according to
which nothing at all exists except the One, is peculiar to the
Māndūkya Upanishad. The 'One' is not the 'All' as it usually is
in the earlier Upanishads, because the 'All' means plurality and
this must be totally denied to the One. In the 'fourth state' there
is experience of oneness only beyond space and time and action
(*karma*) of any kind.

For the *Chāndogya* Upanishad, however, the 'fourth state' is
very different indeed. What it envisages is not an absolutely
motionless oneness but a true 'liberation' or 'release' from space
and time, a form of existence that can only be compared to the
wind in its freedom to roam at will, unhampered by material
things. Brahman, indeed, is frequently identified with the breath
of life (*prāṇa = spiritus*, breath) or with infinite space. It is an
eternal mode of existence in which, paradoxically, timelessness
does not preclude freedom to move in time and spacelessness
does not preclude freedom to roam at will in space. These are
deep waters indeed, and no words can adequately describe this
state of 'liberation'. So let the *Chāndogya* Upanishad speak for
itself:

This body is mortal [it says], held in the grip of death. Yet it is the dwelling-place of the immortal, incorporeal self. [And this self,] while still in the body, is held in the grip of pleasure and pain; and so long as it remains in the body there is no means of ridding it of pleasure and pain. But once it is freed from the body, pleasure and pain cannot [so much as] touch it.

The wind has no body. Clouds, thunder and lightning—these too have no body. So, just as these arise from [the broad expanse of] space up there and plunge into the highest light, revealing themselves each in its own form, so too does this deep serenity arise out of this body and plunge into the highest light, revealing itself in its own form. Such a one is a superman; and there he roves around, laughing, playing, taking his pleasure with women, chariots, or friends and remembering no more that excrescence [which was] his body.   (p. 130.)

This is the extreme pluralist view, and between this and the wholly monistic view every gradation and nuance will be found in the Upanishads. Brahman is both a state of Being—is indeed Being itself—and the source of multiplicity and manifestation; He or It, then, is both One and many, and, seen from the point of view of ordinary mortals who have not yet tasted his immortality, He is the one supreme Lord. He is the real core and centre of both the human being or microcosm and the universe or macrocosm, yet He is also their ruler:

This Self indeed is Lord of all contingent beings, king of all beings. Just as the spokes of a wheel are together fixed on to the hub and felly, so are all contingent beings, all gods, all worlds, all vital breaths and all these selves together fixed in this Self.   (p. 49.)

The supreme principle, as we have seen, is indifferently referred to as *Brahman* (originally 'sacred word' or 'sacred power'), *Ātman* ('Self') or *Purusha* ('male Person'). The words *Ātman* and *Purusha*, however, are also used to mean the individual 'self', and this leads to considerable confusion, since we can rarely be sure whether any particular passage envisages a plurality of 'selves' or only one, nor can we be sure whether—when, for example, the *Mundaka* Upanishad speaks of Brahman, Ātman and Purusha—it makes a distinction between them or not. In that Upanishad (p. 191) the Self (*ātman*) can be won only by him whom He elects, and the 'self' so elected then enters the Brahman-home and 'draws near to the divine Person who is beyond the beyond'. Here it seems that the 'Person', that is, the personal God, is elevated above Brahman in so far as Brahman means (as it does in those passages which speak of 'becoming Brahman') an eternal mode of existence which is at the same time God's mode of existence.

This tendency to elevate the personal God above the usually impersonal Brahman becomes even more marked in the *Katha*

Upanishad. In the *Śvetāśvatara* the process has gone further still, and the ancient Rig-Vedic god, Rudra-Śiva, now emerges as the supreme ruler of the universe, ruler of both the imperishable and the perishable modes of being (p. 204). The 'imperishable' is Brahman, the 'perishable' the whole phenomenal world.

In these later verse Upanishads a new conception of the cosmos makes itself felt—that of the philosophic or rather psychological school called Sāṃkhya-Yoga. According to this school of thought existence is neatly divided up between two separate and totally distinct modes of being. On the one hand you have a plurality of *purushas*, 'persons', 'spirits' or 'souls', the essence of which is timeless being. On the other hand you have *prakriti* or Nature from which the whole phenomenal world derives. Originally Nature is in a state of pure equilibrium and rest—it is as yet 'unmanifest'. Yet even in this 'unmanifest' state Nature is made up of three 'constituents' called 'Goodness' (*sattva*), 'Passion' or 'Energy' (*rajas*) and 'Darkness' (*tamas*). When Nature begins to evolve, the *purushas*, for no apparent reason, become involved in Nature; in other words, they become incarnate in men and other living creatures. This is regarded as a terrible misfortune; they are ensnared in space and time and the world of action (*karma*). Each *purusha* now indwells a psychophysical organism which develops out of 'unmanifest' Nature, and this organism in turn is equipped with faculties—soul (*buddhi*, see below, p. xxi), ego, mind, five organs of sense and five organs of action. Through all of these the three constituents of Nature act, that is to say, they involve the *purushas* in an endless cycle of works (*karma*) which, as we have seen, bind the *purusha* or, in the terminology more usual to the Upanishads, the 'self' or *ātman* to this world of never-ending coming to be and passing away. The self's only true salvation consists in its return to its original state, which is one of timeless bliss in perfect isolation both from Nature and also from all other *purushas*.

Most of this is taken over in the later Upanishads, and very much more markedly in the Bhagavad-Gītā; but whereas in the Sāṃkhya system proper there is no God and no Brahman, this is emphatically not so in the later Upanishads and the Gītā. The *Śvetāśvatara* Upanishad accepts unreservedly the two orders of existence, that of becoming and that of pure Being, but places the supreme God above both. Brahman is still the pantheistic indwelling God which is pure Being on the one hand and the source of all becoming on the other; but God, in this case Rudra-Śiva, transcends and controls both orders of existence. Here self, Brahman and God are distinguished: by realizing 'self' as being eternal and 'isolated' as in the Sāṅkhya system the 'embodied soul' knows Brahman since Brahman as eternal Being is the ambience in which the 'self' moves, and by knowing

Brahman in its essence he comes to know God who is beyond all essences, and by knowing Him thus he is set free from all the fetters of mortal life:

> Even as a mirror with dirt begrimed
> Shines brightly once it is well cleaned,
> So too the embodied soul, once it has seen
> Self as it really is,
> Becomes one, its goal achieved, from sorrow free.
>
> When by means of self as it really is as with a lamp
> An integrated man sees Brahman as It really is,
> [Then will he know] the unborn, undying God, the Pure,
> Beyond all essences as they really are,
> [And] knowing Him, from all fetters he'll be freed.
>
> (p. 207.)

It will be noticed that even in this fully theistic Upanishad 'liberation' is not interpreted as 'union with God'; it is having access to Brahman (VI. 10), being merged in Brahman (I. 7), 'isolation' (I. 11) as in the Sāṁkhya system, or it is 'to know [God] with the heart and mind as dwelling in the heart (IV. 20)'. It is to experience God's immanence in the human heart, but it is not yet felt to be union with a *transcendent* God who is 'beyond all essences as they really are'.

The earlier Upanishads' principal preoccupation was with the nature of Brahman as the eternal ground of the universe. It was intuitively realized that this Brahman was identical with the inmost self of man. In the later ones (*Katha* (VI. 11), *Śvetāśvatara* (II. 8–17), and *Maitri* (VI. 18 ff.)) we learn about the *method* used to bring this realization about. This is the technique called *Yoga*, and if it is properly carried out it will, under the guidance of a competent spiritual director, lead to complete liberation from this conditioned world and the experience of timeless bliss—'becoming Brahman', as the Upanishads put it, or 'isolation' from all created things, as the Sāṁkhya phrases it. This is something that can be achieved by unaided human effort, and, with but a few exceptions, the Upanishads say that it can be achieved by human effort alone.

To sum up: the Upanishads investigate the nature of reality and their main conclusion is that in both the universe at large and in the individual human being there is a ground of pure Being which is impervious to change. To realize this Being in oneself means salvation. Once this is done, re-birth and re-death are done away with, and man realizes himself as at least participating in eternal Being. Even when he comes to a knowledge of God as being transcendent as well as immanent, he does not interpret this realization as union with God. The immanent God is everything, the transcendant largely irrelevant. This is the position as we find it at the end of the Upanishadic period, and it is from here that the Bhagavad-Gītā takes on.

THE BHAGAVAD-GĪTĀ

Unlike the Upanishads, the Bhagavad-Gītā does not form part of the Veda which Hindus believe to have been breathed forth by the deity in an immemorial past and 'heard' by ancient seers who then passed it on from father to son by oral tradition. It does not, then, in a legalistic sense have quite the same authority as the Upanishads which form the end of the Veda. In actual fact it is not only the most popular but the most commented on of all the sacred texts of Hinduism. There is scarcely a sage or saint in India who has not commented on this most influential of all Hindu religious texts, from the time of Śankara in the ninth century to Vinoba Bhave of our own day.

The Bhagavad-Gītā forms a minute part of India's enormous epic, the *Mahābhārata*. The Mahābhārata is an account of the origins, the actual course and the aftermath of a great war between the five sons of Pāndu and their cousins, the hundred sons of Dhritarāshtra. The kingdom of the sons of Pāndu has been usurped by the sons of Dhritarāshtra, but the former agree to accept only five villages as a token payment for the usurped kingdom. This offer Duryodhana, the eldest of the sons of Dhritarāshtra, contemptuously turns down, even after Krishna, who is God (Vishnu) incarnate and the close friend of the sons of Pāndu, has made one last desperate effort to keep the peace. The war then is about to begin, and Krishna, who had elected to act as the charioteer of Arjuna, the third of the five brothers, is now driving the latter into battle. Krishna is determined to finish off the sons of Dhritarāshtra and their allies once and for all, but at the last moment Arjuna's nerve fails him because he is appalled at the carnage he knows must ensue among his kinsmen. Krishna is greatly distressed by his friend's sudden *volte-face* and proceeds to tell him why he should and must fight. The Bhagavad-Gītā is the dialogue between the two on this momentous occasion, and it is reported to the blind king, Dhritarāshtra, by his minister Sanjaya, who overhears the dialogue by miraculous means.

This, then, is the setting of the poem, but Krishna discourses on topics so remote from the immediate situation that scholars have thought that the original Gītā must have been very much shorter than it is now. This is pure speculation, and we need not let it detain us now.

The ostensible cause of Krishna's discourse, then, is to persuade Arjuna to fight. In the course of doing so, however,

Krishna resumes most of the doctrines that we have already met with in the Upanishads, as well as some Buddhistic ideas such as *nirvāna*, the Buddhist term for what the Upanishads call 'liberation' or 'release' from mortal existence. To all this, however, he adds something that is quite new, namely the message that the transcendent God (Himself) is to be adored, loved and worshipped. This, it is usually alleged, is one of the three 'ways' or 'yogas' taught in the Gītā—the way of *bhakti*, or 'loving devotion', as opposed to the ways of 'knowledge' or contemplation, and of action (*karma*). On reading and re-reading the Gītā, however, it seems each time more clear to me that, although a distinction is made between the contemplative and the active life, there is no hard and fast line that divides them from the life of love and devotion to God. It is love, on the contrary, that brings both to fruition. This comes out only gradually, but on each repetition it is made clearer that to 'become Brahman' or to 'reach Nirvāna', which is the aim of both the Upanishads and the Buddhists, is not enough; it must be supplemented by an active love of God.

The Gītā falls naturally into three distinct parts. Chapters I–VI are concerned mainly with the nature of the self, its timeless quality, and its ultimate identity with Brahman here used in the Buddhistic sense of the word and meaning '*static* timeless bliss' (e.g. II. 72). Once this is achieved, then 'works' (*karma*) are transcended:

> Nay, let a man take pleasure in self alone,
> In self his satisfaction find,
> In self alone content:
> [Let him do this, for then]
> There is naught he needs to do. (III. 17.)

The Upanishadic idea is accepted, but Krishna immediately goes on to say that a man must even so perform his caste duty (in Arjuna's case go to war) because God himself is tirelessly engaged in works in order to keep the world in being. Man, then, must do his caste duty and do it well, for by so doing he will resemble God not only in his timeless essence (Brahman), but also in his activity. At the same time—and this is drummed in again and again,—he must never feel attachment to the goal (even if it is a good one) to which his actions tend. It is, then, meaningless to speak of *karma-yoga* or 'Yoga of works' in the context of the Gītā. Works can never bring salvation; this comes only from a total detachment from what you are doing and what you are doing that thing *for* (IV. 19). This is the way God operates, and man must imitate him in this, for Vishnu's various incarnations have the purpose of re-establishing righteousness (*dharma*) on earth, yet without being in any way committed to or affected by the process (IV. 7–8). Moreover, right living itself will lead a man on to wisdom which means the eternal state of Being which is Brahman. This is a state of complete detachment in which works have no more relevance. In it:

> Attachments gone, deliverance won,
> His thoughts are fixed on wisdom:
> He works for sacrifice [alone],
> And all the work [he ever did]
>   Entirely melts away. . . .   (IV. 23.)

It cannot be denied that there is a contradiction here. Works should be done in a spirit of complete detachment, but it is the detachment that counts, not the works. Detachment leads to 'liberation', and the self, once liberated, sees the essential irrelevance of works; and yet Krishna, in a supreme paradox, goes on to say:

> Let a man in spiritual exercise (*yoga*) all works renounce,
> Let him by wisdom his doubts dispel,
>   Let him be himself, and then
> [Whatever] his works [may be], they will never bind him [more].
>
> And so, [take up] the sword of wisdom, cut
> This doubt of thine, unwisdom's child,
> Still lurking in the heart:
> Prepare for action (*yoga*) [now], stand up!   (IV. 41–2.)

Krishna here uses the word *yoga* in two senses; in the first verse he uses it in the sense of what *we* understand by Yoga, that is, 'spiritual exercise', and in the second verse he uses it in its mundane sense—*yogam ātiṣṭha*, which could be exactly translated in colloquial English as 'Get cracking'. And yet in the next chapter we are again told that detachment is the one virtue that ultimately leads to the Nirvāna of Brahman, and this in turn enables the aspirant to know Krishna, the personal God, as 'Lord of all the worlds, friend of all contingent beings'. This is new, for obviously Krishna is making a distinction between himself and the Nirvāna of Brahman. The transition between the older idea of 'becoming Brahman' and partaking in (for that is the root meaning of *bhakti*) the essence of the personal God has now been made. In chapter VI. 15 we are shown that there is no contradiction between the two ideas. 'Becoming Brahman' means the integration (*yuj-*, 'uniting', from the same root as *yoga*) of all a man's faculties into the immortal 'self': this is Nirvāna, and Nirvāna in the Gītā, so far from being a state independent of any personal God as it is with the Buddhists, in fact subsists in Him.

> Thus let the Yogin ever integrate [him]self,
>   His mind restrained;
> Then will he approach that peace
> Which has Nirvāna as its end
> And which subsists in Me.   (VI. 15.)

> With self by Yoga integrated, [now] he sees
>   The self in all beings standing,
>   All beings in the self:
> The same in everything he sees.

> Who sees Me everywhere,
> Who sees the All in Me,
> For him I am not lost,
> Nor is he lost for Me.

> Who loves and worships Me, embracing unity,
>   As abiding in all beings,
>   In whatever state he be,
> That man of Yoga abides in Me.   (VI. 29-31.)

The point of this seems obvious, but it is all too frequently missed. The 'integrated' man who feels himself to be omnipresent, who has 'become Brahman', *thinks* he has won a 'prize beyond all others' (VI. 22). It is only when he sees that his newly won omnipresence is dependent on God's omnipresence, that he comes to love and worship God as the author of his new, timeless mode of being, and so he 'abides in' Him. To integrate oneself and thereby to realize one's own eternity is not the end, but the only valid beginning, of true *bhakti*—true love and true worship. This comes out with unmistakable clarity at the end of this chapter:

> But of all the men of Yoga
> The man of faith who loves and honours Me,
>   *His inmost self absorbed in Me,*
> He is the most fully integrated: this do I believe.

From this point on, 'liberation' is no longer regarded as the ultimate goal. Total detachment from the world is still rigorously insisted on, for this brings one to the Nirvāna of Brahman, but this is not enough; for the very first words of the next chapter are: '*Attach* thy mind to Me.' God must not only be experienced in his timeless eternity, He must be actively loved and worshipped; and this brings us to the second section of the Gītā (chapters VII–XI) which tells us of the positive qualities of God and culminates in the terrific theophany of chapter XI which shakes Arjuna's 'inmost self' out of any complacency it might have had of resting securely in the Nirvāna of Brahman.

This is the climax of the poem, and from now on Arjuna, as yet
not wholly convinced that he must fight, submits. He has no
choice, for he has seen God in his awful majesty and he knows
that he is powerless against his will; for Krishna tells him that
the sons of Dhritarāshtra are as good as killed already since this
is his irrevocable decision: Arjuna himself can be no more than
the occasion. The lesson of the theophany is that while the still,
static, eternal state of Brahman can be gained by anyone who can
completely detach himself from this world, the fulness of the god-
head as it is tirelessly active in time can only be seen and experienced by God's loving devotees:

> By worship of love addressed to Me alone
>   Can I be known and seen
> In such a form and as I really am:
> [So can my lovers] enter into Me.   (XI. 54.)

The tremendous theophany over, it must be admitted that the
rest of the poem is an anticlimax. Old themes are again taken up
and further elaborated. Chapter XII tells us for the first time the
kind of man God particularly loves, while chapters XIII–XVII
contain matter predominantly based on Sāṁkhya thinking, a
great deal of analysis of how the 'constituents' of Nature operate
in practice, and the reiterated conclusion that Krishna, the
personal God, stands higher than the Sāṁkhya *purushas* and
Nature, and higher too than the Brahman of the Upanishads.
For in God the eternal Being, which is Brahman, and righteous
living (*dharma*), as it must be practised while man is still in time,
meet:

> For I am the base supporting Brahman,
> Immortal [Brahman] Which knows no change,
> [Supporting too] the eternal law of righteousness
>   And absolute beatitude.   (XIV. 27.)

Krishna has now nothing to teach until we reach the very end
of this wonderful poem: then he reveals what to a Christian is
taken for granted but which is so rarely really understood,
namely, that God loves man. Man, however, can only love God
as He deserves to be loved if and when he has passed into
eternity, only when he has 'become Brahman'. And so He sums
up his whole teaching in these words:

> Let him give up all thought of 'I', force, pride,
> Desire and hatred and possessiveness,
> Let him not think of anything as 'mine', at peace—
> [If he does this,] to becoming Brahman he's conformed.

Brahman become, with self serene,
    He grieves not nor desires;
The same to all contingent beings,
He gains the highest love and loyalty to Me.

By love and loyalty he comes to know Me as I really am,
    How great I am and who;
And once he knows Me as I am,
    He enters [Me] forthwith.   (xvIII. 53–5.)

And then, right at the end, comes the crowning mystery:

And now again give ear to this my all-highest Word,
    Of all the most mysterious:
        'I love thee well.'
Therefore will I tell thee thy salvation.

Bear Me in mind, love Me and worship Me,
Sacrifice, prostrate thyself to Me:
So shalt thou come to Me, I promise thee
Truly, for thou art dear to Me.   (xvIII. 64–5.)

This is the final message of the Gītā. The ideal of 'liberation'
common to the Upanishads and the Buddhists is not enough: it
must be consummated in a total loving self-surrender to Krishna,
the personal God.

THE TRANSLATION

The present translation differs considerably from that
previously published in Everyman's Library. I can only hope that
it is an improvement. I have tried to vary the style in accordance
with the individual text translated, but, so far as I have been able,
I have endeavoured to give a faithful rendering of the Sanskrit
without being literalistic to the point of being incomprehensible
— a defect apparent in some modern translations of the Upanishads and the Bhagavad-Gītā. In the translations of the hymns
from the Rig-Veda and Atharva-Veda, of the verse Upanishads
and the Gītā I have made my translation as metrical as I could.
The charitable will, I hope, read it as free verse. On no occasion,
however (I hope), have I allowed questions of style to obscure
what I conceive to be the true meaning of the texts. For the prose
Upanishads I have adopted an almost colloquial style, for that
seemed to me the most suitable to their *genre.*
When there are important variants I have noted them in a
footnote. Sometimes, again, the Sanskrit can be rendered in
different ways, in which case I have put the alternative translation
in a footnote. For instance, in Bhagavad-Gītā xIII. 12 the same

Sanskrit words can be read to mean 'All-highest Brahman is it called', or as, 'It is called Brahman, dependent on Me'. Theologically it makes a great deal of difference which we read. I hope that none of these theologically important alternative translations have been overlooked.

I have not tried to render key Sanskrit words by one single English equivalent, as this seems to me quite unrealistic. Very occasionally I leave the Sanskrit word untranslated if, in my opinion, there simply is no adequate English equivalent. The most obvious example of this is the word *brahman* itself. I could have adopted this rather unsatisfactory procedure for other key concepts such as *purusha*, *ātman*, *yoga*, *bhakti* and *dharma*, but I have not done so, preferring to add the word in brackets after the individual translation. *Purusha* I sometimes translate as 'man', but when it refers to the supreme Being I have usually retained 'Person', since Christian readers will already be familiar with the 'Persons' of the Holy Trinity.

Yoga has a vast number of meanings, and in chapters v and vi of the Gītā particularly these meanings and all the nuances between them are most skilfully played on, as are the meanings of *yukta*, the past participle of the same root. Thus *yoga* can mean 'practice, spiritual exercise, integration, moderation, method, power', to quote only the most obvious meanings. In each case I have tried to choose the appropriate one. *Bhakti* too has a wide variety of meanings, prominent among which are 'loyalty, devotion, worship, love'. Frequently I have combined two of these words to render the idea, and I have followed this practice (occasionally) with other words too. *Ātman* I have nearly always translated as 'self' or 'Self' depending on context, or when it is simply a reflexive pronoun, as '[him]self', the square brackets being used to distinguish it from other reflexive pronouns which do not have the theological and philosophic connotations possessed by the word *ātman*.

Ātman, then, appears as 'self', not as 'soul', and this is because there is another key concept that corresponds fairly exactly to our word 'soul', and that is *buddhi*. For this most translators use such words as 'intellect' or 'intelligence', and this, of course, is what it often means; but the concept seems to be broader than this, for in Bhagavad-Gītā II. 41 we read that 'the essence of *buddhi* is will'. *Buddhi*, then, is the combination of intellect and will, and this is almost exactly what Catholic Christianity understands by 'soul'; and this is how I translate it in the later Upanishads and the Gītā. For in our Western tradition it is the soul that is the responsible and perduring element in man: it is the soul that is saved or damned. This is equally true of *buddhi*; it is man's highest faculty and ultimately responsible for whether a man continues to be reborn or is finally released. It is not the 'self', or *ātman*, which has no responsibilities and is a mere onlooker at the drama of 'works' enacted in this world. *Buddhi* and *ātman* are nevertheless closely interconnected, and in the Upanishads and Gītā it is never quite certain whether the *ātman* is wholly dissociated from *buddhi* even when it attains liberation. For *buddhi*, then, I have stuck to 'soul', for *ātman* to 'self'. The reader must firmly bear this distinction in mind.

This must suffice by way of introduction. The reader will be able to judge for himself how far the translation is successful: the Sanskritist will, I hope, let me know where it is incorrect. If none of the magic of the originals comes through, then I have surely failed.

R. C. Z.

1966.

CONTENTS

xxiii

From the Rig-Veda

From the Rig-Veda

III, lxii, 10: THE 'GĀYATRĪ' (THE BRĀHMAN'S DAILY PRAYER)

We meditate on the lovely light of the god, Savitri: [1]
  May it stimulate our thoughts!

I, xxiv : TO VARUNA AND OTHERS
[Strophes 1–5 are omitted]

§ 6. None hath attained to thy sovereignty and power,
None to thine undaunted spirit,—[none,—]
Nor swift-winged bird, nor restless-moving water,
Nor [mountain] curbing wind's impulsive might.

§ 7. In the bottomless [abyss] king Varuna
By the power of his pure will upholds aloft
The [cosmic] tree's high crown. There stand below
[The branches], and above the roots. Within us
May the banners of his light be firmly set!

§ 8. For the sun hath king Varuna prepared
A broad path that he may roam along it:
For the footless he made feet that he might move:
And he it is who the stricken of heart absolves.

§ 9. A hundred and a thousand men of healing
Hast thou, O king: how wide, profound thy grace (*sumati*)!
Ward off and drive away unjust decay (*nirṛti*):
From the sin (*enas*) we have incurred deliver (*pramuc-*) us.

§ 10. The stars of the Bear at night are set on high
[For all] to see; by day where do they go?
Of the laws of Varuna there's no deceiving:
At night the moon rides forth, herself displaying.

§ 11. Praising thee with holy prayer (*brahman*), I beg thee,—
The sacrificer by his oblation begs thee:
O Varuna, be not enraged,—thy words
Are widely heard, so rob us not of life.

[1] A sun-god.
3

§ 12. By night, by day they tell me, as tells me too
This longing of my heart: 'Whom Śunahśepa
Called upon, bound [and captive as he was],
Varuna, the king, may he release (*muc-*) us!'

§ 13. For Śunahśepa, captive, manacled
To three stakes, called upon the son of Aditi,
Varuna, the king, that he might free him:
May the wise one, undeceived, all fetters loose!

§ 14. With obeisance, sacrifice, oblations we
Would pray away thine anger, Varuna:
Wise sovereign (*asura*), king, make loose our sins,—
For thou hast power,—[the sins] we have incurred.

§ 15. Make loose our fetters,—[loose] the uppermost,
[Loose] the nethermost, and [loose] the midmost:
Then, son of Aditi, [firm] in thy covenant (*vrata*)
Will we sinless stand before [thy mother] Aditi!

I, cliv : TO VISHNU

§ 1. I will now proclaim the manly powers of Vishnu
Who measured out earth's broad expanses,
Propped up the highest place of meeting:
Three steps he paced, the widely striding!

§ 2. For [this], his manly power is Vishnu praised.
Like a dread beast he wanders where he will,
Haunting the mountains: in his three wide paces
All worlds and beings (*bhuvana*) dwell.

§ 3. May [this] my hymn attain to Vishnu and inspire him,
Dwelling in the mountains, widely striding Bull,
Who, one and alone, with but three steps this long
And far-flung place of meeting measured out.

§ 4. The marks of his three steps are filled with honey;
Unfailing they rejoice each in its own way.[1]
Though one, in threefold wise he has propped up
Heaven and earth, all beings [and all worlds].

§ 5. Fain would I reach that well-loved home
Where god-devoted men are steeped in joy,
For that is kith and kin of the Wide-strider,—
The honey's source in Vishnu's highest footstep!

[1] Following Geldner.

§ 6. To the dwellings of you two we fain would go
Where there are cattle, many-horned and nimble(?).
There indeed the widely striding Bull's
Highest footstep, copious, downward shines.

II, xxxiii : TO RUDRA (ŚIVA)

§ 1. Father of the Maruts! May thy grace (*sumna*) come [down]:
Do not withhold from us the vision of the sun!
May our warriors on horseback remain unscathed: [1]
Rudra, may we bring forth progeny abounding!

§ 2. Most healing are the remedies thou givest;
By these for a hundred years I'd live!
Hatred, distress, disease drive far away,
Rudra, dispel them,—away, on every side!

§ 3. Most glorious in glory, in strength most strong art thou
Of all that's born, O Rudra, wielder of the bolt!
Ferry us in safety to the shore beyond distress;
Fend off [from us] all assaults of injury [and disease].

§ 4. May we not, Bull Rudra, provoke thy wrath
    By bowing down to thee,
    By praising thee ineptly,
    By invoking thee with others.
Raise up our men with healing remedies,
Best of physicians,—so do I hear of thee.

§ 5. To him are offered up
    Oblations—invocations:
    Him would I appease,
    Rudra, with songs of praise.

    Compassionate is he,
    Easy to invoke;
    Tawny [his body],
    Lovely his lips:
    May he not deliver us
    Up to his fearful wrath!

§ 6. With tough, compelling force
The Bull, the Maruts' lord
Hath cheered my suppliant's heart.

---

[1] Following Geldner.

As shade in torrid heat,
Would I, unhurt, [my Lord] attain,
Win Rudra's [saving] grace (*sumna*).

§ 7. O Rudra, where is thy caressing hand,
[The hand] that heals, [the hand] that cools,
[The hand] that bears away god-given hurt?
  [Great] Bull, forbear with me!

§ 8. The tawny Bull with white beflecked,—for him,
The great,—great, goodly praise I offer.
I will bow down—deep is my prostration—
To radiant (?) Rudra: his awful name we praise.

§ 9. Right firm his limbs, manifold his forms;
Tawny and strong, he hath bedecked himself
  With ornaments of lustrous gold.

Lord of this far-flung world is he:
  Rudra [is his name].
May never celestial sovereignty (*asurya*)
  Part company with him!

§ 10. How fit it is that thou shouldst bear
  Arrows and bow:
How fit [that thou shouldst bear]
A many-coloured necklace, adored [of men]:
How fit it is that thou shouldst so dispose
  Of all this shattering power:
None is there, Rudra, more vast in strength than thou!

§ 11. Praise him, the stripling widely famed,
Enthroned in his chariot,—like unto a beast,
Fearful and strong, all ready for the kill(?).
Praised by the singer, Rudra, show him mercy;
Let thine armies lay another low,—not us!

§ 12. As a son bows down to a father who esteems him,
So, Rudra, [bow I] to thee as thou draw'st nigh:
[Thee,] giver of much, the lord of truth I praise,—
And praised, thou givest us thy healing remedies.

§ 13. Pure are your remedies, ye Marut-bulls;
Healing they bring, gladness they inspire:
Our father, Manu, chose them; these do I desire
  With health and Rudra's blessing.

§ 14. May Rudra's arrow pass us by;
May the great ill-will of the awful one pass on!
For our patrons' sake slacken thy taut [bow-string]:
O rich in grace (*mīḷvat*), have mercy on our children!

§ 15. O God, O tawny Bull, who knowest all(?),
Let thy fury be restrained, do us no hurt!
Hearken thou here to this our invocation:
Rich in warriors, loud would we speak out
In [this] assembly [devoted to thy worship]!

X, lxxxi : TO VIŚVAKARMAN (THE 'ALL-MAKER')

§ 1. The seer, our father, sacrificing all these worlds,
   Sat on the high priest's throne:
Pursuing wealth by [offering] prayer, he made away
With what came first, entering into the latter things.

§ 2. What was the primal matter (*adhiṣṭhāna*)? What the
   beginning?
How and what manner of thing was that from which
The Maker of All, see-er of all, brought forth
The earth, and by his might the heavens unfolded?

§ 3. His eyes on every side, on every side his face,
On every side his arms, his feet on every side—
With arms and wings he together forges
Heaven and earth, begetting them, God, the One!

§ 4. What was the wood? What was the tree
From which heaven and earth were fashioned forth?
Ask, ask, ye wise in heart, on what did he rely
That he should [thus] support [these] worlds?

§ 5. Teach us thy highest dwelling-places (*dhāma*), thy lowest too;
[Teach us] these, thy midmost, Maker of All:
Teach thy friends at the oblation, O thou, self-strong;
Offer sacrifice thyself to make thy body grow!

§ 6. Maker of All, grown strong by the oblation,
Offer heaven and earth in sacrifice thyself!
Let others hither and thither, distracted, stray,
But for us let there be a bounteous patron here.

§ 7. Let us today invoke the Lord of Speech,
Maker of All, inspirer of the mind,
To help us at the [time of] sacrifice.
Let him take pleasure in all our invocations,
Bring us all blessing, working good to help us!

X, lxxxii : TO VIŚVAKARMAN

§ 1. The father of the eye—for wise of mind is he—
Begat these twain [1] like sacrificial ghee,
  And they bowed to him [in worship].
Not till the ancient [2] bounds were firmly fixed
  Were heaven and earth extended.

§ 2. Maker of All, exceeding wise, exceeding strong,
Disposer,[3] Ordainer, highest Exemplar (*saṁdṛś*):
Their sacrifices [4] exult in nourishment
There where, they say, the One is—beyond the Seven Seers.[5]

§ 3. He is our father, he begat us,
[He] the Ordainer: [he all] dwellings (*dhāma*) knows,
All worlds [he knows]: the gods he named,
[Himself] One only: other beings go to question him.

§ 4. As [now our] singers [give] of their abundance,
So did the ancient seers together offer him wealth:
After the sunless and the sunlit spaces
Had been set down, together they made these beings.

§ 5. Beyond the heavens, beyond this earth,
Beyond the gods, beyond the Asuras,
What was the first embryo the waters bore
  To which all the gods bore witness?

§ 6. He [6] was the first embryo the waters bore
  In whom all gods together came,
The One implanted in the Unborn's navel
  In which all the worlds abode.

§ 7. You will not find him who [all] these begat:
  Some other thing has stepped between you.
Blinded by fog and [ritual] mutterings
Wander the hymn-reciters, robbers of life!

X, xc : THE SACRIFICE OF PRIMAL MAN
(*puruṣa* = 'male person')

§ 1. A thousand heads had [primal] Man,
A thousand eyes, a thousand feet:
Encompassing the earth on every side,
He exceeded it by ten fingers' [breadth].

---

[1] i.e. heaven and earth.   [2] Or, 'eastern'.   [3] Or, 'Creator'.
[4] Or 'wishes'.   [5] i.e. the Great Bear.   [6] i.e. Viśvakarman.

§ 2. [That] Man is this whole universe,—
What was and what is yet to be,
The Lord of immortality
Which he outgrows by [eating] food.

§ 3. This is the measure of his greatness,
But greater yet is [primal] Man:
All beings form a quarter of him,
Three-quarters are the immortal in heaven.

§ 4. With three-quarters Man rose up on high,
A quarter of him came to be again [down] here:
From this he spread in all directions,
Into all that eats and does not eat.

§ 5. From him was Virāj born,
From Virāj Man again:
Once born,—behind, before,
He reached beyond the earth.

§ 6. When with Man as their oblation
The gods performed the sacrifice,
Spring was the melted butter,
Summer the fuel, and autumn the oblation.

§ 7. Him they besprinkled on the sacrificial strew,—
[Primeval] Man, born in the beginning:
With him [their victim], gods, Sādhyas, seers
    Performed the sacrifice.

§ 8. From this sacrifice completely offered
The clotted ghee was gathered up:
From this he fashioned beasts and birds,
Creatures of the woods and creatures of the village.

§ 9. From this sacrifice completely offered
Were born the Rig- and Sāma-Vedas;
From this were born the metres,
From this was the Yajur-Veda born.

§ 10. From this were horses born, all creatures
That have teeth in either jaw:
From this were cattle born,
From this sprang goats and sheep.

§ 11. When they divided [primal] Man,
Into how many parts did they divide him?
What was his mouth? What his arms?
What are his thighs called? What his feet?

§ 12. The Brāhman was his mouth,
The arms were made the Prince,
His thighs the common people,
And from his feet the serf was born.

§ 13. From his mind the moon was born,
And from his eye the sun,
From his mouth Indra and the fire,
From his breath the wind was born.

§ 14. From his navel arose the atmosphere,
From his head the sky evolved,
From his feet the earth, and from his ear
The cardinal points of the compass:
So did they fashion forth these worlds.

§ 15. Seven were his enclosing sticks,
Thrice seven were made his fuel-sticks,
When the gods, performing sacrifice,
Bound Man, [their sacrificial] beast.

§ 16.   With sacrifice the gods
Made sacrifice to sacrifice:
These were the first religious rites (*dharma*),
To the firmament these powers went up
Where dwell the ancient Sādhya gods.

X, cxxi : PRAJĀPATI (THE 'GOLDEN EMBRYO')

§ 1. In the beginning the Golden Embryo
   [Stirred and] evolved:
Once born he was the one Lord of [every] being;
This heaven and earth did he sustain. . . .
What god shall we revere with the oblation?

§ 2. Giver of life (*ātman*), giver of strength,
   Whose behests all [must] obey,
   Whose [behests] the gods [obey],
   Whose shadow is immortality,
   Whose [shadow] death. . . .
What god shall we revere with the oblation?

§ 3. Who by his might has ever been the One
King of all that breathes and blinks the eye,
Who rules all creatures that have two feet or four. . . .
What god shall we revere with the oblation?

§ 4. By whose might the snowy peaks,
By whose [might], they say, the sea
With Rasā, [the earth-encircling stream,]
By whose [might] the cardinal directions
Which are his arms, [exist] . . .
What god shall we revere with the oblation?

§ 5. By whom strong heaven and earth are held in place,
By whom the sun is given a firm support,
By whom the firmament, by whom the ether (*rajas*)
Is measured out within the atmosphere. . . .
What god shall we revere with the oblation?

§ 6. To whom opposing armies, strengthened by his help,
   Look up, though trembling in their hearts,
By whom the risen sun sheds forth its light. . . .
What god shall we revere with the oblation?

§ 7. When the mighty waters moved, conceived the All
As an embryo, giving birth to fire,
Then did he evolve, the One life-force (*asu*) of the gods. . . .
What god shall we revere with the oblation?

§ 8. Who looked upon the waters, [looked on them] with power,
As they conceived insight,[1] brought forth the sacrifice;
Who, among the gods, was the One God above. . . .
What god shall we revere with the oblation?

§ 9. May he not harm us, father of the earth,
Who generated heaven, for truth is his law,
Who gave birth to the waters,—shimmering, strong. . . .
What god shall we revere with the oblation?

§ 10. Prajāpati! None other than thou hath comprehended
   All these [creatures] brought to birth.
Whatever desires be ours in offering up
The oblation to thee, may that be ours!
   May we be lords of riches!

X, cxxix : 'IN THE BEGINNING . . .'

§ 1. Then neither Being nor Not-being was,
Nor atmosphere, nor firmament, nor what is beyond.
What did it encompass? Where? In whose protection?
What was water, the deep, unfathomable?

[1] Or 'strength', or a proper name (*Daksha*).

§ 2. Neither death nor immortality was there then,
　　No sign of night or day.
That One breathed, windless, by its own energy (*svadhā*):
　　Nought else existed then.

§ 3. In the beginning was darkness swathed in darkness;
All this was but unmanifested water.
Whatever was, that One, coming into being,
　　Hidden by the Void,
Was generated by the power of heat (*tapas*).

§ 4. In the beginning this [One] evolved,
Became desire, first seed of mind.
Wise seers, searching within their hearts,
Found the bond of Being in Not-being.

§ 5.　Their cord was extended athwart:
Was there a below? Was there an above?
Casters of seed there were, and powers;
Beneath was energy, above was impulse.

§ 6. Who knows truly? Who can here declare it?
Whence it was born, whence is this emanation.
By the emanation of this the gods
　　Only later [came to be].
Who then knows whence it has arisen?

§ 7. Whence this emanation hath arisen,
Whether [God] disposed [1] it, or whether he did not,—
Only he who is its overseer in highest heaven knows.
[He only knows,] or perhaps he does not know!

[1] Or, 'created'.

From the Atharva-Veda

From the Atharva-Veda

¶ 1. Who formed the heels of Man (*puruṣa*)?
Who formed his flesh, his ankles?
Who his well-formed fingers?
Who [opened up his] apertures?
Who [formed] the testicles (??) in his middle part?
Who [gave him] a firm basis?

¶ 2. Of what were made the ankles down below,
And the knee-caps of Man above them?
[Whence] were the shanks produced [and where] inserted?
Where were the knee-joints? Who can understand it?

¶ 3. [To the body] four [arms and legs] are joined
With ends welded thereinto.
Above the knees the flabby trunk;
The buttocks and the thighs,—who then produced them,
By which the trunk was firmly propped?

¶ 4. How many gods and which were they
Who built the breast and neck of Man?
How many arranged the breasts? Who [made] the nipples(?)?
How many [built] the shoulder-blades?
How many built the ribs?

¶ 5. Who brought together his two arms
That he might do manly deeds?
What god attached the shoulders to his trunk?

¶ 6. Who bored the seven apertures in the head,—
These ears, the nostrils, eyes and mouth?
By mastering which with power four-footed and two-footed
   beasts
Pursue their several ways in many a direction.

¶ 7. For he placed the many-sided tongue between the jaws,
And made to dwell therein the mighty [power of] speech.
Within the worlds he roves abroad, dwelling in the waters:
   Who can understand it?

[1] Cf. p. 8.
15

¶ 8. Who [fashioned] first the brain of Man,
His forehead, nape and skull, and built
What had to be built between the jaws,
Then heavenward ascended. Which god is that?

¶ 9. By whom (or what) does mighty Man endure
So much that's pleasing, so much displeasing,
Dream, affliction, weariness,
Joys and satisfactions?

¶ 10. Whence [comes] to Man distress, depression and decay,
And mindlessness; and whence [comes] affluence,
Success, prosperity, thought and exaltations?

¶ 11. Who arranged in Man the waters, flowing variously,
Wide-flowing, born to course in streams,
Pungent, brown, red and the colour of smoky copper,
    Upward, down, athwart?

¶ 12. Who gave Man form, who gave him name and stature?
Who [gave him] gait, consciousness and legs?

¶ 13. Who wove in Man his breathing-in, who his breathing-out,
His breath 'diffused', his 'concentrated' breath?
What god made them dwell within him?

¶ 14. What single (eka) God put sacrifice in Man?
Who [planted] truth, untruth within him?
[And] whence is death, whence immortality?

¶ 15. Who wrapped him round with clothing? Who devised his
    life (āyu)?
Who gave him strength? Who made him fleet of foot?

¶ 16. Through whom [1] did he spread the waters out?
Through whom did he make the day to shine?
Through whom did he kindle the [light of] dawn?
Through whom did he grant the gift of eventide?

¶ 17. Who planted the semen in him
That his thread might be further spun?
Who brought him wisdom? Who in him put music, dance?

¶ 18. Through whom did he bedeck this earth?
Through whom the heavens encompass?
Through what power [2] does Man surpass the mountains?
Through whom are his works (karma) [performed]?

---

[1] Or, 'what'. So too in the following lines and stanzas.
[2] Or, 'through whom in greatness'.

¶ 19. Through whom does he seek the rain-filled cloud
(*parjanya*)?
Through whom the Soma, wise?
Through whom [does he seek] sacrifice and faith?
By whom was mind installed within him?

¶ 20. Through whom does he acquire one learned in the scrip-
tures?
Through whom [does he win] the highest Lord?
Through whom does Man [acquire] this fire?
Through whom did he measure out the year?

¶ 21. Brahman [it is who] acquires one learned in the scriptures;
Brahman [wins] the highest Lord:
Brahman [as] Man [acquires] this fire;
Brahman [it is who] measured out the year.

¶ 22. Through whom does he dwell beside the gods?
Through whom beside the common people (*viś*) among the gods?
Through whom beside this other [class], not princely?
By whom is the princely [class] called Being (*sat*)?

¶ 23. Brahman [it is who] dwells beside the gods;
Brahman beside the common people among the gods;
Brahman beside this other [class], not princely;
Brahman is called Being, the princely [class].

¶ 24. By whom was this earth established?
By whom were the heavens fixed on high?
By whom was this atmosphere, this wide expanse,
Established above, athwart?

¶ 25. By Brahman was this earth established;
Brahman the heavens fixed on high;
Brahman this atmosphere, this wide expanse,
Established above, athwart.

¶ 26. Atharvan sewed up his head and heart:
A wind, rising above the brain, expelled [it] from the head.

¶ 27. Atharvan's head assuredly
Is a casket of the gods, close sealed:
This head the breath of life (*prāṇa*) protects;
So too do food and mind.

¶ 28. Brought forth above, brought forth athwart,
All cardinal points did Man pervade,—
[Yes, Man] who Brahman's city (*pur*) knows,
By which he is called 'Man' (*puruṣa*).

¶ 29. Whoso that city of Brahman truly (*vai*) knows
As swathed in immortality,
To him do Brahman and the Brāhmans give
Sight, life (*prāṇa*), and progeny.

¶ 30. Neither sight nor life desert the man
Before old age sets in,
Who the city of Brahman knows
By which he is called 'Man'.

¶ 31. The city of the gods which none lays low in battle
Has circles eight and portals nine:
In it is a golden treasure-chest,—
Celestial, suffused with light.

¶ 32. In this golden treasure-chest, three-spoked and thrice
supported,—
In this there is a being strange (*yakṣa*) possessed of self
(*ātmanvat*):
That is what knowers of Brahman know.

¶ 33. Into this radiant [city],—yellow, gold,
Compassed with glory round about,
The city unsubdued
Brahmā has entered in!

X, vii : SKAMBHA (THE SUPPORT)

¶ 1. In which of his limbs does fervour (*tapas*) dwell?
In which of his limbs is the law (*ṛta*) set down?
Where is the ordinance? Where in him does faith abide?
In which of his limbs is truth established?

¶ 2. From which of his limbs does the fire blaze forth?
From which of his limbs does Mātariśvan (the wind) blow?
From which of his limbs does the moon measure out,—
Measuring a limb of mighty Skambha?

¶ 3. In which of his limbs does the earth abide?
In which of his limbs does the atmosphere dwell?
In which of his limbs are the heavens set and so abide?
In which of his limbs does the higher than heaven dwell?

¶ 4. Yearning for whom [1] does the fire blaze up on high?
Yearning for whom does Mātariśvan blow?—
Yearning for whom their courses(?) go towards him:
Tell forth that Skambha: which and what is he?

[1] Or, 'what'; and so in the following stanzas.

¶ 5. Whither go the half-months, whither go the months
In mutual understanding with the year?—
To where the seasons go, to where the seasons' fruits(?):
Tell forth that Skambha: which and what is he?

¶ 6. Yearning for whom [1] do those maidens of differing form,
Day and night, run forth in mutual understanding?—
Yearning for whom the waters forward flow:
Tell forth that Skambha: which and what is he?

¶ 7. On whom Prajāpati propped up the worlds
    And sustained them all [thereby]?
Tell forth that Skambha: which and what is he?

¶ 8. That which Prajāpati brought forth in every form
    Above, below, and in between,—
With how much [of himself] did Skambha enter in?
What he did not enter, how much was that?

¶ 9. With how much [of himself] did Skambha enter the past?
How much of him extends into the future?
That one limb which he made a thousand-fold,—
With how much [of himself] did Skambha enter in?

¶ 10. Wherein, men know, are worlds and what contains them
    (kośa),
The waters and Brahman in which are Being and Not-being:
Tell forth that Skambha: which and what is he?

¶ 11. Wherein ascetic fervour, striding forth, upholds the
    highest ordinance,
Wherein are law (rta) and faith, the waters and Brahman set
    together:
Tell forth that Skambha: which and what is he?

¶ 12. In whom are earth and atmosphere,
In whom the heavens are set, wherein the sun and moon
And fire and wind are fixed and so abide:
Tell forth that Skambha: who and what is he?

¶ 13. In a limb of whom all three and thirty gods are welded,
Tell forth that Skambha: who and what is he?

¶ 14. Wherein are the first-born seers,
The Vedas [three], Rig-, Sāma-, and great Yajus,
In whom the Single Seer is fixed:
Tell forth that Skambha: which and what is he?

¶ [1] Or, 'what'; and so in the following lines and stanzas.

¶ 15. Wherein, in Man (*puruṣa*), immortality and death are held
   together,
To whom belongs the ocean, the veins together held in Man:
Tell forth that Skambha: which and what is he?

¶ 16. Of whom the four cardinal directions are the swelling
   veins,
Wherein the sacrifice has mightily strode forth:
Tell forth that Skambha: which and what is he?

¶ 17. Whoso in Man knows Brahman, knows the highest Lord
   (*parameṣṭhin*),
Whoso knows the highest Lord, whoso Prajāpati,
Whoso knows that the Brahman-power (*brāhmaṇa*) is best,
   Knows Skambha by analogy (*anu-*).

¶ 18. Whose head is the universal fire,
Whose eye the Angirases became,
Whose limbs are sorcerers (*yātu*):
Tell forth that Skambha: which and what is he?

¶ 19. Whose mouth, they say, is Brahman,
Whose tongue the honeyed whip,
Whose udder is Virāj:
Tell forth that Skambha: which and what is he?

¶ 20. From whom the Rig-Veda was carved out,
From whom the Yajur-Veda was drawn forth,
Whose hairs the Sāma-Veda is, whose mouth
The Atharva-Veda and [the songs of] the Angirases:
Tell forth that Skambha: which and what is he?

¶ 21. A branch of Not-being, jutting out, men take to be the
   highest.
Inferior men who this thy branch revere,
   Think that it is Being too.

¶ 22. Wherein Ādityas, Rudras, Vasus are together held,
Wherein is what was and what is yet to be,
[Wherein] are all the worlds established:
Tell forth that Skambha: which and what is he?

¶ 23. Whose treasure-trove the three and thirty gods forever
   guard:
Today, ye gods, who knows that treasure-trove ye guard?

¶ 24. Whereas the gods who Brahman know
Revere Brahman as the highest, best,
Whoso thus knows them face to face
Is a Brahman-priest (*brahmā*) who knows.

¶ 25. Great indeed are the gods
Who from Not-being came to birth.
Men say that that Not-being is but one limb
   Of Skambha: beyond [is he].

¶ 26. When Skambha generated and evolved the Ancient One,
Men knew then by analogy that this Ancient One
   Is but one limb of Skambha.

¶ 27. Whereas in [that one] limb of his the three and thirty gods
Parcelled out legs [between themselves],
Some knowers of Brahman [came to] know
   Those three and thirty gods.

¶ 28. Men [think they] know the Golden Embryo [1]
   As the unutterable, supreme:
[No,] in the beginning Skambha poured it forth,
   [Pure] gold within the world.

¶ 29. In Skambha are the worlds, in Skambha ascetic fervour,
In Skambha is the law (rta) set down:
I know thee, Skambha, face to face
In Indra wholly concentrated!

¶ 30. In Indra are the worlds, in Indra ascetic fervour,
In Indra is the law set down:
I know thee, Indra, face to face,
On Skambha wholly founded!

¶ 31. Again and again name after name a man invokes
Before [the rising of] the sun, before the dawn.
When the Unborn first grew and came to birth (sambhū-),
Forth did he stride to sovereignty:
No other being is higher than he!

¶ 32. Whose measure is the earth, whose belly the atmosphere,
Who made the sky his head,—to him be homage,—Brahman,
   best!

¶ 33. Whose eye is the sun, and the moon forever new,
Who made the fire his mouth,—to him be homage,—Brahman,
   best!

¶ 34. Whose breathing in and breathing out are wind,
Whose eye the Angirases became,
Who made the cardinal points his wisdom,
   To him be homage,—Brahman, best!

[1] See p. 10.

¶ 35. Firmly did Skambha hold in place heaven and earth,—
      both these,
Firmly did Skambha hold in place the far-flung atmosphere,
Firmly did Skambha hold in place the six wide-spread directions:
Into this whole world hath Skambha entered in.

¶ 36. Who came to birth by fervour, toil,
Who mastered all the worlds,
Who made the Soma all his own (*kevala*),—
      To him be homage,—Brahman, best!

¶ 37. How [is it that] the wind doth never come to rest?
How [is it that] the mind doth never cease from thinking?
How [is it that] the waters, yearning for the truth,
      Are never, never still?

¶ 38. A being great and strange (*yakṣa*) in the middle of the
      world
Strode forth in holy fervour on the waters' crest:
In it whatever gods there be found refuge
Like branches clustered round the tree-trunk.

¶ 39. To whom with hands and feet, with voice and ear and eye
The gods forever offer up a measureless sacrifice
In a [place of sacrifice well] measured out:
Tell forth that Skambha: who and what is he?

¶ 40. From him is darkness far removed: untouched by evil he:
In him are all the lights,—in Prajāpati but three.

¶ 41. Whoso doth know the golden reed standing in the waters,
      He is indeed Prajāpati, though hidden.

¶ 42. Two single maidens of differing form
Weave a web on six pegs set,
      Approaching it in turn:
The one draws forth the threads,
The other sets them in their place.
They do not break them off:
[Their labour] has no end.

¶ 43. They seem to dance around, and I cannot distinguish
Which of them came first. A male [now] weaves it, ties it up:
A male hath borne it [up] unto the firmament.

¶ 44. These pegs prop up the sky: the chants were made the
      shuttle for the weaving.

X, viii : SKAMBHA AGAIN

¶ 1. Who supervises all that was and that is yet to be,
To whom the sun alone belongs,—to him be homage,—Brahman,
   best!

¶ 2. By Skambha are these two held apart,—
Heaven and earth,—and so they stand:
In Skambha [dwells] this whole universe, possessed of self
   (ātmanvat),—
What breathes and blinks the eye.

¶ 3. Three generations have passed away and gone;
Others have entered in around the [sacrificial] fire.[1]
Great [is the sun which] stood [there], measuring out the firma-
   ment:
The golden-yellow male has entered the golden-yellow females.[2]

¶ 4. Twelve fellies, a single wheel, three naves:
   Who can understand it?
Three hundred pegs have there been hammered in,
   And sixty nails which none can move.

¶ 5. This, Savitri, do thou understand:
Six twins there are, another born alone:
In him among their number who alone was born
   They crave association.

¶ 6. Though manifest, it is yet hidden, secret:
The 'ageing' is its name, a mighty mode of being (pada).[3]
Therein is this universe [firm] fixed;
Therein is [all] that moves and breathes established.

¶ 7. With a single wheel it turns, with a single felly,
With a thousand syllables, up to the east, down to the west:
With a half [of itself] it brought the whole world forth:
   Its [other] half, oh, what has that become?

¶ 8. In front of these the five-horsed [chariot] moves on:
Trace-horses yoked to it help to draw it.
The path it has not traversed some have seen;
   What it has traversed none.
The nearer [sees it] high above,
   The further down below.

---

[1] Or 'sun', or 'praise'.   [2] i.e. the plants?   [3] Or, 'place'.

¶ 9. A bowl there is, a hole [pierced] in its side, its bottom
   upward turned;
In it is glory stored, [glory] in all its forms:
Thereon together sit the Seven Seers
Who became this mighty one's protectors.

¶ 10. [The Rig-Vedic verse] which is yoked in front,
That [yoked] behind, that yoked on every side,
And that on all sides [yoked], by which
The sacrifice is forward stretched,—of that
I ask thee: which of [those] verses is that?

¶ 11. What moves, what falls, what stands, what breathes,
What does not breathe, what blinks, becomes,
This keeps the world in being,—many are its forms,—
This, growing together, becomes just One.

¶ 12. The infinite is extended out in many places:
Infinite and finite [meet] at a common edge.
The guardian of the firmament moves,—discriminates between
   them,—
Knowing what of it was and what is yet to be.

¶ 13. The Lord of Creatures (*prajāpati*) stirs within the womb:
Unseen he comes to birth in many forms and places:
With a half [of himself] he brought the whole world forth:
   His [other] half, oh, what is the mark of that?

¶ 14. Like a woman bearing water in her pitcher
   He bears the water up:
All see him with the eye; not all know him with the mind.

¶ 15. Far off he dwells with what is full,
Far off he lacks what is deficient,
A being great and strange (*yakṣa*) in the middle of the world:
To him do kings bring tribute.

¶ 16. From which the sun arises,
In which [the sun] doth set;
That, I think, is the highest, best:
There is none that can surpass it.

¶ 17. When recently, or in the middle past, or long ago
Men speak about the man who knows the Veda,
It is the sun of which they one and all do speak,
Of fire as second and of the threefold swan.

¶ 18. For a thousand-day journey the wings of the yellow swan
Are spread abroad as heavenward it flies:
Gathering all the gods into its bosom, it
    Flies on, surveying all the worlds.

¶ 19. By truth he gives heat on high,
By Brahman he looks below:
He breathes obliquely by the breath
In which the Best has found a home.

¶ 20. Who knows the fire-sticks from which, by rubbing, wealth
    is won,
He, knowing, ponders on the highest, best:
He knows the mighty Brahman-power.

¶ 21. In the beginning he, footless, came to be;
In the beginning he bore the heavenly light:
He acquired four feet and became of use;
All enjoyment took he for himself.

¶ 22. Whoso reveres the eternal God who reigns on high
[Himself] becomes of use, an eater of much food.

¶ 23. Eternal do they call him, and yet e'en now
    Is he ever again renewed.
Day and night are each from the other born
    Each in its different form.

¶ 24. A hundred, a thousand, a myriad, a hundred million,—
What is his own, what has entered him, how can it be counted?
All that is his they slay as he looks on:
On this account this god approves it!

¶ 25. The One is finer than a hair:
The One, it seems, cannot be seen.
Hence is that deity so dear to me,
    Most fit to be embraced.

¶ 26. In the house of mortal man there is [a maiden,]
    Fair, unageing and immortal.
He for whom she was made lies flat;
He who made her has grown old.

¶ 27. Thou art woman, thou art man,
Thou art the lad and the maiden too,
Thou art the old man tottering on his staff:
Once born thou comest to be, thy face turned every way!

¶ 28. He is their father, he their son,
He their eldest brother and their youngest:
The One God, entering the mind,
Is the first-born; [yet] he is in the womb.

¶ 29. From the full the full he raises up;
With the full is the full besprinkled:
Would that today we knew from whence
That [full] is sprinkled round about.

¶ 30. She, the eternal, was born in right olden times;
She, the primeval, all things encompassed:
The great goddess, lighting up the dawn,
Looks out from each single thing that blinks the eye.

¶ 31. The deity whose name is 'Helpful' sits
    Encompassed by the law (rta):
Because its hue is such, these trees
Are green, and green their garlands.

¶ 32. Near though he is, one cannot leave him;
Near though he is, one cannot see him.
Behold the god's wise artistry!
He does not die, he grows not old.

¶ 33. Words uttered by him than whom there's nothing earlier
    Speak of things as they really are:
The place to which they, speaking, go
    Men call the mighty Brahman-power (brāhmaṇa).

¶ 34. That wherein gods and men were set
    As spokes within the hub,
Wherein the waters' flower by some uncanny power (māyā)
    Was laid, of that I ask thee.

¶ 35. [The gods] by whom impelled the wind blows forth,
Who cause the five points of the compass to converge,
These gods who the oblations spurned,
Guides to the waters,—which were they?

¶ 36. Of these one clothes himself in this [our] earth,
    And one encompasseth the atmosphere;
One of them, the Disposer, gives the sky,
Others protect all the cardinal directions.

¶ 37. Who knows the thread extended
On which these creatures are spun;
Who knows the thread of the thread,
Would know the mighty Brahman-power.

¶ 38. I know the thread extended
On which these creatures are spun;
I know the thread of the thread,
Hence the mighty Brahman-power.

¶ 39. When between heaven and earth the fire
Rushed onward, burning, everything consuming,
To where the wives of but one husband stood far off,
    Where was Mātariśvan then?

¶ 40. Into the waters had Mātariśvan entered,
Into the waters the gods had entered.
Great [is the sun which] stood [there], measuring out the spaces:
The cleansing [Soma] [1] has entered the golden-yellow females.[2]

¶ 41. Higher, it seems, than the Gāyatrī [3]
He strode forth in immortality:
Who chant with chant together know,—
[Can they know] where the Unborn saw it?

¶ 42. The bringer of rest, hoarder of wealth,
Whose law (dharma), like the god Savitri, is true,
Like Indra in the war for riches stood.

¶ 43. A lotus with nine gates [4] enveloped by three strands
    (guṇa),—
In it is a being strange (yakṣa), possessed of self (ātmanvat):
That [it is that] knowers of Brahman know.

¶ 44. Free from desire, immortal, wise and self-existent,
With [its own] savour satisfied, and nothing lacking,—
Whoso knows him, the Self,—wise, ageless, [ever] young,—
    Of death will have no fear.

XI, iv : TO THE BREATH OF LIFE ('PRĀNA')

¶ 1. Homage to the Breath of Life, for this whole universe obeys
it,
Which has become the Lord of all, on which all things are based.

¶ 2. Homage to thee, O Breath of Life, [homage] to thy
    crashing;
Homage to thee, the thunder; homage to thee, the lightning;
Homage to thee, O Breath of Life, when thou pourest rain.

---

[1] Or, '[wind]'.   [2] i.e. the plants?
[3] See p. 3.   [4] i.e. the body.

¶ 3. When upon the plants the Breath of Life in thunder roars,
They [then] conceive and form the embryo;
    Then manifold are they born.

¶ 4. When upon the plants the Breath of Life, the season come,
    roars loud,
All things soever upon [this] earth rejoice with great rejoicing.

¶ 5. When the Breath of Life [this] mighty earth with rain
    bedews,
Then do the cattle [too] rejoice: 'Great [strength] will be our
    portion.'

¶ 6. Rained upon by the Breath of Life, the plants gave voice:
'Thou hast prolonged for us our life; fragrance hast thou given.

¶ 7. Homage to thee, O Breath of Life, when thou comest, when
    thou goest:
Homage to thee when standing still; homage to thee when
    sitting!

¶ 8. Homage to thee, O Breath of Life, when breathing in,
    Homage when breathing out:
Homage to thee when thou turnest aside, homage to thee when
    thou facest [us]!
To all of thee, [yea, all,] is this [our] homage [due].

¶ 9. O Breath of Life, that form of thine so dear [to us],
O Breath of Life, that [form] which is yet dearer,
And then that healing which [too] is thine,
Place it in us that we may live.

¶ 10. The Breath of Life takes [living] creatures as its garment,
    As father [takes] his beloved son.
The Breath of Life is the Lord of all,
Of whatever breathes and what does not.

¶ 11. The Breath of Life is death, is fever;
The Breath of Life the gods revere.
In the highest world hath the Breath of Life
Set the man who speaks the truth.

¶ 12. The Breath of Life is Virāj, the Breath of Life is guide,
The Breath of Life all things revere.
The Breath of Life is sun and moon;
The Breath of Life they call Prajāpati.

¶ 13. The breathing in and the breathing out are rice and barley:
    Draught-ox [too] is [this] breath called:
The breathing in is placed in barley,
The breathing out is surnamed rice.

¶ 14. Within the womb a man (*puruṣa*) breathes in and out:
When, Breath of Life, thou quickenest him,
  Then is he born again.

¶ 15. The Breath of Life some call the wind (*mātariśvan*);
  Again it's called the breeze (*vāta*).
In the Breath of Life is what is past and what is yet to be;
On the Breath of Life all things are based.

¶ 16. Atharvan plants, Angiras [plants, plants] derived from
  gods or men,
O Breath of Life, are born when thou dost quicken them.

¶ 17. When the Breath of Life [this] mighty earth with rain
  bedews,
The plants are born,—whatever herbs there are.

¶ 18. Who this of thee knows, O Breath of Life,
And what it is that forms thy base,
To him all [men] shall tribute bring
  In yonder highest world.

¶ 19. As all these creatures here, O Breath of Life,
  Bring tribute unto thee,
So too shall they to him bring tribute
Who hears thee,—thou, so good to hear.

¶ 20. As an embryo he stirs within the deities;
He comes to be, has been, is born again.
What was,[1] what is and what is yet to be
Hath he entered with his powers, as father [enters] son.

¶ 21. [Like] a swan from the ocean he rises up,
  Withdrawing not his single foot:
Should he withdraw it, there would not be
Todays, to-morrows, nights or days;
  It would never dawn again.

¶ 22. With eight wheels he turns, with a single felly,
With a thousand syllables, up to the east, down to the west.
With half [of himself] he gave birth to the whole world:
  His [other] half, oh, what is the mark of that?

¶ 23. To him who rules all births, all moving things,
To him whose bow is swift among the rest,
To him, to thee, O Breath of Life, be homage!

¶ 24. May he who rules all births, all moving things,
Unwearied, wise by Brahman, the Breath of Life, stand by me!

---

[1] Reading *bhūtam*.

¶ 25. Erect, he stays awake when others sleep,
   He never falls down prone:
That he should sleep while others sleep,
   None has ever heard.

¶ 26. O Breath of Life, turn not thy back on me:
   None other than I shalt thou be.
As an embryo in the waters, so I within myself
   Bind thee, that I may live!

From the Upanishads

Brihadāranyaka Upanishad[1]

I, i

[Chapter i, which identifies the universe with the sacrificial horse, is omitted.]

I, ii

¶ 1. In the beginning nothing at all existed here. This [whole world] was enveloped by Death,—by Hunger. For what is death but hunger? And [Death] bethought himself: 'Would that I had a self!' He roamed around, offering praise; and from him, as he offered praise, water was born. And he said [to himself]: 'Yes, it was a joy (*ka*) to me to offer praise (*arc-*).' And this is what makes fire (*arka*) fire. And joy is the lot of him who understands that this is what makes fire fire.

¶ 2. Water too is *arka*. And the froth of the water was churned together and became the earth. And on this [earth] he wore himself out. And the heat (*tejas*) and sap [generated] by him, worn out and consumed by fierce penances (*tapta*) as he was, turned into fire.

¶ 3. He divided [him]self (*ātman*) into three parts: [one third was fire,] one third the sun, one third the wind. He too is the breath of life (*prāṇa*) threefold divided.

The east is his head. The north-east and south-east [2] are his two arms. The west is his tail. The north-west and south-west [2] are his two buttocks. The south and north are his flanks. The sky is his back, the atmosphere his belly, this [earth] his chest. Firmly is he based on the waters; and firmly is that man based who thus knows, wherever he may go.

¶ 4. [Then] he longed that a second self might be born to him; [and so he who is] Hunger and Death copulated with Speech by means of mind. What was the seed became the year; for there was no year before that. For so long did he bear him [within himself], —for a whole year; and after so long a time did he bring him forth. When he was born, [Death] opened his mouth [as if to swallow him]. 'Bhān,' said he, and that became speech.

---

[1] The *Kānva* text is followed throughout.
[2] So Sankara: the text has simply 'that and that'.

¶ 5. He considered [within himself]: 'If I should try to take his life, I should make less food for myself.' By this word, by this self, he brought forth this whole universe,—everything that exists,—Rig-Veda, Yajur-Veda, Sāma-Veda, metres, sacrifices, men and beasts.

And whatever he brought forth he began to eat: for he eats up everything. And that is what makes Aditi Aditi (*ad-* = 'to eat'). Whoso thus knows what makes Aditi Aditi becomes an eater of everything here: everything is his food.

¶ 6. He longed to sacrifice with a yet greater sacrifice. He wore himself out, performing fierce penances. And from him, worn out and consumed by fierce penances, glory and strength issued forth. Glory and strength are the vital breaths. And as these vital breaths issued forth, the body began to swell; and the mind was in his body.

¶ 7. He longed for his [body] to become fit for sacrifice and that thereby he might come to possess a self. And from this [longing of his] a horse (*aśva*) came to be because he had swelled (*aśvat*). 'Now it has become fit for sacrifice,' thought he. That is what makes the horse-sacrifice the horse-sacrifice. Whoso knows him thus, knows the horse-sacrifice.

Without penning the [horse] in, he kept it in mind and after a year he sacrificed it to [him]self (*ātman*). The [other] animals he distributed among the deities. That is why the victim besprinkled and offered up to Prajāpati is [really] sacrificed to all the gods.

This horse-sacrifice is the same as the burning [sun]; and the year is its self.

This fire [here] is *arka*, the sacrificial fire. These worlds are its selves.

Two they are,—the sacrificial fire and the horse-sacrifice. Yet he is only one deity,—Death. He [who knows this] overcomes the second death (*punarmṛtyu*); death cannot touch him; death becomes his [very] self: he becomes one of these deities.

I, iii

[Verses 1–27, concerning the bodily functions, the superiority of the breath of life, and the power of the Sāma-Veda, are omitted.]

¶ 28. Now [we come to] the recital of the formulas of purification.

The priest whose function is to praise begins his praises with the *Sāman* chant. When he begins his praises he should mutter these [words]:

> From the unreal lead me to the real!
> From darkness lead me to the light!
> From death lead me to immortality!

When he says, 'From the unreal lead me to the real', by the unreal [he means] death, by the real immortality. [When he says,] 'From death lead me to immortality', he means, 'Make me immortal', And when he says, 'From darkness lead me to the light', by darkness [he means] death, and by light immortality. [When he says,] 'From death lead me to immortality', he means, 'Make me immortal'.

'From death lead me to immortality!' There is nothing obscure about that.

[The remainder is omitted.]

I, iv

¶ 1. In the beginning this [universe] was the Self alone,—in the likeness of a man (*puruṣa*). Looking around, he saw nothing other than [him]self. First of all he said: 'This is I.' Hence the name 'I' came to be. So, even now when a man is addressed, he says first, 'This is I,' and then speaks out any other name he may have. And because he had first (*pūrva*) burnt up (*uṣ-*) all evils from this whole universe, he is [called] 'man' (*puruṣa*). So too does the man who thus knows burn up anyone who tries to get the better of him.

¶ 2. He was afraid. So, [even now] a man who is all alone is afraid.

He took thought and said [to himself]: 'Since nothing exists other than I, of whom (or what) am I afraid?' And his fear then departed [from him]; for of whom (or what) should he have been afraid? It is of a second that one is afraid.

¶ 3. He found no pleasure at all. So, [even now] a man who is all alone finds no pleasure. He longed for a second.

Now he was of the size of a man and a woman in close embrace. He split (*pat-*) this Self in two: and from this arose husband (*pati*) and wife (*patnī*). Hence we say, 'Oneself (*sva*) is like half a potsherd', as indeed Yājñavalkya used to say. That is why space is filled up with woman. He copulated with her, and thence were human beings born.

¶ 4. She took thought and said [to herself]: 'How is it that he copulates with me, although he generated me from his very Self? Very well, I will disappear.'

She became a cow: he a bull. He copulated with her, and thence were cattle born.

She became a mare: he a stallion. She [became] a she-ass: he a he-ass. He copulated with her, and thence were single-hoofed animals born.

She became a she-goat: he a he-goat. She [became] a ewe: he a ram. He copulated with her, and thence were goats and sheep born.

So did he bring forth all couples that exist, even down to the ants: [so did he bring forth] this whole universe.

¶ 5. He knew that he was [the whole of] creation [1], for he had brought it all forth. Hence he became [all] creation.[1] Whoso thus knows comes to be in that creation [1] of his.

¶ 6. Then he rubbed [backwards and forwards],—like this,—and with his hands and from his mouth [as] from the womb [2] he brought forth fire. That is why both (hands and mouth) are hairless on the inside; for the womb [too] is hairless on the inside.

Now, when people say, 'Sacrifice to this [god], sacrifice to that [god],'—one god after another, they mean this creation [1] of his; for he himself *is* all the gods.

Now, whatever is moist, he brought forth from semen, and that is Soma. The whole extent of this universe is nothing but food and what eats food. Soma is food: fire eats it.

This is the super-emanation of Brahman [3], namely, that he brought forth the gods, his betters; so too, though he [himself] was mortal, he brought forth immortals. That is why it is [called] a super-emanation. Whoso thus knows comes to be in that super-emanation of his.

¶ 7. Now, at that time this [world] was undifferentiated. What introduces differentiation is name and form (individuality), so that we can say: 'A man has this name; he has this form.' For even now it is name and form that introduce differentiation, so that we can say: 'A man has this name, he has this form.'

He entered in here (into the body), right up to the finger-tips just as a razor fits into a razor-case or fire into a brazier. [Yet] he cannot be seen, for he is incomplete. When breathing his name is breath; when speaking, voice; when seeing, the eye; when hearing, the ear; when thinking, the mind. These are the names of his [various] works (*karma*). The man who reveres any of these individually has no [right] knowledge: for he is incomplete in any of these individually.

Let a man revere Him rather as the 'Self', for therein do all these [works] become one. The Self is [as it were] a trace of all this, for it is by It that one knows all this [universe]. And just as a man can find [another] by his footprints, so does the man who thus knows find good fame and praise.

¶ 8. This [Self] is dearer than a son, dearer than wealth, dearer than all else, for the Self is what is most inward. Were one to speak of a man who says that there is some other thing dearer than the Self, [and say]: 'He will weep for what he holds dear,' he would very likely do so. So, let a man revere the Self as dear. For one who reveres the Self alone as dear, what he holds dear will never perish.

---

[1] *Sṛṣṭi*: more accurately 'emanation'.
[2] Or, 'fire-hole'.   [3] Or, 'Brahmā'.

¶ 9. It has been said: 'Since men think that by knowing Brahman they will become the All,' what was it that Brahman knew by which he became the All?

¶ 10. In the beginning this [universe] was Brahman alone, and He truly knew [him]self (*ātman*), saying: 'I am Brahman.' And so he became the All. Whichever of the gods became aware of this, also became that [All]: so too with seers (*ṛṣi*) and men. Seeing this, Vāmadeva, the seer, realized [this, saying]:

'I became Manu and the sun!'

This is true even now. Whoso thus knows that he is Brahman, becomes this whole [universe]. Even the gods have not the power to cause him to un-Be, for he becomes their own self.

So, whoever reveres any other deity, thinking: 'He is one, and I am another,' does not [rightly] understand. He is like a [sacrificial] animal for the gods; and just as many animals are of use to man, so is each single man of use to the gods. To be robbed of even a single animal is disagreeable. How much more to be robbed of many! And so the [gods] are not at all pleased that men should know this.

¶ 11. In the beginning this [universe] was Brahman,—One only. Being One only, he had not the power to develop. By a supreme effort (*ati*) he brought forth a form of the Good (*śreyo-rūpa*), [namely], princely power (*kṣatra*),—that is to say, those princely powers among the gods called Indra, Varuna, Soma, Rudra, Parjanya, Yama, Death and Iśāna (the Lord). Hence there is nothing higher than princely power, and so the Brāhman [priest] sits below the prince at the ceremonial anointing of a king, thereby conferring glory on the princely office. Brahman, (the quality that makes a Brāhman a Brāhman,) is the womb and source of princely power. Hence, even though the king enjoys supremacy, in the end he must return to Brahman, which is his [mother's] womb. And so whoever injures a [Brāhman] does violence to his [mother's] womb. He becomes more evil in that he has injured one who is better [than himself].

¶ 12. He had no power to develop further. He brought forth the common people (*viś*), that is, those types of gods which are referred to in groups,—the Vasus, the Rudras, the Ādityas, the All-gods and the Maruts.

¶ 13. He had no power to develop further. He brought forth the class [1] of serfs,—Pūshan. Pūshan is this [earth], for the [earth] nourishes everything that exists.

¶ 14. He had no power to develop further. By a supreme effort (*ati*) he brought forth a form of the Good,—right and law (*dharma*). This is the princely power of the princely class, namely, right and law. Hence there is nothing higher than right and law.

[1] Lit. 'colour'.

And so it is that a weaker man lords it over a stronger one by means of right and law, as by a king. Right and law are the same as truth. And so, of the man who speaks the truth it is [also] said that he speaks right, and of the man who speaks right it is said that he speaks the truth; for both of these are the same thing.

¶ 15. This Brahman, [then,] is [at the same time] the princely power and class, the common people, and the serfs.[1]

Among the gods this Brahman appeared (*abhavat*) as fire, among men as the Brāhman. He is a prince [too] through the princely power [inherent in him], a member of the common people through the virtue of the common people [inherent in him], and a serf through the quality of serf [inherent in him]. And so people wish for a state of being (*loka*) among the gods through [2] the [sacrificial] fire, among men through [2] a Brāhman. For it was in these two forms that Brahman appeared (*abhavat*).

Now whoever departs this world without having caught a glimpse of the state of being appropriate to himself will have no part in it because it will have no knowledge of him,—just like the Veda if it is not recited, or any other work (*karma*) left undone.

Yes, even if a man were to perform a great and holy work (*karma*) without knowing this,—this, in the end, would be lost for him indeed.

Let a man revere the Self only as a state of being [appropriate to himself]. Whoso reveres the Self only as a state of being [appropriate to himself], his deeds are not lost for him, for out of this very Self he brings forth whatever he desires.

¶ 16. Now this Self is the state of being (*loka*) of all contingent beings. In so far as a man pours libations and offers sacrifice, he is the sphere (*loka*) of the gods; in so far as he recites [the Veda], he is [the sphere] of the seers; in so far as he offers cakes and water to the ancestors, desiring offspring the while, he is [the sphere] of the ancestors; in so far as he gives food and lodging to men, he is [the sphere] of men; in so far as he finds grass and water for domestic animals, he is [the sphere] of domestic animals; in so far as wild beasts and birds, even down to the ants, find something to live on in his house, he is their sphere. For just as one would wish for security in one's own sphere [of activity] (*loka*), so do all contingent beings desire the security of the man who has this knowledge. This indeed is well known and has been [thoroughly] investigated.

¶ 17. In the beginning this [universe] was the Self alone,—One only. He longed to have a wife so that he might procreate, win

---

[1] Or, 'There are, [then,] this Brahman, the princely power and class, the common people, and the serfs.'
[2] Lit. 'in'.

wealth for himself and perform [good] works.[1] This was the extent of [his] desire. Not even by longing for it would a man obtain more than that. And so even today a man who is all alone longs to have a wife so that he may procreate, win wealth for himself and perform [good] works.[1] In so far as he does not obtain any one of these, he considers himself incomplete. Now, his wholeness [lies in this]: mind is his very self; the voice his wife; breath his offspring; the eye his worldly wealth, for it is by the eye that one finds it; the ear his heavenly [wealth], for by the ear does one hear it. Self [2] is his work (*karma*), for it is through the self that a man performs works.

This sacrifice is fivefold; cattle are fivefold; man is fivefold; this whole universe is fivefold,—everything that exists. Whoso thus knows wins this whole universe.

I, v

[Verses 1–2, on the different kinds of food produced by Prajāpati; 3–13, on the whole universe being composed of mind, the voice and breath; 14–15 on Prajāpati as the year; and 16, on the three worlds and how to win them, are omitted.]

¶ 17. Now next [comes] the handing over.

When a man thinks he is on the point of death, he says to his son: 'You are Brahman (the Veda, handed from father to son), you are the sacrifice, you are the world.' The son answers: 'I am Brahman, I am the sacrifice, I am the world.'

Whatever has been learnt (from the Veda) is summed up in the one word, 'Brahman'. Whatever sacrifices [have been offered] are summed up in the one word, 'sacrifice'. Whatever worlds (or states of being) there are, are summed up in the one word, 'world'. Such is the extent of this whole universe.

[Then the father thinks:] 'Since he is this whole universe, let him help me on my way from this world.' That is why a well-instructed son is called *lokya*, 'experienced in the world'. It is for this that he is instructed.

When [a father] who has this knowledge departs this world, he enters into his son with [all] these faculties (*prāṇa*). Whatever wrong he may have done, his son frees him from it all. Hence he is called a 'son'. It is through his son that a father is firmly established in this world. Then those divine, immortal faculties enter him (the father).

¶ 18. From earth and fire a divine voice enters into him. This is the divine voice by which whatever he says comes true.

---

[1] Or, 'perform sacrificial acts'.   [2] Meaning 'the body'?

¶ 19. From sky and sun a divine mind enters into him. This is the divine mind by which he experiences bliss and knows no sorrow.
¶ 20. From water and moon a divine spirit (breath) enters into him. This is the divine breath which, whether moving or at rest, neither quavers nor is hurt.

The man who possesses this knowledge becomes the Self of all contingent beings. As is that deity, so too is he. As all contingent beings contribute to that deity, so too do all contingent beings contribute to the man who has this knowledge. Whatever sorrows these creatures endure remain with them; only good (*puṇya*) follows after him, for evil cannot reach the gods.

¶ 21. Next [comes] the investigation of observances (*vrata*).

Prajāpati brought forth the faculties (*karma*). Once they had been brought forth, they entered into competition. 'I shall speak,' the voice began. 'I shall see,' said the eye. 'I shall hear,' said the ear. And so said [all] the other faculties each in accordance with the work [that is proper to it].

Death in the form of exhaustion laid hold of them and took possession of them. Death, on taking possession of them, penned them in. And so the voice becomes exhausted, the eye becomes exhausted and the ear becomes exhausted. But of that one known as the 'middle breath' he could not take possession. These [other faculties] began to understand it.

'This one indeed is the best of us,' [they thought,] 'for, whether moving or at rest it neither quavers nor is hurt. Come, let us all become a form of it.'

And they did all become a form of it. That is why they are called 'vital breaths' after it. In whatever family there is a man who has this knowledge, the family is called after him; but whoever sets himself up in rivalry with him, withers away; and after withering away, he finally dies. So much with regard to the self.
¶ 22. Now with regard to natural phenomena (*adhidaivata*).

'I shall blaze up,' began the fire. 'I shall generate heat,' said the sun. 'I shall shine,' said the moon. And so said [all] the other natural phenomena each in accordance with its nature.

Just as breath holds the midmost position among the human faculties (*prāṇa*), so does the wind among natural phenomena; for the other natural phenomena fade away; not so the wind. The natural phenomenon known as wind never sets [as does the sun].
¶ 23. On this there is the following verse:

> From whence the sun arises
> To whither it goes down—

This means that it rises out of the breath of life and sets in the breath of life.

> Him the gods made right and law (*dharma*):
> He is today, tomorrow too!

What those [faculties] started in olden times they still do today. So a man should follow but one observance. He should breathe in and breathe out, saying: 'May not the evil one, may not Death take possession of me!' And whatever [observance] he follows, he should want to see it through to the end. Thereby will he win union (*sāyujya*) with that natural phenomenon and will share in its state of being (*salokatā*).

I, vi

¶ 1. This [universe] is a triad,—name, form and work (*karma*).

Among names the voice is the hymn of praise (*ùk-tha*), for all names arise (*ut-thā*-) out of it. It is their chant (*sāman*), for it is the same (*sama*) as all names. It is their *brahman* (sacred utterance), for it bears (*bhṛ*-) all names.

¶ 2. Again, among forms the eye is the hymn of praise, for all forms arise out of it. It is their chant, for it is the same as all forms. It is their Brahman, for it bears all forms.

¶ 3. Again, among works the self is the hymn of praise, for all works arise out of it. It is their chant, for it is the same as all works. It is their Brahman, for it bears all works.

This, though a triad, is yet one,—the self. The self, though one, is yet a triad. That is the immortal hidden in the real (*satya*). The breath of life is the immortal, name and form are the real. By them is the breath of life hidden.

BOOK TWO

II, i

¶ 1. Driptabālāki was a learned member of the Gārgya clan. He said to Ajātaśatru, [king] of Benares: 'Shall I tell you about Brahman?' And Ajātaśatru said: 'I will give you a thousand [cows] for your teaching. In fact people do come running [to this place] saying, "A [second] Janaka [1] is here."'

¶ 2. The Gārgya said: 'It is the Person in the sun whom I revere as Brahman.'

Ajātaśatru said: 'Do not speak to me about him in this way. I revere him as sovereign Lord, the head and king of all contingent beings. Whoso reveres him thus [himself] becomes a sovereign Lord, the head and king of all contingent beings.'

---

[1] A king renowned for his generosity.

¶ 3. The Gārgya said: 'It is the Person in the moon whom I revere as Brahman.'

Ajātaśatru said: 'Do not speak to me about him in this way. I revere him as the great king Soma, robed in white. Whoso reveres him thus, for him is the Soma-juice pressed out day after day: he never lacks for food.'

¶ 4. The Gārgya said: 'It is the Person in the lightning whom I revere as Brahman.'

Ajātaśatru said: 'Do not speak to me about him in this way. I revere him as the effulgent. Whoso reveres him thus [himself] becomes effulgent, and effulgent is his offspring.'

¶ 5. The Gārgya said: 'It is the Person in space whom I revere as Brahman.'

Ajātaśatru said: 'Do not speak to me about him in this way. I revere him as the full,—inactive, undeveloping (*apravartin*). Whoso reveres him thus is full filled with offspring and cattle; nor does his offspring die out from this world.'

¶ 6. The Gārgya said: 'It is the Person in the wind whom I revere as Brahman.'

Ajātaśatru said: 'Do not speak to me about him in this way. I revere him as invincible Indra, an unconquerable army. Whoso reveres him thus [himself] becomes a conqueror, unconquered, conqueror of others.'

¶ 7. The Gārgya said: 'It is the Person in fire whom I revere as Brahman.'

Ajātaśatru said: 'Do not speak to me about him in this way. I revere him as the all-powerful (? *viśāsahin*). Whoso reveres him thus [himself] becomes all-powerful, and all-powerful is his offspring.'

¶ 8. The Gārgya said: 'It is the Person in water whom I revere as Brahman.'

Ajātaśatru said: 'Do not speak to me about him in this way. I revere him as the reflection [in the water]. Whoso reveres him thus is attended by what reflects [his own nature], not by what does not; and offspring reflecting [his own nature] are born to him.'

¶ 9. The Gārgya said: 'It is the Person in a mirror whom I revere as Brahman.'

Ajātaśatru said: 'Do not speak to me about him in this way. I revere him as the brilliant. Whoso reveres him thus [himself] becomes brilliant, and brilliant is his offspring. Moreover, he outshines all with whom he comes into contact.'

¶ 10. The Gārgya said: 'It is the sound that follows after a man as he walks that I revere as Brahman.'

Ajātaśatru said: 'Do not speak to me about him in this way. I revere him as life (*asu*). Whoso reveres him thus, to him does all the life-force (*āyu*) in the world accrue, nor does the breath of life leave him before his time.'

¶ 11. The Gārgya said: 'It is the Person in the points of the compass whom I revere as Brahman.'

Ajātaśatru said: 'Do not speak to me about him in this way. I revere him as the second that is inseparable [from the One]. Whoso reveres him thus acquires a "second"; plurality (*gaṇa*) is not cut away from him.'

¶ 12. The Gārgya said: 'It is the Person that consists of shadow whom I worship as Brahman.'

Ajātaśatru said: 'Do not speak to me about him in this way. I revere him as death. Whoso reveres him thus,—to him does all the life-force in the world accrue, nor does death approach him before his time.'

¶ 13. The Gārgya said: 'It is the Person in the self whom I revere as Brahman.'

Ajātaśatru said: 'Do not speak to me about him in this way. I revere him as one who possesses a self (*ātmanvin*). Whoso reveres him thus will [himself] come to possess a self, as will his offspring.' And the Gārgya held his peace.

¶ 14. Ajātaśatru said: 'Is that all?'

'That is all.'

'That is not enough for knowing [Brahman].'

'Then may I come to you as a pupil?' said the Gārgya.

¶ 15. Ajātaśatru said: 'It goes against the grain that a Brāhman should come to a prince and ask him to discourse on Brahman. Even so, I shall bring you to know [him] clearly.'

He took him by the hand and stood up; and the two of them went up to a man who was asleep and addressed him in these words: 'O great King Soma, robed in white!' But he did not get up. Then Ajātaśatru rubbed him with his hand and woke him up. He stood up.

¶ 16. Ajātaśatru said: 'When this man was asleep, where was the "person" who consists of consciousness (*vijñāna*) then? And from where did he return?' But the Gārgya did not know.

¶ 17. Ajātaśatru said: 'When this man was asleep, the "person" who consists of consciousness, with consciousness [as its instrument], took hold of the consciousness of the senses (*prāṇa*) and lay down in the space which is within the heart. When he takes hold of them [in this way], that means that the man is asleep. Then is the breath his captive,—captive too the voice, the eye and ear and mind.

¶ 18. 'When he moves around in dream, the worlds [of dream] are his. It seems to him that he has become a great king or a great Brāhman; regions high and low he seems to visit. As a great king, taking his people with him, might move at will within his kingdom, so does [this "person"] take the senses with him and rove at will throughout his own body.

¶ 19. 'But when he has fallen into a deep sleep and is conscious (*vid-*) of nothing at all, then does he slip out [from the heart] into the pericardium, [passing] through the seventy-two thousand channels called *hitā* which lead from the heart to the pericardium, and there he lies. Just as a youth or a great king or a great Brāhman might lie down on reaching the highest peak of bliss, so does he lie.

¶ 20. 'As a spider emerges [from itself] by [spinning] threads [out of its own body], as small sparks rise up from a fire, so too from this Self do all the life-breaths, all the worlds, all the gods, and all contingent beings rise up in all directions. The hidden meaning (*upaniṣad*) of this is the "Real of the real". The life-breaths are the real, and He is their Real.'

[Chapter ii is omitted.]

II, iii

¶ 1. Assuredly there are two forms of Brahman, the formed and the unformed, the mortal and the immortal, the static and the moving, the actual (*sat*) and the beyond (*tya*).

¶ 2. What is called the 'formed' is [all] that is other than the wind and atmosphere. This is the mortal, the static, the actual. The essence of this formed, mortal, static, actual [Brahman] is [the sun] which gives out heat; for this is the essence of the actual.

¶ 3. Now, the unformed is the wind and atmosphere. This is the immortal, the moving, the beyond. The essence of this unformed, immortal, moving [Brahman] beyond is the Person in the disc [of the sun]; for this is the essence of the beyond. So much with regard to natural phenomena.

¶ 4. Now with regard to the self.

The formed is what is other than the breath of life and the space within the self. This is the mortal, the static, the actual. The essence of this formed, mortal, static, actual [Brahman] is the eye; for this is the essence of the actual.

¶ 5. Now the unformed is the breath of life and the space within the self. This is the immortal, the moving, the beyond. The essence of this unformed, immortal, moving [Brahman] beyond is the Person in the right eye; for this is the essence of the beyond.

¶ 6. The form of this Person is like a saffron-coloured robe, or like white wool, or an *indragopa* beetle, or a flame of fire, or a white lotus, or a sudden flash of lightning. Like a sudden flash of lightning too is the good fortune of the man who thus knows.

From this follows the teaching [summed up in the words]: 'No, no!' For there is nothing higher than this 'No'. Or again it can be named the 'Real of the real'. The life-breaths are the real and He is their Real.

II, iv

¶ 1. 'Maitreyī,' said Yājñavalkya, 'I am about to give up my status [as a householder]. Well then, let me make a settlement for you and [your co-wife] Kātyāyanī.'

¶ 2. But Maitreyī said: 'If, sir, this whole earth, filled as it is with riches, were to belong to me, would I be immortal thereby?'

'No,' said Yājñavalkya. 'As is the life of the rich, so would your life be. For there is no hope of immortality in riches.'

¶ 3. And Maitreyī said: 'What should I do with something that does not bring me immortality? Tell me, good sir, what you know.'

¶ 4. And Yājñavalkya said: 'Dearly do I love you,—oh, that is certain,—and lovely are the words you speak. Come, sit down, and I will explain it to you; and as I am discoursing, ponder on it well.'

¶ 5. [Thus] did he discourse:

'Mark well, it is not for the love (*kāma*) of a husband that a husband is dearly loved (*priya*). Rather it is for the love of the Self that a husband is dearly loved.

'Mark well, it is not for the love of a wife that a wife is dearly loved. Rather it is for the love of the Self that a wife is dearly loved.

'Mark well, it is not for the love of sons that sons are dearly loved. Rather it is for the love of the Self that sons are dearly loved.

'Mark well, it is not for the love of riches that riches are dearly loved. Rather it is for the love of the Self that riches are dearly loved.

'Mark well, it is not for the love of the Brāhman class (*brahman*) that the Brāhman class is dearly loved. Rather it is for the love of the Self that the Brāhman class is dearly loved.

'Mark well, it is not for the love of the princely class that the princely class is dearly loved. Rather it is for the love of the Self that the princely class is dearly loved.

'Mark well, it is not for the love of the worlds that the worlds are dearly loved. Rather it is for the love of the Self that the worlds are dearly loved.

'Mark well, it is not for the love of the gods that the gods are dearly loved. Rather it is for the love of the Self that the gods are dearly loved.

'Mark well, it is not for the love of contingent beings that contingent beings are dearly loved. Rather it is for the love of the Self that contingent beings are dearly loved.

'Mark well, it is not for the love of the All that the All is dearly loved. Rather it is for the love of the Self that the All is dearly loved.

'Mark well, it is the Self that should be seen, [the Self] that should be heard, [the Self] that should be thought on and deeply pondered, Maitreyī.

'Mark well, by seeing the Self and hearing It, by thinking of It and knowing It, this whole [universe] is known.

¶ 6. 'A Brāhman's high estate (*brahman*) forsakes the man who thinks of a Brāhman's high estate as other than the Self.

'A prince's high estate forsakes the man who thinks of a prince's high estate as other than the Self.

'The worlds forsake the man who thinks of the worlds as other than the Self.

'The gods forsake the man who thinks of the gods as other than the Self.

'Contingent beings forsake the man who thinks of contingent beings as other than the Self.

'The All forsakes the man who thinks of the All as other than the Self.

'The high estate of Brāhmans, the high estate of princes, these worlds, these gods, these contingent beings, this All are nothing but the Self!

¶ 7. 'As, when a drum is beaten, you cannot grasp the sounds that issue from it; only by grasping the drum [itself] or the drummer can you grasp the sound:

¶ 8. 'As, when a conch is blown, you cannot grasp the sounds that issue from it; only by grasping the conch [itself] or the blower of the conch can you grasp the sound:

¶ 9. 'As, when a lute is played, you cannot grasp the sounds that issue from it; only by grasping the lute or the player of the lute can you grasp the sound:

¶ 10. 'As clouds of smoke surge up in all directions from a fire kindled from damp fuel, so too, I say, was this [whole universe] breathed forth from that great Being (*bhūta*),—Rig-Veda, Yajur-Veda, Sāma-Veda, the Atharva-Veda, [the hymns of] the Angi-rases, the collections of stories, the ancient tales, wisdom (*vidyā*), the secret doctrines (*upaniṣad*), the verses, aphorisms, com-mentaries and commentaries on commentaries,—all these were breathed forth from It.

¶ 11. 'As all the waters meet in one place only,—in the sea; as all sensations meet in one place only,—in the skin; as all scents meet in one place only,—in the nose; as all tastes meet in one place only,—in the tongue; as all forms meet in one place only,—in the eye; as all sounds meet in one place only,—in the ear; as all concepts meet in one place only,—in the mind; as all wisdom meets in one place only,—in the heart; as all actions (*karma*) meet in one place only,—in the hands; as all ecstasies (*ānanda*) meet in one place only,—in the phallus; as all excretions meet in

one place only,—in the anus; as all paths meet in one place only,
—in the feet; as all the Vedas meet in one place only,—in the
voice:

¶ 12. 'As a lump of salt dropped into water dissolves in it and
cannot be picked out [again], yet from whatever part of the water
you draw, there is still salt there, so too, I say, is this great Being,
—infinite, boundless, a mass of understanding (*vijñāna*). Out of
these elements (*bhūta*) do [all contingent beings] arise and along
with them are they destroyed. After death there is no consciousness (*saṁjñā*): this is what I say.' Thus spake Yājñavalka.

¶ 13. But Maitreyī said: 'In this, good sir, you have thrown me
into confusion in that you say that after death there is no consciousness.'

And Yājñavalkya said: 'There is nothing confusing in what I
say. This is surely as much as you can understand now.

¶ 14. 'For where there is any semblance of duality, then does one
smell another, then does one see another, then does one hear
another, then does one speak to another, then does one think of
another, then does one understand another. But when all has
become one's very (*eva*) Self, then with what should one smell
whom? With what should one see whom? With what should one
hear whom? With what should one speak to whom? With what
should one think of whom? With what should one understand
whom? With what should one understand Him by whom one
understands this whole universe? With what indeed should one
understand the Understander?'

II, v

¶ 1. This earth is the honey of all beings (*bhūta*), and all beings
are honey for this earth. That radiant, immortal Person who
indwells this earth and, in the case of the [human] self, that
radiant, immortal Person who consists of the body, is indeed that
very Self: this is the Immortal, this Brahman, this the All.

¶ 2. The waters are the honey of all beings and all beings are
honey for the waters. That radiant, immortal Person who
indwells these waters and, in the case of the [human] self, that
radiant, immortal Person who consists of semen, is indeed that
very Self: this is the Immortal, this Brahman, this the All.

¶ 3. Fire is the honey of all beings and all beings are honey for
fire. That radiant, immortal Person who indwells this fire and, in
the case of the [human] self, that radiant, immortal Person who
consists of the voice, is indeed that very Self: this is the Immortal,
this Brahman, this the All.

¶ 4. The wind is the honey of all beings and all beings are honey
for the wind. That radiant, immortal Person who indwells this

wind and, in the case of the [human] self, that radiant, immortal Person who is breath, is indeed that very Self: this is the Immortal, this Brahman, this the All.

¶ 5. The sun is the honey of all beings and all beings are honey for the sun. That radiant, immortal Person who indwells that sun and, in the case of the [human] self, that radiant, immortal Person who consists of sight, is indeed that very Self: this is the Immortal, this Brahman, this the All.

¶ 6. The points of the compass are the honey of all beings and all beings are honey for the points of the compass. That radiant, immortal Person who indwells these points of the compass and, in the case of the [human] self, that radiant, immortal Person who consists of hearing and echo, is indeed that very Self: this is the Immortal, this Brahman, this the All.

¶ 7. The moon is the honey of all beings and all beings are honey for the moon. That radiant, immortal Person who indwells that moon and, in the case of the [human] self, that radiant, immortal Person who consists of mind, is indeed that very Self: this is the Immortal, this Brahman, this the All.

¶ 8. Lightning is the honey of all beings and all beings are honey for the lightning. That radiant, immortal Person who indwells this lightning and, in the case of the [human] self, that radiant, immortal Person who consists of radiance (*tejas*) [itself], is indeed that very Self: this is the Immortal, this Brahman, this the All.

¶ 9. Thunder is the honey of all beings and all beings are honey for the thunder. That radiant, immortal Person who indwells this thunder and, in the case of the [human] self, that radiant, immortal Person who consists of sound and tone, is indeed that very Self: this is the Immortal, this Brahman, this the All.

¶ 10. Space is the honey of all beings and all beings are honey for space. That radiant, immortal Person who indwells this space and, in the case of the [human] self, that radiant, immortal Person who is the space within the heart, is indeed that very Self: this is the Immortal, this Brahman, this the All.

¶ 11. [Cosmic] law (*dharma*) is the honey of all beings and all beings are honey for the law. That radiant, immortal Person who indwells this law and, in the case of the [human] self, that radiant, immortal Person who consists of duty (*dhārma*), is indeed that very Self: this is the Immortal, this Brahman, this the All.

¶ 12. Truth is the honey of all beings and all beings are honey for truth. That radiant, immortal Person who indwells this truth and, in the case of the [human] self, that radiant, immortal Person who consists of truthfulness (*sātya*), is indeed that very Self: this is the Immortal, this Brahman, this the All.

¶ 13. Humanity is the honey of all beings and all beings are honey for humanity. That radiant, immortal Person who indwells humanity and, in the case of the [human] self, that radiant, immortal Person who consists of humanity, is indeed that very Self: this is the Immortal, this Brahman, this the All.

¶ 14. The Self is the honey of all beings and all beings are honey for the Self. That radiant, immortal Person who indwells the Self and that radiant, immortal Person who *is* the Self,—he is that very Self indeed: this is the Immortal, this Brahman, this the All.

¶ 15. This Self is indeed the Lord of all contingent beings, king of all beings. Just as the spokes of a wheel are together fixed on to the hub and felly, so are all contingent beings, all gods, all worlds, all vital breaths and all these selves together fixed in this Self.

[Verses 16–19a, which are purely mythological, are omitted.]

¶ 19b. Seeing this, a seer has said:

> He conformed himself to every form:
> This is [one] form of him [for all] to see.
> By his uncanny powers (*māyā*) does Indra
> Rove round in many a form:
> Yoked are his thousand steeds!

This [Self] is [those] steeds indeed. It is tens and thousands, many and infinite. This is Brahman,—without an earlier or a later, without inside or outside. This Self is Brahman,—all-experiencing (*anubhū-*). Such is the teaching.

[Chapter vi, which gives the chain of the teachers of this doctrine, is omitted.]

BOOK THREE

III, i

¶ 1. Janaka, [king] of Videha, was offering a sacrifice at which the fees [paid to the officiating Brāhmans] were to be copious. There Brāhmans of the Kurupancālas had assembled.

Janaka, [king] of Videha, was curious to know which of [all] these Brāhmans was the most learned in scripture. So he penned in a thousand cows, to the horns of each of which ten *pādas* [of gold] were attached.

¶ 2. He said to them: 'Venerable Brāhmans, let whichever of you is the most conversant with Brahman (*brahmiṣṭha*) drive away these cows.'

Not one of these Brāhmans dared to. But Yājñvalkya said to his pupil: 'Sāmaśravas, my dear, drive them away.' So he drove them away.

The [other] Brāhmans were greatly vexed. 'How dare he claim to be the most conversant with Brahman among us?' said they.

At that time [one] Aśvala was the officiating priest of Janaka,

[king] of Videha. He questioned Yājñavalkya and said: 'So you are the most conversant with Brahman, are you?'

'Let us do homage to whoever is the most conversant with Brahman,' said he. 'But surely [all] of us would like to have the cows.' Then Aśvala, the officiating priest, began to question him.

[Verses 3 to end, which deal with magic correspondences between various classes of priest, natural phenomena and human faculties, are omitted.]

III, ii

[Verses 1-9, on the senses and their objects, are omitted.]

¶ 10. 'Yājñavalkya,' said [Jāratkārava Ārtabhāga]: 'Since all things are food for death, which is the natural phenomenon (*devatā*) of which death is the food?'

'Death is fire and the food of water. [Whoso knows this] overcomes repeated death.'

¶ 11. Yājñavalkya,' said he, 'when a man dies, do his vital breaths depart from him or not?'

'No,' said Yājñavalkya. 'They are brought together here [in the body], and [the body] swells and inflates. Once inflated it lies [there] dead.'

¶ 12. 'Yājñavalkya,' said he, 'when a man (*puruṣa*) dies, what [is it that] does not leave him?'

'Name,' he said; 'infinite is the name; infinite are the All-gods; and infinite is the state of being (*loka*) he wins thereby.'

¶ 13. 'Yājñavalkya,' he said, 'when a man is dead and his voice enters the fire, his breath the wind, his eye the sun, his mind the moon, his ear the points of the compass, his body the earth, his self space, the hairs of his body the plants, the hairs of his head the trees, and his blood and seed are laid to rest in the waters, where is that man then?'

'Ārtabhāga, my friend,' said he, 'take my hand. We two alone will know about this. It is not for us [to speak of this] in public.'

Together they went away and conversed together. What they were discussing was 'works' (*karma*): what they were praising was 'works'. By good (*puṇya*) works a man becomes holy (*puṇya*), by evil [works] evil. Then did Jāratkārava Ārtabhāga hold his peace.

[Chapter iii, on the fate of the Pārikshitas, is omitted.]

III, iv

¶ 1. Then Ushasta Cākrāyana questioned him, saying: 'Yājña-valkya, explain to me that Brahman which is evident and not obscure, the Self that indwells all things.'

'This Self that indwells all things is within you (*te*).'
'[But] which one [is it], Yājñavalkya, [that] indwells all things?'
'Who breathes in with the in-breath, he is the Self within you that indwells all things; who breathes out with the out-breath, he is the Self within you that indwells all things; who breathes along with your "diffused breath" (*vyāna*), he is the Self within you that indwells all things; who breathes along with your "upper breath" (*udāna*), he is the Self within you that indwells all things: he is the Self within you that indwells all things.'

¶ 2. Ushasta Cākrāyana said: 'Your teaching on this subject is exactly like [that of] a man who says: "That is a cow, and that is a horse." Explain to me that Brahman which is really (*eva*) evident and not obscure, the Self that indwells all things.'
'This Self that indwells all things is within you.'
'[But] which one [is it], Yājñavalkya, [that] indwells all things?'
'How should you see the seer of seeing? How should you hear the hearer of hearing? How should you think on the thinker of thought? How should you understand (*vijñā-*) the understander of understanding? This Self that indwells all things is within you. What is other than It suffers (*ārta*).' Then Ushasta Cākrāyana held his peace.

III, v

Then Kahola Kaushītakeya questioned him, saying: 'Yājña-valkya, explain to me that Brahman which is evident and not obscure, the Self that indwells all things.'
'The Self that indwells all things is within you (*te*).'
'[But] which one [is it], Yājñavalkya, [that] indwells all things?'
'He who transcends hunger and thirst, sorrow, confusion, old age and death. Once Brāhmans have come to know this Self, they rise above their desire for sons, their desire for riches, their desire for [exalted] states of being (*loka*), and wander forth to lead a beggar's life. For there is no difference between a desire for sons and a desire for riches; and there is no difference between a desire for riches and a desire for [exalted] states of being: all of them are nothing more than desire.
'So let a Brāhman put away learning with disgust and lead a childlike life. Let him then put away both the childlike life and learning with disgust, and [become] a silent sage (*muni*). Let him then put away both silence and its opposite with disgust, and [become a true] Brāhman (a man who really knows Brahman).'
'And what is it that makes him a Brāhman?'
'Whatever really makes him such. What is other than [the Self] suffers (*ārta*).' Then Kahola Kaushītakeya held his peace.

III, vi

Then Gārgī Vācaknavī questioned him, saying: 'Yājñavalkya, since this whole universe is woven, warp and woof, on water, what is it on which water is woven, warp and woof?'
'On the wind, Gārgī,' said he.
'What is it, then, on which the wind is woven, warp and woof?'
'On the worlds of the atmosphere, Gārgī.'
'What is it, then, on which the worlds of the atmosphere are woven, warp and woof?'
'On the worlds of the Gandharvas, Gārgī.'
'What is it, then, on which the worlds of the Gandharvas are woven, warp and woof?'
'On the worlds of the sun, Gārgī.'
'What is it, then, on which the worlds of the sun are woven, warp and woof?'
'On the worlds of the moon, Gārgī.'
'What is it, then, on which the worlds of the moon are woven, warp and woof?'
'On the worlds of the stars, Gārgī.'
'What is it, then, on which the worlds of the stars are woven, warp and woof?'
'On the worlds of the gods, Gārgī.'
'What is it, then, on which the worlds of the gods are woven, warp and woof?'
'On the worlds of Indra, Gārgī.'
'What is it, then, on which the worlds of Indra are woven, warp and woof?'
'On the worlds of Prajāpati, Gārgī.'
'What is it, then, on which the worlds of Prajāpati are woven, warp and woof?'
'On the worlds of Brahman, Gārgī.'
'What is it, then, on which the worlds of Brahman are woven, warp and woof?'
'Gārgī,' he said, 'do not question overmuch lest your head should fall off. You are asking too many questions about a deity about which too many questions should not be asked. Do not question overmuch.' Then Gārgī Vācaknavī held her peace.

III, vii

¶ 1. Then Uddālaka Āruni questioned him, saying: 'Yājña-valkya, we were living among the Madras in the house of Patañjala Kāpya, studying the sacrifice. His wife was possessed of a spirit (*gandharva*), and we asked him who he was. He answered that he was Kabandha Ātharvana, and, addressing

Patañjala Kāpya and the students of the sacrifice, he said: "Kāpya, do you know that thread by which this world and the next world and all beings (*bhūta*) are strung together?"

'Patañjala Kāpya said: "No, sir, I do not."

'Addressing Patañjala Kāpya and the students of the sacrifice [again], he said: "Kāpya, do you know the Inner Controller who controls this world and the next world and all beings from within?"

'Patañjala Kāpya said: "No, sir, I do not."

'Addressing Patañjala Kāpya and the students of the sacrifice [again], he said: "Kāpya, whoever knows that thread and that Inner Controller, will [also] know Brahman, [all] worlds, gods, Vedas, contingent beings, the Self,—everything." So did he speak to them.

'Now I do know this. If you, Yājñavalkya, drive away the Brahman-cows without knowing the thread and the Inner Controller, your head will fall off.'

'Certainly, Gautama, I know that thread and that Inner Controller.'

'Anyone might say, "I know, I know." Tell me *what* you know.'

¶ 2. 'Wind, Gautama, is that thread,' said he. 'By this thread which is the wind, this world and the next world and all beings are strung together. So it is, Gautama, that it is said of a dead man that his limbs are unstrung, for they are strung together, Gautama, by the wind as by a thread.'

'Very true, Yājñavalkya: [now] tell [us] about the Inner Controller.'

¶ 3. 'He who, abiding in the earth, is other than the earth, whom the earth does not know, whose body is the earth, who controls the earth from within,—he is the Self within you (*te*), the Inner Controller, the Immortal.

¶ 4. 'He who, abiding in water, is other than water, whom water does not know, whose body is water, who controls the water from within,—he is the Self within you, the Inner Controller, the Immortal.

¶ 5. 'He who, abiding in fire, is other than fire, whom fire does not know, whose body is fire, who controls fire from within,—he is the Self within you, the Inner Controller, the Immortal.

¶ 6. 'He who, abiding in the atmosphere, is other than the atmosphere, whom the atmosphere does not know, whose body is the atmosphere, who controls the atmosphere from within,—he is the Self within you, the Inner Controller, the Immortal.

¶ 7. 'He who, abiding in the wind, is other than the wind, whom the wind does not know, whose body is the wind, who controls the wind from within,—he is the Self within you, the Inner Controller, the Immortal.

¶ 8. 'He who, abiding in the sky, is other than the sky, whom the sky does not know, whose body is the sky, who controls the sky from within,—he is the Self within you, the Inner Controller, the Immortal.

¶ 9. 'He who, abiding in the sun, is other than the sun, whom the sun does not know, whose body is the sun, who controls the sun from within,—he is the Self within you, the Inner Controller, the Immortal.

¶ 10. 'He who, abiding in the points of the compass, is other than the points of the compass, whom the points of the compass do not know, whose body is the points of the compass, who controls the points of the compass from within,—he is the Self within you, the Inner Controller, the Immortal.

¶ 11. 'He who, abiding in the moon and stars, is other than the moon and stars, whom the moon and stars do not know, whose body is the moon and stars, who controls the moon and stars from within,—he is the Self within you, the Inner Controller, the Immortal.

¶ 12. 'He who, abiding in space, is other than space, whom space does not know, whose body is space, who controls space from within,—he is the Self within you, the Inner Controller, the Immortal.

¶ 13. 'He who, abiding in darkness, is other than darkness, whom darkness does not know, whose body is darkness, who controls darkness from within,—he is the Self within you, the Inner Controller, the Immortal.

¶ 14. 'He who, abiding in light (*tejas*), is other than light, whom light does not know, whose body is light, who controls light from within,—he is the Self within you, the Inner Controller, the Immortal.

'So much with regard to natural phenomena (*adhidaivata*). Now with regard to contingent beings (*adhibhūta*).

¶ 15. 'He who, abiding in all contingent beings, is other than all contingent beings, whom all contingent beings do not know, whose body is all contingent beings, who controls all contingent beings from within,—he is the Self within you, the Inner Controller, the Immortal.

'So much with regard to contingent beings. Now with regard to the self.

¶ 16. 'He who, abiding in breath, is other than breath, whom breath does not know, whose body is breath, who controls breath from within,—he is the Self within you, the Inner Controller, the Immortal.

¶ 17. 'He who, abiding in the voice, is other than the voice, whom the voice does not know, whose body is the voice, who controls the voice from within,—he is the Self within you, the Inner Controller, the Immortal.

¶ 18. 'He who, abiding in the eye, is other than the eye, whom the eye does not know, whose body is the eye, who controls the eye from within,—he is the Self within you, the Inner Controller, the Immortal.

¶ 19. 'He who, abiding in the ear, is other than the ear, whom the ear does not know, whose body is the ear, who controls the ear from within,—he is the Self within you, the Inner Controller, the Immortal.

¶ 20. 'He who, abiding in the mind, is other than the mind, whom the mind does not know, whose body is the mind, who controls the mind from within,—he is the Self within you, the Inner Controller, the Immortal.

¶ 21. 'He who, abiding in the skin, is other than the skin, whom the skin does not know, whose body is the skin, who controls the skin from within,—he is the Self within you, the Inner Controller, the Immortal.

¶ 22. 'He who, abiding in the understanding (*vijñāna*), is other than the understanding, whom the understanding does not know, whose body is the understanding, who controls the understanding from within,—he is the Self within you, the Inner Controller, the Immortal.

¶ 23. 'He who, abiding in semen, is other than semen, whom semen does not know, whose body is semen, who controls semen from within,—he is the Self within you, the Inner Controller, the Immortal.

'He is the unseen seer, the unheard hearer, the unthought thinker, the unununderstood understander. No other seer than He is there, no other hearer than He, no other thinker than He, no other understander than He: He is the Self within you, the Inner Controller, the Immortal. What is other than He suffers.'

Then Uddālaka Āruni held his peace.

III, viii

¶ 1. Then [Gārgī] Vācaknavī said: 'Venerable Brāhmans, look, I will ask him two questions. If he answers them for me, then not one of you will defeat him in argument about Brahman.'

'Ask on, Gārgī,' said he.

¶ 2. She said: 'Yājñavalkya, like a young hero from the Kāsyas or the Videhas who, having strung his unstrung bow and grasped in his hand two arrows, murderous to his foe, advances [against his enemy], so too do I advance against you with two questions. Answer them for me.'

'Ask on, Gārgī,' said he.

¶ 3. She said: 'Yājñavalkya, that which is above the sky, which is below the earth, which is between sky and earth,—that which men speak of as past, present and future: on what is *that* woven, warp and woof?'

¶ 4. He said: 'Gārgī, that which is above the sky, which is below the earth, which is between sky and earth,—that which men speak of as past, present and future: that is woven on space, warp and woof.'

¶ 5. She said: 'All honour to you, Yājñavalkya, in that you have solved this [question] for me. Hold yourself ready for another.'

'Ask on, Gārgī,' said he.

¶ 6. She said: 'Yājñavalkya, that which is above the sky, which is below the earth, which is between sky and earth,—that which men speak of as past, present and future: on what is *that* woven, warp and woof?'

¶ 7. He said: 'Gārgī, that which is above the sky, which is below the earth, which is between sky and earth,—that which men speak of as past, present and future: that is woven on space, warp and woof.'

'On what, then, is space woven, warp and woof?' said she.

¶ 8. He said: 'Gārgī, that is what Brāhmans call the "Imperishable".

'It is not coarse nor fine; not short nor long; not red (like fire) nor adhesive (like water). It casts no shadow, is not [1] darkness. It is not [1] wind nor is it space. It is not attached to anything. It is not [1] taste or smell; it is not [1] eye or ear; it is not [1] voice or mind; it is not [1] light (*tejas*) or life (*prāṇa*); it has no face [2] or measure; it has no "within", no "without". Nothing does It consume nor is It consumed by anyone at all.

¶ 9. 'At the behest of this Imperishable, Gārgī, sun and moon are held apart and so abide. At the behest of this Imperishable, Gārgī, sky and earth are held apart and so abide. At the behest of this Imperishable, Gārgī, seconds and minutes, days and nights, fortnights and months, seasons and years are held apart and so abide. At the behest of this Imperishable, Gārgī, some rivers flow from the [snow-]white mountains to the east, others to the west, each pursuing its [appointed] course. At the behest of this Imperishable, Gārgī, men praise the open-handed, gods depend upon the sacrificer and the ancestors on the rites offered for the dead.

¶ 10. 'Whatever oblations a man may offer up in this world, Gārgī, whatever sacrifice he may perform, whatever penances he may impose upon himself [even though they last] for many thousands of years, all this must have an end unless he knows this Imperishable.

---

[1] 'Not' can here equally be translated 'without'.
[2] Or 'mouth'. One recension adds here: 'It has no personal or family name: it does not age or die; it is free from fear, immortal, immaculate: it is not revealed nor hidden.'

'Gārgī, whoso departs this world without knowing this Imperishable, pitiable is he! But, Gārgī, whoso departs this world, knowing this Imperishable, he is a Brāhman [indeed] (for he thereby knows Brahman).

¶ 11. 'Gārgī, this same Imperishable [it is who] is the unseen seer, the unheard hearer, the unthought thinker, the ununderstood understander. No other seer than It is there, no other hearer than It, no other thinker than It, no other understander than It. In this Imperishable, indeed, Gārgī, is space woven, warp and woof.'

¶ 12. [And Gārgī] said: 'Venerable Brāhmans, you should count yourselves lucky if you manage to rid yourselves of this man [simply] by paying him homage, for not one of you will defeat him in argument about Brahman.' Then [Gārgī] Vācaknavī held her peace.

III, ix

¶ 1. Then Vidagdha Śākalya questioned him, saying: 'How many gods are there, Yājñavalkya?'

He answered by [reciting] this invocatory formula:

'As many as are mentioned in the invocatory formula in the hymn to the All-gods,—three hundred and three and three thousand and three (= 3306).'

'Yes (oṁ),' said he, 'but how many gods are there really (eva), Yājñavalkya?'

'Thirty-three.'

'Yes,' he said, 'but how many gods are there really, Yājña-valkya?'

'Six.'

'Yes,' he said, 'but how many gods are there really, Yājña-valkya?'

'Three.'

'Yes,' he said, 'but how many gods are there really, Yājña-valkya?'

'Two.'

'Yes,' he said, 'but how many gods are there really, Yājña-valkya?'

'One and a half.'

'Yes,' he said, 'but how many gods are there really, Yājña-valkya?'

'One.'

'Yes,' he said, 'but which are those three hundred and three and those three thousand and three?'

¶ 2. [Yājñavalkya] said: 'These are only their attributes of majesty (mahiman). There are only thirty-three gods.'

'Which are those thirty-three?'

'The eight Vasus, the eleven Rudras, the twelve Ādityas. That makes thirty-one. [Add] Indra and Prajāpati, [and that] makes thirty-three.'

¶ 3. 'Which are the Vasus?'

'Fire, earth, wind, atmosphere, sun, sky, moon and stars. These are the Vasus. For to these all wealth (*vasu*) is entrusted. That is why they are [called] Vasus.'

¶ 4. 'Which are the Rudras?'

'The ten breaths in man (*puruṣa*), and the eleventh is the self. When they depart this mortal body, they make [men] weep; and because they make them weep (*rud*-), they are [called] Rudras.'

¶ 5. 'Which are the Ādityas?'

'The twelve months of the year are the Ādityas, for they carry off everything,[1] though going on [themselves]; and because they carry off (*ādā*-) everything,[1] though going on (*yanti*) [themselves], they are [called] Ādityas.'

¶ 6. 'Which is Indra? Which Prajāpati?'

'Indra is thunder, Prajāpati the sacrifice.'

'Which is thunder?'

'The thunderbolt.'

'Which is the sacrifice?'

'Cattle.'

¶ 7. 'Which are the six?'

'Fire, earth, wind, atmosphere, sun and sky. These are the six. These six are everything.[1]

¶ 8. 'Which are the three gods?'

'These three worlds, for all these gods are in them.'

'Which are the two gods?'

'Food and the breath of life.'

'Which is the one and a half?'

'The purifying [2] [wind].'

¶ 9. 'It has been asked: "Since the purifying [2] [wind] appears to be one, how can it be [called] one and a half?"'

'Because everything[1] grows to maturity (*adhyārdhnot*) in it, it is [called] one and a half (*adhyardha*).'

'Which is the one God?'

'The breath of life, and that is Brahman, the beyond (*tya*). So have [we] been taught.'

¶ 10. [Śākalya said:] 'If a man were to know that "person" whose dwelling is the earth, whose sphere (*loka*) is fire, whose light is the mind, and who is the goal of every self, then would he be one who really knows, Yājñavalkya?'

[Yājñavalkya said:] 'I do know that "person", the goal of

---

[1] Or, 'this whole universe'.   [2] Or, 'blowing'.

every self of whom you speak. It is the "person" in the body. But tell [me], Śākalya, what is his [tutelary] deity?'

'The Immortal,' said he.

[Verses 11–18, which give a list of similar 'persons' and the corresponding 'deities', and verses 19–25, on the points of the compass, their 'deities' and 'bases', are omitted.]

¶ 26. [Śākalya said:] 'On what are you and [your] self based?'

[Yājñavalkya said:] 'On the in-breath.'

'On what is the in-breath based?'

'On the out-breath.'

'On what is the out-breath based?'

'On the "diffused" breath.'

'On what is the "diffused" breath based?'

'On the "upper" breath.'

'On what is the "upper" breath based?'

'On the "concentrated" breath.

'This Self—[what can one say of it but] "No, no!" It is impalpable, for it cannot be grasped; indestructible, for it cannot be destroyed; free from attachment, for it is not attached [to anything], not bound. It does not quaver nor can it be hurt.

'These are the eight dwellings, the eight spheres (loka), the eight gods, the eight "persons".[1] Who splits apart and puts together these "persons" and then passes beyond them, he is the "Person" of the Upanishads about whom I question you. If you do not tell me who he is, your head will fall off.'

But Śākalya did not know him, and so his head did fall off. And robbers made away with his bones, thinking they were something else.

¶ 27. Then [Yājñavalkya] said: 'Venerable Brāhmans, let any one of you who so wishes question me; or do you all question me. Or I will question any of you who so wishes, or I will question all of you.'

But none of the Brāhmans dared to [question him].

¶ 28. Then he questioned them with these verses:

'As a mighty tree, the forest's lord,
So, in very truth, is Man.
His hairs are [like] the leaves,
His skin the outer bark.

From his skin the blood flows forth
[As] sap from the bark [of the tree]:
When he is wounded, sap goes out
As from a stricken tree.

[1] Enumerated in verses 10–17.

His flesh is [like] the mass of wood(?),
His sinews tough [like] the inner bark;
His bones are the wood within,
His marrow wrought like pith.

As a tree, when felled, grows up again
From the root, a new [creation],
So mortal [Man], when felled by death—
From what root will *he* grow up?

Say not "from seed", for that springs forth
From one who is alive.
The tree, it seems, grows up from grain;
When dead, it straightway comes to be.

Along with the tree tear out the roots,—
It will not rise again:
So mortal [Man], when felled by death—
From what root will *he* grow up?

Once born, he is not born [again],
Who should again beget him?

Brahman is understanding (*vijñāna*), bliss,
[Self-]giving, giver's goal,
[The goal] of him who [patient] stands,
    Knowing It the while.'

BOOK FOUR

IV, i

¶ 1. Janaka, [king] of Videha was sitting down when Yājñavalkya
approached him. [The king] said to him: 'Yājñavalkya, what have
you come for? Is it cows you want or subtle arguments?'
    'Both, Your Majesty,' said he.
¶ 2. 'Let us hear what people have been telling you,' [continued
Yājñavalkya.]
    'Jitvan Śailini told me that Brahman is speech.'
    'For Śailini to say that Brahman is speech is [about as signi-
ficant] as for him to say that he has a mother or a father or a
teacher; for what is the use of a man who cannot speak? But did
he tell you its home and support?'
    'No, he did not.'
    'Your Majesty, [such a Brahman as this stands] on one leg
only.'
    'Well, Yājñavalkya, tell us yourself.'

'Its home is speech itself, and space is its support. It should be revered as cognition (*prajñā*).'

'What is the essence of cognition, Yājñavalkya?'

'Again speech, Your Majesty,' said he. 'It is by speaking, sire, that a friend is recognized (*prajñā*-). By speech, Your Majesty, the Rig-Veda, Yajur-Veda, Sāma-Veda, the Atharva-Veda, [the hymns of] the Angirases, the collections of stories, the ancient tales, wisdom (*vidyā*), the secret doctrines (*upaniṣad*), the verses, aphorisms, commentaries and commentaries on commentaries, what is offered up in sacrifice and as an oblation, food and drink, this world and the next and all contingent beings are cognized. Speech it is, sire, that is the highest Brahman. [And] speech does not forsake the man who, thus knowing, reveres it; all beings (*bhūta*) flow into him. He becomes a god and goes to the gods.'

'I will give you a thousand [cows] with a bull the size of an elephant,' said Janaka, [king] of Videha.

'My father [always] thought', said Yājñavalkya, 'that one should not accept [gifts] without first imparting instruction.'

¶ 3. 'Let us hear what people have been telling you,' [continued Yājñavalkya.]

'Udanka Śaulbāyana told me that Brahman is the breath of life.'

'For Śaulbāyana to say that Brahman is the breath of life is [about as significant] as for him to say that he has a mother or a father or a teacher; for what is the use of a lifeless man? But did he tell you its home and support?'

'No, he did not.'

'Your Majesty, [such a Brahman as this stands] on one leg only.'

'Well, Yājñavalkya, tell us yourself.'

'Its home is the breath of life itself, and space is its support. It should be revered as love (*priyam*).'

'What is the essence of love, Yājñavalkya?'

'Again the breath of life, Your Majesty,' said he. 'For love (*kāma*) of life, sire, a man will offer in sacrifice what should not be sacrificed, and will accept [gifts] from one from whom he should not accept [them]. For love of life, Your Majesty, a man lives in fear of being killed wherever he may go. The breath of life it is, sire, that is the highest Brahman. [And] the breath of life does not forsake the man who, thus knowing, reveres it; all beings flow into him. He becomes a god and goes to the gods.'

'I will give you a thousand [cows] with a bull the size of an elephant,' said Janaka, [king] of Videha.

'My father [always] thought', said Yājñavalkyra, 'that one should not accept [gifts] without first imparting instruction.'

¶ 4. 'Let us hear what people have been telling you,' [continued Yājñavalkya.]

'Barku Vārshna told me that Brahman is sight.'

'For Vārshna to say that Brahman is sight is [about as signifi-cant] as for him to say that he has a mother or a father or a teacher; for what is the use of a sightless man? But did he tell you its home and support?'

'No, he did not.'

'Your Majesty, [such a Brahman as this stands] on one leg only.'

'Well, Yājñavalkya, tell us yourself.'

'Its home is the eye, and space is its support. It should be revered as truth.'

'What is the essence of truth, Yājñavalkya?'

'Again sight, Your Majesty,' said he. 'If you say to a man who can see, "Can you see?" and he replies, "I can", that is the truth. Sight it is, sire, that is the highest Brahman. [And] sight does not forsake the man who, thus knowing, reveres it; all beings flow into him. He becomes a god and goes to the gods.'

'I will give you a thousand [cows] with a bull the size of an elephant,' said Janaka, [king] of Videha.

'My father [always] thought', said Yājñavalkya, 'that one should not accept [gifts] without first imparting instruction.'

¶ 5. 'Let us hear what people have been telling you,' [continued Yājñavalkya.]

'Gardabhīvipīta Bhāradvāja told me that Brahman is hearing.'

'For Bhāradvāja to say that Brahman is hearing is [about as significant] as for him to say that he has a mother or a father or a teacher; for what is the use of a deaf man? But did he tell you its home and support?'

'No, he did not.'

'Your Majesty, [such a Brahman as this stands] on one leg only.'

'Well, Yājñavalkya, tell us yourself.'

'Its home is the ear, and space is its support. It should be revered as the infinite.'

'What is the essence of the infinite, Yājñavalkya?'

'The points of the compass, Your Majesty,' said he. 'That is why, sire, in whatever direction one goes, there is no end to it, for the points of the compass are infinite. Sire, the points of the compass are the same as hearing. Hearing it is, sire, that is the highest Brahman. [And] hearing does not forsake the man who, thus knowing, reveres it; all beings flow into him. He becomes a god and goes to the gods.'

'I will give you a thousand [cows] with a bull the size of an elephant,' said Janaka, [king] of Videha.

'My father [always] thought', said Yājñavalkya, 'that one should not accept [gifts] without first imparting instruction.'

¶ 6. 'Let us hear what people have been telling you,' [continued Yājñavalkya.]

'Satyakāma Jābāla told me that Brahman is mind.'

'For Jābāla to say that Brahman is mind is [about as significant] as for him to say that he has a mother or a father or a teacher; for what is the use of a mindless man? But did he tell you its home and support?'

'No, he did not.'

'Your Majesty, [such a Brahman as this stands] on one leg only.'

'Well, Yājñavalkya, tell us yourself.'

'Its home is the mind itself, and space is its support. It should be revered as bliss.'

'What is the essence of bliss, Yājñavalkya?'

'Again mind, Your Majesty,' said he. 'With the mind a man betroths himself to a woman, and a son is born by her in his own likeness; and [a son] is [very] bliss. The mind it is, sire, that is the highest Brahman. [And] the mind does not forsake the man who, thus knowing, reveres it; all beings flow into him. He becomes a god and goes to the gods.'

'I will give you a thousand [cows] with a bull the size of an elephant,' said Janaka, [king] of Videha.

'My father [always] thought', said Yājñavalkya, 'that one should not accept [gifts] without first imparting instruction.'

¶ 7. 'Let us hear what people have been telling you,' [continued Yājñavalkya.]

'Vidagdha Śākalya told me that Brahman is the heart.'

'For Śākalya to say that Brahman is the heart is [about as significant] as for him to say that he has a mother or a father or a teacher; for what is the use of a heartless man? But did he tell you its home and support?'

'No, he did not.'

'Your Majesty, [such a Brahman as this stands] on one leg only.'

'Well, Yājñavalkya, tell us yourself.'

'Its home is the heart itself, and space is its support. It should be revered as stability (*sthiti*).'

'What is the essence of stability, Yājñavalkya?'

'Again the heart, Your Majesty,' said he. 'Of all contingent beings, sire, the heart is the home; for, Your Majesty, of all contingent beings the support is the heart: all contingent beings are established on the heart. The heart it is, sire, that is the highest Brahman. [And] the heart does not forsake the man who, thus knowing, reveres it; all beings flow into him. He becomes a god and goes to the gods.'

'I will give you a thousand [cows] with a bull the size of an elephant,' said Janaka, [king] of Videha.

'My father [always] thought', said Yājñavalkya, 'that one should not accept [gifts] without first imparting instruction.'

IV, ii

¶ 1. Janaka, [king] of Videha, came down from his couch and said: 'All honour to you, Yājñavalkya. Will you instruct me?'

[And Yājñavalkya] said: 'As a man about to set out on a long journey might make ready (*samādhā-*) a chariot or a ship, so too has your [own] self been made ready (and concentrated upon itself, *samāhita*) by these secret teachings (*upaniṣad*). You are highly respected and wealthy, you have studied the Veda and been told the secret teachings. [Even so,] when you are set free (*vimuc-*) from this world, where will you go?'

'Good sir, I do not know where I shall go.'

'Then I will tell you where you will go.'

'Speak on, good sir.'

¶ 2. 'The "person" in the right eye is named Indha, the "kindler", but though he really *is* Indha, men call him Indra,—obscurely. For the gods, it seems, love the obscure and hate the obvious.

¶ 3. 'Now that semblance of a "person" in the left eye is his wife, Virāj. The place where they meet in mutual praise is the space within the heart. Their food is the clot of blood within the heart. Their covering is something like a fine mesh within the heart. The path they move along is the channel that goes up from the heart. Like a hair a thousandfold divided are these channels, called *hitā*, which are established in the heart. Through these this liquid flows. That is why this [self composed of Indha and Virāj] seems to eat a more refined [form of] food than the bodily self.

¶ 4. 'The eastern quarter is his eastward breaths; the southern quarter is his southward breaths; the western quarter is his westward breaths; the northern quarter is his northward breaths; the zenith is his upward breaths; the nadir is his downward breaths. All the quarters are all his breaths.

'This Self—[what can one say of it but] "No, no!" It is impalpable, for it cannot be grasped; indestructible, for it cannot be destroyed; free from attachment, for it is not attached [to anything], not bound. It does not quaver, nor can it be hurt.

'Now indeed, Janaka, freedom from fear is yours!' Thus spake Yājñavalkya.

'May freedom from fear be yours, venerable Yājñavalkya,' said Janaka, [king] of Videha, 'for it is you, sir, who teach freedom from fear. All honour to you. Here are the Videhas and here am I [at your service].'

IV, iii

¶ 1. Yājñavalkya was going to visit Janaka, [king] of Videha and he thought [within himself]: 'I will not speak.'

But later Janaka, [king] of Videha and Yājñavalkya held converse together at the oblation of the fire, and Yājñavalkya granted him a boon. He chose to ask any question he wished, and [Yājñavalkya] granted him this [boon]. This was the first question the king asked him:

¶ 2. 'Yājñavalkya, what is the light of man (*puruṣa*)?'

'The sun is his light, Your Majesty,' said he. 'Lighted by the sun alone a man sits down, moves away, does his work and comes back.'

'Very true, Yājñavalkya.'

¶ 3. 'When the sun has set, Yājñavalkya, what is the light of man then?'

'The moon becomes his light then. Lighted by the moon alone he sits down, moves away, does his work and comes back.'

'Very true, Yājñavalkya.'

¶ 4. 'When both sun and moon have set, Yājñavalkya, what is the light of man then?'

'Fire becomes his light then. Lighted by fire alone he sits down, moves away, does his work and comes back.'

'Very true, Yājñavalkya.'

¶ 5. 'When both sun and moon have set, Yājñavalkya, and the fire has gone out, what is the light of man then?'

'The voice becomes his light then. Lighted by the voice alone he sits down, moves away, does his work and comes back. That is why, sire, even when a man cannot distinguish his own hands, he will go towards [any place] where a voice is raised.'

'Very true, Yājñavalkya.'

¶ 6. 'When both sun and moon have set, Yājñavalkya, when the fire has gone out and [all] voices are stilled, what is the light of man then?'

'The self becomes his light then. Lighted by the self alone he sits down, moves away, does his work and comes back.'

¶ 7. 'Which one is the self?'

'[Abiding] among the senses there is a "person" who consists of understanding (*vijñāna*), a light within the heart: this is he. Remaining ever the same (*samāna*), he skirts both worlds, seemingly thinking, seemingly moving. For, having fallen asleep, he transcends this world,—the forms of death.

¶ 8. 'This "person", on being born and on being embodied, is conjoined with evil things. When he departs and dies he leaves evil things behind.

¶ 9. 'This "person" has two states [of consciousness] (*sthāna*), that of this world and that of the other world. There is a third twilight state [of consciousness],—that of sleep. Standing in this twilight state, he sees the [other] two, that of this world and that of the other world. Now, however, when he approaches the state [of consciousness] of the other world, he fares forth [towards it] and descries both evil and joyful (*ānanda*) things.

'When he falls asleep, he takes with him [all] the materials (*mātrā*) of this all-embracing world. Himself, he destroys them and himself builds them up [again]; and he dreams [in a world lighted] by his own brilliance, by his own light. Then is this "person" light by his own light.

¶ 10. 'There there are no chariots, no spans, no paths; but he brings forth [from himself] chariots, spans and paths. There there are no joys, no pleasures, no delights; but he brings forth [from himself] joys, pleasures and delights. There there are no tanks, no lotus-pools, no rivers; but he brings forth [from himself] tanks, lotus-pools and rivers: for he is a creator (*kartr*).

¶ 11. 'On this there are these verses:

By sleep he mashes down the things of body;
Unsleeping, the sleeping [senses] he surveys:
White light (*śukra*) assuming, back to his [former] state
He returns,—the Golden Person, lonely swan.

¶ 12. Guarding his lower nest with the breath of life,
Forth from the nest, immortal, on he flies.
Where'er he will, immortal, on he goes—
The Golden Person, lonely swan!

¶ 13. In the realm of dream aloft, beneath, he roams,
A god,—how manifold the forms he fashions!
With women he takes his pleasure, laughs,—or else
Sees dreadful sights: so does it seem to him.

There are some who see his pleasure-grove:
Him no one sees at all.

¶ 14. 'There is a saying: "You should not awaken a man stretched out [in sleep]." Hard to cure indeed is the man to whom this ["person"] does not return.

'Now, some say that this is no different from (*eva*) the state of wakefulness, for he sees the same things whether awake or asleep. [But the difference is that] there (in sleep) this "person" is light by his own light.'

[Said Janaka:] 'Venerable sir, I will give you a thousand [cows]. Say on, [for your words show the way] to liberation [from our earthly state].'

¶ 15. 'In this deep serenity [1] he finds his joy, roams around, seeing good and evil. Then he hurries back in whatever manner suits him (*pratinyāya*), in accordance with his original nature (*pratiyoni*), to [the realm of] dream. Whatever he sees there, he is not followed by it; for this "person" is free from attachment.'

---

[1] i.e. 'dreamless sleep'.

'Very true, Yājñavalkya. Venerable sir, I will give you a thousand [cows]. Say on, [for your words show the way] to liberation.'

¶ 16. 'In dream he finds his joy, roams around, seeing good and evil. Then he hurries back in whatever manner suits him, in accordance with his original nature, to the realm of wakefulness. Whatever he sees there, he is not followed by it; for this "person" is free from attachment.'

'Very true, Yājñavalkya. Venerable sir, I will give you a thousand [cows]. Say on, [for your words show the way] to liberation.'

¶ 17. 'In this realm of wakefulness he finds his joy, roams around, seeing good and evil. Then he hurries back in whatever manner suits him, in accordance with his original nature, to the realm of dream.

¶ 18. 'As a great fish might skirt both banks [of a river], both the nearer and the farther, so does this "person" skirt both realms,—the realm of sleep and the realm of wakefulness.

¶ 19. 'As a falcon or some [other] bird, flying round in space, tires, folds its wings and is carried [down] to its nest, so too does this "person" hasten to this realm where, sleeping, he desires nothing whatever, and where he sees no dream.

¶ 20. 'Like a hair a thousand times divided are the channels [in] his [heart] called *hitā*, so minute are they, full of white, blue, yellow, green and red.

'Now, when it seems to him that he is being killed, or over-powered, or chased by an elephant, or that he is falling into a pit, he is [only] imagining in ignorance the horrors he sees when he is awake. But when, like a god or king, he thinks, 'I surely am this [whole universe: I am] whole,' that is his highest state of being (*loka*).

¶ 21. 'This is that form of his which is beyond desire, free from evil, free from fear.

'Just as a man, closely embraced by his loving wife, knows nothing without, nothing within, so does this "person", closely embraced by the Self that consists of wisdom (*prājña*), know nothing without, nothing within. That is his [true] form in which [all] his desires are fulfilled, in which Self [alone] is his desire, in which he has no desire, no sorrow.

¶ 22. 'There a father is no longer a father, a mother no longer a mother; states of being (*loka*) are no longer states of being, gods are no longer gods, the Vedas no longer Vedas. There a thief is no longer a thief, a slayer of an embryo no longer a slayer of an embryo, an outcaste no longer an outcaste,[1] a wandering friar no longer a wandering friar, an ascetic no longer an ascetic. He is

---

[1] Two types of outcaste are mentioned.

not followed by good, not followed by evil; for then he will have passed beyond all sorrow of the heart.

¶ 23. 'Though he does not see, yet it is by seeing that he does not see; for there is no disjunction between seer and sight since [both] are indestructible. But there is no second thing other than himself and separate that he might see it.

¶ 24. 'Though he does not smell, yet it is by smelling that he does not smell; for there is no disjunction between smeller and smell since [both] are indestructible. But there is no second thing other than himself and separate that he might smell it.

¶ 25. 'Though he does not taste, yet it is by tasting that he does not taste; for there is no disjunction between taster and taste since [both] are indestructible. But there is no second thing other than himself and separate that he might taste it.

¶ 26. 'Though he does not speak, yet it is by speaking that he does not speak; for there is no disjunction between speaker and speech since [both] are indestructible. But there is no second thing other than himself and separate that he might speak to it.

¶ 27. 'Though he does not hear, yet it is by hearing that he does not hear; for there is no disjunction between hearer and hearing since [both] are indestructible. But there is no second thing other than himself and separate that he might hear it.

¶ 28. 'Though he does not think, yet it is by thinking that he does not think; for there is no disjunction between thinker and thought since [both] are indestructible. But there is no second thing other than himself and separate that he might think on it.

¶ 29. 'Though he does not touch, yet it is by touching that he does not touch; for there is no disjunction between toucher and touch since [both] are indestructible. But there is no second thing other than himself and separate that he might touch it.

¶ 30. 'Though he does not understand (vijñā-), yet it is by understanding that he does not understand; for there is no disjunction between understander and understanding since [both] are indestructible. But there is no second thing other than himself and separate that he might understand it.

¶ 31. 'When there seems to be another, then one can see another, one can smell another, one can taste another, one can speak to another, one can hear another, one can think on another, one can touch another, one can understand another.

¶ 32. 'An ocean, One, the seer becomes, without duality: this, sire, is the Brahman-world.[1]'

Thus did Yājñavalkya teach him.

'This is his highest path,[2] this his highest prize (sampat), this his highest world, this his highest bliss. This is that bliss of his on but a fraction of which other beings (bhūta) live.

[1] Or, 'the man whose world is Brahman'.   [2] Or, 'goal'.

¶ 33. 'Take a man who is rich and prosperous, master over others, possessing everything possible that could minister to human enjoyment: that is the highest [measure of] bliss on the human scale.

'Now, a hundred [measures of] bliss on the human scale make one [measure of] bliss on the scale of the world-conquering ancestors.

'A hundred [measures of] bliss on the scale of the world-conquering ancestors make one [measure of] bliss of the world of the Gandharvas.

'A hundred [measures of] bliss of the world of the Gandharvas make one [measure of] bliss of the gods who have won divinity by their works (*karma*).

'A hundred [measures of] bliss of the gods who have won divinity by their works make one [measure of] bliss of the gods who are destined to be gods by birth and of the man well-versed in scripture who is not crooked nor smitten with desire.

'A hundred [measures of] bliss of the gods destined to be gods by birth make one [measure of] bliss of the world of Prajāpati and of the man well versed in scripture who is not crooked nor smitten with desire.

'A hundred [measures of] bliss of the world of Prajāpati make one [measure of] bliss of the Brahman-world and of the man well versed in scripture who is not crooked nor smitten with desire.

'This, sire, is indeed the highest bliss—the Brahman-world, (that state of being which is Brahman).'

Thus spake Yājñavalkya.

'Venerable sir,' [said Janaka,] 'I will give you a thousand [cows]. Say on, [for your words show the way] to liberation.'

Then Yājñavalkya was afraid. 'The king is wise [indeed,' thought he], 'he has driven me out of every position (from which I could conceal the highest truth from him).'

¶ 34. [But he continued.] 'In this realm of dream,' [said he,] 'he finds his joy, roams around, seeing good and evil. Then he hurries back in whatever manner suits him, in accordance with his original nature, to the realm of wakefulness.

¶ 35. 'As a heavily-loaded cart moves along creaking, so does the bodily self, mounted by the self who consists of wisdom (*prājña*), move along groaning as he breathes his last.

¶ 36. 'When this "person" grows thin from old age, grows thin through fever, then does he detach (*pramuc-*) himself from his limbs as a mango or a fig or a berry detaches itself from its stalk. He hurries back in whatever manner suits him, in accordance with his original nature, to the breath of life (*prāṇa*).

¶ 37. 'As policemen, magistrates, charioteers and village headmen wait for the king when he comes [back from a journey] with food and drink and dwelling-places [all ready], saying, "Here he comes, here he comes," so do all contingent beings wait for the man who thus knows, saying, "Here comes Brahman, here he comes."

¶ 38. 'As policemen, magistrates, charioteers and village headmen gather round the king as he is about to go away, so at the time of death do all the bodily faculties (*prāṇa*) gather round this self when he is about to breathe his last.'

IV, iv

¶ 1. [And Yājñavalkya went on:] 'When this self grows weak and seems all confused, then do the bodily faculties (*prāṇa*) gather round him. He collects around him those elements of light (*tejas*) [1] and descends right down (*eva*) into the heart. When the "person" present in the eye turns away, back [towards the sun], he no longer recognizes forms.

¶ 2. '"He is becoming one, he does not see," they say. "He is becoming one, he does not smell," they say. "He is becoming one, he does not taste," they say. "He is becoming one, he does not speak," they say. "He is becoming one, he does not hear," they say. "He is becoming one, he does not think," they say. "He is becoming one, he does not feel," they say. "He is becoming one, he does not understand (*vijñā*)," they say.

'The apex of the heart lights up, and [lighted] by this light the self departs through the eye or the head or some other part of the body. As he departs, the breath of life follows after him; and as the breath of life departs, all the bodily faculties follow after it. He is then [re-]united with the understanding (*vijñāna*, ability to recognize things), and follows after the understanding.[2] His wisdom (*vidyā*) and his works (*karma*) and his knowledge of the past (*pūrvaprajñā*) lay hold of him.

¶ 3. 'As a caterpillar, drawing near to the tip of a blade of grass, prepares its next step and draws [it]self up towards it, so does this self, striking the body aside and dispelling ignorance (*avidyā*), prepare its next step and draw [it]self up (for its plunge into the Brahman-world).

¶ 4. 'As a goldsmith, making use of the material of a [golden] object, forges another new and more beautiful form, so does this self, striking the body aside and dispelling ignorance, devise (*kṛ-*) another new and more beautiful form,—be it [the form] of

---

[1] Or, 'heat' or 'energy'.

[2] Reading *sa vijñānam*. If *savijñānam* is read, the translation must be, 'he follows after what has understanding'.

one of the ancestors or of a Gandharva or of a god or of one in
the Prajāpati[-world] or of one in the Brahman[-world] or of any
other being (bhūta).

¶ 5. 'This Self is Brahman indeed: it consists of understanding
(vijñāna), mind, breath, sight and hearing; of earth, water, wind
and space, light (tejas) and darkness (atejas),[1] desire and desire-
lessness, anger and the lack of it, right (dharma) and wrong: it
consists of all things. This is what is meant by the saying: "It
consists of this: it consists of that."

'As a man acts (karma), as he behaves, so does he become.
Whoso does good, becomes good: whoso does evil, becomes
evil. By good (puṇya) works (karma) a man becomes holy
(puṇya), by evil [works] he becomes evil.

'But some have said: "This 'person' consists of desire alone.
As is his desire, so will his will (kratu) be; as is his will, so will he
act (karma kṛ-); as he acts, so will he attain."

¶ 6. 'On this there is this verse:

To what his mind [and] character (liṅga) are attached,
To that attached a man goes with his works (karma).
Whatever deeds he does on earth,
Their rewards he reaps.
From the other world he comes back here,—
To the world of deed and work (karma).

'So much for the man of desire.

'Now [we come to] the man without desire:
'He is devoid of desire, free from desire; [all] his desires have
been fulfilled: the Self [alone] is his desire. His bodily functions
(prāṇa)[2] do not depart [when he departs this world]. Being very
Brahman to Brahman does he go.

¶ 7. On this there is this verse:

When all desires which shelter in the heart
Detach themselves (pramuc-), then does a mortal man
Become immortal: to Brahman he wins through.

'As the slough of a snake lies on an ant-hill, dead, cast off, so
too does this body lie. Then is this incorporeal, immortal spirit
(breath of life, prāṇa) Brahman indeed, light (tejas) indeed.'

'Venerable sir, I will give you a thousand [cows],' said Janaka,
[king] of Videha.

¶ 8. [And Yājñavalkya continued:] 'On this there are these
verses:

---

[1] Or, 'heat and cold', or 'energy and the lack of it'.
[2] Or, 'vital breaths'.

The ancient narrow far-flung path
Has touched me: I have found it!
Knowers of Brahman, wise, proceed along it
[From this world] freed and raised on high,
    Along to Paradise.

¶ 9. On it, they say, are white and blue,
        Yellow and green and red:
    This is the path that Brahman [1] found:
    Knowers of Brahman proceed along it,
        Workers of good—irradiant (*taijasa*).

¶ 10. Blind darkness enter they
    Who reverence unwisdom (*avidyā*):
    Into darkness blinder yet
    [Go they] who delight in wisdom.

¶ 11. Some worlds there are called "void of bliss",
        Within blind darkness swathed:
    To these at death such folk pass on
    As know not wisdom—unawake.

¶ 12. Should a man [truly] understand the Self,
    Knowing this that: "I am He,"
    What could he wish for,—what desire
    That he should to this body cleave?

¶ 13. Whoso has found the Self and wakened It
    Deep buried in this abyss of ambiguity:
    All-maker he—for everything he makes and does:
    His is the world: the world itself is he!

¶ 14. While yet on earth we may come to know It.
    If thou hast here not known [It], great is the destruction!
    Whoso knows This becomes immortal,
    The rest must suffer misery indeed.

¶ 15. Should a man descry Him suddenly,
        This Self, this God,
    Lord of what was and what is yet to be,
        How should he shrink from Him?

¶ 16.   Before whose face the year
        Revolves with [all] its days,—
        To Him the gods pay homage,—
    Life, light of lights, and immortality.

[1] Or, 'Brahmā'.

¶ 17.   On whom the peoples five
           And space [itself] are founded,—
         Myself immortal, wise (*vidvān*), I know Him
           The Self—Immortal—Brahman!

¶ 18.   Breath of breath, eye of eye,
           Ear of ear, and mind of mind:
         Who knows him thus, has understood
           Primeval Brahman who from the beginning is.

¶ 19.   Descry This with your mind:
           Herein there's no diversity at all.
         Death beyond death is all the lot
           Of him who sees in This what seems to be diverse.

¶ 20.   Descry It in its Oneness (*ekadhā*),
           Immeasurable, firm (*dhruva*),
         Transcending space, immaculate,
           Unborn, abiding (*dhruva*), great,—
             [This is] the Self!

¶ 21.   Let a wise Brāhman, knowing Him,
           Bend his mind towards Him:
         Let him not meditate on many words;
           These can but tire the voice.

¶ 22. 'This is indeed the great unborn Self which consists of understanding (*vijñāna*) among the human faculties (*prāṇa*). In the space within the heart lies the Ruler of all, the Lord of all, the King of all. He neither increases by good works nor does he diminish by evil ones. He is the Lord of all, He the King of beings, He their Protector. He is the causeway which holds these worlds apart lest they should split asunder.

'He it is whom Brāhmans strive to know by reciting the Veda, by sacrifice and the giving of alms, by fierce austerities and fasting. Once a man has come to know Him, he becomes a "silent sage" (*muni*). Desiring Him alone as a state of being (*loka*), wandering friars leave their homes.

'This is what the men of old knew well, [and knowing it,] they had no wish for offspring. "What should we do with offspring?" [so they said,] "for we possess this Self,—this [immortal] state of being (*loka*)." Rising above their desire for sons, their desire for riches, their desire for [exalted] states of being, they wander forth to lead a beggar's life. For there is no difference between a desire for sons and a desire for riches; and there is no difference between a desire for riches and a desire for [exalted] states of being: all of them are nothing more than desire.

'This Self—[what can one say of it but,] "No, no!" It is

impalpable, for it cannot be grasped; indestructible, for it cannot
be destroyed; free from attachment, for it is not attached [to
anything], not bound. It does not quaver, nor can it be hurt.

'Whoso [thus knows],—these two thoughts do not occur to
him, "So I have done evil," or, "So I have done what is [good
and] fair." He shrugs them off (*tar-*). What he has done and what
he has left undone does not torment him.

¶ 23. 'This is laid down in a Rig-Vedic verse:

Such is a Brāhman's eternal majesty:
By works (*karma*) he grows no greater, grows no less.
Seek out the track of it! for knowing Him,
By no evil work wilt thou be defiled.

'Hence the man who thus knows will be at peace, tamed,
quietly contented, long-suffering, recollected (*samāhita*), for he
will see the Self in [him]self: he will see all things as the Self. Evil
does not touch (*tar-*) him: all evil he shrugs off (*tar-*). Evil does
not torment (*tap-*) him: all evil he burns (*tap-*) out. Free from evil,
free from doubt, immaculate, he becomes a Brāhman (in very
truth, for Brahman now indwells him). This, sire, is the Brahman-
world, (this the state of being which *is* Brahman). This it is that
has been granted *you*.'

Thus spake Yājñavalkya.

'Venerable sir,' [said Janaka,] 'I will give you the whole of my
kingdom [1] and myself to be your slave.'

¶ 24. [But Yājñavalkya continued:] 'This indeed is the great,
unborn Self, eater of food, giver of good things; and good things
will that man find who thus knows.

¶ 25. 'This indeed, the great, unborn Self, that knows neither
age nor death nor fear, is Brahman,—yes, Brahman, free from
fear! Whoso knows this becomes Brahman, free from fear.'

IV, v

¶ 1. Now, Yājñavalkya had two wives, Maitreyī and Kātyāyanī.
Of these Maitreyī liked to discuss Brahman while Kātyāyanī
possessed only such knowledge as is proper to a woman. At that
time Yājñavalkya was about to adopt another way of life (that is,
he was about to give up the way of life of a householder and
retire to the forest to pursue a life of meditation).

¶ 2. 'Maitreyī,' said Yājñavalkya, 'I will shortly be giving up my
present way of life in order to pursue the life of a wandering friar.
Well then, let me make a settlement between you and Kātyāyanī
here.'

---

[1] Text, 'the Vedehas'.

[Verses 3–12 are omitted as they are almost identical with II, iv. 2–11. Verses 13–15 round off what Yājñavalkya had left undisclosed in the earlier version.]

¶ 13. 'As a mass of salt [dissolved in water] has neither a "within" nor a "without", but is wholly a mass of taste, so too this Self has neither a "within" nor a "without", but is wholly a mass of wisdom (*prajñāna*). Out of the elements (*bhūta*) do [all contingent beings] arise and along with them are they destroyed. After death there is no consciousness (*saṁjñā*): this is what I say.' Thus spake Yājñavalkya.

¶ 14. But Maitreyī said: 'In this, good sir, you have thrown me into the utmost confusion. Indeed, I really do not understand this [Self].'

But he said: 'There is surely nothing confusing in what I say. The Self is wholly indestructible: of its very nature (*dharma*) it cannot be annihilated.

¶ 15. 'For where there is any semblance of duality, there does one see another, there does one smell another, there does one taste another, there does one speak to another, there does one hear another, there does one think of another, there does one touch another, there does one understand another. But when all has become one's very Self, then with what should one see whom? With what should one smell whom? With what should one taste whom? With what should one speak to whom? With what should one hear whom? With what should one think of whom? With what should one touch whom? With what should one understand whom? With what should one understand Him by whom one understands this whole universe?

'This Self—[what can one say of it but,] "No, no!" It is impalpable, for it cannot be grasped; indestructible, for it cannot be destroyed; free from attachment, for it is not attached [to anything], not bound. It does not quaver, nor can it be hurt.

'With what indeed should one understand the Understander?

'Maitreyī, [now] you have been told the [full] teaching. Of such is immortality.'

So saying, Yājñavalkya took his leave.

[Chapter vi, which gives the chain of the teachers of this doctrine, is omitted.]

BOOK FIVE

V, i

Oṁ.

> Fullness beyond, fullness here:
> Fullness from fullness doth proceed.
> From fullness fullness take away:
> Fullness yet remains.

Oṁ. 'Brahman is space (*kha*),—primeval windy space.' So said the son of Kauravyāyanī. This is the knowledge which Brāhmans know: by this I know [all] that is to be known.

V, ii

¶ 1. The threefold offspring of Prajāpati,—gods, men and demons,—dwelt with their father, Prajāpati, as chaste students of sacred knowledge. After they had stayed [with him for some time] as students, the gods said: 'Speak to us, sir.'

To them he uttered this [one] syllable: '*Da*. Did you understand?'

'We did understand,' they said. 'What you said to us was "*dāmyata*, restrain yourselves."'

'Yes (*oṁ*),' he said, 'you did understand.'

¶ 2. Then the men said to him: 'Speak to us, sir.'

To them he uttered this [one] syllable: '*Da*. Did you understand?'

'We did understand,' they said. 'What you said to us was "*datta*, give."'

'Yes,' he said, 'you did understand.'

¶ 3. The demons said to him: 'Speak to us, sir.'

To them he uttered this [one] syllable: '*Da*. Did you understand?'

'We did understand,' they said. 'What you said to us was "*dayadhvam*, be compassionate."'

'Yes,' he said, 'you did understand.'

This is indeed what the divine voice, the thunder, echoes: '*Da—da—da*: restrain yourselves, give, be compassionate.' This threefold lesson must be learnt: restraint, giving and compassion.

V, iii

The heart is the same as Prajāpati, it is Brahman, it is the All. The word *hṛdayam*, 'heart', has three syllables.

Hṛ is one syllable. Both his own people and strangers bring offerings (*abhi-hṛ-*) to the man who thus knows.

Da is one syllable. Both his own people and strangers give (*dā-*) to the man who thus knows.

Yam is one syllable. He who thus knows goes to Paradise.

V, iv

This indeed is that. It was that, the truth.[1] He who knows this great and strange being (*yakṣa*), the first-born, [who is] the truth and Brahman, overcomes these worlds.

'Could he be overcome who thus knows that this great and strange being, the first-born, is the truth and Brahman?'

'[No,] for Brahman is Truth.'

[Chapter v, a creation story full of magical correspondences, and chapter vi are omitted.]

V, vii

It is said that lightning (*vidyut*) is Brahman. [It is called] *vidyut* because it destroys (*vidāna*). For the man who knows that lightning is Brahman, it destroys [all] evil: for lightning *is* Brahman.

[Chapters viii and ix are omitted.]

V, x

When a man departs from this world, he goes to the wind. There [the wind] opens up before him like the hole in a chariot-wheel. Through it he rises aloft till he comes to the sun. [The sun] then opens up before him like the hole in a musical instrument. Through it he rises aloft till he comes to the moon. [The moon] then opens up before him like a hole in a drum. Through it he rises aloft till he comes to a world where there is neither heat [2] nor snow, and there he dwells for countless years.

[Chapter xi is omitted.]

V, xii

Some say that Brahman is food. But this is not so, for food goes bad without the breath of life.

---

[1] Or, 'the real'.   [2] Or, 'sorrow'.

Others say that Brahman is the breath of life. But this is not so, for without food the breath of life dries up.

Only when these two natural phenomena (*devatā*) become one single substance (*ekadhā*), do they reach the highest state.

In this connection Prātrida said to his father: 'What good could I do to one who knows this? What evil could I do?'

[His father] replied [beckoning] with his hand: 'Do not [talk like that,] Prātrida, for who could reach the highest state by becoming a single substance with these two?'

He also said to him: '[The syllable] *vi* is food, for all these contingent beings indwell (*viś-*) food; [the syllable] *ram* is the breath of life, for all these contingent beings take pleasure (*ram-*) in life. So all contingent beings indwell and take pleasure in the man who thus knows.'

[Chapters xiii, xiv and xv (which is identical with *Iśā*, 15–18, pp. 166–7) are omitted.]

Book Six

[Chapter i, verses 1–6 are omitted.]

VI, i

¶ 7. These bodily organs (*prāṇa*) were disputing among themselves, each vaunting its own superiority. They went to Brahman and asked him which of them was the best. He replied: 'That one is the best on whose departure the body seems to be at its worst.'

¶ 8. The voice went off and stayed away for a year. On its return it said: 'How did you manage to live without me?'

They replied: '[We were] like the dumb, not speaking with the voice, [but] breathing with breath, seeing with the eye, hearing with the ear, knowing with the mind, begetting with semen. That is how we lived.' The voice entered [the body again].

¶ 9. The eye went off and stayed away for a year. On its return it said: 'How did you manage to live without me?'

They replied: '[We were] like the blind, not seeing with the eye, [but] breathing with breath, speaking with the voice, hearing with the ear, knowing with the mind, begetting with semen. That is how we lived.' The eye entered [the body again].

¶ 10. The ear went off and stayed away for a year. On its return it said: 'How did you manage to live without me?'

They replied: '[We were] like the deaf, not hearing with the ear, [but] breathing with breath, speaking with the voice, seeing with the eye, knowing with the mind, begetting with semen. That is how we lived.' The ear entered [the body again].

¶ 11. The mind went off and stayed away for a year. On its return it said: 'How did you manage to live without me?'

They replied: '[We were] like the feeble-minded, not knowing with the mind, [but] breathing with breath, speaking with the voice, seeing with the eye, hearing with the ear, begetting with semen. That is how we lived.' The mind entered [the body again].

¶ 12. The semen went off and stayed away for a year. On its return it said: 'How did you manage to live without me?'

They replied: '[We were] like eunuchs, not begetting with semen, [but] breathing with breath, speaking with the voice, seeing with the eye, hearing with the ear, knowing with the mind. That is how we lived.' The semen entered [the body again].

¶ 13. The breath of life was on the point of going off. As a great and goodly stallion from the Indus country might tear up the pegs to which it is tethered all together, so was the breath of life [on the point of] tearing up the [other] bodily organs. They said: 'Good sir, do not go away; for we will never manage to live without you.'

'Then make me an offering,' [said the breath of life.]

'So be it,' [said they].

¶ 14. The voice said: 'In so far as I am most excellent, you [too] are most excellent.'

'In so far as I am a prop and support, you [too] are a prop and support,' said the eye.

'In so far as I am success, you [too] are success,' said the ear.

'In so far as I am a home, you [too] are a home,' said the mind.

'In so far as I am procreation, you [too] are procreation,' said the semen.

'Then what is my food, what my dwelling?' [said the breath of life.]

'Everything that exists is your food, right down to dogs, worms and the insects that crawl and fly; and your dwelling is water.'

What is not food is not eaten or accepted by one who thus knows this food of the breath of life. Men who are conversant with scripture and who know this, take a sip [of water] before they eat and do the same when they have finished eating. In so doing they believe that they cover the nakedness of that breath of life.

VI, ii

¶ 1. Śvetaketu Āruneya once went to an assembly of the Pancālas. He approached [a certain] Jaivali Pravāhana, who was surrounded by servants. Looking up, [Jaivali] addressed him thus:

'Young man!'

'Sir,' he replied.

'Have you been instructed by your father?'

'Yes indeed (*oṁ*),' said he.

¶ 2. 'Do you know how these creatures here go off in different directions when they depart?'

'No,' he said.

'Do you know how they come back again to this world?'

'No,' he said.

'Do you know how [it is that] that world up there is not filled up with all those many [souls] which depart [from here] again and again?'

'No,' he said.

'Do you know at which oblation offered up water comes to have a human voice, rises up and speaks?'

'No,' he said.

'Do you know [how one obtains] access to the "path of the gods" or the "path of the ancestors", that is, what must one do to arrive at these two paths? For we have heard the word of the seer:

Two paths there are for mortal man, I've heard,—
The path of the ancestors and the path of the gods:
On these all things that move converge,
[All things] that between the Father and the Mother [1] [dwell].'

'I do not know [the answer to] a single one of these [questions],' said he.

¶ 3. [Jaivali] then invited him to stay on, but the boy brushed [the invitation] aside and hurried away. He went up to his father and said to him: 'Formerly, sir, you used to speak of us as being instructed.'

'What is the matter now, you clever [boy?' the father said].

'Some fellow of the princely class asked me five questions, and I did not know [the answer to] one of them.'

'What were they?'

'These,' and he repeated the [various] heads.

¶ 4. [The father] said: 'You should know me, child, and how I have [always] told you everything I know. But come, let us go there and stay, leading the chaste life of a student of sacred knowledge.'

'Sir, go there yourself!'

So Gautama [Āruni] went to where Jaivali Pravāhana's house was. He offered him a seat, ordered water to be brought for him and gave him the customary offerings. Then he said: 'We will grant a boon to the venerable Gautama.'

¶ 5. [The other] said: 'You have promised me this boon. Well then, tell me the words you said in the young man's presence.'

[1] i.e. 'heaven and earth'.

¶ 6. 'Gautama,' he said, 'that is a boon appropriate to the gods; mention one appropriate to men.'

¶ 7. 'It is well known', said [Gautama], 'that I have my full share of gold, cattle, horses, maidservants, carpets and clothing. Please do not ungenerously measure out for me something that is great, infinite and boundless.'

'Then, Gautama, you should ask properly.'

'Sir, I come to you as a pupil.' This is the formula used by the men of old when they came as pupils [to a teacher]. Having [thus] acknowledged himself a pupil, he stayed on.

¶ 8. 'May neither you nor your forefathers do us harm!' said [Jaivali]. 'Although this wisdom has never dwelt with any Brāhman at all hitherto, I shall nevertheless tell it to you; for who could refuse you when you speak as you do?'

[Verses 9-12, which are almost identical with *Chāndogya* v, iv–vii (p. 99), and describe the next world, the rain-cloud, this world, and man as fires, are omitted.]

¶ 13. 'Woman is a fire, Gautama: the phallus is her fuel; the hairs are her smoke; the vulva is her flame; when a man penetrates her, that is her coal; the ecstasy is her sparks.

'In this very fire the gods offer semen; from this oblation man (*puruṣa*) comes to be. He lives out his allotted span. And when he dies he is carried off to the [funeral] pyre. His fire becomes [real] fire, his fuel [real] fuel, his smoke [real] smoke, his flame [real] flame, his coal [real] coal, his sparks [real] sparks. In this very fire the gods offer up man. From this oblation a [new] man arises, bright in colour.

¶ 14. 'Those who know this and those too who in the forest revere faith as truth, merge into the flame. From the flame [they pass on] into the day, from the day into the half-month of the full moon, from the half-month of the full moon into the six months during which the sun moves northwards, from [those] months to the world of the gods, from the world of the gods to the sun, from the sun to the realm of lightning. [Then] a Person who is [all] mind draws near to these realms of lightning and leads them on to the Brahman-worlds. In those Brahman-worlds they live for long ages. For them there is no return.

¶ 15. 'But those who win for themselves many a world by sacrifice, the giving of alms and self-mortification merge into the smoke. From the smoke [they pass on] into the night, from the night into the half-month in which the moon wanes, from the half-month in which the moon wanes into the six months in which the sun moves southwards, from [those] months to the world of the ancestors, from the world of the ancestors to the moon. When they reach the moon, they turn into food, and the gods then eat them up even as [they eat] King Soma, (the moon,) with cries of "Wax! Wane!" When this [experience] passes away from them, they pass on into space, from space into the wind, from the wind into rain, from rain into the earth. When they reach the earth, they turn into food. Then they are again offered up in the fire of a man, and after that in the fire of a woman, [and then] they are born, only to face [these] worlds again: and so they are caught up in the cycle [again and again].

'But those who do not know these two paths become insects that crawl or fly, or else snakes.'

[Chapters iii (an incantation for obtaining a wish), iv (an incantation for fruitful sexual intercourse) and v, which gives the chain of teachers, are omitted.]

Chāndogya Upanishad

[Chapter i, extolling the syllable Oṁ, is omitted.]

I, ii

[Verses 1–6 discuss the battle between the gods and demons. The gods revere the syllable Oṁ as the breath in the nose, as speech, the eye, the ear and the mind. All these the demons succeed in corrupting.]

¶ 7. Then [the gods] revered this breath in the mouth as the syllable Oṁ (*udgīthā*). When the demons struck it, they were smashed to pieces, just as [a clod of earth] would be smashed to pieces on striking a solid stone.

¶ 8. Just as [a clod of earth] would be smashed to pieces on striking a solid stone, so too would anyone who bears ill-will towards one who knows this or who does him harm, be smashed to pieces, for he is a solid stone.

¶ 9. With this [breath in the mouth] he does not distinguish what is fragrant from what is foul-smelling, for it is devoid of [all] evil. With whatever he eats or drinks by means of it, he supports the other vital breaths. When at the last he can no longer find that [breath] he departs, leaving the mouth open.

[Verses 10–14 are omitted.]

I, iii

¶ 1. Now [we shall speak of the syllable Oṁ] in connection with natural phenomena (*adhidaivata*).

Let a man revere [the sun] up there which radiates heat as the syllable Oṁ; for on rising it sings aloud for the sake of [all] creatures; on rising it strikes down darkness and fear. So too shall he who knows this smite down darkness and fear.

¶ 2. This, [the breath in the mouth,] and that, [the sun in the sky,] are the same (*samāna*). This is hot, and that is hot: this is called *svara*,[1] sound, and that is called *svara*, *pratyāsvara*, 'sound and

---

[1] A pun on *svara*, 'sound', and *svar*, 'sun'.

echo'. That is why a man should revere both this and that as the syllable Om̐.

[The remainder of this chapter, as well as chapters iv to viii, which deal with technicalities of the sacred chant, are omitted.]

I, ix

¶ 1. 'What is the goal of this world?'[1] said [Śilaka Śalavatya].

'Space,' said [Pravāhana]; 'for all these contingent beings originate from space, and to space do they return. For space is greater (and more ancient) than they: space is the final goal.

¶ 2. 'This is the supremely desirable (*parovarīyān*) [manifestation of] the syllable Om̐: [and] it is infinite. Whoso thus knows and reveres this supremely desirable [manifestation of] the syllable Om̐, wins what is supremely desirable and conquers supremely desirable states of being (*loka*).'

¶ 3. Atidhanvan Śaunaka, after expounding this [manifestation of the syllable Om̐] to Udaraśāndilya, said: 'To the extent that this supremely desirable [manifestation of] the syllable Om̐ shall be known among your offspring, to that extent will they enjoy a supremely desirable life in this world [¶ 4] and an [exalted] state (*loka*) in the next. Whoso thus knows and reveres it, shall enjoy a supremely desirable life in this world and an [exalted] state in the next,—an [exalted] state in the next.'

[Chapters x and xi, 1–3, are omitted. A beggar, Ushasti Cākrāyana, is called upon to perform the sacrifice.]

I, xi

¶ 4. Then the priest who sings the introductory words approached him and said: 'Sir, you said to me: "Your reverence, if you sing the introductory words without knowing to what natural phenomenon (*devatā*) they refer, your head will fall off." Which [then] is that natural phenomenon?'

¶ 5. 'Breath,' said he; 'for all contingent beings here merge into breath, (the air,) [when they die] and rise up into breath [when they are born]. This is the natural phenomenon referred to by the introductory words. Had you sung them without knowing this, your head would have fallen off, just as I told you.'

¶ 6. Then the priest who chants the hymns approached him and said: 'Sir, you said to me: "Your reverence, if you chant the hymns without knowing to what natural phenomenon they refer, your head will fall off.' Which [then] is that natural phenomenon?'

---

[1] Or, 'What does this world go back to?'

¶ 7. 'The sun,' said he; 'for all contingent beings here chant the praises of the sun when it is up. That is the natural phenomenon referred to by the hymns. Had you chanted them without knowing this, your head would have fallen off, just as I told you.'

¶ 8. Then the assistant of the priest who chants the hymns approached him and said: 'Sir, you said to me: "Your reverence, if you chant your part of the ritual without knowing to what natural phenomenon it refers, your head will fall off." Which [then] is that natural phenomenon?'

¶ 9. 'Food,' said he; 'for all contingent beings here live by absorbing food. That is the natural phenomenon referred to by your part of the ritual. Had you chanted it without knowing this, your head would have fallen off, just as I told you,—just as I told you.'

I, xii

¶ 1. Next we come to the chant of the dogs.

Baka Dālbhya or, [as he was also called,] Glāva Maitreya, retired to study the Veda. [¶ 2] [One day] a white dog appeared on the scene, and other dogs gathered round him saying: 'Venerable sir, get us some food by singing; we are hungry.'

¶ 3. [The white dog] said to them: 'Gather round me here tomorrow morning.' So Baka Dālbhya, that is, Glāva Maitreya, kept watch.

¶ 4. [The next day] the dogs appeared making the same motions as [priests] make when, hand in hand, they start chanting the hymn of praise called *Bahishpavamāna*. Then they sat down together and said: 'Hiṅ! Oṁ, let us eat; Oṁ, let us drink! Oṁ, may the god Varuna, may Prajāpati and Savitri bring food here! O Lord of food, bring food here,—bring it here!'

[Chapter xiii, on magical correspondences between various sounds and natural phenomena, is omitted.]

BOOK TWO

[Chapters i–xxii, which describe magical correspondences between various sounds and natural phenomena, are omitted.]

II, xxiii

¶ 1. There are three branches of religion (*dharma*). The first consists of sacrifice, study of the Veda and the giving of alms. The

second is mortification. The third is to dwell as a student of
sacred knowledge in the house of a teacher and to behave with
the utmost humility in his house. All these gain the worlds
allotted to the virtuous [as their reward]. He who stands firm in
Brahman wins through to immortality.

¶ 2. Prajāpati brooded over the worlds. From these, thus
brooded on, welled up the threefold wisdom, (the three Vedas).
He brooded on this [too]; [and] from it, thus brooded on, welled
up these syllables,—*bhūr, bhuvas, suvar*.
¶ 3. He brooded upon these, [and] from these, thus brooded on,
the syllable Oṁ welled up. Just as a whole pile of leaves might be
pierced through and held together by a stake, so is all speech
pierced through and held together by the syllable Oṁ. Surely Oṁ
is this whole universe,—Oṁ is this whole universe!

[Chapter xxiv, on the rewards of sacrifices, is omitted.]

BOOK THREE

[Chapters i–x, dealing with the sun seen as honey extracted
from the Vedas, are omitted.]

III, xi

¶ 1. Thenceforth [the sun], after rising up on high, will never
again rise or set: all alone will it stand in the midst. On this there
is this verse:

> There indeed it never sets,
> Nor does it ever rise at all:
> By the truth of this, ye gods,
> May I never be robbed of Brahman!

¶ 2. For the man who knows the secret doctrine (*upaniṣad*) of
Brahman it neither rises nor sets: it is always day for him.
¶ 3. Brahmā told this to Prajāpati, Prajāpati to Manu, Manu to
his offspring. This is the Brahman that his father taught to
Uddālaka Āruṇi, his eldest son.
¶ 4. This is the Brahman that a father may teach to his eldest son
or to a worthy pupil, but to no one else at all. Even if a man were
to be given the [whole earth], girdled [as it is] by the waters and
full of treasure, he should yet say: 'Assuredly, this is more than
that,—this is more than that.'

III, xii

¶ 1. The Gāyatrī verse (p. 3) is the whole universe, whatever has come to be; and the Gāyatrī is voice, for voice sings forth and protects this whole universe that has come to be.

¶ 2. What the Gāyatrī is, that is what this earth is, for it is on the [earth] that this whole universe has come to be, on it is it established; it does not extend beyond it.

¶ 3. What the earth is, that is what this body in man is here; for these vital breaths are established on it; they do not extend beyond it.

¶ 4. What this body in man is, that is the heart within the self-same man; for on it these vital breaths are established; they do not extend beyond it.

¶ 5. This Gāyatrī has four quarters and is sixfold. A verse of the Rig-Veda has commented on this:

¶ 6.   This is the measure of his greatness,
         But greater yet is Man (*puruṣa*):
         All beings form a quarter of him,
         Three quarters are the immortal in heaven.   (p. 9)

¶ 7. What is called Brahman, that is what this space outside a man is; and what that space outside a man is, [¶ 8] that is what this space within a man is; and what that space within a man is, [¶ 9] that is what this space within the heart is. That is the 'full', —inactive, undeveloping (*apravartin*). Whoso knows this wins good fortune (*śrī*), full, inactive, undeveloping.

[Chapter xiii; verses 1–6, on the vital breaths, are omitted.]

III, xiii

¶ 7. Now, the light which shines beyond the heavens, on to the back of all things, on to the back of every single thing, in the highest and most exalted worlds, that is indeed the same as the light within man.

¶ 8. When a man feels the heat in the body [of another] by touching it, he sees that [light]. When he stops up his ears and hears something like a rumbling or the crackling of a blazing fire, he hears that [light]. So it should be revered as something seen and heard. Whoso knows this will be [well-]seen and [his name will be] noised abroad,—whoso knows this.

III, xiv

¶ 1. This whole universe is Brahman. Let a man in all tranquillity revere it as *tajjalān*,—(as that from which all things are

born, into which they dissolve and in which they breathe and
move).[1]

¶ 2. Now, man (*puruṣa*) is possessed of an active will (*kratu*). As
is his will in this world, so does he, on departing hence, become.
Let a man exercise his will.

¶ 3. He who consists of mind, whose body is the breath of life
(*prāṇa*), whose form is light, whose idea (*saṅkalpa*) is the real,
whose self is space, through whom are all works, all desires, all
scents, all tastes, who encompasses all this universe, who does not
speak and has no care,—[¶ 4] he is my Self within the heart,
smaller than a grain of rice or a barley-corn, or a mustard-seed,
or a grain of millet, or the kernel of a grain of millet; this is my
Self within my heart, greater than the earth, greater than the
atmosphere, greater than the sky, greater than all these worlds.

¶ 5. All works, all desires, all scents, all tastes belong to it: it
encompasses all this universe, does not speak and has no care.
This my Self within the heart is that Brahman. When I depart
from hence I shall merge into it. He who believes this will never
doubt.

So did Śāndilya say,—so did he say.

[Chapters xv (taking refuge in various 'deities') and xvi (life
seen as the Soma sacrifice) are omitted.]

III, xvii

¶ 1. When a man hungers and thirsts, taking no pleasure, that is
the initiatory rite (*dīkshā*).

¶ 2. When he eats and drinks and takes his pleasure, he takes
part in the *Upasada* ceremonies (in which it is permitted to eat).

¶ 3. When he laughs and eats and copulates, he takes part in the
chants and recitations.

¶ 4. Mortification, the giving of alms, uprightness, refusal to do
harm (*ahiṁsā*), truthfulness,—these are one's gifts to the priests.

¶ 5. Hence it is said: 'He will procreate, he has procreated,'[2]
that is his second birth. Death is the ablution he performs after
the ceremony.

¶ 6. When Ghora Āngirasa told this to Krishna, son of Devakī,
he also said—for he had passed beyond thirst: 'When the end
approaches, let a man lay hold of these three [thoughts]: "You
are something that can never be destroyed; you are something
that can never fall or fail; you are something quickened (*saṁśita*)
by the breath of life."'

---

[1] So, according to the commentary of Sankara.

[2] This also means: 'He will press out [the Soma-juice], he has pressed
it out.'

On this there are the following two verses from the Rig-Veda:

> Of the primordial seed
> [The early-morning light they see
> That higher than heaven gleams].

> [Emerging] from the darkness round about
>   We see the highest light,
>   The [all-]highest sun we see:
> To the sun, God among [all the] gods
> We have attained,—to the highest light,—
>   Yes, to the highest light.

III, xviii

¶ 1. Let a man revere Brahman as mind. So much with reference to the self.

Next with reference to natural phenomena (*adhidaivata*).

[Let a man revere] Brahman as space. This is the twofold teaching with reference both to the self and to natural phenomena.

¶ 2. This Brahman has four quarters,—one quarter is voice, one breath, one the eye and one the ear. So much with reference to the self.

Next with reference to natural phenomena: one quarter is fire, one wind, one the sun, one the points of the compass. This is the twofold teaching with reference both to the self and to natural phenomena.

¶ 3. The voice is one quarter of Brahman. It shines and gives warmth with fire as its light. Whoever knows this shines and gives warmth by his renown and glory and the vital power (*varcas*) of Brahman.

¶ 4. Breath too is one quarter of Brahman. It shines and gives warmth with the wind as its light. Whoever knows this shines and gives warmth by his renown and glory and the vital power of Brahman.

¶ 5. The eye is one quarter of Brahman. It shines and gives warmth with the sun as its light. Whoever knows this shines and gives warmth by his renown and glory and the vital power of Brahman.

¶ 6. The ear is one quarter of Brahman. It shines and gives warmth with the points of the compass as its light. Whoever knows this shines and gives warmth by his renown and glory and the vital power of Brahman,—whoever knows this.

III, xix

¶ 1. 'The sun is Brahman,' so runs the teaching. Now follows an amplification of this:

In the beginning this [universe] was Not-Being: [Yet] it was Being [too]. It developed. It turned into an egg. For the measure of a year it lay [there]. It was split [in two]. These two egg-shells became [the one] silver, [the other] gold.

¶ 2. The silver one is this earth, the golden one the sky up there. The outer membrane is the mountains, the inner membrane cloud and mist. The veins are the rivers. The fluid like goat's milk(?) is the ocean.

¶ 3. Now what was then born was the sun up there. When it was born, shouts and cries of joy rose up towards it, as did all contingent beings and all [their] aspirations (*kāma*). And so at its rising and whenever it returns, shouts and cries of joy rise up towards it, as do all contingent beings and all [their] aspirations.

¶ 4. Whoever knows this in this way and reveres the sun as Brahman may expect heartening shouts to follow and encourage him,—to follow and encourage him.

BOOK FOUR

IV, i

¶ 1. [Once upon a time] there lived one Jānaśruti, the great-grandson [of Janaśruta], a man of faith and generous, who gave away much in alms and supplied many a cooked meal [to his people]. He built rest-houses everywhere, hoping that people would [thus] everywhere be eating his food.

¶ 2. One night some flamingoes flew by, and one flamingo was saying to another: 'Hey, hey! Short-sight, Short-sight! The light of Jānaśruti, the great-grandson [of Janaśruta], is as extensive as the sky. Do not touch it if you do not want to get burnt!'

¶ 3. The other one then answered [saying]: 'Now, what has this man got that you speak of him as if he was Raikva, the man with a cart?'

'Tell me about this Raikva, the man with a cart.'

¶ 4. 'Just as [in a game of dice] the lower throws go to the highest, to the winner, so do all the good deeds performed by [living] creatures go to him; and I say the same about whoever knows what he knows.'

¶ 5. Now Jānaśruti, the great-grandson [of Janaśruta], over-heard this. Rising up, he said to an attendant: 'Well, my friend, do *you* speak of me as if I were Raikva, the man with a cart?'

'Tell me about Raikva, the man with a cart.'

¶ 6. 'Just as [in a game of dice] all the lower throws go to the highest, to the winner, so do all the good deeds performed by [living] creatures go to him; and I say the same about whoever knows what he knows.'

¶ 7. The attendant went to look for him, but came back saying he
could not find him. So [Jānaśruti] said to him: 'Well, then, go
wherever you would [naturally] look for a Brāhman.'
¶ 8. [So the attendant] approached a man who was scratching his
scabs under a cart, and said to him: 'Venerable sir, are you
Raikva, the man with a cart?'

'That's who I am,' he admitted, and the attendant went back
and told [the king] that he had found him.

IV, ii

¶ 1. So Jānaśruti, the great-grandson [of Janaśruta], took six
hundred cows, a golden necklace, and a chariot drawn by she-
mules, went up to [Raikva] and said to him:
¶ 2. 'Raikva, here are six hundred cows, a golden necklace, and
a chariot drawn by she-mules. Now, venerable sir, teach me
about the divinity you revere.'
¶ 3. The other answered him and said: 'You can keep your
necklace and cows, you low creature (śūdra)!'

Then again did Jānaśruti, the great-grandson [of Janaśruta],
take a thousand cows, a golden necklace, a chariot drawn by she-
mules, and his daughter [too], and went up [to him] and said to
him:
¶ 4. 'Raikva, here are a thousand cows, a golden necklace, and
this chariot drawn by she-mules, and here is a wife, and here is the
village in which you live. Now, venerable sir, will you teach me?'
¶ 5. Lifting up her face, he said: 'You low creature, though you
have brought [all] these [cows] along, it is only because of this face
that you will make me talk.'

So [the villages] in the country of the Mahāvrishas where
Raikva lived were, with the permission of Jānaśruti, called
Raikvaparna.

Then he said to him:

IV, iii

¶ 1. 'It is the wind that consumes all (saṁvarga); for when a fire
blows out, it simply goes to the wind; when the sun sets, it too
goes to the wind; and when the moon sets, it also goes to the
wind.
¶ 2. 'When water dries up, it goes to the wind; for it is the wind
that consumes all these. So much for natural phenomena
(adhidaivata).
¶ 3. 'Now with regard to the self:
   'It is the breath of life that consumes all; for when a man is

asleep, the voice simply enters [this] breath, as do eye, ear and mind; for it is the breath of life that consumes all these.

¶ 4. 'These are the two all-consumers, the wind among natural phenomena (*deva*), the breath of life among bodily functions (*prāṇa*).

¶ 5. 'Now, [once upon a time] when Śaunaka Kāpeya and Atiprātarin Kākshaseni were [at table] surrounded [by attendants], a student of sacred knowledge came begging, but they gave him nothing.

¶ 6. 'Then he said:

"One God, protector of the world, has swallowed up
    Four great-souled beings: Kāpeya, who is He?
Him mortal men do not discern, Atiprātarin,
    Though manifold his dwellings.

"Indeed, no food was given to a man to whom it rightfully belongs."

¶ 7. 'Then Śaunaka Kāpeya, pondering [on this] retorted:

"The Self [it is], father of the gods and [every] creature,
    With tusks of gold devouring, truly wise:
Great is his majesty, they say:
    Himself uneaten he devours
Even what is not food.

"Student of sacred knowledge, thus do we revere it (Brahman)." [And turning to the attendants,] he said: "Give him alms." [¶ 8] So they gave to him.

'These five [1] and the other five make ten, and that is the highest throw at dice. And so, in all regions, ten, the highest throw, is food. That [food] is primal matter (*virāj*), the eater of food, by which the whole universe was seen. Whoso knows this, comes to see the whole universe: he becomes an eater of food,—whoso knows this.'

IV, iv

¶ 1. [Once upon a time] Satyakāma, son of Jabālā, addressed his mother, Jabālā: 'Madam, I wish to lead the life of a chaste student of sacred knowledge. What is my parentage?'

¶ 2. She said to him: 'My poor boy, I do not know what your parentage is. In my youth I used to wander round a good deal serving as a maid, and it was then that I conceived you: so I do not know what your parentage is. But [at least] my name is

---

[1] The natural phenomena and bodily functions mentioned in verses 1–3.

Jabālā, and yours is Satyakāma; so you might as well call yourself Satyakāma Jābāla.'

¶ 3. So he went off to [a certain] Hāridrumata Gautama and said: 'I wish to live the life of a chaste student of sacred knowledge with you and I would like to be your pupil.'

¶ 4. [Gautama] said to him: 'What is your parentage, my dear boy?'

'I do not know, sir, what my parentage is,' he replied. 'I did ask my mother, and she answered and told me that in her youth she used to wander round a good deal serving as a maid, and it was then that she conceived me: so she did not know what my parentage was. Her name, [she said,] was Jabālā, and mine was Satyakāma. So, sir, I am Satyakāma Jābāla.'

¶ 5. 'No one but a Brāhman could put the matter so clearly,' said [Gautama]. 'Bring fuel, my dear boy; I will accept you as a pupil. You have not deviated from the truth.'

After he had accepted him as a pupil, he selected four hundred lean and feeble cows and told him to keep an eye on them. As he drove them on, he said: 'I shall not come back with less than a thousand.' So he lived away for many years, and when the number [of cows] had reached a thousand,—

IV, v

¶ 1. The bull [of the herd] spoke to him [saying], 'Satyakāma!'
'Sir?' he replied.

'My dear boy, there are now a thousand of us; take us to the teacher's house, [¶ 2] and I will tell you a quarter of Brahman.'

'Tell me, sir.'

He told him. 'One part [of it] is the East, one part the West, one part the South and one part the North. You see, my dear boy, this quarter of Brahman is in four parts; "luminous" is its name.

¶ 3. 'Whoever thus knows that this quarter of Brahman is in four parts and that it is called the "luminous", whoever reveres it as such, himself becomes luminous in this world. Yes, whoever thus knows that this quarter of Brahman is in four parts and that it is called the "luminous", whoever reveres it as such, wins [for himself] luminous states of being (loka).'

IV, vi

¶ 1. 'The fire will tell you [another] quarter.'

On the following day he drove the cows on. At the place where they bivouacked in the evening, he built up a fire, penned in the cows, put fuel [on the fire] and sat down behind it, facing east.

¶ 2. [And] the fire spoke to him [saying], 'Satyakāma!'
'Sir?' he replied.
¶ 3. 'My dear boy, I will tell you a quarter of Brahman.'
'Tell me, sir,'
It told him. 'One part [of it] is the earth, one part the atmosphere, one part the sky and one part the sea. You see, my dear boy, this quarter of Brahman is in four parts: "infinite" is its name.
¶ 4. 'Whoever thus knows that this quarter of Brahman is in four parts and that it is called "infinite", whoever reveres it as such, himself becomes infinite in this world. Yes, whoever knows that this quarter of Brahman is in four parts and that it is called "infinite", whoever reveres it as such, wins [for himself] infinite states of being.'

IV, vii

¶ 1. 'A flamingo will tell you [another] quarter.'
On the following day he drove the cows on. At the place where they bivouacked in the evening, he built up a fire, penned in the cows, put fuel [on the fire] and sat down behind it, facing east.
¶ 2. [Sure enough] a flamingo flew down towards him and spoke to him [saying], 'Satyakāma!'
'Sir?' he replied.
¶ 3. 'My dear boy, I will tell you a quarter of Brahman.'
'Tell me, sir.'
It told him. 'One part [of it] is fire, one part the sun, one part the moon and one part the lightning. You see, my dear boy, this quarter of Brahman is in four parts: "effulgent" is its name.
¶ 4. 'Whoever thus knows that this quarter of Brahman is in four parts and that it is called "effulgent", whoever reveres it as such, himself becomes effulgent in this world. Yes, whoever thus knows that this quarter of Brahman is in four parts and that it is called "effulgent", whoever reveres it as such, wins [for himself] effulgent states of being.'

IV, viii

¶ 1. 'A diver-bird will tell you [yet another] quarter.'
On the following day he drove the cows on. At the place where they bivouacked in the evening, he built up a fire, penned in the cows, put fuel [on the fire] and sat down behind it, facing east.
¶ 2. [Sure enough] a diver-bird flew down towards him and spoke to him [saying], 'Satyakāma!'
'Sir?' he replied.

¶ 3. 'My dear boy, I will tell you a quarter of Brahman.'
'Tell me, sir.'
It told him. 'One part [of it] is breath, one part sight, one part
hearing, and one part the mind. You see, my dear boy, this
quarter of Brahman is in four parts: "homely" (*āyatanavat*,
"possessing a home") is its name.
¶ 4. 'Whoever thus knows that this quarter of Brahman is in four
parts and that it is called "homely", whoever reveres it as such,
himself becomes "homely" in this world. Yes, whoever knows
that this quarter of Brahman is in four parts and that it is called
"homely", whoever reveres it as such, wins [for himself] homely
states of being.'

IV, ix

¶ 1. Then he reached the house of [his] teacher. The teacher
spoke to him [saying], 'Satyakāma!'
'Sir,' he replied.
¶ 2. 'My dear boy, you are radiant as is a man who knows
Brahman. Now, who has been instructing you?'
'Not human beings,' he confessed, 'but it is you alone whom I
should like to teach me; [¶ 3] for I have heard from men like you
that wisdom learnt from a teacher produces the best results.'
Then [the teacher] repeated the very [words the others had
spoken]. None of it was omitted,—nothing was omitted.

IV, x

¶ 1. [Later] Upakosala Kāmalāyana lived with Satyakāma
Jābāla as a student of sacred knowledge. For twelve years he
tended his [sacred] fires. Then [Satyakāma] sent his other pupils
home, but he did not send [Upakosala] home.
¶ 2. His wife said to him: 'This student of sacred knowledge has
[duly] mortified himself and tended the fires splendidly. Do not
let the fires reproach you,[1] but teach him.' But he went away on
a journey without having taught him.
¶ 3. But [Upakosala] fell ill and lost his appetite; and the
teacher's wife said to him, 'Eat, young man; why do you not
eat?' But he [only] said: 'Many are the desires in man, distracting
him in all directions. I am riddled with every kind of illness; I
will not eat.'
¶ 4. Then the fires said among themselves: '[This] student of
sacred knowledge has [duly] mortified himself and tended us
splendidly. Come, let us teach him.' And they said to him:

---

[1] Or, 'Do not let the fires speak [to him] before you.'

'The breath of life is Brahman; pleasure (*ka*) is Brahman; space (*kha*) is Brahman.'

¶ 5. 'I understand how the breath of life is Brahman,' he said, 'but I do not understand how pleasure and space are so.'

'What pleasure is,' they said, 'that too is space. What space is, that too is pleasure.' And they explained to him about the breath of life and space (*ākāśa*).

IV, xi

¶ 1. Then did the householder's fire instruct him.

'Earth—fire—food—sun:' so did it say. 'The Person who is seen in the sun—He am I: He am I indeed.'

¶ 2. [All the fires speak:] 'Whoever thus knows and reveres this [fire] wards off evil deeds, wins [exalted] states of being (*lokibhū-*), lives a long and vigorous life, lives long and gloriously (*jyok*). His progeny is not cut short. In him—the man who knows and reveres this [fire]—we are well pleased and serve him (*upabhuñj-*) in this world and the next.'

IV, xii

¶ 1. Then did the southern sacrificial fire instruct him.

'Water—the points of the compass—stars—moon:' so did it say. 'The Person who is seen in the moon—He am I: He am I indeed.'

¶ 2. [All the fires speak:] 'Whoever thus knows and reveres this [fire] wards off evil deeds, wins [exalted] states of being, lives a long and vigorous life, lives long and gloriously. His progeny is not cut short. In him—the man who knows and reveres this [fire]—we are well pleased and serve him in this world and the next.'

IV, xiii

¶ 1. Then did the eastern sacrificial fire instruct him.

'Breath of life—space—sky—lightning:' so did it say. 'The Person who is seen in the lightning—He am I: He am I indeed.'

¶ 2. [All the fires speak:] 'Whoever thus knows and reveres this [fire] wards off evil deeds, wins [exalted] states of being, lives a long and vigorous life, lives long and gloriously. His progeny is not cut short. In him—the man who knows and reveres this [fire] —we are well pleased and serve him in this world and the next.'

IV, xiv

¶ 1. [The fires] said: 'Upakosala, my dear, now you know about us and about [your]self; [1] but it is for your teacher to tell you the way (*gati*).'

His teacher came back and spoke to him thus: 'Upakosala,' he said.

¶ 2. 'Sir,' he replied.

'My dear boy, your face is radiant as is [the face] of one who knows Brahman. Now, who has been instructing you?'

'Who do you think should have instructed me, sir?' Here he seemed to deny [what had happened to him]. 'They look like this now, though they can look quite different.' Here he alluded to the fires.

'Well, my dear boy, what did they tell you?'

'This——,' he confessed.

¶ 3. 'Indeed, my boy, they spoke to you of [exalted] states of being. But I will tell you something too: As water does not stick to a lotus leaf, so do evil deeds (*karma*) not stick to the man who knows this.'

'Please speak out, then,' he said.

And then to him he said:

IV, xv

¶ 1. 'This Person who is seen in the eye,—he is the Self,' said he: 'He is immortality, freedom from fear: Brahman is He. Even if they were to pour ghee or water on to the [eye], it would flow away towards the edges.

¶ 2. '"Convergence of the Beautiful" (*saṁyadvāma*) they call him; for all beauteous things converge upon him [as] all beauteous things converge on the man who knows this.

¶ 3. '"Bringer of the Beautiful" (*vāmānīḥ*) is he too, for all beauteous things he brings [as] the man who knows this brings [with him] all beauteous things.

¶ 4. '"Bringer of Light" (*bhāmanīḥ*) is he too, for in all the worlds he shines [as] the man who knows this shines in all the worlds.

¶ 5. 'Now, whether or not the funeral rites are performed for such men as these, they merge into a flame, from the flame into the day, from the day into the half-month of the full moon, from the half-month of the full moon into the six months during which the sun moves northwards, from [those] months into the year, from the year into the sun, from the sun into the moon, from the moon into lightning. There there is a Person who is other than

[1] Or, 'the Self'.

human. He leads them on to Brahman. This is the path of the
gods, the path of Brahman. Those who follow this [path] never
come back to human life,—they never come back.'

[Chapters xvi and xvii, on aspects of the sacrifice, are omitted.]

BOOK FIVE

[Chapters i and ii are omitted, being almost identical with
Brihadāranyaka Upanishad vi, chapters i and ii.]

V, iii [1]

¶ 1. Śvetaketu Āruneya once went to an assembly of the Pan-
cālas, and [a certain] Pravāhana Jaibali addressed him thus:
'Young man, has your father instructed you?'
'Yes indeed, sir,' he said.

¶ 2. 'Do you know where [living] creatures go [when they depart]
from here?'
'No, sir.'
'Do you know how they come back again?'
'No, sir.'
'Do you know the partings of the two paths, the way of the
gods and the way of the ancestors?'
'No, sir.'

¶ 3. 'Do you know how [it is that] that world up there is not
filled up?'
'No, sir.'
'Do you know how [it is that] at the fifth oblation water comes
to have a human voice?'
'No indeed, sir.'

¶ 4. 'Then, how could you say that you had been instructed?
How, indeed, could anyone who does not know these things say
that he has been instructed?'

Much depressed, he returned to his father's house and said to
him:
'You have not instructed me at all and yet, sir, you said that
you had done so. [¶ 5] Some fellow of the princely class asked me
five questions, and I could not unravel one of them.'

'As you have repeated them to me', [the father] said, 'I do not
know [the answer to] one of them. Had I known of them, how
should I not have told you?'

¶ 6. Then Gautama [i.e. Śvetaketu's father] went off to the

---

[1] cf. *Brihadāranyaka*, vi, ii.

king's house, and on his arrival [the king] paid him due honour.
Next morning he went up to him as he was entering the assembly-
hall and said to him:
'Venerable Gautama, choose a boon from among such things
as men possess.'
'Keep such things for yourself, Your Majesty,' said he.
'Rather, tell me the words you said in this young man's presence.'
¶ 7. [But the king] was troubled. Then he bade him stay [with
him] awhile and said: 'As to what you have said, this wisdom has
never yet reached the Brāhmans before you, and that is why in
all the worlds sovereignty (*praśāsana*)[1] has belonged to the
princely class alone.' Then he said to him:

V, iv

¶ 1. 'Gautama, the world up there is a fire: the sun is its fuel; the
sun's rays its smoke; the day its flame; the moon its coal; the
stars its sparks.
¶ 2. 'In this very fire the gods offer faith; from this oblation
King Soma comes to be.'

V, v

¶ 1. 'Gautama, the rain-cloud is a fire: the wind is its fuel; cloud
its smoke; lightning its flame; the thunderbolt its coal; hail-
stones its sparks.
¶ 2. 'In this very fire the gods offer King Soma; from this
oblation rain comes to be.'

V, vi

¶ 1. 'Gautama, the earth is a fire: the year is its fuel; space its
smoke; night its flame; the points of the compass its coal; the
intermediate points of the compass its sparks.
¶ 2. 'In this very fire the gods offer rain; from this oblation food
comes to be.'

V, vii

¶ 1. 'Gautama, man is a fire: the voice is his fuel; breath his
smoke; the tongue his flame; the eyes his coal; the ears his sparks.
¶ 2. 'In this very fire the gods offer food; from this oblation
semen comes to be.'

---

[1] Or, 'teaching'.

V, viii

¶ 1. 'Gautama, woman is a fire: the phallus is her fuel; when a man solicits her, this is her smoke; the vulva is her flame; when he penetrates her, this is her coal; the ecstasy is her sparks.

¶ 2. 'In this very fire the gods offer semen; from this oblation the embryo comes to be.'

V, ix

¶ 1. 'So [it is that] at the fifth oblation water comes to have a human voice.

'Enveloped in the membrane the embryo lies within [the womb] for nine, ten, or however many months it may be, and is then born.

¶ 2. 'Once born he lives out his allotted span. When dead he is carried off from here to the [funeral] pyre [to go from there to that] allotted [place] from which he came, from which he arose.'

V, x

¶ 1. 'Those who know thus as well as those who worship in the forest knowing that self-mortification is the same as faith, merge into the flame [of the funeral pyre]; from the flame [they pass on] into the day, from the day into the half-month of the full moon, from the half-month of the full moon into the six months during which the sun moves northwards, [¶ 2] from [those] months into the year, from the year into the sun, from the sun into the moon, from the moon into the lightning. There, there is a Person who is other than human. He leads them on to Brahman. This path is the "way of the gods".

¶ 3. 'But those who in their villages lay great store by sacrifice, good works and the giving of alms, merge into smoke, from smoke [they pass on] into the night, from the night into the latter half of the month, from the latter half of the month into the six months in which the sun moves southwards. These do not reach the year. [¶ 4] From [those] months they [merge] into the world of the ancestors, from the world of the ancestors into space, from space into the moon which is King Soma, the food of the gods. This the gods eat up.

¶ 5. 'There they remain until the residue [of their good works] is exhausted, and then they once again return on the same path. [They merge] into space, and from space into the wind. After becoming wind, they become smoke; after becoming smoke, they become mist; [¶ 6] after becoming mist, they become cloud; after becoming cloud, they pour forth as rain. [Then] they are born

here as rice or barley, herbs or trees, sesame or beans. To emerge
from these is very difficult. For only if someone or other eats
[him as] food and pours [him out as] semen, can he be born
again.

¶ 7. 'Those whose conduct on earth has given pleasure, can hope
to enter a pleasant womb, that is, the womb of a Brāhman, or a
woman of the princely class, or a woman of the peasant class; but
those whose conduct on earth has been foul can expect to enter
a foul and stinking womb, that is, the womb of a bitch or a pig
or an outcaste. [¶ 8] But those small and continually returning
creatures (like flies and worms) are not to be found on either of
these two paths: [theirs is] a third condition, [for of them it is
said:] "Be born and die."

'That is why the world up there is not filled up, and that is why
a man should take good care of himself. On this there is the
following verse:

¶ 9.   Stealer of gold, drinker of wine,
               Defiler of his teacher's bed,
               Slayer of Brāhmans, these are the four
               Who fall [in the scale of being]; the fifth
               Is he who associates with these.

¶ 10. 'But whoever thus knows these five fires is not defiled by
evil even though he associate with such people. Pure and clean, he
reaches the world of the good and pure (puṇya),—whoever thus
knows, whoever thus knows.'

        V, xi

¶ 1. Prācīnaśāla Aupamanyava, Satyayajña Paulushi, Indra-
dyumna Bhāllaveya, Jana Śārkarākshya and Budila Āśvatarāśvi,
all of them owners of stately mansions and greatly learned in the
scriptures, once came together to consider [the problem of] what
the Self is and what Brahman is.

¶ 2. [Knowing that] Uddālaka Āruni was just then making a
study of the universal (vaiśvānara) Self, they agreed to approach
him, and did so.

¶ 3. He, however, thought to himself: 'These owners of stately
mansions, who are so greatly learned in the scriptures, are going
to ask me questions all of which I may not be able to answer.
Well, I shall direct them to another teacher.'

¶ 4. So he said to them: 'Gentlemen, Aśvapati Paikeya is just
now making a study of the universal Self; let us approach him.'
And so they did.

¶ 5. When they arrived he saw to it that they were received with
all due honour. On getting up the following morning he said:

'Within my realm there is no thief,
No miser, no drinker of wine,
No man without a sacred fire,
No dunce, no lecher, no whore!

¶ 6. 'Gentlemen, I am about to arrange for the performance of a sacrifice, and I will give you gentlemen as much wealth as I give to each of the priests. Please stay [with me], sirs.'

¶ 7. But they said: 'A man should speak only about the subject with which he is conversant. At the moment you are making a study of the universal Self; please tell us about that.'

¶ 8. 'I shall give you your answer tomorrow morning,' said he. The following morning they came back with fuel in their hands, but he, without accepting them officially as pupils, spoke to them as follows:

V, xii

¶ 1. 'Aupamanyava, what is the Self that you revere?'

'The sky, Your Majesty,' he said.

'The brilliant [sky] which you revere as the Self is certainly the universal Self. That is why the Soma-juice is seen to be pressed out again and again in your family.

¶ 2. 'You eat food and see what is agreeable [to you]; and whoever thus reveres this universal Self eats food and sees what is agreeable [to him]. [Moreover,] the vital power (varcas) of Brahman abides in his family. But this is only the head of the Self,' said he. 'Your head would have fallen off if you had not come to me.'

V, xiii

¶ 1. Then he said to Satyayajña Paulushi: 'Prācīnayogya, what is the Self that you revere?'

'The sun, Your Majesty,' he said.

'[The sun] which possesses every form and which you revere as the Self is certainly the universal Self. That is why things of every shape and form are seen in your family, [¶ 2] such as a chariot drawn by a she-mule all ready to set out, a maidservant and a golden necklace.

'You eat food and see what is agreeable [to you]; and whoever thus reveres this universal Self eats food and sees what is agreeable [to him]. [Moreover,] the vital power of Brahman abides in his family. But this is only the eye of the Self,' said he. 'You would have gone blind if you had not come to me.'

V, xiv

¶ 1. Then he said to Indradyumna Bhāllaveya: 'Vaiyāghrapadya, what is the Self that you revere?'

'The wind, Your Majesty,' he said.

'[The wind] which follows various paths and which you revere as the Self is certainly the universal Self. That is why the offerings to you are so various, and various are the rows of chariots that follow you.

¶ 2. 'You eat food and see what is agreeable [to you]; and whoever thus reveres this universal Self eats food and sees what is agreeable [to him]. [Moreover,] the vital power of Brahman abides in his family. But this is only the life-breath of the Self,' said he. 'Your life-breath would have departed if you had not come to me.'

V, xv

¶ 1. Then he said to Jana: 'Sārkarākshya, what is the Self that you revere?'

'Space, Your Majesty,' he said.

'Broad [space] which you revere as the Self is certainly the universal Self. That is why you have a broad [quiver of] offspring and wealth.

¶ 2. 'You eat food and see what is agreeable [to you]; and whoever thus reveres this universal Self eats food and sees what is agreeable [to him]. [Moreover,] the vital power of Brahman abides in his family. But this is only the body of the Self,' said he. 'Your body would have wasted away if you had not come to me.'

V, xvi

¶ 1. Then he said to Budila Āśvatarāśvi: 'Vaiyāghrapadya, what is the Self that you revere?'

'Water, Your Majesty,' he said.

'That treasure which you revere as the Self is certainly the universal Self. That is why you are rich in treasure and prosperous.

¶ 2. 'You eat food and see what is agreeable [to you]; and whoever thus reveres this universal Self eats food and sees what is agreeable [to him]. [Moreover,] the vital power of Brahman abides in his family. But this is only the bladder of the Self,' said he. 'Your bladder would have burst if you had not come to me.'

V, xvii

¶ 1. Then he said to Uddālaka Āruni: 'Gautama, what is the Self that you revere?'
'The earth, Your Majesty,' he said.
'This firm basis which you revere as the Self is certainly the universal Self. That is why you are firmly based as far as offspring and cattle are concerned.
¶ 2. 'You eat food and see what is agreeable [to you]; and whoever thus reveres this universal Self eats food and sees what is agreeable [to him]. [Moreover,] the vital power of Brahman abides in his family. But this is only the feet of the Self,' said he. 'Your feet would have withered away if you had not come to me.'

V, xviii

¶ 1. Then he said to them [all]: 'You know, you eat food, although you [only] know this universal Self as if it were something separate. But whoever reveres this universal Self, as having the measure of a span and [yet] as having limitless dimensions(?), eats food in all worlds, all creatures, all selves.
¶ 2. 'The head of this universal Self is indeed the brilliant [sky], its eye is [the sun] which possesses every form, its breath is [the wind] whose nature is to follow various paths, its body is broad [space], its bladder is the wealth [of water], its feet are the earth, its breast is the sacrificial altar, its hair is the sacrificial strew, its heart is the householder's fire, its mind is the southern sacrificial fire and its mouth is the eastern sacrificial fire.'

[Chapters xix to xxiv, concerning various oblations, are omitted.]

Book Six

VI, i

¶ 1. [Once upon a time] there lived [a man called] Śvetaketu Āruneya. To him his father said: 'Śvetaketu, you should [now] live the life of a chaste student of sacred knowledge. No one in our family, my dear boy, is uneducated, a [mere] hanger on, as you might say, of the Brāhman class.'
¶ 2. So at the age of twelve he went to [a master], and when, at the age of twenty-four, he had studied all the Vedas, he returned, conceited, priding himself on his learning, and obdurate.
¶ 3. Then his father said to him: 'Śvetaketu, my boy, since you are now conceited and obdurate, and pride yourself on your

learning, did you also ask about that teaching by which what had [hitherto] not been heard, is heard; what had [hitherto] not been thought of, is thought of; and what had [hitherto] not been known, is known?'

'Now, sir, what manner of teaching is that?'

¶ 4. 'My dear boy, just as all that is made up of clay can be known by one lump of clay—its modifications are verbalizations, [mere] names,—the reality is just "clay-ness".

¶ 5. 'And, dear boy, just as all that is made of copper can be known by one copper ornament,—its modifications are verbalizations, [mere] names,—the reality is just copper.

¶ 6. 'And, dear boy, just as all that is made of iron can be known by one pair of nail-scissors,—its modifications are verbalizations, [mere] names,—the reality is just iron,—so, dear boy, is that teaching.'

¶ 7. 'Now, I am sure those venerable gentlemen did not know this; for if they had known it, why should they not have told me? Do you, sir, then tell me.'

'My dear boy, I will,' said he.

VI, ii

¶ 1. 'In the beginning, my dear, this [universe] was Being only,—one only,—without a second. True, some say that in the beginning this [universe] was Not-Being only,—one only,—without a second, and that from that Not-Being Being was born.

¶ 2. 'But, my dear, whence could this be?' said he. 'How could Being be born from Not-Being? No, it was Being alone that was this [universe] in the beginning,—one only, without a second.

¶ 3. 'It had this thought: "Would that I were many; fain would I procreate!" It emitted light-and-heat (*tejas*). This light-and-heat [too] had the thought: "Would that I were many; fain would I procreate!" And it emitted water. So whenever a man is very hot [1] or sweats from the heat (*tejas*), water is produced.

¶ 4. 'This water [too] had the thought: "Would that I were many; fain would I procreate!" It emitted food. So whenever it rains, there is food in abundance; for it is from water that edible food is produced.

VI, iii

¶ 1. 'There are only three origins [2] of all these beings, [whether they be] born of an egg, a living being, or a sprout.

¶ 2. 'That same [primal] substance (*devatā*) had this thought: "Come, let me enter into these three [secondary] substances with

---

[1] Or, 'grieves'.   [2] Lit. 'seed'.

this [my] living Self and [thereby] differentiate name and form (individuality).

¶ 3. 'Let me make each of them threefold.' [So] that same [primal] substance entered into these three [secondary] substances with his own (*eva*) living Self and [thereby] differentiated name and form. [¶ 4] Each one of them he made threefold.

'Now, my dear boy, learn from me how each one of these three substances becomes threefold.

VI, iv

¶ 1. 'In fire whatever is red in colour (*rūpa*) is the form (*rūpa*) of light-and-heat; whatever is white is [the form] of water; whatever is black is [the form] of food. The essence of fire [1] has [now] left the fire; the modification is a verbalization, a [mere] name. The reality is just the three forms (*rūpa*).

¶ 2. 'In the sun whatever is red in colour is the form of light-and-heat; whatever is white is [the form] of water; whatever is black is [the form] of food. The essence of the sun has [now] left the sun; the modification is a verbalization, a [mere] name. The reality is just the three forms.

¶ 3. 'In the moon whatever is red in colour is the form of light-and-heat; whatever is white is [the form] of water; whatever is black is [the form] of food. The essence of the moon has [now] left the moon; the modification is a verbalization, a [mere] name. The reality is just the three forms.

¶ 4. 'In the lightning whatever is red in colour is the form of light-and-heat; whatever is white is [the form] of water; whatever is black is [the form] of food. The essence of lightning has left the lightning; the modification is a verbalization, a [mere] name. The reality is just the three forms.

¶ 5. 'It is precisely this that those owners of stately mansions who were greatly learned in the scriptures [2] knew in olden times when they said: "No one today can bring up any [idea] which has never been heard of, thought of, or known before." [Starting] from these [three forms] they knew [everything].

¶ 6. 'They knew that whatever appeared red was the form of light-and-heat; they knew that whatever appeared white was the form of water; they knew that whatever appeared black was the form of food.

¶ 7. 'What seemed to be unknown, they knew, was a compound of these same substances (*devatā*).

'Now, my dear boy, learn from me how each of these three substances [itself] becomes threefold when it enters into the sphere of man.

---

[1] *Agnitva*, 'fire-ness'.   [2] *See* v, xi. 1.

VI, v

¶ 1. 'Food, when eaten, is disposed of in three ways. Its coarsest element becomes faeces, the intermediate one flesh and the finest one the mind.

¶ 2. 'Water, when drunk, is disposed of in three ways. Its coarsest element becomes urine, the intermediate one blood and the finest one breath.

¶ 3. 'Light-and-heat, when absorbed, is disposed of in three ways. Its coarsest element becomes bone, the intermediate one marrow and the finest one voice.

¶ 4. 'For the mind, dear boy, is composed of food, breath is composed of water, while the voice is composed of light-and-heat.'

'Good sir, will you kindly instruct me further?'

'I will, my dear child,' said he.

VI, vi

¶ 1. 'My dear boy, when curds are churned, the finest part rises upwards and turns into butter. [¶ 2] So too, dear boy, when food is eaten, the finest part rises upwards and becomes mind. [¶ 3] When water is drunk, dear boy, the finest part rises upwards and becomes breath. [¶ 4] When light-and-heat is absorbed, dear boy, the finest part rises upwards and becomes the voice.

¶ 5. 'For, my dear child, the mind is composed of food, breath is composed of water, while the voice is composed of light-and-heat.'

'Good sir, will you kindly instruct me further?'

'I will, my dear child,' said he.

VI, vii

¶ 1. 'A human being, dear boy, consists of sixteen parts.

'Do not eat for fifteen days, but drink as much water as you like, for the breath of life is composed of water and will not be cut off so long as you drink.'

¶ 2. So for fifteen days he ate nothing. He then approached [his father] and said: 'Sir, what shall I recite?'

'Recite verses from the Rig-Veda, the Sāma-Veda and the Yajur-Veda,' said he.

'I am afraid they do not come to my mind,' he replied.

¶ 3. 'My dear boy,' he said to him, 'if a single piece of coal the size of a firefly was all that was left of a large [fire] which had already been lighted, then [the fire] would not burn much by means of it. So too, my dear, only one of your sixteen parts may be left, and that is not enough for you to remember the Vedas by. Eat, and then you will [be able to] learn from me.'

¶ 4. [The boy] ate, and approached [his father]; and he [was able to] answer anything he asked him.

¶ 5. [The father] said to him: 'My dear boy, if a single piece of coal the size of a firefly was all that was left of a large [fire] which had already been lighted, and if it was then made to blaze up by putting straw on it, then by these means there would be quite a big fire. [¶ 6] So too, my dear, although only one of your sixteen parts was left, that [part,] once it had been strengthened by food, blazed up, and that was enough for you to remember the Vedas by,—for the mind is composed of food, dear boy, breath is composed of water, while the voice is composed of light-and-heat.'

This, then, did he learn from him,—this did he learn.

VI, viii

¶ 1. Uddālaka Āruni said to his son, Śvetaketu: 'My child, learn from me the true nature of sleep.

'When a man is properly (nāma) asleep (svapiti), then, dear boy, is he suffused in Being,—he will have returned to his own (svam apīta). That is why it is said of him "svapiti, he is asleep"; for he will have returned to his own (svam apīto bhavati).

¶ 2. 'Just as a bird, tied to a string, will fly around in all directions and finding no resting-place anywhere else, will resort to the very [string] that keeps it captive, so too, my dear, the mind will fly around in all directions and, finding no resting-place anywhere else, will come to rest in the breath of life; for, my child, the mind is the captive of the breath of life.

¶ 3. '[Now,] dear boy, learn from me about hunger and thirst. When a man is really hungry, it is the water that carries off what he has eaten. For just as we speak of a carrier off of cattle or a carrier off of horses or a carrier off of men, so do we speak of water as a carrier off of food.

'In this context, my dear boy, you must know that this [body] is a sprout which has sprung up; and there is no [sprout] without a root.

¶ 4. 'What could its root be but food? So too, my child, [if you think of] food as a sprout, then you must look for water as its root; and, dear boy, [if you think of] water as the sprout, then you must look for light-and-heat as its root; and, dear boy, [if you think of] light-and-heat as the sprout, you must look for Being as its root.

'My dearest child, all these creatures [here] have Being as their root, Being as their resting-place (āyatana), Being as their foundation.

¶ 5. 'Now, when a man is really thirsty, it is the light-and-heat that carries off what he has drunk. For just as we speak of a carrier off of cattle or a carrier off of horses or a carrier off of men, so too do we speak of light-and-heat as a carrier off of water.

'In this context, my dear boy, you must know that this [body] is a sprout which has sprung up; and there is no [sprout] without a root.

¶ 6. 'What could its root be but water? And, my child, [if you think of] water as the sprout, you must look for light-and-heat as its root; and, dear boy, [if you think of] light-and-heat as the sprout, you must look for Being as its root.

'My dearest child, all these creatures [here] have Being as their root, Being as their resting-place, Being as their foundation.

'My dear boy, I have already told you how each of these substances (*devatā*) [itself] becomes threefold when it enters into the sphere of man.

'My dear boy, when a man dies, his voice is absorbed (*sampad-*) into the mind, his mind into breath, breath into light-and-heat and light-and-heat into the highest substance.

¶ 7. 'This finest essence,—the whole universe has it as its Self: That is the Real: That is the Self: That *you* are, Śvetaketu!'

'Good sir, will you kindly instruct me further?'

'I will, my dear child,' said he.

VI, ix

¶ 1. 'As bees, dear boy, make honey by collecting the juices of many trees and reduce the juice to a unity, [¶ 2] yet [those juices] cannot perceive any distinction there [so that any of them might know:] "I am the juice of this tree," or "I am the juice of that tree," [so too], my dearest boy, all these creatures [here], once they have merged (*sampad-*) into Being do not know that they have merged into Being.

¶ 3. 'Whatever they are in this world, whether tiger or lion, wolf or boar, worm or moth, gnat or fly, that they become again (*ā-bhū-*).

¶ 4. 'This finest essence,—the whole universe has it as its Self: That is the Real: That is the Self: That *you* are, Śvetaketu!'

'Good sir, will you kindly instruct me further?'

'I will, my dear child,' said he.

VI, x

¶ 1. '[Look at] these rivers, my dear: from east to west, from west to east they flow,—from ocean to ocean they go. They become the ocean itself so that, once there, they no longer know: "This one am I, that one am I."

¶ 2. 'Even so, my dear, all these [living] creatures, arising out of Being, do not know that they have arisen out of Being.

'Whatever they are in this world, whether tiger or lion, wolf or boar, worm or moth, gnat or fly, that they become again.

¶ 3. 'This finest essence,—the whole universe has it as its Self: That is the Real: That is the Self: That *you* are, Śvetaketu!'

'Good sir, will you kindly instruct me further?'

'I will, my dear child,' said he.

VI, xi

¶ 1. '[Look at] this great tree, my dear. If you were to strike at its root, it would bleed but live on; if you were to strike it in the middle, it would bleed but live on; if you were to strike it at the top, it would bleed but live on. Strengthened [1] by the living Self, it still stands, drinking in the moisture and exulting.

¶ 2. 'If life leaves one of its branches, it dries up; if it leaves a second, that too dries up; if it leaves a third, that too dries up. If it leaves the whole [tree], the whole [tree] dries up. This, my dear boy, is how you ought to understand it,' said he.

¶ 3. 'When the life has gone out of it, this [body] dies; [but] the life does not die.

'This finest essence,—the whole universe has it as its Self: That is the Real: That is the Self: That *you* are, Śvetaketu!'

'Good sir, will you kindly instruct me further?'

'I will, my dear child,' said he.

VI, xii

¶ 1. 'Bring me a fig from over there.'

'Here you are, sir.'

'Cut it open.'

'[There it is,] cut open, sir.'

'What do you see there?'

'These rather small seeds, sir.'

'Would you, please, cut one of them up?'

'[Here is one,] cut up, sir.'

'What do you see there?'

'Nothing at all, sir.'

¶ 2. Then he said to him: 'My dear boy, it is true that you cannot perceive this finest essence, but it is equally true that this huge fig tree grows up from this same finest essence.

¶ 3. 'My dear child, have faith.

---

[1] Or, 'pervaded' (*anuprabhūta*).

'This finest essence,—the whole universe has it as its Self: That is the Real: That is the Self: That *you* are, Śvetaketu!'

'Good sir, will you kindly instruct me further?'

'I will, my dear child,' said he.

VI, xiii

¶ 1. 'Put this piece of salt in the water and come to me tomorrow morning.'

[Śvetaketu] did as he was told. [Then his father] said to him: '[Do you remember] that piece of salt you put in the water yesterday evening? Would you be good enough to bring it here?'

He groped for it but could not find it. It had completely dissolved.

¶ 2. 'Would you please sip it at this end? What is it like?' he said.

'Salt.'

'Sip it in the middle. What is it like?'

'Salt.'

'Sip it at the far end. What is it like?'

'Salt.'

'Throw it away, and then come to me.'

He did as he was told; but [that did not stop the salt from] remaining ever the same.

[His father] said to him: 'My dear child, it is true that you cannot perceive Being here, but it is equally true that it *is* here.

¶ 3. 'This finest essence,—the whole universe has it as its Self: That is the Real: That is the Self: That *you* are, Śvetaketu!'

'Good sir, will you kindly instruct me further?'

'I will, my dear child,' said he.

VI, xiv

¶ 1. 'And now a parable.

'A certain man was led blindfold from [the land of] the Gandhāras and left in an uninhabitated place. He was tossed around, whether east or north or south or west [he did not know], for he had been brought there blindfold and been abandoned blindfold.

¶ 2. '[Then a certain man came up to him and] removed the bandage [from his eyes], saying, "[The land of] the Gandhāras is in that direction; that is the direction you should take."

'[And so,] being a sensible man, he [went] from village to village asking [his way], and once he had been shown the way he arrived home in [the land of] the Gandhāras.

'So too does the man who has a teacher [to show him the way] know that he will remain [in this phenomenal world] only so long as he is not released (*vimuc-*): then he will arrive home.

¶ 3. 'This finest essence,—the whole universe has it as its Self: That is the Real: That is the Self: That *you* are, Śvetaketu!'

'Good sir, will you kindly instruct me further?'

'I will, my dear child,' said he.

VI, xv

¶ 1. 'Again, my dear boy, when a man is gravely ill, his relatives gather round him and ask him again and again if he recognizes them. So long as his voice does not merge into his mind, his mind into breath, breath into light-and-heat, and light-and-heat into the highest substance (*devatā*), he will recognize (*jñā-*) [them].

¶ 2. 'Then, when his voice does merge into his mind, his mind into breath, breath into light-and-heat, light-and-heat into the highest substance, then he will not recognize [them].

¶ 3. 'This finest essence,—the whole universe has it as its Self: That is the Real: That is the Self: That *you* are, Śvetaketu!'

'Good sir, will you kindly instruct me further?'

'I will, my dear child,' said he.

VI, xvi

¶ 1. 'Again, my dear boy, people bring a man handcuffed [to face the ordeal], crying out, "He has committed a robbery, he has stolen, heat the axe for him!" If he is guilty, he makes himself out to be what he is not (*anṛtam ātmānaṁ kurute*), speaks untruly (*anṛta*), clothes [him]self (*ātmānam*) in untruth. He takes hold of the red-hot axe and is burnt. Then he is killed.

¶ 2. 'If, however, he is innocent, he shows himself to be what he is (*satya*), speaks the truth (*satya*), clothes [him]self in truth. He takes hold of the red-hot axe and is not burnt. Then he is released (*muc-*).

¶ 3. 'So, just as such a man is not burnt [because he embodies Truth], so does this whole universe have this [Truth] as its Self. That is the Real (*satya*, Truth): That is the Self: that *you* are, Śvetaketu!'

This did he understand from him,—this did he understand.

BOOK SEVEN

VII, i

¶ 1. Nārada approached Sanatkumāra and said to him: 'Teach [me], sir.'

[Sanatkumāra] said: 'Tell me what you know, and I will then develop it further for you.'

¶ 2. [Nārada] said: 'I know the Rig-Veda, sir, the Yajur-Veda and the Sāma-Veda; fourthly [I know] the Atharva-Veda and fifthly the ancient collections of stories (*itihāsa-purāṇa*). [I also know] the "Veda of Vedas" (grammar), the funeral rites for the dead, arithmetic, divination, chronometry, logic, politics, the etymological interpretation (*devavidyā*) and semantic interpretation (*brahmavidyā*) of the scriptures, the way to approach disembodied spirits, archery,[1] astronomy, the art of dealing with snakes, and the fine arts. [All] this, sir, do I know.

¶ 3. 'And so, sir, I am conversant with the sacred writings (*mantra*), but I do not know the Self. But I have heard from men like you that any man who knows the Self transcends unhappiness; and I *am* unhappy, sir. Do you then, sir, enable me to transcend unhappiness.'

[Sanatkumāra] replied: 'Everything that you have been studying is no more than a name.

¶ 4. 'The Rig-Veda, the Yajur-Veda and the Sāma-Veda are no more than a name. Your fourth and fifth, that is, the Atharva-Veda and the ancient collections of stories [are no more than a name. And no more than a name are] the "Veda of Vedas" (grammar), the funeral rites of the dead, arithmetic, divination, chronometry, logic, politics, the etymological and semantic interpretations of the scriptures, the way to approach disembodied spirits, archery,[1] astronomy, the art of dealing with snakes, and the fine arts. All this is merely a name. Revere the name.

¶ 5. 'Whoso reveres the name as Brahman, gains freedom of movement (*kāmacāra*) in the whole sphere of name,—whoso reveres the name as Brahman.'

'Is there anything greater than the name, sir?'

'There is indeed something greater than the name.'

'Then, sir, will you please tell me what it is?'

VII, ii

¶ 1. 'Speech is greater than the name; for speech makes the Rig-Veda, the Yajur-Veda and the Sāma-Veda known; so too your fourth and fifth, that is, the Atharva-Veda and the ancient collections of stories, grammar, the funeral rites of the dead, arithmetic, divination, logic, politics, the etymological and semantic interpretations of the scriptures, the way to approach disembodied spirits, archery,[1] astronomy, the art of dealing with snakes, and the fine arts. [Speech too makes known]

[1] Or, 'the art of rulership'.

heaven and earth, wind and space, water and fire (*tejas*), gods and
men, beasts and birds, grasses and trees, animals right down to
worms, moths and ants, right (*dharma*) and wrong, truth and
falsehood, good and evil, pleasant and unpleasant. Were it
indeed not for speech, there would be no knowledge of right and
wrong, truth and falsehood, good and evil, pleasant and unpleasant: for it is speech that makes all this known. Revere
speech.

¶ 2. 'Whoso reveres speech as Brahman gains freedom of
movement in the whole sphere of speech,—whoso reveres speech
as Brahman.'

'Is there anything greater than speech, sir?'

'There is indeed something greater than speech.'

'Then, sir, will you please tell me what it is?'

VII, iii

¶ 1. 'Mind is greater than speech. For just as a man's fist can
contain two acorns or two berries or two nuts, so does mind
contain both speech and name. If a man by his mind has a mind
to study the sacred texts (*mantra*), he then studies them; [if he
has a mind] to perform any [sacred] action, he then performs it;
[if he has a mind] to wish for sons and cattle, he then wishes for
them; [if he has a mind] to wish for this world and the next, he
then wishes for them. Mind is the Self; for mind is the [whole]
world: mind is Brahman. Revere mind.

¶ 2. 'Whoso reveres mind as Brahman gains freedom of movement in the whole sphere of mind,—whoso reveres mind as
Brahman.'

'Is there anything greater than mind, sir?'

'There is indeed something greater than mind.'

'Then, sir, will you please tell me what it is?'

VII, iv

¶ 1. 'Will [1] is greater than mind. For when a man wills something, then he has it in mind, then he utters speech and formulates it in a name. In the name the sacred formulas become one
as do [sacred] actions in the sacred formulas.

¶ 2. '[All] these meet in one place only,—in the will. Will is their
very self, and will is their foundation. Heaven and earth were
willed into existence; wind and space were willed into existence;
water and fire were willed into existence. Because these were

---

[1] Or, 'conception'. Śankara comments: 'Ability to distinguish between
what ought to be and what ought not.'

willed into existence,[1] rain was willed into existence; because rain was willed into existence, food was willed into existence; because food was willed into existence, living creatures (*prāna*) were willed into existence; because living creatures were willed into existence, the sacred formulas were willed into existence; because the sacred formulas were willed into existence, [sacred] actions were willed into existence; because [sacred] actions were willed into existence, the world was willed into existence; because the world was willed into existence, all is willed into existence. Such is will. Revere will.

¶ 3. 'Whoso reveres will as Brahman [attains to] states of being (*loka*) ordered and willed (*klpta*); being himself abiding, firmly based and unperturbed, he attains to states of being that are [likewise] abiding, firmly based and unperturbed. He gains freedom of movement in the whole sphere of will,—whoso reveres will as Brahman.'

'Is there anything greater than will, sir?'

'There is indeed something greater than will.'

'Then, sir, will you please tell me what it is.'

VII, v

¶ 1. 'Thought is greater than will. For when a man thinks, then he wills, then he has it in mind, then he utters speech and formulates it in a name. In name the sacred formulas become one as do [sacred] actions in the sacred formulas.

¶ 2. '[All] these meet in one place only,—in thought. Thought is their very self, and thought is their foundation. And so even if a man knows a great deal but is unthinking, people say of him: "He is nothing, whatever he may know. For if he were [really] wise, he would not be so very unthinking." On the other hand, even if a man knows only a little but knows how to think, people are anxious to listen to him. For thought is the one point at which [all] these [other faculties] meet: thought is [their] self, thought [their] foundation. Revere thought.

¶ 3. 'Whoso reveres thought as Brahman [attains to] states of being (*loka*) that have been properly thought out; being himself abiding, firmly based and unperturbed, he attains to abiding, firmly based and unperturbed states of being. He gains freedom of movement in the whole sphere of thought,—whoso reveres thought as Brahman.'

'Is there anything greater than thought, sir?'

'There is indeed something greater than thought.'

'Then, sir, will you please tell me what it is.'

---

[1] Or, 'by the will of these'. So, too, in the following clauses.

VII, vi

¶ 1. 'Meditation (*dhyāna*) is greater than thought. The earth seems to meditate; atmosphere and sky seem to meditate; the waters and the mountains seem to meditate, as do gods and men. That is why whenever men achieve greatness on earth, they may be said to have received their [due] portion of the fruits of meditation. So, while small men are quarrelsome, slanderous gossips, the great may be said to have received their [due] portion of the fruits of meditation. Revere meditation.

¶ 2. 'Whoso reveres meditation as Brahman gains freedom of movement in the whole sphere of meditation,—whoso reveres meditation as Brahman.'

'Is there anything greater than meditation, sir?'

'There is indeed something greater than meditation.'

'Then, sir, will you please tell me what it is?'

VII, vii

¶ 1. 'Understanding (*vijñāna*) is greater than meditation. For it is with the understanding that one understands the Rig-Veda, the Yajur-Veda and the Sāma-Veda, the Atharva-Veda and the ancient collections of stories as fourth and fifth, grammar, the funeral rites of the dead, arithmetic, divination, chronometry, logic, politics, the etymological and semantic interpretations of the scriptures, the way to approach disembodied spirits, archery,[1] astronomy, the art of dealing with snakes, and the fine arts. It is with the understanding too that one understands heaven and earth, wind and space, water and fire, gods and men, beasts and birds, grasses and trees, animals right down to worms, moths and ants, right and wrong, truth and falsehood, good and evil, pleasant and unpleasant, food and taste,[2] this world and the next. Revere the understanding.

¶ 2. 'Whoso reveres the understanding as Brahman, attains to states of being characterized by understanding and wisdom (*jñāna*). He gains freedom of movement in the whole sphere of understanding,—whoso reveres the understanding as Brahman.'

'Is there anything greater than understanding, sir?'

'There is indeed something greater than understanding.'

'Then, sir, will you please tell me what it is.'

VII, viii

¶ 1. 'Strength is greater than understanding. For one strong man can make a hundred men of understanding tremble. If a man is strong, he will engage in manly effort (*utthātā*); and, so engaged,

---

[1] Or, 'the art of rulership'.   [2] Or, 'drink'.

he will serve [the wise]. Serving [the wise], he will become familiar [with them, and] once familiar [with them], he will become one who [truly] sees, hears, thinks (*mantṛ*), is aware (*boddhṛ*), acts and understands. It is by strength alone that the earth and atmosphere and sky subsist, that the mountains subsist, that gods and men subsist, that beasts and birds subsist, that grasses and trees subsist, that animals right down to worms, moths and ants subsist, that the world [itself] subsists. Revere strength.

¶ 2. 'Whoso reveres strength as Brahman gains freedom of movement in the whole sphere of strength,—whoso reveres strength as Brahman.'

'Is there anything greater than strength, sir?'

'There is indeed something greater than strength.'

'Then, sir, will you please tell me what it is.'

VII, ix

¶ 1. 'Food is greater than strength. For if a man should abstain from food for ten days, although he might still live, he would not be able to see, hear, think, be aware [of anything], act or understand. Once he starts to eat again, however, he will be able to see, hear, think, be aware [of things], act and understand. Revere food.

¶ 2. 'Whoso reveres food as Brahman attains to states of being (*loka*) rich in food and drink. He gains freedom of movement in the whole sphere of food,—whoso reveres food as Brahman.'

'Is there anything greater than food, sir?'

'There is indeed something greater than food.'

'Then, sir, will you please tell me what it is?'

VII, x

¶ 1. 'Water is greater than food. This being so, if the rains are deficient, living creatures become ill, thinking that there will be a dearth of food; but if the rains are abundant, living creatures will be overjoyed, thinking that there will be plenty of food. Truly, earth and atmosphere and sky are nothing but water transmuted into different forms; the mountains, gods and men, beasts and birds, grasses and trees, animals right down to worms, moths and ants are nothing but water transmuted into different forms. Revere water.

¶ 2. 'Whoso reveres water as Brahman, obtains all his desires and will be well satisfied. He gains freedom of movement in the whole sphere of water—whoso reveres water as Brahman.'

'Is there anything greater than water, sir?'

'There is indeed something greater than water.'

'Then, sir, will you please tell me what it is?'

VII, xi

¶ 1. 'Heat (*tejas*) is greater than water. For heat seizes hold of the wind and warms up space. Then people say: "It is hot: it is burning hot: it is going to rain." It is heat that gives the first indication [of the coming rains] and that pours down water. Then, with the lightning flashing upwards and sideways, the thunder roars. And so people say: "There is thunder and lightning: it is going to rain." It is heat that gives the first indication [of the coming rains] and that pours down the water. Revere heat.

¶ 2. 'Whoso reveres heat as Brahman, himself becomes brilliant (*tejasvin*) and attains to brilliant, shining states of being from which all darkness has been expelled. He gains freedom of movement in the whole sphere of heat,—whoso reveres heat as Brahman.'

'Is there anything greater than heat, sir?'

'There is indeed something greater than heat.'

'Then, sir, will you please tell me what it is?'

VII, xii

¶ 1. 'Space is greater than heat. For in space are both the sun and moon, lightning, stars and fire. Through space a man calls, through space he hears and through space he answers. In space does a man take his pleasure and in space is he distressed: in space is he born and for space is he born. Revere space.

¶ 2. 'Whoso reveres space as Brahman, attains to states of being that are spacious, luminous, unconfined, broadly extended. He gains freedom of movement in the whole sphere of space,—whoso reveres space as Brahman.

'Is there anything greater than space, sir?'

'There is indeed something greater than space.'

'Then, sir, will you please tell me what it is?'

VII, xiii

¶ 1. 'Memory is greater than space. This being so, if there was a crowd of people who had no memory, they would hear nothing, have a mind to nothing, recognize (*vijñā-*) nothing. But if their memory was intact, then they would hear, have a mind [to do something] and recognize [people and things]; for it is by memory that one recognizes one's sons and cattle. Revere memory.

¶ 2. 'Whoso reveres memory as Brahman, gains freedom of movement in the whole sphere of memory,—whoso reveres memory as Brahman.'

'Is there anything greater than memory, sir?'

'There is indeed something greater than memory.'

'Then, sir, will you please tell me what it is?'

VII, xiv

¶ 1. 'Hope is greater than memory. For it is only when kindled by hope that memory learns the sacred formulas, performs [sacred] actions, wishes for sons and cattle, wishes for this world and the next. Revere hope.

¶ 2. 'Whoso reveres hope as Brahman,—all his desires are fulfilled by hope, all his prayers come true; he gains freedom of movement in the whole sphere of hope,—whoso reveres hope as Brahman.'

'Is there anything greater than hope, sir?'

'There is indeed something greater than hope.'

'Then, sir, will you please tell me what it is?'

VII, xv

¶ 1. 'The breath of life is greater than hope. For just as the spokes [of a wheel] are fixed in the hub, so is everything fixed in this breath of life. By life (*prāṇa*) does life [itself] go on: life gives life,—gives [it back] to life.[1] Life is father, life mother, life brother and sister, life the teacher and life the Brāhman.

¶ 2. '[And so,] if a man, showing even a little harshness, answers back his father or mother, brother or sister, teacher or a Brāhman, people will say to him: "A curse on you, you have killed your father," or "You have killed your mother,"—or your brother or sister or teacher or a Brāhman.

¶ 3. 'But if, when the breath of life has left such as he, someone were [to strike them] with a stake, cast them aside(?) and burn them up completely, no one would say to him: "You have killed your father," or "You have killed your mother,"—or your brother or sister or teacher or a Brāhman.

¶ 4. 'For truly the breath of life is all these things; and the man who sees that this is so, has it thus in mind and understands that it is so, becomes a master of dialectic (*ativādin*). Should people say to him, "You are a master of dialectic," he should reply, "That is perfectly true." He should not deny it.

VII, xvi

'Now the man who shows himself a master of dialectic shows it by [speaking] the truth.'

'I too, sir, would show myself to be a master of dialectic by [speaking] the truth.'

'Then [you] should really want to understand the truth.'

'Sir, I do want to understand the truth.'

---

[1] Or, 'a living creature'.

VII, xvii

'When one understands, then one speaks the truth. No one speaks the truth without understanding. Only by understanding does one speak the truth. So [you] should really want to understand understanding (*vijñāna*).'

'Sir, I do want to understand understanding.'

VII, xviii

'When one thinks, then one understands. No one understands without thinking. Only by thinking first can one understand. So [you] should really want to understand thought.'

'Sir, I do want to understand thought.'

VII, xix

'When one has faith, then one thinks. No one thinks until he has faith. Only by having faith does one think. So [you] should really want to understand faith.'

'Sir, I really do want to understand faith.'

VII, xx

'When one has an ideal (? *nististhati*),[1] then one has faith. No one has faith without having an ideal. Only by having an ideal does one have faith. So [you] should really want to understand what it is to have an ideal.'

'Sir, I really do want to understand such an ideal.'

VII, xxi

'When one acts, then one has an ideal. No one has an ideal without acting first. Only by acting first has one an ideal. So [you] should really want to understand action (*kṛti*).'

'Sir, I really do want to understand action.'

VII, xxii

'When one is blessed with happiness (*sukha*), then does one act. No one acts without being blessed with happiness first. Only by being blessed with happiness first, does one act. So [you] should really want to understand happiness.'

'Sir, I really do want to understand happiness.'

[1] Or, 'grows forth'.

VII, xxiii

'Happiness is nothing less than the Infinite (*bhūman*): there is no happiness in what is small (finite). Only the Infinite is happiness. So [you] should really want to understand the Infinite.'

'Sir, I do want to understand the Infinite.'

VII, xxiv

'Where one sees nothing else, hears nothing else, knows (*vijñā-*) nothing else, that is the Infinite. But where one sees something else, hears something else, knows something else, that is something small [because finite]. The Infinite is the same as the immortal; the small [and finite] is the same as what is mortal.'

'Sir, on what is this [Infinite] based?'

'On its own greatness, or else,—not on any greatness at all. Cows and horses men here on earth call "greatness",—so too elephants, gold, slaves, wives, fields and dwelling-places. This is not the way I talk: this is not the way I talk,' said he, 'for [in these cases] one is based on another.'

VII, xxv

¶ 1. 'This [Infinite] is below, it is above, it is to the west, to the east, to the south, to the north. Truly it is this whole universe.

'Next the teaching concerning the ego.

'I am below, I am above, I am to the west, to the east, to the south, to the north. Truly I am this whole universe.

¶ 2. 'Next the teaching concerning the Self. The Self is below, the Self is above, the Self is to the west, to the east, to the south, to the north. Truly the Self is this whole universe.

'The man who sees and thinks and understands (*vijñā-*) in this way has pleasure in the Self, plays with the Self, lies with the Self and has his joy with the Self: he becomes an independent sovereign. In all the worlds (and in every state of being) freedom of movement is his. But [all] those who understand [reality] in any way that if different from this, are subjects of another sovereign: [1] their states of being (*loka*) are perishable, and in all the worlds (and states of being) they have no freedom of movement.'

VII, xxvi

¶ 1. 'For the man who sees and thinks and understands in this way, life (*prāṇa*) [wells up] from the Self; hope and memory [well

[1] Or, 'sovereign over others'.

up] from the Self; space, heat and water [well up] from the Self;
appearance and disappearance, food and strength [well up] from
the Self; understanding, meditation, thought, will,[1] mind, speech
and name [well up] from the Self; sacred formulas and [sacred]
actions, nay, this whole universe [wells up] from the Self. [¶ 2] On
this there are the following verses:

> The seer does not see death,
> Nor sickness nor yet sorrow:
> Seeing the All, the seer
> Attains the All in every way.
> Onefold, threefold it becomes,
> Fivefold, sevenfold, nine,—
> Again they say elevenfold,
> One hundred-and-elevenfold,
> And twenty-thousandfold.

'If your food is pure, your whole nature will be pure: if your
whole nature is pure, your memory will be unfailing: if you have
mastered your memory, all the knots [of doubt within your heart]
will be loosened. To such a one from whom all stains have been
wiped away the blessed Sanatkumāra shows the [further] shore
beyond darkness. He is called "Skanda," "he who leaps [from
shore to shore]"—Skanda is he called.'

BOOK EIGHT

VIII, i

¶ 1. [The teacher speaks:]
  'Now, in this city of Brahman there is a dwelling-place, a tiny
lotus-flower; within that there is a tiny space. What is within that
is what [you] should seek: that is what [you] should really want to
understand.'
¶ 2. If [his pupils] should say to him: '[Granted that] there is a
dwelling-place, a tiny lotus-flower, within this city of Brahman,
and that within that there is a tiny space, what, then, is to be
found there that [we] should seek out and really want to understand?'
¶ 3. Then he should say: 'As wide as this space [around us], so
wide is this space within the heart. In it both sky and earth are
concentrated, both fire and wind, both sun and moon, lightning
and the stars, what a man possesses here on earth and what he
does not possess: everything is concentrated in this [tiny space
within the heart].'

[1] Or, 'conception'.

¶ 4. If they should say to him: 'If all this is concentrated within this city of Brahman,—all beings and all desires,—what is left of it all when old age overtakes it and it falls apart?'

¶ 5. Then should he say: 'It does not grow old with [the body's] ageing nor is it slain when [the body] is slain. This is the true city of Brahman; in it are concentrated [all] desires. This is the Self, exempt from evil, untouched by age or death or sorrow, untouched by hunger or thirst: [this is the Self] whose desire is the real, whose idea [1] is the real.

'As here on earth people act as they are bidden, living out their lives [conditioned] by the ends on which they have set their hearts, be it a kingdom or [only] a plot of land,—

¶ 6. 'As here on earth the worldly station (*loka*) that is won by work (*karma*) must perish, so too must the [heavenly] state (*loka*) won by merit perish in the next world.

'[All] those who go hence without having found the Self and these real [objects of] desire, will have no freedom of movement in any state of being (*loka*). But those who go hence, having found the Self and these real [objects of] desire, will have freedom of movement in every state of being.'

VIII, ii

¶ 1. If a man should desire the world of fathers, by a mere act of will [2] fathers will rise up together before him. By possessing the world of fathers he will be magnified.[3]

¶ 2. And if he should desire the world of mothers, by a mere act of will mothers will rise up together before him. By possessing the world of mothers he will be magnified.

¶ 3. And if he should desire the world of brothers, by a mere act of will brothers will rise up together before him. By possessing the world of brothers he will be magnified.

¶ 4. And if he should desire the world of sisters, by a mere act of will sisters will rise up together before him. By possessing the world of sisters he will be magnified.

¶ 5. And if he should desire the world of comrades, by a mere act of will comrades will rise up together before him. By possessing the world of comrades he will be magnified.

¶ 6. And if he should desire the world of perfumes and garlands, by a mere act of will perfumes and garlands will rise up together before him. By possessing the world of perfumes and garlands he will be magnified.

¶ 7. And if he should desire the world of food and drink, by a

---

[1] Or, 'will' (*saṅkalpa*).
[2] Or, 'conception' (*saṅkalpa*), and so in the following verses.
[3] Or, 'happy', and so in the following verses.

mere act of will food and drink will rise up together before him.
By possessing the world of food and drink he will be magnified.
¶ 8. And if he should desire the world of song and music, by a
mere act of will song and music will rise up together before him.
By possessing the world of song and music he will be magnified.
¶ 9. And if he should desire the world of women, by a mere act of
will women will rise up together before him. By possessing the
world of women he will be magnified.
¶ 10. On whatever end a man sets his heart, whatever [object of]
desire he desires, by a mere act of will that same [end and object]
rises up before him and, possessed of it, he is [duly] magnified.

VIII, iii

¶ 1. 'These desires,[1] [though directed to what is] real,[2] are
[nonetheless] covered over with unreality.[2] Though they are real
themselves, their covering is unreal.
    'Never on earth can a man bring back one close to him once he
has departed this life so that he can see him. [¶ 2] Yet whatever he
may long for among the living and the dead, or whatever else he
may long for and cannot obtain, all that will he find if he will but
go to that [city of Brahman within the heart]; for there it is that
his real desires are, [though now they are] covered over with unreality.
    'For, just as [a group of people] who do not know the country
(akṣetrajña) might wander about and pass over a hidden hoard of
gold time and again without finding it, so too do all these
creatures go on day after day without finding the Brahman-
world within them (eta), for they are led astray by unreality.
¶ 3. 'Truly, this Self is in the heart. And the etymology of
hṛdayam, "heart", is this: hṛdy ayam, "He is in the heart".
Hence it is [called] hṛdayam, "heart". Whoever understands it in
this way, day in and day out, goes to the heavenly world.
¶ 4. 'Then this deep serenity which, rising up from this body,
attains the highest light, reveals itself in its own [true] form: this
is the Self.' So said he. 'This is the immortal, [this] freedom from
fear: this is Brahman. And the name of Brahman is this,—
Reality: [and Reality is Truth].
¶ 5. 'In this word satiyam, "Reality and Truth", there are three
syllables: sat, which means "immortal", ti, which means
"mortal", and yam, which means "by this the two are held
together". Because the two are held together by this [element, it
is called] yam (√yam, meaning to "control" or "hold together").
Whoever understands it in this way day in and day out, goes to
the heavenly world.'

    [1] Enumerated in VIII, ii.
    [2] Satya and anṛta. These words also mean 'true' and 'false'.

VIII, iv

¶ 1. Now, the Self is a causeway [1] which holds these worlds apart lest they should split asunder. On this causeway there passes neither day nor night, neither old age nor death nor sorrow, neither deeds well done nor deeds ill done. All evils recoil from it, for in this Brahman-world evil has ever been laid low.

¶ 2. And so, let the blind pass along this causeway and he will regain his sight; let the wounded [pass along it] and he will be healed; let the fevered [pass along it] and his fever will be calmed. And so it is that once a man has passed along this causeway, night will reveal itself as day indeed, for this Brahman-world is once and for all (*sakṛt*) light [by its own light].

¶ 3. To them alone belongs this Brahman-world who discover it by living the Brahman-life.[2] In all the worlds they have [full] freedom of movement.

VIII, v

¶ 1. What is commonly called sacrifice is really the chaste life of student of sacred knowledge, for only by leading such a life can a wise man (*jñātr*) find the [Brahman-world].

What is commonly called the sacrificial offering is really the chaste life of a student of sacred knowledge, for only by leading such a life and after having searched for it [3] can a man find the Self.

¶ 2. What is commonly called the protracted sacrifice is really the chaste life of a student of sacred knowledge, for only by leading such a life can a man win the protection of the real (*sat*) Self.

What is commonly called a vow of silence (*mauni*) is really the chaste life of a student of sacred knowledge, for only by leading such a life can a man discover the Self and [thereby learn how to] think.

¶ 3. What is commonly called a vow of perpetual fasting is really the chaste life of a student of sacred knowledge, for the Self that a man finds by leading such a life is never destroyed.

What is commonly called the vow of the forest-dweller is really the chaste life of a student of sacred knowledge.

In the Brahman-world, in the third heaven from here, there are two seas called Ara and Nya. There too is the lake *Airam Madīyam* ('Refreshment and Ecstasy'). There too is the fig-tree *Somasavana* ('Soma-dripping'), the city of Brahman called

---

[1] Or, 'bridge'.
[2] i.e. the chaste life of a student of sacred knowledge.
[3] Or, 'sacrificed'.

Aparājita ('Unconquered') and the golden [palace] built by the Lord (*prabhuvimita*).

¶ 4. But only those who, by leading the chaste life of a student of sacred knowledge, find these two seas, Ara and Nya, in the Brahman-world, enjoy this Brahman-world and [full] freedom of movement in all states of being (*loka*).

VIII, vi

¶ 1. Now, these channels within the heart arise from a minute substance which is reddish-brown,—white, blue, yellow and red. So too the sun up there,—it too is reddish-brown, white, blue, yellow and red.

¶ 2. Just as a broad highway leads to two villages,—this one here and that one over there,—so do these rays of the sun lead to the two worlds,—this one down here and that one up there. [And] these [rays] stretch out from the sun up there and filter into these channels down here, [and, reversing the process,] they stretch out from these channels and filter [back] to the sun.

¶ 3. Now, when a man is sound asleep, integrated within himself (*samasta*) and quite serene, and when he is not conscious of dreaming, then he slips into these channels and no evil can touch him, for he is then swathed in the light (*tejas*) [of the sun].

¶ 4. Again, when a man is reduced to a state of [great] weakness, people will gather round him, sitting [at his bedside], and will ask him again and again whether he recognizes (*jñā-*) them. So long as he has not left the body, he [still] recognizes [them].

¶ 5. But when he leaves the body behind, then, surrounded by these same rays of light, he strides on upwards. Uttering [the sacred syllable] Oṁ, he ascends aloft.[1] In as short a time as it takes to think of it (*kṣipyen manas*) he reaches the sun: for this, truly, is the gate of the world by which the wise may enter, by which the unwise are held back. On this there is the following verse:

> One hundred and one are the channels of the heart.
> Of these but one extends right up to the head:
> Ascend thereby to immortality!
>   The rest, at thy departing,
>   Everywhere get lost.

VIII, vii

¶ 1. 'The Self is exempt from evil, untouched by age or death or sorrow, untouched by hunger or thirst: its desire is the real, its idea [2] is the real. This is what [you] must seek out, this is what

---
[1] Text corrupt.   [2] Or, 'will'.

[you] must want to understand. Whoso has found this Self and understands it, wins all states of being (*loka*) and all [objects of] desire.' Thus spake Prajāpati.

¶ 2. Both the gods and the demons were apprised [of what he had said]. They said: 'Come, let us seek out that Self; for once a man has sought him out he will win all states of being and all [objects of] desire.'

Then Indra from among the gods and Virocana from among the demons sallied forth, and these two, without knowing what the other did, came with fuel in hand into the presence of Prajāpati.

¶ 3. For thirty-two years they lived the chaste life of a student of sacred knowledge. And Prajāpati said to them: 'What is it you seek by living [here so long]?'

Then the two of them replied: 'The Self is exempt from evil, untouched by either age or death or sorrow, untouched by hunger or thirst: its desire is the real, its idea is the real. This is what [you] must seek out, this is what [you] must want to understand. Whoso has found this Self and understands it, wins all states of being and all [objects of] desire. Good sir, such were your words, or so do men report them. This is what we sought when we came to live [here].'

¶ 4. And Prajāpati said to them: 'This Person who can be seen in the eye is that very Self.' So said he. 'This is the immortal, [this] the free from fear: this is Brahman!'

'But, good sir, what of that [Person] who can be observed in water or in a mirror, which is he?'

'The very same is observed in all these cases.'

VIII, viii

¶ 1. 'Look at [your]selves in a dish of water, and report to me anything you do not understand about [your]selves.'[1]

So the two of them looked into a dish of water; and Prajāpati said to them: 'What do you see?'

And they said: 'We see all of it, good sir,—a self corresponding exactly [to our own bodies] right up to the hairs on our bodies and the finger-nails.'

¶ 2. And Prajāpati said to them: 'Attire yourselves gorgeously, put on fine raiment, adorn yourselves and then look [again] into the dish of water.' And so did they do.

And Prajāpati said to them: 'What did you see?'

¶ 3. And they said: 'Just as we ourselves here, good sir, are gorgeously attired, clad in fine raiment and [richly] adorned, so are they gorgeously attired, clad in fine raiment and [richly] adorned.'

[1] Or, 'the Self'.

'This is the Self,' said he; 'this the immortal, [this] the free from fear: this is Brahman!'

And the two of them, their hearts at peace, went their way.

¶ 4. And Prajāpati, gazing after them, said: 'There they go, understanding nothing and without having discovered the Self. All who hold *such* a doctrine (*upaniṣad*), be they gods or demons, can but go down to defeat.'

And Virocana, his heart at peace, returned to the demons and preached to them this doctrine: 'Let [one]self [1] be magnified! [2] Let [one]self be carefully tended! Whoso magnifies [him]self and carefully tends [him]self here and now, wins the two worlds, both this one and the next.'

¶ 5. That is why even now men say on earth [when they run across] a man who gives no alms, has no faith, and offers no sacrifice: 'Oh! what a demon!' for such is the doctrine of the demons. They deck out the body of the dead with what they have begged, [adorning it] with clothes and ornaments,—for that is what they call them,—thinking that they will win the next world thereby.

VIII, ix

¶ 1. But Indra, even before he had rejoined the gods, saw this danger. ['True,' he thought,] 'when this body is gorgeously attired, clad in fine raiment and [richly] adorned, so too will that [self] be gorgeously attired, clad in fine raiment and [richly] adorned; but should this [body] be blind or lame or maimed, then that [self] too will be blind or lame or maimed; and when once this body is destroyed, it too must follow it in its destruction. I see nothing enjoyable in this.'

¶ 2. [So,] with fuel in hand back he went.

And Prajāpati said to him: 'Bountiful [Indra], with heart at peace you went your way together with Virocana, yet now you have returned. What is it you want?'

But [Indra] said: 'Good sir, when this body is gorgeously attired, clad in fine raiment and [richly] adorned, so too will that [self] be gorgeously attired, clad in fine raiment and [richly] adorned; but should this [body] be blind or lame or maimed, then that [self] too will be blind or lame or maimed; and when once this body is destroyed, it must follow it in its destruction. I see nothing enjoyable in this.'

¶ 3. 'Such indeed must be his fate, Bountiful [Indra],' said [Prajāpati], 'but I shall explain this [Self] to you further. Stay [with me] for another thirty-two years.' So he stayed [with him] for another thirty-two years. And [then Prajāpati] spoke to him:

---

[1] i.e. the body.   [2] Or, 'be happy'.

VIII, x

¶ 1. 'He who roams abroad in dream, glorying in himself,—this is the Self,' said [Prajāpati], 'this the immortal, [this] the free from fear: this is Brahman.'

And with heart at peace he went his way. But even before he had rejoined the gods, he saw this danger.

['True,' he thought,] 'even if this body is blind or lame, that [other self] will be neither blind nor lame; it is not in any way harmed by the body's ailments; [¶ 2] it is not killed when the [body] is killed, nor lame when the [body] is lame; and yet it does have the impression of being killed, of being stripped, of undergoing unpleasant experiences and even of weeping. I see nothing enjoyable in this.'

¶ 3. [So,] with fuel in hand back he went.

And Prajāpati said to him: 'Bountiful [Indra], with heart at peace you went your way, yet now you have returned. What is it you want?'

But [Indra] said: 'Good sir, now even if this body is blind and lame, that [other self] will be neither blind nor lame; it is not in any way harmed by the body's ailments; [¶ 4] it is not killed when the [body] is killed, nor lame when the [body] is lame; and yet it does have the impression of being killed, of being stripped, of undergoing unpleasant experiences and even of weeping. I see nothing enjoyable in this.'

'Such indeed must be his fate, Bountiful [Indra],' said [Prajāpati,] 'but I shall explain this [Self] to you further. Stay [with me] for another thirty-two years.' So he stayed [with him] for another thirty-two years. And [then Prajāpati] spoke to him:

VIII, xi

¶ 1. 'Now, when a man is sound asleep, integrated within himself (*samasta*) and quite serene, and when he is not conscious of dreaming,—this is the Self,' said [Prajāpati], 'this the immortal, [this] the free from fear: this is Brahman!'

And with heart at peace he went his way. But even before he had rejoined the gods he saw this danger.

[He thought:] 'Such a man, it seems to me, has no present knowledge of [him]self so that he could say, "This I am," nor, for that matter, [has he any knowledge] of these creatures [here]. Surely he might as well be a man annihilated. I see nothing enjoyable in this.'

¶ 2. [So,] with fuel in hand back he went.

And Prajāpati said to him: 'Bountiful [Indra], with heart at peace you went your way, yet now you have returned. What is it you want?'

But [Indra] said: 'Good sir, such a man, it seems to me, has no present knowledge of [him]self so that he could say, "This I am," nor, for that matter, [has he any knowledge] of these creatures [here]. Surely he might as well be a man annihilated. I see nothing enjoyable in this.'

¶ 3. 'Such indeed must be his fate, Bountiful [Indra],' said Prajāpati, 'but I shall explain this [Self] to you further, for it is not otherwise than this. Stay [with me] for another five years.' So he stayed [with him] for another five years, which makes a hundred and one years altogether. Hence we have the saying: 'For a hundred and one years the Bountiful [Indra] lived the life of a chaste student of sacred knowledge with Prajāpati.'

And [then Prajāpati] spoke to him:

VIII, xii

¶ 1. 'Bountiful one! For sure this body is mortal, held in the grip of death. Yet it is the dwelling-place of the immortal, incorporeal Self. [And this Self,] while still in the body, is held in the grip of pleasure and pain; and so long as it remains in the body there is no means of ridding it of pleasure and pain. But once it is freed from the body, pleasure and pain cannot [so much as] touch it.

¶ 2. 'The wind has no body. Clouds, thunder and lightning,— these too have no body. So, just as these arise from [the broad expanse of] space up there and plunge into the highest light, revealing themselves each in its own form, [¶ 3] so too does this deep serenity arise out of this body and plunge into the highest light, revealing itself in its own form. Such a one is a superman (uttara puruṣa); and there he roves around, laughing, playing, taking his pleasure with women, chariots, or friends and remembering no more that excrescence [which was] his body.[1]

'As a draught-animal is yoked to a wagon, so is this breath of life yoked to the body.

¶ 4. 'Now, when the eye gazes upon space, it is the Person in the eye [who actually sees]: the eye itself [is merely the instrument] of sight.

'Again, when a man is conscious of smelling something, it is the Self [that smells], the nose [is only the instrument] of smell.

'And when a man is conscious of wanting to say something, it is the Self [that is so conscious], the voice [is only the instrument] of speech.

'And when a man is conscious of hearing something, it is the Self [that hears], the ear [is only the instrument] of hearing.

¶ 5. 'And when a man is conscious of thinking of something, it is

[1] Or, 'the body into which he was born'.

the Self [that thinks], the mind is its divine eye. With this divine eye, the mind, this Self sees these [objects of] desire and rejoices. ¶ 6. 'Assuredly, the gods in the Brahman-world revere this Self. And so all states of being (*loka*) and all [objects of] desire are in their hands. Let a man but discover this Self and understand it, then will he make his own all states of being and all [objects of] desire.' Thus spake Prajāpati: thus spake Prajāpati.

VIII, xiii

From the dark I go to the dappled: from the dappled I go to the dark.

Shaking off evil as a horse [shakes off] its hairs, shaking off the body as the moon delivers herself from the eclipse, with self perfected (*kṛtātman*), I merge into the unmade Brahman-world, —I merge [into the Brahman-world].

VIII, xiv

Space it is indeed which brings out name and form. That within which they are, is Brahman, the immortal, the Self.

I go to the palace and assembly-hall of Prajāpati.

I am the glory (*yaśas*) of the Brāhmans, the glory of princes, the glory of the people.

Glory have I won! Glory of glories am I! May I never go near the white and toothless,—the toothless, white and slimy.[1] To that drivelling thing may I never go!

VIII, xv

This did Brahmā tell to Prajāpati, Prajāpati to Manu, and Manu to his descendants.

The man who has studied the Veda in his teacher's family in accordance with the prescribed ordinances and in the time left over after he has performed his duties for his teacher; and who, after returning home, has continued his Vedic studies in his house and in a clean place; who has produced virtuous [sons]; and who has concentrated all his faculties (*indriya*) on the Self, taking care to hurt no living thing (*ahiṁsan*) except in sacrifice,— such a man, if he perseveres in this throughout life, will reach the Brahman-world and will not return again,—he will not return again.

[1] i.e. old age.

Taittirīya Upanishad

I

¶ 1. Homage to Brahman! Homage to thee, O wind; for thou art Brahman manifest. Of thee who art Brahman [made] manifest shall I surely speak. I shall speak of the cosmic law (*ṛta*); I shall speak of truth. May it help me, may it help the speaker! May it help me, may it help the speaker!

Oṁ. Peace—peace—peace.

¶ 2. Oṁ. We will [now] explain about pronunciation: pitch, tone, quantity, force, articulation, length. So much for the lesson on pronunciation.

¶ 3. [1] May glory [come] to both of us together! May the splendour of Brahman [1] [come] to both of us together!

Next we will explain the secret teaching (*upaniṣad*) of the combined phrase (*saṁhitā*) under five heads;—as it is applied to the world,—to the luminaries,—to knowledge,—to offspring,—and to the self. These are called the 'great combinations'.

Now, with regard to the world:

The earth is the first element (*rūpa*), heaven the last element, space the connection [between the two], [2] wind the operative conjunction (*sandhāna*). So much for its application to the world.

Now, with regard to the luminaries:

Fire is the first element, the sun the last element, water the connection [between the two], lightning the operative conjunction. So much for its application to the luminaries.

Now, with regard to knowledge:

The teacher is the first element, [3] the pupil the last element, knowledge the connection [between the two], teaching the operative conjunction. So much for its application to knowledge.

Now, with regard to offspring:

The mother is the first element, the father the last element, offspring the connection [between the two], procreation the operative conjunction. So much for its application to offspring.

[4] Now, with regard to the self:

The lower jaw is the first element, the upper jaw the last element, speech the connection [between the two], the tongue the operative conjunction. So much for its application to the self.

These are the great combinations. He who knows the great

---

[1] This could mean the Veda.

133

combinations explained in this way, will [himself] be conjoined
with offspring, cattle, the vital power of Brahman, with food and
the heavenly world.

¶ 4. [1] Exalted is he in the Vedic hymns, possessor of every form,
　　　Sprung from the immortal, he surpasses the hymns [them-
　　　selves].
　　　May he, [great] Indra, deliver [me] by wisdom!
　　　May I, O God, become a carrier of immortality!
　　　May my body be robust and vigorous,
　　　　My tongue exceeding sweet!
　　　May I hear abundantly with my ears!
　　　Thou art the sheath of Brahman in wisdom swathed:
　　　Preserve for me what I have heard!

　　　[2] She it is, [prosperity,] who ever and anon
　　　Brings, spreads out, swiftly appropriates to me
　　　Garments and kine and food and drink,—
　　　　So bring me prosperity
　　　Rich in wool and rich in flocks. All hail!

May students of sacred knowledge (*brahmacārin*) come to me!
All hail!
May students of sacred knowledge come to me from every
side! All hail!
May students of sacred knowledge come forward to me! All
hail!
May students of sacred knowledge be self-restrained! All hail!
May students of sacred knowledge be at peace! All hail!
[3] May I be glorious among men! All hail!
May I excel the very rich! All hail!
May I enter into thee, O Lord (*bhaga*)! All hail!
Do thou enter into me, O Lord! All hail!
In thee, possessed of a thousand branches,
In thee, O Lord, I'm cleansed! All hail!
As waters follow a downward course, as the months [are
merged] in the year, so may students of sacred knowledge, O
Ordainer (*dhātṛ*),[1] come to me from everywhere! All hail!
Thou art [my] refuge; shine upon me; make me thy home!

¶ 5. [1] *Bhūr—Bhuvas—Suvar*. These are the three ejaculations.
Apart from these Māhācamasya made known a fourth called
Mahas ('greatness'). That is Brahman: that is the Self. The other
deities are [only] limbs.
　　Bhūr: this means this world; *bhuvas*, the atmosphere; *suvar*,
the other world; [2] *mahas*, the sun. By the sun, assuredly, all
worlds are magnified.

　　　　　　　　　　　[1] Or, 'Creator'.

Bhūr: this means fire; *bhuvas,* wind; *suvar,* the sun; *mahas,* the moon. By the moon assuredly all lights are magnified.

Bhūr: this means the Rig-Veda; *bhuvas,* the Sāma-Veda; *suvar,* the Yajur-Veda; [3] *mahas,* Brahman ('sacred knowledge'). By Brahman, assuredly, are all the Vedas magnified.

Bhūr: this means the in-breath; *bhuvas,* the out-breath; *suvar,* the diffused breath; *mahas,* food. By food, assuredly, all modes of breathing are magnified.

These four are thus themselves fourfold, and the ejaculations are four times four. To know these is to know Brahman. To It all the gods pay tribute.

¶ 6. [I] In this space that is within the heart dwells the 'person' made of mind,—golden, immortal. Between the sides of the palate [the uvula] hangs like a nipple; this is the seat (*yoni*) of Indra. Thrusting aside the two bone-structures of the skull at the point where the roots of the hair are separated, he takes his stand on fire by saying *bhūr,* on wind by saying *bhuvas,* [2] on the sun by saying *suvar,* on Brahman by saying *mahas.* He attains to independent sovereignty (*svārājya*), attains to the lord of the mind. Lord of speech, eye, ear and understanding, [all] this he becomes, and, [after that,] Brahman [itself] whose body is space, whose self is the real (*satya*), whose pleasure-ground is the breath of life (*prāṇa*), whose joy is mind, immortal, in whom there is peace abounding. O adept of the ancient spiritual exercise (*prācīnayogya*), do homage to It as such!

¶ 7. Earth, atmosphere, sky, the points of the compass and the intermediate points: fire, wind, sun, moon and constellations: water, plants, trees, space, the Self:—so much for the material world (*adhibhūta*).

Now [we come] to the [individual] self.

In-breath, out-breath, diffused breath, upper breath, concentrated breath: sight, hearing, mind, speech, touch: skin, flesh, muscle, bone, marrow:—after breaking it down into these categories an ancient seer remarked: 'Surely the universe is [made up] of fives. By the fivefold one preserves the fivefold.'

¶ 8. [The syllable] Oṁ is Brahman. Oṁ is the whole universe.

Oṁ means consent. At the call 'Oṁ',[1] recite,' [the priests] duly recite. The chants of the Sāma-Veda [begin] with Oṁ; the laudatory hymns [begin] with 'Oṁ, śoṁ'. [Starting] with Oṁ the priest in charge of the sacrificial action pronounces the response; saying 'Oṁ' the Brāhman priest gives his consent; with the word Oṁ permission is given [to proceed] with the daily fire-sacrifice. Saying 'Oṁ' the Brāhman who is about to recite [the Veda]

---

[1] The text has *o.*

proceeds to say, 'May I attain to Brahman.' And he does attain to Brahman.

¶ 9. There is the cosmic law (*rta*) and the study and recitation [of the Veda].

There is the real (*satya*) and the study and recitation [of the Veda].

There is asceticism and the study and recitation [of the Veda].

There is self-control and the study and recitation [of the Veda].

There is calm and the study and recitation [of the Veda].

There are the [sacrificial] fires and the study and recitation [of the Veda].

There is the daily fire-sacrifice and the study and recitation [of the Veda].

There are guests and the study and recitation [of the Veda].

There is mankind and the study and recitation [of the Veda].

There is offspring and the study and recitation [of the Veda].

There is procreation and the study and recitation [of the Veda].

There is progeny and the study and recitation [of the Veda].

'The real (truth),' said Rāthītara who spoke the truth. 'Asceticism,' said Pauruśishti, the permanent ascetic. 'Study and recitation [of the Veda] only,' said Nāka Maudgalya, 'for that is asceticism, that is [really] asceticism.'

¶ 10. I am the shaker of the tree,
      My fame is like a mountain's ridge:
      Surpassing pure, I am like goodly nectar in the sun.
      [I am] a dazzling treasure,
      Most wise and bathed in deathlessness.[1]

This is Triśanku's interpretation of the Veda.

¶ 11. [1] Once he has given instruction in the Veda, the teacher should proceed to instruct his pupil [as follows]:

Speak the truth.

Do what is right (*dharma*).

Do not neglect study [of the Veda].

After you have given your teacher an acceptable sum, do not let your family line die out.

Do not be careless about truth.

Do not be careless about what is right.

Do not be careless about welfare.

Do not be careless about prosperity.

Do not be negligent in the study and recitation [of the Veda].

[2] Do not neglect your duties to the gods and ancestors.

Let your mother be a god to you.

Let your father be a god to you.

---

[1] Or, 'immortal, imperishable'.

Let your teacher be a god to you.

Let a guest be a god to you.

Perform only deeds to which no blame attaches, no others.

Respect such deeds of ours as have been well done, [3] no others.

Offer the comfort of a seat to whatever Brāhmans may be better than we.

Give with faith: do not give without faith. Give plentifully: [1] give modestly: give with awe; give with sympathy.[2]

Now, if you are in doubt about how to act or how to behave, then behave as Brāhmans of good judgment would behave if they were present,—[Brāhmans] who are competent, versed in these matters, not harsh, and devoted to what is right (*dharma*).

Again, in matters [3] that have given rise to criticism, behave as Brahmans of good judgment would behave if they were present, —[Brāhmans] who are competent, versed in these matters, not harsh, devoted to what is right. This is the rule, this the teaching, this the secret doctrine (*upaniṣad*) of the Veda, this the instruction. And so it should be respected; yes, this should be respected even so.

¶ 12. May Mitra be propitious to us, propitious Varuna,
　　　　Propitious Aryaman,
　　　Propitious Indra [and] Brihaspati,
　　　Propitious Vishnu, the wide strider!

Homage to Brahman! Homage to thee, O wind! For thou art Brahman manifest. Of thee who art Brahman [made] manifest have I spoken. Of cosmic law have I spoken. Of truth have I spoken. It has helped me, helped the speaker. It has helped me, helped the speaker!

Oṁ. Peace—peace—peace.

II

¶ 1. Oṁ. Whoso knows Brahman wins the all-highest.
　　On this the following [verse] has been recorded:

The real (*satya*), [true] wisdom, infinite is Brahman:
Whoso knows It hidden in a secret place, in the highest
　　firmament,
All he desires is his;
His too is Brahman, the discerning (*vipaścit*) [seer].

From It, from this Self, space came to be, from space the wind, from wind fire, from fire water, from water earth, from earth the

---

[1] Or, 'with grace'.　　　[2] Or, 'conscientiously'.　　　[3] Or, 'with people'.

plants, from the plants food, from food [transformed into semen] man (*puruṣa*). Man, indeed, essentially consists of choice food. This is his head, this his right side, this his left side, this his trunk (*ātman*), this his tail and seat.

On this too there are the following verses:

¶ 2.   From food indeed do creatures come to birth,
         Whatever [creatures] dwell on earth.
         Then again by food they live,
         And again pass into it in the end.
         For food is the chief of beings,
         Hence is it called the elixir of all.
         All food most certainly do they attain
         Who reverence Brahman as food.
         For food is the chief of beings,
         Hence is it called the elixir of all.
         From food do beings come to birth,
         When born, by food they grow.
         Eaten, it eats [all] beings;
         Hence is it known as food (*an-na*, 'eatable').

Quite other than [this man] who essentially consists of choice food and interior to him is the self that consists of breath. The one is filled with the other. The first has the likeness of a man (*puruṣa*), and because it has the likeness of a man, the second follows it and itself takes on the likeness of a man. The in-breath is his head, the diffused breath his right side, the out-breath his left side, space his trunk (*ātman*), earth his tail and seat.

On this there are the following verses:

¶ 3.   In sympathy with breath do the gods breathe,
         As do [all] men and beasts:
         For breath is the life (*āyu*) of beings,
         And so is it called the 'life of all'.
         All life do they obtain
         Who reverence Brahman as breath:
         For breath is the life of beings,
         And so is it called the 'life of all'.

This [self consisting of breath] shares the same bodily self [1] with the former.

Quite other than this [self] that consists of breath and interior to it is the self that consists of mind. The one is filled with the other. The first has the likeness of a man, and because it has the likeness of a man, the second follows it and itself takes on the likeness of a man. The Yajur-Veda is its head, the Rig-Veda its

---

[1] i.e. 'is located in the same body'.

right side, the Sāma-Veda its left side, teaching its trunk (ātman),
the Atharva-Veda its tail and seat.
On this there are the following verses:

¶ 4. That from which [all] words recoil together with the mind,
     Unable to attain It,—
    That is the bliss of Brahman; knowing It,
    A man has naught to fear from anywhere.

This [self consisting of mind] shares the same bodily self with
the former [self consisting of breath].
Quite other than this [self] that consists of mind and interior to
it is the self that consists of understanding (vijñāna). The one is
filled with the other. The first has the likeness of a man, and
because it has the likeness of a man, the second follows it and
itself takes on the likeness of a man. Faith is its head, cosmic
order (rta) is its right side, the real (truth) its left side, spiritual
exercise (yoga) its trunk (ātman), greatness (mahas) its tail and
seat.
On this too there are the following verses:

¶ 5. Understanding [it is that] spins forth the sacrifice,
    Spins forth the [ritual] action (karma) too.
    As chiefest Brahman all the gods
    Revere the understanding.
    Should a man know understanding as Brahman
      And persevere therein,
    He'll leave [all] evils in the body,
    All he desires is his!

This [self consisting of the understanding] shares the same
bodily self with the former [self consisting of mind].
Quite other than this [self] that consists of understanding and
interior to it is the self that consists of bliss. The one is filled with
the other. The first has the likeness of a man, and because it has
the likeness of a man, the second follows it and itself takes on the
likeness of a man. The pleasant is its head, enjoyment (moda) its
right side, delight (pramoda) its left side, bliss its trunk (ātman),
Brahman its tail and seat.
On this too there are the following verses:

¶ 6. Non-existent (asat) does he become who thinks
    That Brahman is Not-Being (asat):
    Who knows that Brahman IS
    Is then known to BE himself.

This [self consisting of bliss] shares the same bodily self with
the former [self consisting of understanding].

Next there are these supplementary questions:

> Does any man who knows not [Brahman]
>   Go at death to the other world?
> Or is it that a man who knows
>   At death attains the other world?

He desired: 'May I become many, may I procreate.' He heated himself by fierce austerities (*tap-*); and having heated himself thus, he emanated this whole universe,—all things whatever [that exist]. Having emanated it, he proceeded to enter into it. And having entered it, he became the actual (*sat*) and what is beyond (*tyat*), the specific and the unspecified, the containable and the uncontainable, the conscious (*vijñāna*) and the unconscious, the real (true) and the false. The real became everything [that exists down] here. That is what they call the real.

On this too there are the following verses:

¶ 7.   In the beginning this [universe] was Not-Being only,
            Therefrom was Being born:
        [And Being] itself made [for itself] a self:
        Hence is it called 'well-done'.

What that 'well-done' really is, is the [essential] savour (*rasa*) [in all things]. Once a man has tasted this savour, he tastes bliss. For who could breathe, who could live, were this bliss not [diffused] throughout space? For this [savour] alone brings bliss.

For when a man finds security from fear and permanence (*pratiṣṭhā*) in this invisible, insubstantial (*an-ātmya*), unspecified, uncontainable [savour], then does he achieve [full] security from [all] fear. But when he excavates a hole in it and splits it into different parts, then will he experience fear,—the fear of a man who thinks he knows.[1]

On this there are the following verses:

¶ 8.   For fear of It the wind doth blow,
           For fear [of It] the sun doth rise,
           For fear of It the gods of fire and storm
           And Death, the fifth, [hither and thither] fly.

What follows is the catalogue of bliss:

Take a young man of noble lineage, well read [in the Vedas], very nimble, tough, and strong; for him the whole world yields up its wealth. Such is a single [measure of] bliss on the human scale.

A hundred such human [measures of] bliss make one [measure of] bliss on the scale of human genii (*gandharva*), and of the man well versed in scripture who is not smitten by desire.

----

[1] Var. 'does not think he knows'.

A hundred such [measures of] bliss on the scale of human genii make one [measure of] bliss on the scale of divine genii, and of the man well versed in scripture who is not smitten by desire.

A hundred such [measures of] bliss on the scale of divine genii make up one [measure of] bliss on the scale of the ancestors in their long-lasting worlds, and of the man well versed in scripture who is not smitten by desire.

A hundred such [measures of] bliss on the scale of the ancestors in their long-lasting worlds make one [measure of] bliss of the gods who are destined to be gods by birth, and of the man well versed in scripture who is not smitten by desire.

A hundred [measures of] bliss on the scale of the gods who are destined to be gods by birth make one [measure of] bliss on the scale of the gods who become gods by [good] works and who join the gods by means of such works, and of the man well versed in scripture who is not smitten by desire.

A hundred [measures of] bliss on the scale of the gods who have become gods by [good] works make one [measure of] bliss of the gods [in their own right], and of the man well versed in scripture who is not smitten by desire.

A hundred [measures of] bliss on the scale of the gods [in their own right] make one [measure of] bliss on the scale of Indra, and of the man well versed in scripture who is not smitten by desire.

A hundred [measures of] bliss on Indra's scale make one [measure of] bliss on the scale of Brihaspati, and the man well versed in scripture who is not smitten by desire.

A hundred [measures of] bliss on Brihaspati's scale make one [measure of] bliss on the scale of Prajāpati, and of the man well versed in scripture who is not smitten by desire.

A hundred [measures of] bliss on Prajāpati's scale make one [measure of] bliss on the scale of Brahman, and of the man well versed in scripture who is not smitten with desire.

This one that is here in a man (*puruṣa*) and that one there in the sun,—He is One.

The man who knows this, on departing from this world, draws near to the self that consists of food, draws near to the self that consists of breath, draws near to the self that consists of mind, draws near to the self that consists of understanding, draws near to the self that consists of bliss.

On this there are the following verses:

¶ 9. That from which [all] words recoil together with the mind,
        Unable to attain it,—
    That is the bliss of Brahman; knowing it,
    A man has naught to fear from anywhere.

Such a man is not worried (*tap-*) [by the thought]: 'Why did I

not do good? Why did I do evil?' [1] Knowing [good and evil] in
this way he saves [him]self: who knows them both as such, he
saves [him]self. Such is the secret teaching.

III

¶ 1. Hari, Oṁ. Bhrigu, son of Varuna, approached his father
Varuna.

'Sir, tell me about Brahman,' he said.

[His father] said to him: 'Food, breath, sight, hearing, mind
and speech.'

He spoke to him [further saying]: 'That from which [all] these
beings are born, by which, once born, they live, into which they
enter when they die,—that is what you must want to understand:
that is Brahman.'

[Bhrigu then] mortified himself, and after mortifying himself
[¶ 2] he understood that Brahman is food. For surely it is from
food that [all] these beings are born, by food that, once born, they
live and into food that they enter when they die.

Realizing this, he again approached his father, Varuna, and
said [again]: 'Sir, tell me about Brahman.'

[His father] said to him: 'Try to understand Brahman by self-
mortification: Brahman is mortification (*tapas*).'

[So Bhrigu] mortified himself [again], and after mortifying
himself [¶ 3] he understood that Brahman is breath (*prāṇa*). For
surely it is from breath that [all] these beings are born, by breath
that, once born, they live and into breath that they enter when
they die.

Realizing this, he again approached his father, Varuna, and
said [again]: 'Sir, tell me about Brahman.'

[His father] said to him: 'Try to understand Brahman by self-
mortification: Brahman is mortification.'

[So Bhrigu] mortified himself [again], and after mortifying
himself [¶ 4] he understood that Brahman is mind. For surely it is
from mind that [all] these beings are born, by mind that, once
born, they live and into mind that they enter when they die.

Realizing this, he again approached his father, Varuna, and
said [again]: 'Sir, tell me about Brahman.'

[His father] said to him: 'Try to understand Brahman by self-
mortification: Brahman is mortification.'

[So Bhrigu] mortified himself [again], and after mortifying
himself [¶ 5] he understood that Brahman is the understanding
(*vijñāna*). For surely it is from the understanding that [all] these
beings are born, by the understanding that, once born, they live
and into the understanding that they enter when they die.

[1] Or, 'What good have I left undone? What evil have I done?'

Realizing this, he again approached his father, Varuna, and said [again]: 'Sir, tell me about Brahman.'

[His father] said to him: 'Try to understand Brahman by self-mortification: Brahman is mortification.'

[So Bhrigu] mortified himself [again], and after mortifying himself [¶ 6] he understood that Brahman is bliss (*ānanda*). For surely it is from bliss that [all] these beings are born, by bliss that, once born, they live and into bliss that they enter when they die.

This is the doctrine (*vidyā*) of Bhrigu, son of Varuna, firmly based (*pratiṣṭhita*) in the highest heaven. He who knows it thus has a firm basis [himself]; he becomes an owner of food, an eater of food, rich in offspring, cattle and the vital force of Brahman, rich in fame.

¶ 7. Food should not be despised. That is the sacred rule (*vrata*).

Breath is food indeed; the body eats food and is itself dependent (*pratiṣṭhita*) on breath, [while] breath [in turn] depends on the body. Food, then, depends on food.

He who knows that food depends [and is firmly based] on food, has [himself] a firm basis; be becomes an owner of food, an eater of food, rich in offspring, cattle and the vital force of Brahman, rich in fame.

¶ 8. Food should not be set at naught. That is the sacred rule.

The waters are food indeed; light eats food and is itself dependent on the waters, [while] the waters [in turn] depend on light. Food, then, depends on food.

He who knows that food depends [and is firmly based] on food, has [himself] a firm basis; he becomes an owner of food, an eater of food, rich in offspring, cattle and the vital force of Brahman, rich in fame.

¶ 9. Food should be multiplied. That is the sacred rule.

The earth is food indeed; space eats food and is itself dependent on the earth, [while] the earth [in turn] depends on space. Food, then, depends on food.

He who knows that food depends [and is firmly based] on food, has [himself] a firm basis; he becomes an owner of food, an eater of food, rich in offspring, cattle and the vital force of Brahman, rich in fame.

¶ 10. [1] One should not refuse anyone in [one's own] home. That is the sacred rule.

And so one should accumulate a large store of food by every possible means. Of such a man people say: 'He has been fortunate in his food [supply]. If this food has been prepared in an exemplary way [1] [for others, it is as if] it has been prepared in an exemplary way for himself; if prepared in a middling way [2] [for others], then it is [as if] prepared in a middling way for

---

[1] Or, 'from the beginning'.   [2] Or, 'in the middle'.

himself; if prepared in a wretched way [1] [for others], then it is [as if] prepared in a wretched way for himself, [2] [that is,] for the man who knows this.'

Ease of speech, acquisition and preservation of the in-breath and the out-breath, action (*karma*) with the hands, movement with the feet, excretion by the anus, these are signs in human beings [of the effects of food].

And now [the signs] in natural phenomena (*deva*): satisfaction in rain, force in the lightning, [3] splendour (*yaśas*) in cattle, light in the constellations, procreative power, immortality and bliss (*ānanda*) in the sexual organs, the All in space.

If one reveres it as the firm foundation (*pratiṣṭhā*), then one becomes firmly founded [oneself]. If one reveres it as great, one becomes great [oneself]. If one reveres it as mind, one becomes mindful [oneself]. [4] If one reveres it as homage, [all] desires will do him homage. If one reveres it as Brahman, one becomes possessed of Brahman [oneself]. If one reveres it as what dies around Brahman [while Brahman lives on], his enemies and rivals, ill-wishers and false friends will die round about him.

This one that is here in a man (*puruṣa*) and that one [up] there in the sun,—He is One.

[5] The man who knows this, on departing from this world, draws near to the self that consists of food, draws near to the self that consists of breath, draws near to the self that consists of mind, draws near to the self that consists of understanding, draws near to the self that consists of bliss; then he roams [at will] throughout these worlds, eating what he will, changing his form at will: and, sitting down, he sings this song:

Bravo! Bravo! Bravo!
I am food! I am food! I am food!
I am an eater of food! I am an eater of food! I am an eater
    of food!
I am a maker of verses! I am a maker of verses! I am a
    maker of verses!
I am the first-born of the universal order (*rta*),
Earlier than the gods, in the navel of immortality!
Whoso gives me away, he, verily, has succoured me!
I who am food eat the eater of food!
I have overcome the whole world!

He who knows this shines with a golden light.

---

[1] Or, 'in the end'.

Aitareya Upanishad

I

¶ 1. In the beginning the Self alone was here,[1]—no other thing that blinks the eye at all.

He thought: 'What if I were to emanate worlds?'

¶ 2. He emanated these worlds,—water, rays of light, death, the waters. Water is [up] there beyond the sky; the sky supports it. The rays of light are the atmosphere; death the earth; what is underneath, the waters.

¶ 3. He thought [again]: 'Here now are these worlds. What if I were to emanate world-rulers?' He raised a man (*puruṣa*) up from water and gave him a form.

¶ 4. He brooded over him: when he had finished brooding over him, a mouth broke open on him in the likeness of an egg. From the mouth [came] speech, and from speech fire.

Nostrils broke open: from the nostrils [came] breath, from breath the wind.

Eyes broke open: from the eyes [came] sight, from sight the sun.

Ears broke open: from the ears [came] hearing, from hearing the points of the compass.

Skin broke out: from skin [grew] hairs, from the hairs plants and trees.

A heart broke out: from the heart [came] mind, from the mind the moon.

A navel broke open: from the navel [came] the out-breath, from the out-breath death.

A phallus broke forth: from the phallus [came] semen, from semen water.

[Chapters II and III, 1–10, on the correlation of natural phenomena and the faculties of man, are omitted.]

III

¶ 11. [The Self] considered: 'How could this [universe] exist without me?'

[Again] he thought: 'By which [way] shall I enter it?'

[And again] he thought: 'If it is uttered as speech, breathed in

---

[1] Or, 'was this universe'.

145

as breath, seen by the eye, heard by the ear, touched by the skin,
thought by the mind, breathed out as out-breath, or ejaculated by
the phallus, then who am I?'

¶ 12. He split this sagittal suture open and entered in through [it
as through] a door. So this door is called *vidriti*, 'splitting open';
it is [a place of] bliss.

He has three dwellings, three places to sleep in,[1]—one here,
one here and one here (pointing to different parts of the body).

¶ 13. Once born, he contemplated the beings [that existed], and
said [to himself]: 'Why should one wish to speak of another?'
He saw that [primal] man (*puruṣa*) as veriest Brahman. 'I have
seen It,' said he.

¶ 14. That is why his name is *Idaṁdra* ('It-seeing'), for that is his
name. Though he is really *Idaṁdra*, people call him Indra,—
obscurely; for the gods seem to love the obscure, yes, the gods
seem to love the obscure.

IV

¶ 1. Within a man (*puruṣa*) one first becomes an embryo, and
that is nothing but semen, the vigour arising from all the members. Thus [a man] bears a self within [him]self. When he injects it
into a woman, he engenders him; and that is his first birth.

¶ 2. He becomes a self in the woman, like one of her members;
and so he does her no harm. She nourishes this self of his which
has entered into her.

¶ 3. Since she nourishes him, she should [herself] be nourished.
The woman carries him as an embryo. The man takes care of the
child from the beginning, even before his birth. In taking care of
the child from even before his birth, he is really taking care of
[him]self in order that the worlds may continue to exist; for it is in
this way that they do continue to exist. This is his second birth.

¶ 4. This self of his is given good works to do. Then this second
self of his (the son), once he has performed his duty and reached
[his appointed] age, passes on. Having passed on from here, he is
really (*eva*) born again. That is his third birth.

¶ 5. On this a seer has said:

> While yet in the womb I knew
> All the generations of these gods:
> A hundred iron ramparts hemmed me in,
> Yet, [like] an eagle, down I swiftly flew.

While yet lying in the womb Vāmadeva spake these words.

¶ 6. Knowing this, he rose up after his separation from the body,
and after enjoying all that he desired in the heavenly world [up
there], he became immortal,—[so] did he become.

---

[1] Or, 'kinds of sleep'.

V

¶ 1. Who is He whom we should revere as the Self? Which is that Self?

[He] by whom one sees, by whom one hears, by whom one smells scents, by whom one utters speech, by whom one distinguishes sweet from what is not sweet.

¶ 2. Heart is He and mind, conscience (*saṁjñāna*), perception (*ājñāna*), discrimination (*vijñāna*), consciousness (*prajñāna*), inspiration (*medhas*), vision, steadfastness, thought, thoughtfulness, impulse, memory, conception (*saṁkalpa*), will (*kratu*), life (*asu*), desire and will-power (*vaśa*). All these are but names of consciousness (*prajñāna*).

¶ 3. He is Brahman; He is Indra; He is Prajāpati,—all the gods and these five gross elements,—earth, wind, space, water, light, —all those things [too] which seem to be compounded of [some] subtle [matter],—all manner of seeds, [all] creatures born from egg or womb or sweat or bud,—horses, kine, men and elephants, —whatever breathes or moves or flies, whatever remains unmoving. All this has consciousness as its eye, is based on consciousness. The eye of the world is consciousness: consciousness is the ground (*pratiṣṭhā*), consciousness is Brahman.

¶ 4. By this Self which is consciousness [Vāmadeva] rose up from this world and after enjoying all that he desired in that heavenly world [up there], he became immortal,—[so] did he become.

Kaushītakī Upanishad

I

¶ 1. Citra Gārgyāyani, when about to sacrifice, chose Āruni [as sacrificial priest], and [Āruni] dispatched his son, Śvetaketu, saying, 'You perform the sacrifice [for me].' When he had arrived, [Citra] asked him: 'Son of Gautama, is [the road] closed in [that other] world in which you will put me? Or are there several paths in [that] world [in which] you will put me?' [1]

[Śvetaketu] said: 'I do not know; however, I will ask my teacher.' So he went to his father and asked him [saying]: 'This is the question he asked me. How am I going to reply?'

[His father] said: 'I too do not know the answer. After studying [the Veda, let us go] to the assembly and pick up whatever [answers] others are giving. Come on, let us both go.'

With fuel in hand he approached Citra Gārgyāyani, saying: 'I should like to come to you as a pupil.'

[Citra] said to him: 'You are fit to receive the sacred word (brahman) since you have come to me.[2] Come, I will teach you.'

¶ 2. He continued: 'Everyone who departs from this world, comes to the moon. In the first fortnight [the moon] waxes on their breath-souls (prāṇa), while in the latter half it prepares them to be born [again]; for the moon is the gateway of the heavenly world. Those who answer it, it allows to pass on, but those who do not answer are turned into rain and [the moon] rains them down on earth. [Then] they are born again here in different places [in a form] which accords with their [former] deeds (karma) and knowledge,—as worms or moths, fish or birds, tigers or lions, boars or rhinoceros, or as men or some other [animal].

When a man reaches [the moon, the moon] asks him, 'Who are you?'

He should answer:

'From [the moon] far-seeing, fifteenfold produced,
  From the world of the fathers, ye seasons, semen was
     produced.
Speed me then forth into a male who fashions [offspring],
And by [this] fashioning male into a mother pour me.'

---

[1] Translation uncertain.
[2] Var. 'since you have not shown pride'.

149

[Or else:]

'I am he who is born and is reborn
Like the twelfth or thirteenth month
Of a father who has twelve or thirteen parts.
This do I know, this do I understand. O seasons,
Lead me to [the land of] immortality!

'Through this truth, through this ascetic fervour I am a season, a son of the seasons.'

'Whe art thou?' [asks the moon].

'I am thou.'

It lets him pass on.

¶ 3. [And so] reaching that path [called] the 'way of the gods' he comes to the worlds of (the fire-god) Agni, of (the wind-god) Vāyu, of Varuna, of the sun, of Indra, of Prajāpati and of Brahman. In this world of Brahman there are the lake Āra, the moments Yeshtiha, the river Vijarā ('ageless'), the tree Ilya, the public place Sālajya, the residence Aparājita ('unconquered'), the door-keepers Indra and Prajāpati, the palace Vibhu ('extensive'), the throne Vicakshanā ('far-seeing'), the couch Amitaujas ('of boundless strength'), the dearly beloved Mānasī ('mental') and her counterpart Cākshushī ('visual'). (It is these two who weave the worlds out of flowers.) [There too are] the nymphs (apsaras) [called] 'mothers' and 'nurses', and the rivers Ambayā.

He who knows about this comes to this [world]. To him Brahman says: 'Run on: by my glory this one has reached the river Vijarā ('ageless'), he will never [more] grow old.'

¶ 4. Five hundred celestial nymphs run to meet him, one hundred with fruits in their hands, one hundred with unguents in their hands, one hundred with garlands in their hands, one hundred with garments in their hands and one hundred with aromatic powders in their hands. They adorn him with Brahman's own adornment, and thus adorned, knowing Brahman, he approaches Brahman.

He reaches the lake Āra and crosses it [simply] by [using his] mind. On reaching it those who know the present [only] are drowned. He reaches the moments [called] Yeshtiha; they fly away before him. He reaches the river Vijarā ('ageless') and crosses it [simply] by [using his] mind. There he shakes off his good and evil works; the relatives he loves succeed to his good works, those he dislikes to the evil.

As a man riding in a chariot looks down on the two chariot-wheels on either side, so does he on either side look down on day and night, deeds good and evil, and all dualities (dvandva). Delivered from both good and evil works, and knowing Brahman, to Brahman he draws near.

¶ 5. He reaches the tree Ilya, and the fragrance of Brahman

enters into him. He reaches the public place Sālajya, and the savour of Brahman enters into him. He reaches the residence Aparājita ('unconquered') and the glory of Brahman enters into him. He reaches the two door-keepers, Indra and Prajāpati; they flee before him. He reaches the palace Vibhu ('extensive'), and the fame of Brahman enters into him. He reaches the throne Vicakshanā ('far-seeing'). Its front legs are the Brihat and Rathantara chants, its back legs the Śyaita and Naudhasa, the lengthwise pieces the Vairūpa and Vairāja, the crosswise pieces the Śākvara and Raivata. [The throne] itself is consciousness (*prajñā*), for by consciousness a man discerns.

He reaches the couch Amitaujas ('of boundless strength'): this is the breath of life (*prāṇa*). Its front legs are the past and future, its back legs are prosperity and refreshment, its arms the Brihat and Rathantara [chants], the head-rests the Bhadra and Yaj-ñāyanīya [chants]; the front part is the verses [of the Rig-Veda] and the chants [of the Sāma-Veda], the cross-section is the sacrificial formulas [of the Yajur-Veda], the cushions are the Soma-stems, the coverlet is the Udgītha, the pillow prosperity. Thereon is Brahmā [1] seated.

The man who knows about this first mounts [the throne] with one foot [only]. Him Brahmā asks, 'Who art thou?' He should answer him thus:

¶ 6. 'I am a season, the son of seasons, arisen from the womb of space, seed of brilliance,[2] glory of the year, the Self of every single being. Thou art the Self of every single being. What thou art, that am I.'

To him he says: 'And who am I?'

He should [then] say: 'The Real (*satya*).'

'And what is the Real?'

'What is other than the organs of sense (*deva*) and the vital breaths is [called] *sat* ("what is"), the organs of sense and the vital breaths are [called] *tyam* ("this"). [All] this is expressed in this [one] word *satyam*, the Real. It comprises this whole universe: thou art this whole universe.'

[Verse 7 is omitted.]

II

¶ 1. 'The breath of life (*prāṇa*) is Brahman,' said Kaushītaki. 'The messenger of the breath of life, of Brahman, is the mind, its guardian is the eye, its herald the ear, its attendant the voice.

'Whoever knows that the mind is the messenger of this breath of life, of Brahman, himself has a messenger; whoever knows that the eye is its guardian, himself has a guardian; whoever

---

[1] Or, 'Brahman'.   [2] Reading *bhāyai*.

knows that the ear is its herald, himself has a herald; whoever knows that the voice is its attendant, himself has an attendant.

'To this breath of life, to Brahman, all these physical organs (*devatā*) bring tribute without its having to ask. So too all beings bring tribute to the man who knows this without his having to ask. The moral (*upaniṣad*) of this is that one should not ask.

'It is just as if a man were to go begging in a village and, receiving nothing, were to sit down and say: "I would not eat anything from here even if it were given away." The people who had previously repulsed him, would [then] summon him saying, "We will give you [something]." This is the custom (*dharma*) [followed in the case of] the man who does not ask,—people willing to give him food summon him saying, "We will give you [something]."'

[Verses 2–4 are omitted.]

¶ 5. Next [we come to] the rule (*saṁyamana*) [enunciated] by Pratardana which has been called the 'inner daily fire-sacrifice'.

For so long as a man is speaking, for just so long he cannot breathe. Then [it is that] he sacrifices breath in the voice. So long as a man is breathing, for just so long he cannot speak. Then [it is that] he sacrifices the voice in breath. These two are infinite and deathless sacrifices; whether awake or asleep one offers them continuously and without interruption. [All] other sacrifices are finite, for they depend on [ritual] actions (*karma*). This is why the ancient sages did not offer the daily fire-sacrifice.

[Verses 6–11 are omitted.]

¶ 12. Now [we come to] the cyclic death of natural phenomena (*deva*).

This Brahman shines when the fire blazes, and dies when it stops blazing: its virtue (*tejas*) goes to the sun, its breath of life to the wind.

This Brahman shines when the sun can be seen and dies when it can no longer be seen: its virtue goes to the moon, its breath of life to the wind.

This Brahman shines when the moon can be seen and dies when it can no longer be seen: its virtue goes to the lightning, its breath of life to the wind.

This Brahman shines when the lightning flashes and dies when it no longer flashes: its virtue goes to the wind,[1] its breath of life to [that same] wind.

So all these natural phenomena (*devatā*) enter the wind and die in [2] in the wind, but they do not congeal (*mūrchante*),[3] for they rise up again from it.[4]

---

[1] Var. 'the points of the compass'.
[2] Var. 'having gone to'.
[3] Or, 'lose consciousness'. Var. 'die(?)'.
[4] Or, 'therefore they rise up again'.

So much for what concerns natural phenomena (*adhidaivata*). Now [we come to] what concerns the [individual] self.

¶ 13. This Brahman shines when one speaks with the voice and dies when one does not speak: its virtue (*tejas*) goes to the eye, its breath of life to [that same] breath of life.

This Brahman shines when one sees with the eye and dies when one does not see: its virtue goes to the ear, its breath of life to [that same] breath of life.

This Brahman shines when one hears with the ear and dies when one does not hear: its virtue goes to the mind, its breath of life to [that same] breath of life.

This Brahman shines when one thinks with the mind and dies when one does not think: its virtue goes to the breath of life, its breath of life to [that same] breath of life.

So all these physical organs (*devatā*) enter the breath of life [1] and die in [2] in the breath of life, but they do not congeal,[3] for they rise up again from it.[4]

And so, even if both these mountains,—the northern and the southern,—were to roll down on the man who has this [secret] knowledge, bent on crushing him, they could not crush him. But those who hate him and those whom he hates himself, all die round about him.

¶ 14. Now [we come to the story of] the winning of supremacy (*niḥśreyasādāna*).

These physical organs (*devatā*) were disputing among themselves, each vaunting its own superiority; so they left the body and [the body] lay there, without breathing, dried up, [as stiff] as a board.

The voice went into it, but it went on lying there though speaking with the voice. The eye went into it, but it went on lying there though speaking with the voice and seeing with the eye. The ear went into it, but it went on lying there though speaking with the voice, seeing with the eye and hearing with the ear. Mind went into it, but it went on lying there though speaking with the voice, seeing with the eye, hearing with the ear and thinking with the mind.

The breath of life went into it: immediately it stood up. So all the physical organs recognized the supremacy of the breath of life, steeped themselves in [5] that same breath of life, in that self which is consciousness (*prajñātman*), and rose up from this body [6] along with all the [other physical organs and faculties]. With

---

[1] Var. 'the points of the compass'.
[2] Var. 'having gone to'.
[3] Or, 'lose consciousness'. Var. 'die(?)'.
[4] Or, 'therefore they rise up again'.
[5] Var. 'praised'.   [6] Var. 'world'.

wind as their firm foundation,[1] with space as their self, they went
to heaven (*svar*).

So too the man who has this [secret] knowledge, recognizing
the supremacy of the breath of life, steeping himself in [2] this
same breath of life, in that self which is consciousness, rises up
from this body along with all the [other physical organs and
faculties]. With wind as his firm foundation,[1] with space as his
self, he goes to heaven. He goes to [3] where these gods are, and
once he has achieved this, he becomes immortal as the gods are
immortal,—the man who has this [secret] knowledge.

[Verse 15 is omitted.]

III

¶ 1. Pratardana Daivodāsi arrived at Indra's well-loved abode
(*dhāma*) because he had shown courage in battle. Indra said to
him: 'Pratardana, choose [4] a boon.'

'Do you rather choose it,' Pratardana replied; 'whatever you
think most beneficial to mankind.'

'Nobody ever chooses a boon for another,' [5] Indra said to
him; 'choose it yourself.'

'Then it is no boon to me,' Pratardana replied.

But Indra did not swerve from the truth, for Indra *is* truth. So
he said:

'Know me, then, as I am. This indeed is what I consider most
beneficial for mankind,—that they should know me. I killed the
three-headed son of Tvashtri, I threw the Arunmukha ascetics to
the hyenas. Transgressing many a compact, I impaled the people
of Prahlāda to the sky, the Paulomas to the atmosphere and the
Kālakānjas to the earth, and I did not lose a single hair in the
process.

'The man who knows me as I am loses nothing that is his
(*loka*) whatever he does (*karma*), even though he should slay his
mother or his father, even though he steal or procure an abortion.
Whatever evil he does, he does not blanch.'

¶ 2. He continued: 'I am the breath of life, the self that consists
of consciousness (*prajñā*): reverence me as life (*āyu*) and immortality. Life is breath (*prāṇa*) and breath is life. The breath of
life (*prāṇa*)', he said, 'is immortality. For so long as the breath
remains in this body, so long is there life. For by this breath [of
life] a man attains immortality in the other [6] world, by consciousness, true conception. Whoso reverences me as life and

---

[1] Var. 'entering the wind'.   [2] Var. 'praising'.
[3] Var. 'becomes'.   [4] Var. 'I will give you'.
[5] Reading *varaṁ parasmai*.   [6] Var. 'this'.

immortality, wins all [his allotted] life in this world and immortality and indestructibility in the heavenly world.'

Now some say that the bodily organs (*prāṇa*) gravitate towards unity, for no one could make a name known simply by calling it once, or [make] a sound [known] by the ear, or a form by the eye, or a thought by the mind. But [these] bodily organs, acting in unison (*ekabhūyaṁ bhūtvā*), make all these things known one by one.

When the voice speaks, all the [other] organs speak along with it. When the eye sees, all the [other] organs see along with it. When the ear hears, all the [other] organs hear along with it. When the mind thinks, all the [other] organs think along with it. When the breath breathes, all the [other] organs (*prāṇa*) breathe along with it.

'That is very true,' said Indra. 'There is, however,' he continued, 'a hierarchy of being (*niḥśreyasādāna*) among the bodily organs.'

¶ 3. A man who has lost the [power of] speech is alive, for we have [all] seen dumb people. A man who has lost his sight is alive, for we have [all] seen blind people. A man who has lost his hearing is alive, for we have [all] seen deaf people. A man who has lost his mind is alive, for we have [all] seen simple-minded people. A man whose arms or legs have been cut off is alive, for we have [all] seen people like that. It is surely the breath of life, the self which consists of consciousness, that takes hold of this body and makes it stand upright (*ut-thā*). It should then be revered as *Uktha*.[1] This [shows] the all-comprehensiveness of the breath of life. What the breath of life is, that is consciousness: what consciousness is, that is the breath of life. For both of them dwell together in this body, and together they depart.

This is the theory of it, this is the way it should be understood:

When a man is asleep and sees no dream, then he becomes single (*ekadhā*) in this breath of life. The voice goes to it along with all names, sight goes to it along with all forms, hearing goes to it along with all sounds, the mind goes to it along with all thoughts.

When he wakes up, the bodily faculties (*prāṇa*) return from this self to their respective seats, just as sparks are scattered in all directions from a blazing fire; [so too] the senses (*deva*) return [to their respective seats] from the faculties, and the objects of sense (*loka*) from the senses.

This is the proof of it, this is how it should be understood:

When a man is ill and on the point of death, he is overcome

[1] i.e. the recitation of praise in the ritual. Pun on *ut-thā* and *uktha*.

with weakness and delirium (*saṁmoha*), and people will say of him: 'His reason has gone, he cannot see or hear or speak with his voice or think.' Then he becomes single in this breath of life. The voice goes to it along with all names, sight goes to it along with all forms, hearing goes to it along with all sounds, the mind goes to it along with all thoughts.[1]

¶ 4. When he departs from this body, he departs along with all these [things].[2]

The voice pours into him [3] all names; by the voice he comes to possess all names. Breath pours into him [3] all scents; by the breath he comes to possess all scents. Sight pours into him [3] all forms; by sight he comes to possess all forms. Hearing pours into him [3] all sounds; by hearing he comes to possess all sounds. The mind pours into him [3] all thoughts; by the mind he comes to possess all thoughts. This [shows] the all-comprehensiveness of the breath of life. What the breath of life is, that is consciousness: what consciousness is, that is the breath of life. For both of them dwell together in the body, and together they depart.

We will now explain how all beings become one in consciousness.

¶ 5. The voice is one organ (*aṅga*) taken out of it: name is the objective element (*bhūtamātrā*) corresponding to it in the outside world (*parastāt prativihitā*).

The nose is one organ taken out of it: scent is the objective element corresponding to it in the outside world.

The eye is one organ taken out of it: form is the objective element corresponding to it in the outside world.

The ear is one organ taken out of it: sound is the objective element corresponding to it in the outside world.

The tongue is one organ taken out of it: taste is the objective element corresponding to it in the outside world.

The two hands are one organ taken out of it: work (*karma*) is the objective element corresponding to them in the outside world.

The body is one organ taken out of it: pleasure and pain are the objective element corresponding to it in the outside world.

The genitals are one organ taken out of it: delight (*ānanda*), pleasure (*rati*) and procreation are the objective element corresponding to them in the outside world.

The two feet are one organ taken out of it: locomotion is the objective element corresponding to them in the outside world.

The mind [4] is one organ taken out of it: thoughts [5] and desires are the objective element corresponding to it in the outside world.

---

[1] One recension adds, 'When he wakes up . . . from the senses', as above.
[2] One recension lacks this phrase.   [3] Var. 'out of him'.
[4] Var. 'consciousness' (*prajñā*).
[5] One recension adds 'what must be known'.

¶ 6. When one has united [1] voice with consciousness (*prajñā*), one comes to possess all names through the voice.

When one has united the nose [2] with consciousness, one comes to possess all scents through the nose.[2]

When one has united the eye with consciousness, one comes to possess all forms through the eye.

When one has united the ear with consciousness, one comes to possess all sounds through the ear.

When one has united the tongue with consciousness, one comes to possess all the tastes of food through the tongue.

When one has united the two hands with consciousness, one comes to possess all works (*karma*) through the hands.

When one has united the body with consciousness, one comes to possess pleasure and pain through the body.

When one has united the genitals with consciousness, one comes to possess delight, pleasure and procreation through the genitals.

When one has united the two feet with consciousness, one comes to possess all modes of locomotion through the feet.

When one has united the mind with consciousness, one comes to possess [all] thoughts.[3]

¶ 7. For without consciousness the voice could not make any name whatever known. 'My mind was elsewhere,' one says; 'I had no consciousness of that name.'

Without consciousness the breath could not make any scent whatever known. 'My mind was elsewhere,' one says; 'I had no consciousness of that scent.'

Without consciousness the eye could not make any form whatever known. 'My mind was elsewhere,' one says; 'I had no consciousness of that form.'

Without consciousness the ear could not make any sound whatever known. 'My mind was elsewhere,' one says; 'I had no consciousness of that sound.'

Without consciousness the tongue could not make the taste of any food whatever known. 'My mind was elsewhere,' one says; 'I had no consciousness of the taste of that food.'

Without consciousness the two hands could not make any work (*karma*) whatever known. 'My mind was elsewhere,' one says; 'I had no consciousness of that work.'

Without consciousness the body could not make any pleasure or pain known. 'My mind was elsewhere,' one says; 'I had no consciousness of that pleasure or pain.'

Without consciousness the genitals could not make any delight, pleasure or procreative power known. 'My mind was elsewhere,'

---

[1] Lit. 'mounted' (like a horse).
[2] Var. 'breath'.
[3] One recension adds, 'what must be known and desired'.

one says; 'I had no consciousness of that delight, pleasure or procreative power.'

Without consciousness the two feet could not make any locomotion whatever known. 'My mind was elsewhere,' one says; 'I had no consciousness of that locomotion.'

For without consciousness no thought whatever could be formulated, nothing cognizable (*prajñātavya*) could be cognized (*prajñā-*).

¶ 8. It is not the voice that one should want to understand; one should know the speaker.

It is not scent that one should want to understand; one should know the smeller.

It is not form that one should want to understand; one should know the seer.[1]

It is not sound that one should want to understand; one should know the hearer.

It is not the taste of food that one should want to understand; one should know him who discerns the taste of food.

It is not work (*karma*) that one should want to understand; one should know the worker.

It is not pleasure and pain that one should want to understand; one should know him who distinguishes between pleasure and pain.

It is not delight, pleasure and procreative power that one should want to understand; one should know him who cognizes delight, pleasure and procreative power.

It is not locomotion that one should want to understand; one should know him who moves [from place to place].

It is not the mind that one should want to understand; one should know the thinker.

These ten objective elements (*bhūtamātrā*) [have meaning only] in the context of consciousness, and these ten elements of consciousness [have meaning only] in the context of objective reality (*adhibhūta*). For if there were no objective elements, there would be no elements of consciousness; and if there were no elements of consciousness, there would be no objective elements.

¶ 9. For no form at all could be realized from either alone.

But this is not diversity. Rather, just as the felly of a chariot-wheel is fixed on to the spokes, and the spokes on to the hub, so too are these objective elements fixed on to the elements of consciousness, and the elements of consciousness on to the breath of life. And this breath of life is nothing else than the Self which consists of consciousness,—bliss, unageing and immortal.

[This Self] neither increases by good works nor diminishes by evil ones. For it is He who makes him whom He would raise up from these worlds [2] perform good works, and it is He again who

---

[1] Var. 'knower of form'.   [2] Var. 'raise up towards Himself'.

makes him whom He would drag down [1] perform evil works. He is the guardian of the worlds,[2] sovereign of the worlds,[2] universal Lord.[3] Let a man know: 'He is my (*me*) Self.' Let a man know: 'He is my Self!'

IV

[Sections 1–18 and the beginning of 19 are omitted. A Brāhman, Gārgya Bālāki by name, volunteers to reveal Brahman to King Ajātaśatru, who was of the princely class. He fails, and the king turns the tables on him. Cf. *Brihadāranyaka* II. i.]

¶ 19. Then Bālāki, fuel in hand, came near saying: 'I should like to come to you as a pupil.'

'This goes against the grain,' Ajātaśatru said to him, 'that a man of the princely class should receive a Brāhman as his pupil. However, come and I will teach you.'

He took him by the hand and started walking. Together they came upon a man who was asleep. Ajātaśatru addressed him [thus]: '[Hail,] great king, Soma, robed in white!' [The other,] however, lay silent. Thereupon [the king] harried him with a stick, at which he promptly got up.

Ajātaśatru said to him: 'Bālāki, where in the world was this man lying? What became of him then? Where has he come from?'

Bālāki did not understand.

Ajātaśatru continued: 'As to where this man was lying, as to what became of him and as to where he came from,—[it was where] the channels of the heart [4] called *hitā* spread out from the heart towards the pericardium. These are as minute as a hair split up a thousand times; their basis is a fine essence,—brown, white, black, yellow and red. [It is] in these [that] the sleeper dwells when he sees no dream at all.

¶ 20. 'Then truly he becomes single (*ekadhā*) in this breath of life. So the voice goes to it along with all names, sight goes to it along with all forms, hearing goes to it along with all sounds, mind goes to it along with all thoughts.

'When he wakes up, the bodily faculties (*prāna*) return from this Self to their respective seats, just as sparks are scattered in all directions: [so too] the senses (*deva*) [return to their respective seats] from the faculties (*prāna*), and the objects of sense (*loka*) from the senses.

'Just as a razor might be put away in a razor-case or a fire in a brazier, so too this Self which consists of consciousness enters into this body [5] right up to the hairs and nails. Around this Self

---

[1] Var. 'drive out from these worlds'.
[2] Or, 'world'.
[3] Var. 'Lord of the world[s].'
[4] Var. 'man, person'.
[5] Var. 'bodily self'.

these [other] selves (voice, etc.) group themselves like serfs around a chief. Just as a chief makes use of his serfs and just as his serfs profit by him, so does this Self which consists of consciousness make use of these [other] selves, and they [in turn] profit by him.

'Indeed, as long as Indra did not recognize this Self, for just so long the demons had the upper hand over him; but once he had recognized [It] he struck down and conquered the demons and won for himself the supremacy over all beings, [he won] independent sovereignty and kingship.

'Likewise he who has this [secret] knowledge, wins for himself supremacy over all beings, [he wins] independent sovereignty and kingship,—he who has this [secret] knowledge.'

Kena Upanishad

I

§ 1. By whom sent forth, [by whom] impelled soars forth the
   mind?
By whom enjoined does the breath go forth, the first?
By whom impelled do men make loud this utterance?
   Eye—ear: what god enjoins them?

§ 2. Ear of the ear, mind of the mind,
Voice of the voice, He too is the breath of breath,
Eye of the eye: transcending [all], the wise,
Departing from this world, become immortal.

§ 3. There no eye can penetrate,
No voice, no mind can penetrate:
We do not know, we do not understand
   How one should teach it.

Other It is, for sure, than what is known,
Beyond [the scope of] the unknown too.
So have we heard from men of old
   Who instructed us therein.

§ 4. That which cannot be expressed by speech,
By which speech [itself] is uttered,
That is Brahman—know thou [this]—
Not that which is honoured here as such.

§ 5. That which thinks not by the mind,
By which, they say, the mind is thought,
That is Brahman—know thou [this]—
Not that which is honoured here as such.

§ 6. That which sees not by the eye,
By which the eyes have sight,
That is Brahman—know thou [this]—
Not that which is honoured here as such.

§ 7. That which hears not by the ear,
By which this ear is heard,
That is Brahman—know thou [this]—
Not that which is honoured here as such.

161

§ 8. That which breathes not by the breath,
By which breath is drawn in,
That is Brahman—know thou [this]—
Not that which is honoured here as such.

II

[The teacher speaks:]
§ 1. Shouldst thou think, 'I know [It] well,' now little indeed
thou knowest,—a form of Brahman,—what of It is thou, what of
It is among the gods. Think then upon It seriously.
   [The pupil:] I think I know It.

[The teacher:]
§ 2. I do not think, 'I know It well,'
I do not know, 'I do not know';
He of us who knows It, knows It,
He does not know, 'I know It not.'

§ 3. Who thinks not on It, by him It's thought:
Who thinks upon It, does not know,—
Ununderstood by those who understand,
By those who understand not understood.

§ 4. Known by an awakening It is seized upon by thought,
And so a man finds immortality:
By the self one valour wins,
By wisdom immortality.

§ 5. If one has known [It] here, then is there truth;
If one has here not known [It], great is the destruction:
Discerning It in each single contingent being,
Wise men, departing from this world, become immortal.

III

§ 1. Now Brahman won a victory for the gods, and the gods were
exulting in the victory of that Brahman. They thought: 'This
victory belongs to us, this majesty belongs to us.'
§ 2. Brahman was well aware of what they [were thinking], and
so he made himself visible to them. They did not recognize Him.
   'What is this strange creature (*yakṣa*)?' they said.
§ 3. They said to Agni, [the fire-god]: 'Jātavedas,[1] look into this
right away [and find out] what this strange creature is.'
   'All right,' said [Agni].
§ 4. He ran off to Him, and He said to him, 'Who are you?' 'I
am Agni,' he replied; 'I am Jātavedas.'

   [1] A name of Agni ('all-knowing' or 'all-possessing').

§ 5. 'Well, if that is so, what powers have you?'

'I could burn up everything here in this [whole wide] world!'

§ 6. [Brahman] put a straw down in front of him and said, 'Burn that.' He rushed at it at full speed, but could not burn it. So he returned and said, 'I could not find out what this strange creature was.'

§ 7. Then they said to Vāyu, [the wind-god]: 'Vāyu, look into this right away [and find out] what this strange creature is.'

'All right,' said [Vāyu].

§ 8. He ran up to Him, and He said to him, 'Who are you?'

'I am Vāyu,' he replied, 'I am Mātariśvan.' [1]

§ 9. 'Well, if that is so, what powers have you?'

'I could carry off everything here in this [whole wide] world.'

§ 10. [Brahman] put a straw down in front of him and said, 'Carry it off.' He rushed at it at full speed but could not carry it off. So he returned and said, 'I could not find out what this strange creature was.'

§ 11. Then they said to Indra: 'Maghavan,[2] look into this right away land find out] what this strange creature is.'

'All right,' said [Indra].

He ran up to Him, but He disappeared from his sight.

§ 12. In that very place he happened to meet a woman of great beauty,—Umā,[3] Himāvat's daughter; and he asked her what that strange creature might be.

IV

§ 1. She said: 'It is Brahman, and it is in Brahman's victory that you have been exulting.' And straightway [Indra] understood that it was Brahman.

§ 2. That is why these [three] gods, Agni, Vāyu and Indra, rank rather higher than the other gods, for they came nearest to touching Him, and it was they [and especially Indra] who first understood that it was Brahman.

§ 3. That is why Indra ranks rather higher than the other gods, for he came nearest to touching Him and was the first to understand that it was Brahman.

§ 4. Now there is this description of Him: 'Ah!'—[what people say] when the lightning flashes,—'Ah!' as they blink their eyes, So much for the sphere of the gods.

§ 5. Now for the sphere of the [individual] self.

When [a thought] occurs to the mind and the mind recollects it repeatedly,—[this is] conceptual thought (saṁkalpa).

---

[1] A name of Vāyu.　　[2] A name of Indra ('bountiful').
[3] Śiva's consort in the later tradition.

§ 6. [Brahman] is called *tadvanam*,[1] and as such should He be revered. All beings pine for the man who has this knowledge.

§ 7. [The pupil:] 'Sir, tell me the secret doctrine (*upaniṣad*).'

[The teacher:] 'You have been told the secret doctrine. We ourselves have told you the secret doctrine concerning Brahman.

§ 8. 'Its basis is ascetic practice, self-restraint, and works (*karma*), the Vedas and all the treatises that depend on them (*vedāṅga*).[2] Truth is [its] dwelling-place.'

§ 9. Whoever knows this [doctrine] in this way will vanquish evil and find his home in the infinite, unconquerable [3] world of heaven—[there] will he find his home.

---

[1] An esoteric word interpreted as 'one who desires it'.
[2] Or, 'the Vedas are all its limbs'.
[3] Reading *ajyeye*.

Iśā Upanishad

§ 1. This whole universe must be pervaded by a Lord,—
Whatever moves in this moving [world].
Abandon it, and then enjoy:
Covet not the goods of anyone at all.

§ 2. Performing [ritual] works on earth a man
May wish to live a hundred years:
This, not otherwise, is true for thee;
A man is not defiled by works.

§ 3. Some worlds there are called 'devilish'
    In blind darkness swathed:
To these at death such folk pass on
    As [seek to] slay the self.

§ 4. Unmoving—One—swifter than thought (*manas*),—
The gods could not seize hold of It as it sped before [them]:
Standing, It overtakes [all] others as they run;
In It the wind incites activity.

§ 5. It moves. It moves not.
It is far, yet It is near:
It is within this whole universe,
And yet It is without it.

§ 6. Those who see all beings in the Self,
And the Self in all beings
Will never shrink from It.[1]

§ 7. When once one understands that in oneself [2]
    The Self's become all beings,
When once one's seen the unity,
What room is there for sorrow? What room for perplexity?

§ 8. He, the wise Sage, all-conquering, self-existent,
Encompassed that which is resplendent,
    Incorporeal, invulnerable.

----
[1] Var. 'will never doubt It'.   [2] Or, 'at what time'.

Devoid of sinews, pure, unpierced by evil:
[All] things He ordered each according to its nature
    For years unending.

§ 9. Blind darkness enter they
Who revere the uncompounded (*asambhūti*): [1]
Into a darkness blinder yet
[Go they] who delight in the compounded. [2]

§ 10. Other, they say, than what becomes (*sambhava*),
Other, they say, than what does not become:
So from wise men have we heard
Who instructed us therein.

§ 11. Coming to be (*sambhūti*) and perishing,—
Who knows these both together,
By 'perishing' surpasses death,
By 'coming to be' [3] wins deathlessness.

§ 12. Blind darkness enter they
Who reverence unwisdom (*avidyā*):
Into a darkness blinder yet
[Go they] who delight in wisdom.

§ 13. Other, they say, than wisdom,
Other than unwisdom [too], they say:
So from wise men have we heard
Who instructed us therein.

§ 14. Wisdom and unwisdom—
Who knows these both together,
By 'unwisdom' surpasses death,
By 'wisdom' reaches deathlessness.

§ 15. Wind and immortal breath,
And then this body whose end is in ashes:
Oṁ, O mind (*kratu*) remember; what's done remember;
O mind, remember; what's done remember. [4]

§ 16. Lead us, O god of fire, along fair paths to riches,
    Thou who knowest every way;
Repel from us the fault that leads astray.
May we compile for thee a most fulsome hymn of homage!

---

[1] Or, 'not coming to be'.   [2] Cf. p. 72.
[3] Var. 'not coming to be'.
[4] Var. 'O mind remember; the world(?) (*klibe*) remember; what's done remember.'

§ 17. The face of truth is hidden
By the golden vessel [of the sun]:
That Person yonder in the sun,
I in truth am He.

§ 18. O Pushan, single seer, O god of death,
O sun, born of Prajāpati,
Display thy rays, diffuse thy light;
That form of thine which is most fair I see:
That Person yonder, I am He.'

Katha Upanishad

I

§ 1. [A certain] Uśan, son of Vajaśravas, gave away all his property. He had a son called Naciketas;

§ 2. And as [the kine to be distributed as] the fee for the sacrifice performed were being brought near, faith entered into him, boy though he was, and he thought:

§ 3. 'They drink water, eat grass, give milk, insensitive:
Joyless the worlds to which the giver of these must go!'

§ 4. He said to his father, 'Daddy, to whom will you give *me*?'
[And he said it] a second and a third time. [His father] said to him,
'I'll give you to death.'

[Naciketas speaks:]
§ 5. Of many the first to go,
Of many the middlemost,
What is Yama (Death) to do with me,
For today I'm his concern?

§ 6. Look back, [how fared] the first,
Look forward, [how fare] the last:
Like corn a man grows up,
Like corn he's born again.

§ 7. Like fire a Brāhman guest
   Enters a house:
To appease [his fiery anger],
Bring water, [Yama,] Vivasvat's son.

§ 8. Hope and expectation, conviviality and good cheer,
Sacrifice, its merit, sons, cattle,—all of this
The Brāhman wrests away from the man of little wit
In whose house he, nothing eating, dwells.

[Yama, the god of death, returning after three days' absence and finding that Naciketas has not received the hospitality due to Brāhmans, says:]

169

§ 9. Since for three nights, O Brāhman, thou hast dwelt
In [this] my house, an honoured guest, [yet] nothing eating,
I now salute thee, Brāhman, may it go well with me.
Three boons [I grant] thee, choose [what thou wilt].

[Naciketas speaks:]
§ 10. Let my father's ill-will (*samkalpa*) be stilled, let him be well
    disposed,
Let his anger with me melt away, O Death:
Let him greet me kindly, dismissed by thee;
Of the three boons this the first I choose.

[Yama speaks:]
§ 11. Thy father, Auddālaka Āruni, as before
Will be well pleased [with thee] dismissed by me; [1]
His anger spent, how sweet his sleep at night will be,
When he [again] beholds thee from the jaws of Death set free!

[Naciketas speaks:]
§ 12. In paradise there's no [such thing as] fear;
Thou art not there, nor shrinks one from old age.
Hunger and thirst, these two transcending,
Sorrow surpassing, a man makes merry in paradise.

§ 13. O death, thou understandest the fire that leads to paradise;
Declare it [then] to me, for I have faith:
The heavenly worlds partake of (*bhaj*-) immortality;
This do I choose as my second boon.

[Yama speaks:]
§ 14. This [too] will I declare to thee,—take note of it;
The fire that leads to paradise, I know it well.
Know that [this fire] can win [thee] worlds unending,
It is the ground (*pratiṣṭhā*) [of all], hidden in secret places.

§ 15. [And so] he told him of [this] fire, the world's beginning,
[He told him] of the firebricks, how many and how to be disposed.
And [Naciketas] repeated [all] just as he had said it:
Well satisfied with him Death spake again.

§ 16. [So] great-souled [Death], well pleased, spake to him
    [again]:
'To thee again today I grant another boon:
This fire shall bear thy name, no other;
Accept this garland [2] variously contrived.

---

[1] Reading *prasṛṣṭe*.   [2] Translation uncertain.

§ 17. Who thrice performs the Nāciketa rite,
With the three [Vedas] concludes a pact,
And performs the three works [prescribed],
He transcends both birth and death:
Knowing that God adorable who knows
What is from Brahman born,
And realizing Him,
He attains to peace and what is absolute.[1]

§ 18. Who thrice performs the Nāciketa rite,
And understands all three,
Who, knowing them, builds up the Nāciketa fire,
He thrusts afar Death's fetters, sorrow surpassing,
And makes full merry in the heavenly world.

§ 19. This is the Nāciketa fire, thy very own,
  Leading to paradise;
This didst thou choose as thy second boon:
This fire will men proclaim as thine indeed.
Naciketas, [now] thy third boon choose!'

[Naciketas speaks:]
§ 20. When a man is dead, this doubt remains:
Some say, 'He is,' others again, 'He is not.'
This would I know, by thee instructed,—
This is the third of the boons [I crave].

[Yama speaks:]
§ 21. Of old the gods themselves this doubt assailed,—
How hard is it to know! How subtle a matter (*dharma*)!
Choose thou another boon, O Naciketas;
Insist not overmuch, hold me excused in this.

[Naciketas speaks:]
§ 22. 'Of old indeed the gods themselves this doubt assailed,—
How hard is it to know!' So, Death, hast thou declared.
Thou alone canst tell it forth; none other is there like thee:
No other boon is there equal to this in any wise.

[Yama speaks:]
§ 23. Choose sons and grandsons to live a hundred years,
[Choose] wealth in cattle, horses, elephants and gold,
Choose wide property in land, and thou thyself
Live out thy years as many as thou wilt.

§ 24. Or shouldst thou think this a boon [at all] equivalent,
  Choose riches and long life;
Be thou of the great ones in the land:
I grant thee enjoyment of all thou canst desire!

[1] Or, 'absolutely'.

§ 25. Whatever a man could possibly desire
    In [this] the world of men,
    However hard to win,
Ask anything thou wilt at thy good pleasure,—
Fair women, chariots, instruments of music.
The like of these cannot be won by [other] men;—
All these I give thee, bend them to thy service.
O Naciketas, ask me no further concerning death.

[Naciketas speaks:]
§ 26. The morrows of a man, O Death, wear down
    The power of all the senses.
A life though [lived] entire is short indeed;
Keep [then] thy chariots, keep thy songs and dances!

§ 27. With riches can man never be satisfied:
When once we've seen thee, [how] shall we riches win?
So long we'll live as thou [for us] ordainest;
This, then, is the only boon that I would claim.

§ 28. What mortal man, grown old and wretched here below,
Could meet immortals, strangers to old age,
Know them, and [still] meditate on colours, pleasures, joys,
Finding [some] comfort in this life however long.

§ 29. Wherein men, puzzled, doubt, O Death, [that tell us];
What [happens] at the great departing tell us!
That is the boon that's hidden in secret places:
Therefore no other [boon] doth Nacitekas choose.

II

[Yama speaks:]
§ 1. The better part is one thing, the agreeable another;
Though different their goals both restrict a man:
For him who takes the better of the two all's well,
But he who chooses the agreeable fails to attain his goal.

§ 2. 'Better' and 'agreeable' present themselves to man:
Considering them carefully the wise man discriminates,
Preferring the better to what only pleasure brings:
Dull men prefer the 'agreeable',—
For the getting and keeping [1] [of what they crave].

§ 3. Thou, Naciketas, has well considered [all objects of] desire,
[All] that's agreeable in form,—thou has rejected them;
Thou wouldst not accept this garland of wealth compacted
In which how many a man has been [dragged down,] submerged!

[1] Reading *yogaksemād.*

§ 4. Different, opposed, wide separated these,—
Unwisdom (*avidyā*) and what men as wisdom know:
Wisdom [it is that] Naciketas seeks, I see;
Not thou to be distracted by manifold desire!

§ 5. Self-wise, puffed up with learning, some
Turn round and round [emprisoned] in unwisdom['s realm];
Hither and thither rushing, round they go, the fools,
Like blind men guided by the blind!

§ 6. No glimmering have such of man's last destiny,—
Unheeding, childish fools, by wealth deluded:
'This world alone exists, there is no other,' so think they;
Again and ever again they fall into my hands.

§ 7. Many there are who never come to hear of Him,[1]
Many, though hearing of Him, know Him not:
Blessed (*āścarya*) the man who, skilled therein, proclaims Him,
    grasps Him;
Blessed the man who learns from one so skilled and knows him!

§ 8. How difficult for man, though meditating much,
To know Him from the lips of vulgar men:
[Yet] unless another tells of Him, the way (*gati*) to Him is
    barred,
For than all subtleties of reason He's more subtle,—
    Logic He defies.

§ 9. No reasoning, [no logic,] can attain to this Idea;
Let another preach it, then is it easily cognized.
[And yet] hast thou achieved it, for steadfast in truth art thou:
May there never be another like thee, Naciketas, dear,
    To question [me about it].

§ 10. I know that what's called treasure is impermanent,
For by things unstable the Stable cannot be obtained.
Have I, then, builded up the Nāciketa fire,—
By things impermanent have I the Permanent attained?

§ 11. The winning of desires is the foundation of the world,
The unending fruit of sacrifice is the bourn of fearlessness:
[All this] hast thou rejected, wise and steadfast,
For thou hast seen that this foundation broadly based
Is [Brahman,] worthy of great praise.

§ 12. Let a wise man think upon that God,
Let him engage in spiritual exercise (*yoga*) related to the Self
    (*adhyātma*):

---

[1] i.e. the Self.

[Let him think upon that God,] so hard to see,
Deep hidden in the depths, dwelling in a secret place,
Firm-fixed (*-stha*) in the abyss, primordial;
Then will he put behind him both sorrow and [unstable] joy.

§ 13. Let a man hear this and understand,
Let him take hold upon this subtile [God],
Let him uproot all things of law,[1]—rejoice,
For he has won That in which [alone] he should find joy:
A house wide open is Naciketas [now], I see.

[Naciketas speaks:]
§ 14. Other than righteousness (*dharma*), other than unrighteous-
ness,
Other than what's done or left undone,
Other than what has been and what is yet to be,—
This that thou seest, tell it forth!

[Yama speaks:]
§ 15. The single word [2] announced by all the Vedas,
Proclaimed by all ascetic practices,
[The word] in search of which men practise chastity,
This word I tell [thee now] in brief.
    Oṁ—this is it.

§ 16. The Imperishable Brahman this,
This the Imperishable Beyond (*para*):
Whoso this Imperishable comes to know,—
What he desires is his.

§ 17. Depend on This, the best;
Depend on This, the ultimate (*para*):
Who knows that on This [alone all things] depend,
In the Brahman-world is magnified.

§ 18. This wise one is not born nor dies;
From nowhere has He [sprung] nor has He anyone become;
Unborn is He, eternal, everlasting and primeval,—
He is not slain when the body is slain.

§ 19. Should the killer think 'I kill',
Or the killed 'I have been killed',
Both these have no [right] knowledge:
He kills not, is not killed.

---

[1] Reading *dharmyam*. Var. *dharmam*: 'Having attained to this subtile
matter, let him uproot [all else]'.
[2] Or, 'state' or 'goal'.

§ 20. More subtile that the subtile, greater than the great,
The Self is hidden in the heart [1] of creatures [here]:
The man without desire (*kratu*), [all] sorrow spent, beholds It,
The majesty of the Self, by the grace of the Ordainer.[2]

§ 21. Seated he strides afar,
Lying down he ranges everywhere:
This God is joy and joylessness,[3]—
Who but I can understand Him?

§ 22. In bodies bodiless,
In things unstable still, abiding,
The Self, the great Lord all pervading,—
Thinking on Him the wise man knows no grief.

§ 23. This Self cannot be won by preaching [Him],
Not by sacrifice [4] or much lore heard;
By him alone can He be won whom He elects:
To him this Self reveals his own [true] form (*tanū*).

§ 24. Not he who has not ceased from doing wrong,
Nor he who knows no peace, no concentration (*asamāhita*),
Nor he whose mind is filled with restlessness,
Can grasp Him, wise and clever though he be.

§ 25. [Though some there be] for whom the dignity
Of both Brāhman and prince are as a dish of rice
With death its sauce [and condiment],—
[Yet] where He is,—[this] who really knows?

III

§ 1. [Like] light and shade [there are] two [selves]:
[One] here on earth imbibes the law (*rta*) of his own deeds: [5]
[The other,] though hidden in the secret places [of the heart],
[Dwells] in the uttermost beyond.
So say [the seers] who Brahman know,
The owners of five fires and of three Nāciketa fires.

§ 2. May we master the Nāciketa fire,
[Sure] bridge for men who sacrifice,
Seeking to reach the [further] shore
Beyond the reach of fear,—
[The bridge that leads to] Brahman,
Imperishable, supreme.

---

[1] Elsewhere translated as 'secret place'.
[2] Or, 'Creator', cf. *Śvetāsvatara*, III. 20. Var. 'with his elements serene'.
[3] Or, 'perpetually joyful'.   [4] Or, 'intellect'.
[5] Var. 'of his deeds well done'.

§ 3. Know this:
The self is the owner of the chariot,
The chariot is the body,
Soul (*buddhi*) is the [body's] charioteer,
Mind the reins [that curb it].

§ 4. Senses, they say, are the [chariot's] steeds,
Their objects the tract before them:
What, then, is the subject of experience?
'Self, sense and mind conjoined,' wise men reply.

§ 5. Who knows not how to discriminate (*avijñānavat*)
With mind undisciplined (*a-yukta*) the while,—
Like vicious steeds untamed, his senses
He cannot master,—he their charioteer.

§ 6. But he who does know how to discriminate
With mind [controlled and] disciplined,—
Like well-trained steeds, his senses
He masters [fully],—he their charioteer.

§ 7. But he who knows not how to discriminate,
    Mindless, never pure,
He reaches not that [highest] state (*pada*), returns
To this round of never-ending birth and death (*saṁsāra*).

§ 8. But he who does know how to discriminate,
    Mindful, always pure,
He gains [indeed] that [highest] state
From which he's never born again.

§ 9. The man whose charioteer is wisdom (*vijñāna*),
Whose reins a mind [controlled],
Reaches the journey's end [indeed],
Vishnu's final state (*pada*).[1]

§ 10. Higher than the senses are the [senses'] objects,
    Higher than these the mind,
    Higher than mind is soul (*buddhi*),
Higher than soul the self, the 'great'.

§ 11. Higher than the 'great' the Unmanifest,
    Higher than that the 'Person':
Than 'Person' there's nothing higher;
He is the goal, He the All-highest Way.[2]

---

[1] Or, 'step, pace' referring to Vishnu's pacing out of the universe (p. 4).
[2] Or, 'refuge'.

§ 12. This is the Self, deep-hidden in all beings,
[The Self that] shines not forth,—
Yet it *can* be seen by men who see things subtle,
By the subtle soul (*buddhi*), [man's] noblest [part].

§ 13. Let the wise man hold tongue and mind in check,
Submit them to the intellectual (*jñāna*) self;
Let him submit this intellect to the self [called] 'great',
And this to [that] Self which is [forever] still (*śānta*).

§ 14. Arise! Awake! Your boons you've won!
[Awake and] understand [them]!
A sharpened razor's edge is hard to cross,—
The dangers of the path,—wise seers proclaim them!

§ 15. Beyond the 'great', abiding, endless, beginningless,
Soundless, intangible, It knows not form or taste or smell,
Eternal, changeless,—[such It is,] discern It!
[For only so] can ye escape the jaws of death.

§ 16. Wise men who hear and utter forth this deathless tale
Concerning Naciketas, told by Death,—
These shall win greatness in the Brahman-world.

§ 17. Whoso, well versed therein, shall spread abroad
    This highest mystery
Among assembled Brāhmans or at the commemoration of the
    dead,
    He is conformed to infinity,—
    To infinity he's conformed!

    IV

§ 1. The self-existent [Lord] bored holes facing the outside world;
Therefore a man looks outward, not into [him]self.
A certain sage, in search of immortality,
Turned his eyes inward and saw the self within.

§ 2. Fools pursue desires outside themselves,
Fall into the snares of widespread death:
But wise men, discerning immortality,
Seek not the Stable here among unstable things.

§ 3. By what [one knows] of form and taste and smell,
Sound, touch and sexual union,
    By that [same thing] one knows:
    'What of all this abides?'
                                        This in truth is That.

§ 4. By what one sees these both,—
The state of sleep, the state of wakefulness,
'That is the self, the "great", the lord,'
So think the wise, unsorrowing.

§ 5. Who knows this honey-eating self,
The living [self] so close at hand,
Lord of what was and what is yet to be,
   He shrinks not from him.

This in truth is That.

§ 6. Who descried him [1] from among contingent beings
As first-born of fervid penance (*tapas*),[2]
As entering into the secret place [and there] abiding,
He is the first-born of the waters.

This in truth is That.

§ 7. Who comes to be by the breath of life (*prāṇa*),
Who entered into the secret place [and there] abodes,
Aditi, pregnant with divinity,
Was born from among contingent beings.[3]

This in truth is That.

§ 8. The all-knowing [fire] concealed between the fire-sticks,
Like an embryo well nurtured by a woman with child,
Should every day be reverenced by wakeful men,
Bearing their offerings to him, the fire.

This in truth is That.

§ 9. From whence the sun arises,
To whither it goes down,
Thereon are all the gods suspended;
None passes beyond this.

This in truth is That.

§ 10. What [we see] here is also there beyond;
What there, that too is here:
Death beyond death does he incur
Who sees in this what seems to be (*iva*) diverse!

§ 11. Grasp this with your mind:
Herein there's no diversity at all.
Death beyond death is all the lot
Of him who sees in this what seems to be diverse.

---

[1] Sc. the 'Golden Embryo' (p. 10).
[2] Or, 'as being born before heat'.
[3] The grammar of this section is peculiar and the translation uncertain.

§ 12. Of the measure of a thumb, the 'Person'
     Abides within the self,
Lord of what was and what is yet to be:
     No need to shrink from Him.

This in truth is That.

§ 13. Of the measure of a thumb, [this] 'Person',
     Resembling a smokeless flame,
Lord of what was and of what is yet to be:
     He is today, tomorrow He.

This in truth is That.

§ 14. As rain that falls in craggy places
Loses itself, dispersed throughout the mountains,
So does the man who sees things (*dharma*) as diverse,
[Himself] become dispersed in their pursuit.

§ 15. As water pure into pure [water] poured
Becomes even as (*tādṛg*) [that pure water] is,
So too becomes the self of him,—
The silent sage who knows.

V

§ 1. Whoso draws nigh to the city of eleven gates [1]
Of him who is not born, whose thought is not perverse,
He grieves not, for he has won deliverance:
     Deliverance is his!

This in truth is That.

§ 2. As swan he dwells in the pure [sky],
As god (*vasu*) he dwells in the atmosphere,
As priest he dwells by the altar,
As guest he dwells in the house:
Among men he dwells, in vows,
In Law (*rta*) and in the firmament;
Of water born, of kine, of Law (*rta*),
Of rock—[He], the great cosmic Law (*rta*)!

§ 3. He leads the out-breath upward
And casts the in-breath downward:
To this Dwarf seated at the centre
     All gods pay reverence.

§ 4. When the embodied soul whose dwelling is the body
Dissolves and from the body is released,
     What then of this remains?

This in truth is That.

---

[1] i.e. the body.

§ 5. Neither by breathing in nor yet by breathing out
  Lives any mortal man:
  By something else they live
On which the two [breaths] depend.

§ 6. Lo! I will declare to thee this mystery
  Of Brahman never-failing,
And of what the self becomes
When it comes to [the hour of] death.

§ 7. Some to the womb return,—
Embodied souls, to receive another body;
Others pass into a lifeless stone (*sthāṇu*)
In accordance with their works (*karma*),
In accordance with [the tradition] they had heard (*śruta*).

§ 8. When all things sleep, [that] Person is awake,
  Assessing all desires:
That is the Pure, that Brahman,
That the Immortal, so they say:
In It all the worlds are stablished;
Beyond it none can pass.

                                        This in truth is That.

§ 9. As the one fire esconced within the house
Takes on the forms of all that's in it,
So the One Inmost Self of every being
Takes on their several forms, [remaining] without [the while].

§ 10. As the one wind, once entered into a house,
Takes on the forms of all that's in it,
So the One Inmost Self of every being
Takes on their several forms, [remaining] without [the while].

§ 11. Just as the sun, the eye of all the world,
Is not defiled by the eye's outward blemishes,
So the One Inmost Self of every being
Is not defiled by the suffering of the world,—
  [But remains] outside [it].

§ 12. One and all-mastering is the Inmost Self of every being;
  He makes the one form manifold:
Wise men who see Him as subsistent in [their] selves,
Taste everlasting joy (*sukha*),—no others.

§ 13. Permanent among impermanents, conscious among the
  conscious,
The One among the many, Disposer of desires:
Wise men who see Him as subsistent in [their] selves,[1]
Taste of everlasting peace,—no others.

                    [1] Or, 'self-subsistent'.

§ 14. 'That is this,' so think [the wise]
Concerning that all-highest bliss which none can indicate.
   How, then, should I discern It?
Does It shine of itself or but reflect the brilliance? [1]

§ 15. There the sun shines not, nor moon nor stars;
These lightnings shine not [there],—let alone this fire.
All things shine with the shining of this light,
This whole world reflects its radiance.

VI

§ 1. With roots above and boughs beneath
This immortal fig tree [stands];
That is the Pure, that Brahman,
That the Immortal, so men say:
In it all the worlds are stablished;
Beyond it none can pass.

                                      This in truth is That.

§ 2. This whole moving world, whatever is,
Stirs in the breath of life (*prāṇa*), deriving from it:
The great fear [this], the upraised thunderbolt;
Whoso shall know it [thus], becomes immortal.

§ 3. For fear of It the fire burns bright,
For fear [of It] the sun gives forth its heat,
For fear [of It] the gods of storm and wind,
And Death, the fifth, [hither and thither] fly.

§ 4. Could one but know It here [and now]
Before the body's breaking up . . .!
[Falling] from such [a state] a man is doomed
To bodily existence in the 'created' (*sarga*) worlds.

§ 5. In the self one sees as in a mirror,
In the world of the ancestors as in a dream,
In the world of the heavenly minstrels as across the waters,
In the world of Brahman as into light and shade.

§ 6. Separately the senses come to be,
[Separately] they rise and fall,
Separately are they produced,—so thinking
The wise man grieves no more.

§ 7. Higher than the senses is the mind,
Higher than mind the soul (*sattva*),
Higher than soul, the self, the 'great',
Higher than [this] 'great' the Unmanifest.

---

[1] Var. 'Does It shine or does It not?'

§ 8. Higher than [this] Unmanifest the 'Person',
Pervading all, untraceable (*aliṅga*): [1]
When once a creature knows Him, he is freed (*muc-*),
And goes on to immortality.

§ 9. His form is not something that can be seen;
No one beholds Him with the eye;
By heart and mind and soul (*maniṣ*) is He conceived of:
    Whoso knows this becomes immortal.

§ 10. When the five senses (*jñāna*) stand, [their action stilled,]
Likewise the mind; and when the soul (*buddhi*)
    No longer moves or acts,—
Such, have men said, is the all-highest Way. [2]

§ 11. 'Yoga,' this is how they think of it,—
[It means] to check the senses firmly, still them:
Then is a man freed from heedlessness,
    For Yoga is origin and end.

§ 12. [This Self] cannot be apprehended
    By voice or mind or eye:
How, then, can He be understood,
    Unless we say—HE IS?

§ 13. HE IS—so must we understand Him,
And as the true essence (*tattva*) of the two: [3]
HE IS—when once we understand Him thus,
The nature of his essence is limpidly shown forth.

§ 14. When all desires that shelter in the heart
Of [mortal] man are cast aside (*pramuc-*),
Then mortal puts on immortality,—
Thence to Brahman he attains.

§ 15. When here [and now] the knots [of doubt]
Are all cut out from the heart,
Mortal puts on immortality:
Thus far the teaching goes.

§ 16. A hundred veins (*nāḍī*) and one pervade the heart;
Of these [but] one extends up to the head:
By ascending this [a self] fares on to immortality;
The rest, at death (*utkramaṇa*) are dissipated everywhere.

----

[1] Or, 'sexless'.   [2] Or, 'goal', or 'state', or 'refuge'.
[3] Sc. the absolute and the relative.

§ 17. Of the measure of a thumb is [this] Person,
The Inmost Self, in the heart of creatures abiding ever.
Stand firm! and from thy body wrench Him out
Like pith extracted from a reed.
Pure and immortal He: so know Him!
So know Him: pure and immortal He!

§ 18. So did Naciketas learn this [holy] science
By Death declared, and all the arts of Yoga: [1]
Immaculate, immortal, to Brahman he won through;
And so shall all who know what appertains to Self.

May he bring aid to both of us, may He bring profit to both of
us. May we together make a manly effort; may this lesson bring
us glory; may we never hate each other. Oṁ. Peace—peace—
peace.

[1] Or, 'all the ways of putting it into practice'.

Mundaka Upanishad

I, i

¶ 1. First of the gods did Brahmā come to be,
Maker of all, protector of the world:
To his eldest son, Atharvan, he made known
The science of Brahman, of all sciences the base.

¶ 2. This science of Brahman which Brahmā to Atharvan had
  proclaimed,
Atharvan to Angir passed on;
[And] he to Bhāradvāja Satyavāha made it known,
Who [passed it on] to Angiras in its higher and its lower form.[1]

¶ 3. Then Śaunaka, the owner of a handsome property, approached Angiras with due formality and asked: 'Sir, what [is it
that] by knowing [it alone] one can obtain knowledge of the
whole universe?'

¶ 4. To him [Angiras] answered: 'There are two sciences that
must be known, so say those who are well versed in Brahman, a
higher and a lower.'

¶ 5. Of these the lower consists of the Rig-Veda, Yajur-Veda,
Sāma-Veda, Atharva-Veda, phonetics, ritual, grammar, ety-
mology, metre and astronomy. The higher is that by which the
Imperishable can be understood.[2]

¶ 6. Invisible, intangible, having neither family nor caste,[3]
Devoid of eye and ear, devoid of hands and feet,
Eternal, [all]-pervading, penetrating everywhere, most subtile,
Changeless,—so do the wise discern It,—
Womb [and origin] of [all] that comes to be.

¶ 7. As a spider emits and re-absorbs [its threads],
As plants grow up upon the earth,
As hair [grows] on the body and head of a living man,
So does everything on earth arise from [this] Imperishable.

¶ 8. By ascetic fervour is Brahman builded up;
Therefrom does food arise:
From food life (*prāṇa*), mind and truth,
[All] worlds and deathlessness in works (*karma*).

---

[1] Or, 'from an earlier to a later generation'.
[2] Or, 'reached'.　　　　　　　　[3] Or, 'colour'.

¶ 9. From Him who, omniscient, knows all,
Whose ascetic fervour consists in wisdom,
This Brahman comes to birth,—
Name, form and food.

I, ii

¶ 1. This is the truth:

The (ritual) acts (*karma*) that the seers beheld in the sacred
    formulas
Were spread abroad on the threefold [fire]: [1]
O ye who long for truth, perform them constantly,
This is for you the path of [work] well done on earth.

¶ 2. For when the flame shows signs of dying down,
Though [the fire] that carries off the offering be lit,
Then should the oblations be offered up
Between the portions of the melted ghee.

¶ 3. The man whose oblation to the fire
Is offered up with no New- or Full-Moon rites,
No four-month rites or harvest rites,
Without guests or [honour to] the universal gods,
Or offered in a manner not prescribed,
Or not offered up [at all],
Forfeits for himself worlds up to the seventh [world].

¶ 4. Black, Gaping, Swift as thought,
Vermilion, [Brown] as smoke,
Emitting sparks, All-radiant divine,—
These are the seven tongues [of the flame] that is dying down.

¶ 5. Whoso performs [the rite] while these are blazing
And receives the oblations at the proper time,—
Him they lead on, [become] the sun's rays [themselves],
To where is the one Lord of the gods, [our] refuge.

¶ 6. 'Come, come!' the oblations say, full-glorious,
Carrying the sacrificial priest on the sun's [bright] rays,
Addressing him with pleasing speech and praising him:
'This is the Brahman-world, pure and well made for you.' [2]

¶ 7· But unstable are these barks, the eighteenfold,
In the form of sacrifice
In which an inferior [ritual] act (*karma*) is uttered:
Deluded men who hail it as the best
Return again to old age and death.

---

[1] Or, '[Veda]', or '[priesthood]'.
[2] Or, 'gained by your good works'.

¶ 8. Self-wise, puffed up with learning,
Passing their days in the midst of ignorance,
They wander round, the fools, doing themselves much hurt,
Like blind men guided by the blind.

¶ 9. Passing their days in ignorance in many and diverse ways,
'Our goal is won,' say they, childish in their conceit.
By that which in their passion they do not recognize [1] as truth,
Though busy (*karmin*) all the while, they are oppressed
And, losing the worlds [for which they long],
They come hurtling down [again].

¶ 10. Thinking that sacrifice and merit are the highest good,
Deluded men, they nothing better know:
On heaven's vault they'll first enjoy their works well done
But then come back to this world,—or to another—worse!

¶ 11. But those who in penance and in faith dwell in the forest,
Tranquil and wise, living a beggar's life,
Pass on, immaculate, through the doorway of the sun
To where that deathless Person dwells, of changeless Self.

¶ 12. When he surveys the worlds built up by ritual works
        (*karma*),
    A Brāhman must despair.
Between what's made and what's unmade there's no connection:
To know [the truth of] this, let him approach an elder (*guru*)
With fuel in hand, and [let the elder be]
Versed in the Veda, Brahman his [only] goal.

¶ 13. Let him approach him properly, tranquil and at peace,
His mind at rest, and then this wise [preceptor]
Will teach him the science of Brahman in its very essence
Whereby he may know the Imperishable Real, the Person.

II, i

¶ 1. This is the truth:

As a thousand sparks from a blazing fire
Leap forth each like the other,
So, friend, from the Imperishable, modes of being (*bhāva*)
Variously spring forth and return again thereto.

¶ 2. For divine and formless is the Person:
What is without and what within are his:
Unborn [is He],—pure, brilliant (*śubhra*).
He is not breath nor mind,[2]
He, the All-highest, beyond the Imperishable [itself].

---

[1] Lit. 'proclaim'.   [2] Or, 'without breath or mind'.

¶ 3. From Him springs forth the breath of life,
Mind and all the senses too,
Sky, wind and light and water
And the earth that all sustains.

¶ 4. Fire is his head, the sun and moon his eyes,
The points of the compass are his ears,
His voice the Vedic revelation;
Wind is his breath, the whole universe his heart;
From his feet the earth [arose],
For He is the Inmost Self of all contingent beings.

¶ 5. From Him is fire,—its fuel the sun;
From the moon come rain and [our] earthly plants.
Into the female the male pours forth his seed:
How many the creatures engendered from [this] Person!

¶ 6. From Him the Vedas three, the consecrations,
The sacrifices, all rites and the Brāhmans' fees,
The year, the sacrificial priest, the worlds
Whether illumined by moon or sun.

¶ 7. From Him the gods, engendered in many a way,
Saints (*sādhya*), human beings, beasts and birds,
The breathing in, the breathing out, rice, barley, hard austerity,
Faith, truth, the sacred rule and chastity.

¶ 8. From Him spring forth the seven kinds of breath,
The seven flames, the [seven kinds of] fuel,
The seven offerings, the seven earths
On which [all] living things (*prāṇa*) subsist,
Close hidden in the heart, in groups of seven ordered.

¶ 9. From Him the oceans, [from Him] the mountains all;
From Him flow forth the rivers in their wide diversity,
From Him all plants together with their savour:
Hence for [all] beings He abides, the Inmost Self [of all].

¶ 10. [That] Person is all this,—works (*karma*), hard austerity,
Brahman, the highest immortality.
Who knows This (neuter) as hidden in a secret place,
He here [and now] cuts open
The knot of ignorance, my friend!

II, ii

¶ 1. The Great Abode (*pada*) has been revealed:
'Hidden, moving in secret places,' is Its name.
On It are fixed what moves and breathes and blinks.

Know that [This] is more to be desired
Than what is and what is not,—
Beyond consciousness (*vijñāna*), of creatures (*prajā*) far the best! [1]

¶ 2. Brilliant [It is], more subtile than [all] subtile things:
In it [all] worlds and [all] the worlds contain indwell:
This is the Imperishable, Brahman [This],
This life (*prāṇa*), This word (*vāc*) and mind,
This truth, This immortality:
This [it is that] must be pierced, my friend; [so] pierce it!

¶ 3. Take up [thy] bow, the Upanishad, a mighty weapon!
Fit in [thine] arrow sharpened by devotion (*upāsā*)!
Stretch it on thought allied to determination (*bhāva*)! [2]
The Imperishable! This is the target, friend: [so] pierce it.

¶ 4. The bow is Oṁ, [the sacred syllable,] the arrow self,
Brahman the target,—so do they say,
As by an arrow, so can It be pierced
By an undistracted man. Its very nature he wins [then].

¶ 5. Heaven and earth and atmosphere
In It are woven,—mind and all the senses (*prāṇa*):
Know This to be the one [real] Self. [All] other names
Let go. This is the bridge of immortality.

¶ 6. In It [all] nerves (*nāḍī*) are [harmoniously] compacted
As spokes in the hub of a chariot-wheel:
He [it is who] operates within,
Coming to birth in many a form and place.
So must you ponder on the Self, [uttering it] as Oṁ:
Good luck to you! May you pass beyond the darkness!

¶ 7. To Him, the omniscient, all-knowing
Belongs [all] this magnificence on earth;
And He it is, the Self, who is established
In Brahman's heavenly city, the firmament.

¶ 8. Made up of mind, guide of the bodily senses,
With food his base, He holds in check the heart:
Wise men who come to know Him see Him shine,
The immortal, revealed as bliss!

¶ 9. The knot of the heart is cut,
All doubts for him dispelled,
All works (*karma*) abolished
When this 'high and low' [3] [by him] are seen.

---

[1] Or, 'best for creatures'; or, 'the best, beyond the ken of creatures'.
[2] Or, 'allied to a loving disposition'; or, 'which has attained Being'.
[3] Cf. I. i. 2.

¶ 10. In the highest golden sheath
Is spotless Brahman, whole,
Resplendent, light of lights:
Who knows the Self, knows It!

¶ 11. There the sun shines not, nor moon nor stars,—
These lightnings shine not there,—let alone this fire;
All things shine with the shining of this light,—
The whole universe reflects its radiance.

¶ 12. Immortal in very truth is Brahman.
East, west, north and south,
Below, above Brahman projects Itself:
Brahman is this whole universe,
[Brahman what is] most to be desired!

III, i

¶ 1. Two birds, close-linked companions,
Cling to the selfsame tree:
Of these the one eats of the sweet fruit,
The other, eating nothing, looks on intent.

¶ 2. On [this] same tree a person [sits] plunged [in grief],
Mourning his lack of mastery, perplexed:
When he sees the Other, the Lord rejoicing
In his magnificence, his sorrow melts away.

¶ 3. When a seer beholds the Maker, Lord,
The Person golden-hued, whose womb is Brahman,[1]
Then does he understand: immaculate
He shakes off good and evil, reaches the highest,
The same manner of being (sāmya) [as is His].

¶ 4. He is the life (prāṇa) that shimmers through all contingent
     beings:
Who knows and understands Him,
Boasts not about Him nor chatters overmuch.
Whose sport is Self, whose joy is Self, a man of works (kriyāvat),
Of all who Brahman know is the most highly to be prized.

¶ 5. By truth may He be won,—this Self,—by grim austerity,
By knowledge sound and right, by constant chastity:
For instinct with light is He, within the body dwelling;
Seers see Him, pure, resplendent, their imperfections gone.

---

[1] Or, 'womb (origin) of Brahman'; but cf. *Bhagavad-Gītā*, XIV. 3.

¶ 6. Truth conquers, not untruthfulness:
By truth is the path laid out that leads up to the gods:
This [is the path] the sages tread, [all] their desires fulfilled,
Leading to that place wherein
Truth's highest treasure lies.

¶ 7. Vast, heavenly, unthinkable its form,
More subtle than the subtle, forth It shines:
More distant than the distant, It is [yet] here, right near;
For those who see It's even here, hidden in a secret place.

¶ 8. It cannot be comprehended by the eye,
By speech or any other sense (*deva*),
Not by strict penance nor by the doing of [ritual] works (*karma*);
With thoughts all stilled (*jñānaprasāda*),[1] the pure of heart
Behold Him at long last; [and] meditating on Him
[They behold Him] partless and entire.

¶ 9. He is the subtle Self, to be known in meditation (*cetas*);
Into Him life (*prāṇa*) entered, divided into five:
On [these five] senses (*prāṇa*) all the thought of living things
    (*prajā*) is woven;
Once this is purified, this Self shines through (*vibhū-*).

¶ 10. Whatever world a man imagines in his mind,
Whatever wish he forms, [all] pure in heart (*sattva*),
That world and that desire he wins:
Therefore the man who seeks prosperity
Must reverence the man who knows the Self.

III, ii

¶ 1. He knows this highest Brahman-home (*dhāma*)
In which is stored all that, resplendent, shines.
Wise men who reverence this Person without desire,
Transcend the semen['s urge to procreate].

¶ 2. Whoso in self-conceit desires desires,
By those desires [themselves] he's born [again] now here, now
    there,
[But] once a man has [all] desires fulfilled, his self perfected,
In him do all desires dissolve,—in this world here [and now].

¶ 3. This Self cannot be won by preaching [Him],
Not by sacrifice [2] or much lore heard:
By him alone can He be won whom He elects;
To him this Self reveals his own [true] form.

---

[1] Or, 'by the grace of wisdom'.   [2] Or, 'intellect'.

¶ 4. This Self cannot be won by one devoid of strength,
By fecklessness or penance lightly undertaken (*aliṅga*);
But the self of him who by these means strives wisely
  Will enter into the Brahman-home (*dhāma*).

¶ 5. Achieving Him completely seers, with wisdom satisfied,
Their self fulfilled, their passion spent, at peace,
Attaining everywhere to Him who everything pervades,
Wise, self-controlled (*yuktātman*), they penetrate the All.

¶ 6. [So] sages, resolute and pure of heart,
By practising (*yoga*) self-surrender,
Make the wisdom of the Veda's end (*vedānta*) their goal,
And so at their last hour, transcending death,
Are all delivered in the Brahman-worlds.

¶ 7. Gone are the fifteen parts to whence they came,
[Gone] all the senses (*deva*) to their corresponding base;
[All] works (*karma*) and the self composed of consciousness
  (*vijñāna*),—
All these become one in the beyond (*para*) that knows no change.

¶ 8. As rivers flowing [downwards] find their home
In the ocean, leaving name and form behind,
So does the man who knows, from name and form released,
Draw near to the divine Person who is beyond the beyond.

¶ 9. Whoever really knows that all-highest Brahman, really
becomes Brahman. In his family none is born who does not know
Brahman. Transcending grief, transcending evil, delivered from
the knots of secret [doubt], he becomes immortal.
¶ 10. Concerning this, this has been said in a sacred verse:

  Performing rites, devoted to the Veda,
  With Brahman as their [only] goal,
  In faith they offer sacrifice themselves to the One [great]
    Seer:
  To those among them who duly observe the 'vow of the
    head',
  This Brahman-science should be taught.

¶ 11. This is the truth. Of old the seer Angiras proclaimed it.
None who do not observe their vows should study it. All hail to
the highest seers! All hail to the highest seers!

Praśna Upanishad

I

¶ 1. Sukeśan Bhāradvāja, Śaibya Satyakāma, Sauryāyanin Gārgya, Kausalya Aśvalāyana, Bhārgava Vaidarbhi and Kabandhin Kātyāyana, [all] these were intent on Brahman, made Brahman their goal and sought after the highest Brahman. So with fuel in hand they approached the Master Pippalāda thinking that he, if anyone, would tell [them] all about It.

¶ 2. That seer said to them: 'You must spend another year in self-mortification, chastity and faith. [Then] ask me any questions you like. If we know [the answers], we will tell you all.'

¶ 3. Then Kabandhin Kātyāyana came up [to him] and asked: 'Master, whence did [all] these creatures arise?'

¶ 4. [The seer] answered him [and said]: 'Prajāpati (the Lord of Creatures and Demiurge), wishing [to reproduce] offspring, mortified himself. When he had done this, he produced a couple, —matter (*rayi*) and the breath of life (*prāṇa*, breath, spirit). "These two will make all manner of offspring for me," he thought.

¶ 5. 'Now the breath of life is the sun, and matter is the moon. Matter is everything here, whether formed or unformed: therefore form (*mūrti*) too is matter.

¶ 6. 'Now when the sun rises it enters the eastern quarter. In so doing it envelops the living creatures (*prāṇa*) in the east within its rays. When it [enters] the southern, the western, the northern, the lower, the upper and the intermediate quarters, when it illumines everything, it thereby envelops all living creatures in its rays.

¶ 7. 'So arises this universal (*vaiśvānara*) life-breath (*prāṇa*) which has every [possible] form,—[I mean] fire. This has been expressed in a sacred verse:

¶ 8.   'Golden, possessed of every form, all-knowing,[1]
       The final goal, the single light, it burns:
       A thousand rays it has, one hundredfold revolving,
       Life-breath of [living] creatures it rises up—the sun!

¶ 9. 'The year too is Prajāpati: it has a southern and a northern path. Those who revere sacrifice and meritorious works [simply]

---

[1] Or, 'all-possessing', an epithet of the fire-god, Agni.

193

as acts (*kṛta*), secure only the lunar world for themselves: they surely come back [here] again. That is why those seers who wish [to reproduce] offspring, betake themselves to the southern [path]. This assuredly is matter, the "path of the ancestors".

¶ 10. 'But those who seek after the Self by self-mortification, chastity, faith and wisdom (*vidyā*), secure the sun for themselves by the northern [path]. That is the abode of living creatures, that is the immortal, that is exempt from fear, the final goal. Thence they never come back again, they say. That is the stopping [of rebirth]. On this there is the following verse:

¶ 11. 'Some call [him] the father of five feet and twelve forms
                  In the upper half of heaven, rich in moisture:
                  Others again call him the clear-sighted
                  Set in a [chariot] with six spokes and seven wheels.

¶ 12. 'The month too is Prajāpati. Its dark half is matter, the light one the breath of life. That is why those sages sacrifice in the light [half] and other people in the other [half].

¶ 13. 'Day and night too are Prajāpati. Of these day is the breath of life, night matter. People who cohabit voluptuously by day waste their life-breath. True chastity consists in cohabiting voluptuously at night.

¶ 14. 'Food too is Prajāpati. Semen proceeds from it, and from semen [all] these creatures are born, they say.

¶ 15. 'Now those who follow this rule of Prajāpati (as in ¶ 13) will produce a pair (a boy and a girl). Theirs indeed is this Brahman-world, [the world of those] who mortify themselves and practise chastity and in whom truth dwells.

¶ 16. 'To these belongs that Brahman-world immaculate, for in them there is neither crookedness nor falsehood nor deceit (*māyā*).'

II

¶ 1. Then Bhārgava Vaidarbhi asked him: 'Master, how many natural phenomena (*deva*) support a creature? Which [of them] illumine it? And again, which is the best of them?'

¶ 2. To him [the Master] answered: 'Space is one such natural phenomenon, [as are] wind, fire, water and earth; the voice, mind, sight and hearing. Illumining it, they say to it: "We prop up this trunk and support it."

¶ 3. 'The best [of them], the breath of life (*prāṇa*), said to them: "Make no mistake about it. It is I who divided [my]self into five parts and who prop this trunk up and support it." They did not believe him.

¶ 4. 'Ruffled in his pride, he made as if (*iva*) to rise up [from the body]; and as he rose up, all the rest of them rose up [with him], and when he settled down [again in the body], they all settled down [with him].

'Just as all the bees [in a hive] rise up after their queen when she rises up, and all of them settle down when she settles down, even so do the voice, the mind, sight and hearing [follow the breath of life]; and, well satisfied, they offer him praise:

¶ 5.   He is the burning fire, the sun,
        He the rain-cloud, scattering bounty,
        Wind, earth, matter (*rayi*), God (*deva*),
        What IS, what is not, the immortal!

¶ 6.   Like spokes in the hub of a wheel,
        All things are welded (*pratiṣṭhita*) into the breath of
            life:
        Rig-, Sāma-, Yajur-Veda,
        The sacrifice, and the Brāhman and princely classes.

¶ 7.   Lord of Creatures, in the womb thou movest,
            Thyself art born again:
        To thee, life's breath (*prāṇa*), these creatures bring
            their offerings,
        [To thee,] whose dwelling is with living creatures
            (*prāṇa*).

¶ 8.   Chief bearer [of oblations] to the gods,
        First offering to the ancestors art thou:
        Truth art thou enacted by the seers
        Of the house of Atharvan and Angiras.

¶ 9.   In glory (*tejas*) Indra, life's breath, art thou;
            Rudra thou art, protector:
        In the atmosphere thou rovest [free],
        The sun thou art, the lord of lights!

¶ 10.   When thou rainest down the rain,
        O breath of life, these creatures
        [All-]blissful stand upright, thus thinking:
        "There will be food as much as we could wish!"

¶ 11.   Vrātya art thou, life's breath, the single seer,
        Eater of all, lord of what IS: [1]
        We are the givers of [thy] food:
        Thou art the father of the wind.

----

[1] 'Or, 'Eater and real lord of all'.

¶ 12. That form (*tanū*) of thine which indwells voice,
      Which indwells ear and eye,
      Which is spread athwart the mind,—
      Make that auspicious: depart not hence!

¶ 13. This whole universe to the breath of life is subject,
      Whate'er in the three heavens has its home:
      Protect us [then] as a mother would her son,
      And grant us wisdom (*prajñā*) and prosperity!'

III

¶ 1. Then Kausalya Aśvalāyana asked him: 'Master, whence is this breath of life born? How does it come into this body? Once it has divided [it]self, how does it settle down? What makes it go away? How does it correlate itself with the outside world? How with itself (*adhyātma*)?'

¶ 2. To him [the Master] answered: 'You ask a great many questions, so you must know a great deal about Brahman.[1] Well, that is a [good] reason for my speaking up.'

  '[Your first question: Whence is this breath of life born?]'

¶ 3. 'This breath of life is born of self. As his shadow is to a man, so in this case there is an extension. It comes into the body with the mind as its artefact.'[2]

  '[Your second question: How does it come into the body?]'

¶ 4. 'As a king commands his officials, saying: "[Go and] govern this group of villages or that group of villages," so does this breath of life allot to each of the other breaths their appointed task.'

  '[Your third question: Once it has divided itself, how does it settle down?]'

¶ 5. 'The breath of life [allots] the out-breath to the organs of generation and excretion, and itself settles in the eye and ear, the mouth and nostrils. In the middle is the "concentrated" (digestive) breath (*samāna*), for it is this ["breath"] that reduces the food offered up [in the body] to the same [consistency]. From this arise the seven flames.'[3]

  '[Your fourth question: What makes it go away?]'

¶ 6. 'The self is in the heart. Here there are a hundred and one channels, each subdivided a hundred times, and these again are divided into seventy-two thousand branches. Within them moves the diffused breath (*vyāna*).

¶ 7. 'Then the upper breath (*udāna*), [rising] up through one [of these], leads [the transmigrating soul] to a good world by means

---

[1] Or, 'are a very good Brāhman'.
[2] Or, 'by the action of the mind'.
[3] Sc. the seven fires of sacrifice (*Mundaka*, II. i. 8).

of his good [deeds], or to an evil [world] by means of his evil [deeds], or to the world of men by means of both.'

'[Your fifth question: How does it correlate itself with the outside world?]'

¶ 8. 'The sun assuredly is the breath of life in the outside world: it rises, and [in so doing] it shows favour to the life-breath in the eye. That power (*devatā*) which [resides] in the earth supports the out-breath in man. What is between [the sun and the earth], that is, space, is the concentrated breath. The wind is the diffused breath.'

'[Your sixth question: How does it correlate itself with itself?]'

¶ 9. 'Heat (*tejas*) is the upper breath; and so when the heat [of the body] is extinguished, one is reborn from it with the senses concentrated in the mind.

¶ 10. 'With whatever thoughts [he may have had in his previous life] he comes [back] to life. [And] this breath of life, combined with heat and accompanied by the self leads [him] on to whatever world he had [previously] conceived of (*saṅkalpita*).

¶ 11. 'Whoever possesses this knowledge knows the breath of life; his offspring will not fail, [while he himself] will become immortal. On this there is the following verse:

¶ 12. 'How did it originate? How approach [the body]?
    How did it [there] remain? How extend itself fivefold?
    What its relation to the self? Whoso should know
    [All this] concerning the breath of life,
    Attains to immortality: to immortality attains!'

IV

¶ 1. Then Sauryāyaṇin Gārgya asked him: 'Master, what [are the elements that] sleep in a man (*puruṣa*)? What are they that stay awake? Which is the faculty (*deva*) that sees dreams? Whose is this happiness? And on what [1] are all [of them] grounded?'

¶ 2. To him [the Master] answered: 'Gārgya, just as the rays of the sun all become one in that circle of light when it sets, and shoot forth again and again when it rises, so too does everything [in the body] become one in its highest faculty (*deva*), the mind. And so [in this condition] a man does not hear or see, smell or taste, touch or speak, grasp or enjoy sexual pleasure, excrete or move about: "He is asleep," they say.

¶ 3. 'The fires of the breath of life remain awake in this city [of the body]. The out-breath is the householder's fire, the diffused breath is the fire for the ancestors, the in-breath (*prāṇa*) is the fire for the gods, so-called because it is taken from the householder's fire,—*pranayanāt*, "by taking away".

---

[1] Or, 'whom'.

¶ 4. 'The concentrated breath is so called because it reduces to the same [consistency] (*samaṁ nayati*) those two oblations,—inhalation and exhalation. It is the mind which is the sacrificial priest, and the fruit of the sacrifice is the upper breath: it daily leads this sacrificial priest on to Brahman.

¶ 5. 'There, in sleep, this faculty (*deva*, the mind) experiences a great expansion (*mahiman*). All that it has ever seen it sees again; all that it has ever heard it hears again. Whatever it has experienced in different parts of the world, it experiences again and again. What it has seen and what it has not seen, what it has heard and what it has not heard, what it has experienced and what it has not experienced, what is and what is not,—everything he sees; as everything (*sarvaḥ*, "entire", masc.) he sees.

¶ 6. 'When he is overcome by glory (*tejas*),[1] then that faculty sees no dreams, and that [well-known] happiness arises in the body.

¶ 7. 'Just as birds settle on the tree in which they nest, my dear, so too does everything there settle in the highest Self;—

¶ 8. 'Even the earth and the elements of earth, water and the elements of water, fire (*tejas*) and the elements of fire, wind and the elements of wind, space and the elements of space, sight and what can be seen, hearing and what can be heard, smell and what can be smelt, taste and what can be tasted, the skin and what can be touched, the voice and what can be spoken, the hands and what can be handled, the genitals and the pleasure that can be had from them, the anus and what can be excreted, the feet and the movement that can be had from them, the mind and what can be conceived (*man-*), the soul (*buddhi*) and what can be intuitively perceived (*bodhitavya*), the ego and what can be egoized, thought and what can be thought, brilliance (*tejas*) and what can be brilliantly lighted up, the breath of life and what can be supported.

¶ 9. 'This one who sees and touches, hears and smells and tastes, conceives, intuitively perceives and acts, he is the self which consists of consciousness, the "person": he comes to rest (*sampratiṣṭhā-*) in the highest imperishable Self.

¶ 10. 'My dear, whoever comes to know that pure Imperishable that has neither shadow nor body nor blood, attains to [that] highest Imperishable indeed. [Thus] knowing all, he becomes all ("entire", masc.). On this there is the following verse:

'My dear, whoso that Imperishable comes to know
In which the self that consists of consciousness
With all its powers (*deva*), [all] breaths of life,
[All] beings take their rest,
He, knowing all, the All has entered!'

[1] Or, 'heat'.

V

¶ 1. Then Śaibya Satyakāma asked him: 'Master, what state of being (*loka*) does a man win by meditating on the syllable "Oṁ" (= *A* + *U* + *M*) right up to the end of his life?'

¶ 2. To him [the Master] answered: 'Satyakāma, the syllable Oṁ is Brahman, both the higher and the lower. Therefore a man who knows can attain to either, if he makes this [syllable] his home.

¶ 3. 'If he meditates on one element [only], enlightened (*saṁvedita*) by that alone, he will come [back] to earth soon enough. The Rig-Vedic verses bring him down to the world of men, and there, naturally endowed with a bent for self-mortification, chastity and faith, he will experience a great [spiritual] expansion (*mahiman*).

¶ 4. 'But if he meditates with two elements, the Yajur-Vedic formulas will lead him up to the atmosphere, to the world of the moon. In the world of the moon he will experience some enlightenment (*vibhūṣita*), but will return again.

¶ 5. 'Again, he who meditates on the highest Person with this syllable Oṁ in [all] its three elements, will be suffused with glory in the sun.

'As a snake sloughs off its skin, so is he set free from evil. The Sāma-Vedic chants lead him up to the Brahman-world. From out of the mass of living beings (*jīva*) he beholds that Person who is higher than the highest [1] and [yet] dwells within the city [of the body]. On this there are the following two verses:

¶ 6. 'Deadly are the three elements when used in rites
External, internal or in between,
If wholly merged together or wholly separate.
The wise man, using them in proportion due, is not
dismayed.

¶ 7. With Rig-Vedic verses [one gains] this world,
With Yajur-Vedic formulas the atmosphere,
With Sāma-Vedic chants that which the sages know:
With the syllable Oṁ as his firm base (*āyatana*), the wise
Attains to the All-highest,
Tranquil, ageless, immortal, free from fear!'

VI

¶ 1. Then Sukeśan Bhāradvāja asked him: 'Master, Hiranyanābha, a prince of the Kosalas, came up to me and asked this question: "Bhāradvāja, do you know about the 'person' of

[1] Or, 'beholds that Person who is higher than the highest mass of living beings'.

sixteen parts?" I said to the young man: "[No,] I do not know about him. Had I done so, how should I not have told you? Without any doubt a man who tells an untruth dries up—right up to his roots. That is why I cannot tell an untruth." Silently he mounted his chariot and drove away. So I am asking you: Where is that "person"?'

¶ 2. To him [the Master] answered: 'My dear, that "person" is right here inside the body; in him, it is said, these sixteen parts arise.

¶ 3. '[This person] thought to himself: "Who is it that when he departs, I depart, and when he remains, I remain?"

¶ 4. '[Then] he emanated the breath of life; from the breath of life faith, space, wind, fire, water, earth, sense, mind and food; from food strength, fervid ascetic practice, the sacred formulas, [sacred] action (*karma*), the worlds; and in the worlds is the name [individual].

¶ 5. 'Just as these rivers flow coursing towards the sea and, when they reach the sea, disappear from sight, and [just as] their name and form are broken up, so that you can only call them "sea", so too these sixteen parts of [him who is] their overseer,[1] coursing towards [that] "Person", on reaching him, disappear from sight; their name and form are broken up, so that you can only call them "Person". Having no parts, [such a man] becomes immortal. On this there is the following verse:

¶ 6.   'In whom the [sixteen] parts are firmly fixed
             Like the spokes in the hub of a wheel,
             Him do I know as the "person" to be known:
             So let not death unnerve thee!'

¶ 7. [Then] to [all of] them he said: 'So much do I know about this highest Brahman: there is nothing beyond It.'

¶ 8. They praised him and said: 'You are indeed our father, for you ferry us across to the [further] shore which is beyond the reach of ingorance.'

  Homage to the highest seers! Homage to the highest seers!

----

[1] i.e. the 'person'.

Māndūkya Upanishad

¶ 1. Hari [1] Oṁ. This syllable 'Oṁ' is this whole universe. And the interpretation thereof is this:

> What was and is and is yet to be,—
>> All of it is Oṁ;
> And whatever else the three times transcends,—
>> That too is Oṁ.

¶ 2. For all this [world] is Brahman. This Self is Brahman. This Self has four quarters.

¶ 3. The waking state, conscious (*prājña*) of what is without, seven-limbed, with nineteen mouths, experiencing what is gross, common to all men (*vaiśvānara*), is the first quarter.

¶ 4. The state of dream, conscious of what is within, seven-limbed, with nineteen mouths, experiencing what is subtle, composed of light (*taijasa*), is the second quarter.

¶ 5. When a man is asleep and desires nothing whatever, dreams no dream, that is deep sleep (*suṣupta*).

The state of deep sleep, unified, a very mass of wisdom (*prajñāna*), composed of bliss, experiencing bliss, with thought as its mouth, wise (*prājña*), is the third quarter.

¶ 6. This is the Lord of all, This the omniscient. This is the Inner Controller: This is the source of all, for it is both the origin and the end of contingent beings.

¶ 7. Conscious (*prājña*) of neither within nor without, nor of both together, not a mass of wisdom (*prajñā*), neither wise nor unwise, unseen, one with whom there is no commerce, impalpable,[2] devoid of distinguishing mark, unthinkable, indescribable, its essence the firm conviction of the oneness of itself, bringing all development (*prapañca*) to an end, tranquil and mild, devoid of duality, such do they deem this fourth to be. That is the Self: that is what should be known.

¶ 8. [Now,] this is the Self in its relationship to syllables: it is Oṁ. As to the letters, the quarters [enumerated above] are the letters; and the letters are the quarters,—*A, U, M*.[3]

¶ 9. The waking state, common to all men, is *A*, the first letter,

---

[1] A name of Vishnu. [2] Or, 'incomprehensible'.
[3] i.e. *Oṁ* analysed as $A + U + M$.

201

signifying *āpti*, 'obtaining', or *ādimattva*, 'what is in the beginning'. For he who knows this obtains all his desires and becomes the beginning.

¶ 10. The state of dream, composed of light, is *U*, the second letter, signifying *utkarṣa*, 'exaltation', or *ubhayatva*, 'partaking of both', He who knows this exalts the continuum of knowledge and becomes like [Brahman]. In his family there is none who does not know Brahman.

¶ 11. The state of deep sleep, the wise, is *M*, the third letter, signifying *miti*, 'building up' [or 'measuring'], or *apīti*, 'absorption'. He who knows this builds up [or measures] the whole universe in very deed and is absorbed [into it].

¶ 12. The fourth is beyond [all] letters: there can be no commerce with it; it brings [all] development to an end; it is mild and devoid of duality. Such is Oṁ, the very Self indeed. He who knows this merges of his own accord (*ātmanā*) into the Self,— yes, he who knows this.

Śvetāśvatara Upanishad

I

Students of Brahman say:

¶ 1. What is the cause? [What] Brahman? Whence did we come to be?
By whom or what do we live? On what are we established?
By whom directed do we pursue our several ways
In pleasure and in pain? Knowers of Brahman, [tell us!]

¶ 2. How is the first origin to be conceived? As time,
Inherent Nature, fate, chance, the elements, a person (*puruṣa*)?
Or a conjunction of these? [I think] not, given the nature of the self;
For the self [itself] is powerless over whatever causes pleasure and pain.[1]

¶ 3. [Sages] well-practised (*yoga*)[2] in meditation have beheld
God's native (*ātma-*) power deep-hidden by his attributes (*guṇa*).
He, the One, surveys, directs all causes,—
All those [we spoke of] from time to self.

¶ 4. [We understand] Him [as a wheel]
With one felly, with a triple tyre,[3]
With sixteen ends and fifty spokes
And twenty counter-spokes,
With six sets of eights:[4]
Its one[5] rope has every form:
Three separate paths[6] it follows;
Its one illusion (*moha*) is doubly caused.[7]

¶ 5. We understand Him as a river of five streams[8]
From five sources,[9]—crooked, cruel,—
Its waves the five vital breaths,
Its primal fount fivefold perception (*buddhi*);
Its five whirlpools swirl wildly
With fivefold misery:
Fifty tributaries it has, five branches.

[1] Or, 'because of the existence of pleasure and pain'.
[2] Or, 'practised in meditation and Yoga'.
[3] i.e. the three constituents of Nature (p. xiii).
[4] The numbers refer to different categories in the Sāṁkhya system.
[5] i.e. desire.   [6] Of righteousness, unrighteousness and wisdom.
[7] i.e. by good and evil actions.
[8] i.e. the senses.   [9] i.e. the five elements.

¶ 6. This is the great wheel of Brahman
Giving life and livelihood to all,
Subsists in all:
In it the swan [of the soul] is hither and thither tossed.
'One is the self, another
He who impels to action,'
So thinking, a man [1] rejoices:
Hence and hereby [1] he passes on to immortality.

¶ 7. [Of old] was this highest Brahman proclaimed in song:
In It there is a trinity, firm-based, imperishable.
Knowers of Brahman, discerning what lies within It,
Merged in Brahman, intent on It,
Were freed from [the bondage of] the womb.

¶ 8. What is here conjoined together,—
Perishable and imperishable,
Manifest and unmanifest,—
All this doth the Lord sustain;
But for lack of mastery the self is bound,
Its [very] nature to enjoy experience:
[But] once it knows [its] God,
From all fetters is it freed!

¶ 9. Two unborn [males] there are: one knows, the other knows
    not;
One Master, Lord, the other lacking mastery.
One unborn female there is too, close linked
To what enjoys experience and to the experience enjoyed.
And there is the self unbounded
Of universal form: it neither works nor acts.
Find out [this] trinity. That is Brahman.

¶ 10. Perishable is Nature (*pradhāna*);
Immortal and imperishable [the self]:
Both the perishable and the self
Doth the One God Hara [2] rule.
By meditating on Him, by constant striving,[3]
By becoming what one really is (*tattvabhāva*),[4]
The whole world of appearance (*māyā*) will once again
Be lost to sight (*nivṛtti*) at last.

---

[1] Or, 'favoured by Him'.
[2] A name of Śiva. Perhaps the whole phrase should be translated thus:
'The immortal and imperishable is Hara: [He,] the One God rules both the
perishable and the self.'
[3] Or, 'by uniting [with Him]'.
[4] Or, 'by becoming [His] essence'.

¶ 11. Once God is known, all fetters fall away,
[All] cares dissolve,
Birth and death are left behind;
And thirdly, by meditating on Him
At [the time of] the body's breaking up
There is mastery supreme (*viśvaiśvarya*): his desires fulfilled
[A man is then] absolute, alone (*kevala*).

¶ 12. This must be known,—the Eternal Self-subsistent: [1]
For than That there's nothing higher to be known.
The enjoyer of experience—the thing experienced—
The one who provides the impulse,—
Know these! and all is said.
This is the triple Brahman.

¶ 13. Just as the form of fire when it returns to its source
Cannot be seen though its subtle form (*linga*) is not destroyed,
For it can again be grasped at its very source, the fire-drill;
So too can both [be grasped] by [uttering]
Within one's body [the single syllable,] Oṁ.

¶ 14. Make thy body the lower fire-stick,
    [The syllable] Oṁ the upper;
Make use of meditation like the friction [of the sticks],
Then wilt thou see God, like hidden [fire].

¶ 15. As oil in sesame, as butter in cream,
As water in river beds, as fire between the fire-sticks,
So is that Self to be grasped within the self
[Of him] who by austerity beholds Him in [very] truth,—

¶ 16. The Self who all pervades
As butter inheres in cream,
Root of [2] self-knowledge, [root of] ascetic practice,—
That is Brahman, [that] the highest teaching (*upaniṣad*). [3]

II

¶ 1. First harnessing his mind and thoughts
    To what is real (*tattva*),
Savitri [4] discerned the light of fire
And brought it to [5] the earth.

¶ 2. With mind [well] harnessed we
Attend on(?) Savitri, the god,
With power directed heavenward.

---

[1] Or, 'subsisting in selves'.   [2] Or, 'rooted in'.
[3] Or, 'that is the highest teaching concerning Brahman.
[4] A sun-god.   [5] Or, 'from'.

¶ 3. By mind has [Savitri] harnessed the gods
That to bright heaven they may go in thought
  To make a mighty light:
  May Savitri urge them on!

¶ 4. The wise sages of the mighty Sage
Harness their minds, harness their thoughts:
The One who knows the ordinances has decreed the [due]
    oblations.
  How mighty is the praise of [this] god, Savitri!

¶ 5. For you I harness the ancient prayer (*brahman*) with
    adoration:
May my verses go forth on the path of the sun!
Let all the sons of the Immortal hearken [to them],—
[The sons of the Immortal] who dwell in celestial abodes!

¶ 6. Where the fire is kindled,
Where the wind is made to serve it (?),
Where the Soma overflows,
There does the mind arise.

¶ 7. With Savitri to urge us on,
Let us take our pleasure in the ancient prayer (*brahman*):
There must thou seek (*kṛ-*) thine origin,
For thy good works have not disdained thee.

¶ 8. Holding the body straight with head, neck and chest in line,
With senses and the mind withdrawn into the heart,
Let a wise man on Brahman's raft cross over
All the rivers [of this life] so fraught with peril.

¶ 9. Restraining here his breath, his movements well controlled,
Let a wise man breathe in through the nostrils, his breath
    reduced;
Free from distraction, let him hold his mind in chcck
Like a chariot harnessed to vicious steeds.

¶ 10. Let him meditate in a clean and level [spot]
From pebbles, fire and gravel free,
Pleasing to the mind by reason of [soft] sounds,
Water and dwelling-places, not offensive to the eye,—
A secret spot protected from the wind.

¶ 11. Fog, smoke, sun, fire and wind,
Fire-flies, lightning, crystal, and the moon,—
In Yoga these are the visions (*rūpa*) that anticipate
The [fuller] revelations [seen] in Brahman.

¶ 12. When the fivefold attributes (*guṇa*) of Yoga come to be and
    grow,
[The attributes] of earth, water, fire, wind and space,—
Then is there no sickness, age or death
For him who has won himself a body of Yogic fire.

¶ 13. Lightness, good health, freedom from harassment,
A clean complexion and a pleasant voice,
A fragrant odour and but slight excretions
Announce the first steps on Yoga['s path].

¶ 14. Even as a mirror with dirt begrimed
Shines brightly once it is well cleaned,
So too the embodied soul, once it has seen
Self as it really is (*tattva*),
Becomes one, its goal achieved, from sorrow free.

¶ 15. When by means of self as it really is as with a lamp
An integrated (*yukta*) man sees Brahman as It really is (*tattva*),
[Then will he know] the unborn,[1] undying [1] God, the Pure,[1]
Beyond all essences as they really are,[1]
[And] knowing Him, from all fetters he'll be freed.

¶ 16. This is the God who pervades all regions:
He is the first-born, He is in the womb.
He is born indeed and will be born again:
Over against [his] creatures does He stand,
His face turned every way.

¶ 17. This is the God in fire and in the waters;
The whole world has He entered;
In healing plants is He, He it is in the trees:
To this God all hail, all hail!

III

¶ 1. He is the One who, spreading wide his net,
Rules with his sovereign powers:
By his sovereign powers these worlds He rules.
He is One [and One abides]
As [others] come to be and grow together.
Whoso knows this becomes immortal.

¶ 2. For One is Rudra,—they stand not for a second,—
Who all the worlds doth rule by his sovereign powers:
Over against [his] creatures stands He, protector;
All worlds He emanated,
[All worlds] will He roll up at the end of time.

---

[1] These epithets could be taken as agreeing with 'Brahman'.

¶ 3. His eyes on every side, on every side his face,
On every side his arms, his feet on every side:
With arms and wings He together forges
Heaven and earth, begetting them, [He,] God, the One! [1]

¶ 4. He, of gods the source and origin,
All-sovereign Rudra, mighty Seer,
Of old begat the Golden Embryo: [2]
May He conjoin us with a lucid mind (*buddhi*)!

¶ 5. Dweller in the mountains, Thyself reveal to us
In thy fairest form (*tanu*), [great] Rudra,
In a form auspicious (*śiva*), [a form] not cruel,
[A form] that displays no evil!

¶ 6. Dweller in the mountains, make thine arrow kind (*śiva*),
[The arrow] Thou carriest in thy hand to shoot it:
Protector of the mountains, do no hurt
    To man or beast.

¶ 7. Higher than this,[3] than Brahman higher,[4] the mighty [God],
Hidden in all beings, in each according to his kind,
The One, all things encompassing, the Lord,—
By knowing Him a man becomes immortal.

¶ 8. I know that mighty Person,
Sun-coloured beyond the darkness:
By knowing Him indeed a man surpasses death;
No other path is there on which to go.

¶ 9. Beyond Him is nothing whatsoever, no other thing;
No one is more minute than He, no one more vast:
Like a sturdy tree firm-fixed in heaven He stands,
The One, the Person, this whole universe full filling!

¶ 10. Than this [5] yet more exalted
Is That which has no form, no imperfection:
Whoso knows this becomes immortal,
The rest must suffer misery.

¶ 11. The face, the head, the neck of all is He,
In the heart of every being He makes his home,
All things pervading, Blessed Lord (*bhagavat*);
Hence is [He called] 'Benign', *Śiva*, penetrating everywhere.

---

[1] *Rig-Veda*, x. lxxxi. 3, p. 7.   [2] *See* p. 10.
[3] Sc. the 'Golden Embryo'.
[4] Or (with a slight variation), 'is the highest Brahman'.
[5] Sc. the universe. It can scarcely refer to Rudra. Or, 'for this reason'.

¶ 12. A mighty Lord indeed is He, the Person;
He speeds existence on its course:
Over this prize [1] immaculate
He rules, a light unchanging.

¶ 13. This Person of the measure of a thumb, the Inmost Self,
Forever dwells within the hearts of men,
By heart and thought and mind to be conceived of: [2]
Whoso knows this becomes immortal.

¶ 14. A thousand heads [this] Person has,
A thousand eyes, a thousand feet:
Encompassing the earth on every side
He outdistances it by ten fingers' breadth.[3]

¶ 15. All this universe [this] Person is,
What was and what is yet to be,
The Lord of immortality
[And of all] that thrives on food.

¶ 16. With hands and feet on every side,
On every side eyes, heads and mouths,
With ears on every side He stands,
All things encompassing that the world contains.

¶ 17. All attributes of sense doth he light up,[4]
[Himself] devoid of all [attributes of] sense,
[He,] sovereign Lord of all,
Of all the mighty shelter.

¶ 18. In the city of nine doors [5] the embodied soul
[Like] a great bird flutters outward,
Though the whole world's in its power,
What moves and what stands still.

¶ 19. Handless and footless He yet speeds and grasps,
Eyeless he sees and earless hears:
[All that is] knowable He knows,
Though of Him there is no knower:
Him men have called the primeval mighty Person.

¶ 20. More subtile than the subtile, greater than the great,
The Self is hidden in the heart of creatures here;
By the Ordainer's [6] grace does a man whose sorrow's spent
Descry the Lord who active will transcends in majesty.

---

[1] Sc. *mukti*, 'spiritual liberation'.　　　　　　[2] Or, 'fashioned'.
[3] *See* p. 8.　　　　[4] Or, 'seems to possess' or 'reflects'.
[5] i.e. the body.　　　　[6] Or, 'Creator's'.

¶ 21. I know this undecaying primal Self of all,
Everywhere roving, for [all things] he pervades:
[Re]birth by Him is ended,[1] so have [the wise] proclaimed;
For students of Brahman say He is eternal.

IV

¶ 1. The One, [himself] uncoloured,
Widely disposes colours manifold
By the practice (*yoga*) of his power
(How hidden is his purpose!):
Into Him all things dissolve at the end [of time],
[As] in the beginning [all things from Him emerged]:
He is God! May He conjoin us with a lucid mind (*buddhi*)!

¶ 2. That assuredly is fire, That the sun,
That the wind, and That the moon;
That is the Pure, That Brahman,
That is the waters, That the Lord of Creatures!

¶ 3. Thou art woman, Thou art man,
Thou art the lad and the maiden too,
Thou art the old man tottering on his staff:
Once born thou comest to be, thy face turned every way![2]

¶ 4. A dark-blue moth art Thou, green [parrot] with red eyes,
Pregnant with lightning,—seasons, seas:
Thyself beginningless, all things dost Thou pervade;
From Thee all worlds were born.

¶ 5. With the one unborn female, red, white and black,
Who gives birth to many a creature like unto herself,
Lies the one male unborn, taking his delight.
Another Male unborn forsakes her, for she has had her pleasure.

¶ 6. Two birds, close-linked companions,
   Cling to the selfsame tree;
Of these the one eats of the sweet fruit,
The other, nothing eating, looks on intent.

¶ 7. On the selfsame tree a person is plunged in [grief],
Mourning his lack of mastery, perplexed;
When he sees the other, the Lord, rejoicing
In his majesty, his sorrow melts away.

---

[1] Or, 'He is exempt from birth'.
[2] *Atharva-Veda*, x. viii. 27, p. 25.

¶ 8. That syllable [1] of the Vedic hymn (*ṛc*) whereon
In highest heaven all the gods are seated,—
What shall the Vedic hymns avail the man
Who knows not Him [who indwells that syllable]?
The men who know it, lo, they are here assembled!

¶ 9. Hymns, sacrifices, rites and ordinances,
What was and what is yet to be,
[All] that the Vedas proclaim,—
All this does He who is possessed of creative power (*māyā*) emit
From that [same syllable]; and by the same creative power
(*māyā*)
The other is therein constrained.

¶ 10. Creative power (*māyā*) is Nature (*prakṛti*), this must be
known,
And He who possesses it (*māyin*) is the Mighty Lord:
By things that are but parts of Him
This whole world is pervaded.

¶ 11. It is He alone who approaches every womb,[2]
In Him [alone] does this universe grow together and dissolve;
He is the Lord who grants [us] favours,
God, the adorable:
Discerning Him a man wins peace for ever.

¶ 12. He, of gods the source and origin,
All-sovereign Rudra, mighty Seer,
Of old beheld the Golden Embryo [3] when he was born:
May He conjoin us with a lucid mind!

¶ 13. King of the gods is He,
All worlds in Him are fixed!
His is the kingdom over fourfooted and twofooted beasts:
To what God shall we offer our oblations?

¶ 14. More subtile than the subtile, in the midst of chaos
All things He emanates,—how manifold his forms!—
All things encompasses [though He is but] One:
Whoso should know Him, *Śiva*, the Benign, wins peace forever.

¶ 15. For sure protector of the world in time is He,
Sovereign of all, hidden in all creatures;
In Him are seers of Brahman and the gods united:
By knowing Him death's fetters are cut loose.

[1] i.e. Oṁ: or, 'imperishable being'.
[2] Or, 'rules over every source'.
[3] *See* pp. 10, 21.

¶ 16. By knowing *Śiva*, the Benign, in all creatures hidden,
Surpassing subtle, even as cream surpasses butter,
By knowing God, the One Encompasser of all,
A man is from all fetters freed.

¶ 17. He is God, All-maker, of exalted Self (*mahātman*),
Forever dwelling in the hearts of men,
By heart and thought and mind to be conceived of: [1]
Whoso knows this becomes immortal.

¶ 18. When there is no darkness, no day nor night,
No Being, no Not-Being,—Śiva alone (*kevala*) [is this];
This the imperishable, this the choice [light] of Savitri:
From this primeval wisdom (*prajñā*) issued forth!

¶ 19. Above, athwart, or in the middle,—
Nowhere hath anyone caught hold of him:
Of Him there is no likeness,
Great Glory is his name.

¶ 20. His form cannot be glimpsed,
None may see Him with the eye:
Whoso should know Him with heart and mind
As dwelling in the heart, becomes immortal!

¶ 21. 'Unborn is He,' so saying,
Let a man in fear approach Him:
O Rudra, [show] thy right [auspicious] cheek,
Protect me with it ever!

¶ 22. Do us no hurt in child or offspring,
In life or kine or horses;
Slay not our men in anger, Rudra!
Bearing oblations we invoke Thee ever.

V

¶ 1. In the imperishable, infinite city [2] of Brahman
            Two things there are,—
Wisdom (*vidyā*) and unwisdom, hidden, established there:
Perishable is unwisdom, but wisdom is immortal:
Who over wisdom and unwisdom rules, He is Another.

¶ 2. It is He alone who approaches every womb, [3]
[Who rules] all forms and every cause,

---

[1] Or, 'fashioned'.   [2] Reading *pure* for *pare*.
[3] Or, 'rules over every source'.

Who bears in his thoughts the tawny seer [1]
As in the beginning he was engendered,
And gazes on him as he is born.

¶ 3. One after another this God spreads wide his many nets
In this [earthly] field only to draw them in [again]:
So too the Lord of Self so great (*mahātman*) sends out
Rulers, though He [alone] wields the all-sovereign power.

¶ 4. As the sun shines forth, illumining
All regions, above, below, athwart,
So does this One God, the Blessed Lord (*bhagavat*), adorable,
Hold sway over whatever creature (*svabhāva*) issues from the
    womb.

¶ 5. Source of all things, He ripens every creature (*svabhāva*),
When ripe transmutes them all:
Over this whole universe He alone holds sway,
Assigning their proper attributes to all.

¶ 6. That which is hidden in the secret Upanishads of the Veda
Brahmā knows to be the source of Brahman: [2]
The ancient gods and seers who knew It
Shared in its nature and became immortal.

¶ 7. Ruler of the vital breaths,[3] [the individual self]
Has attributes, does works and reaps their fruits,
Enjoys what he has done, assuming all manner of forms:
He's made of Nature's three constituents,[4]
Three paths are open to him: [5]
So does he roam [the world, conditioned] by his works.

¶ 8. Of the measure of a thumb, the sun's equal in appearance,—
When conjoined with will (*saṅkalpa*) and ego, such is he;
But with soul (*buddhi*) and self as his [only] attributes (*guṇa*)
He seems another,—no larger than the fine point of an awl.

¶ 9. Think of this living (*jīva*) self as but a part
Of a hundredth part of the tip of a hair
    Divided a hundred times!
And [yet] to infinity is it conformed.

¶ 10. It is not male, not female,
Nor yet hermaphrodite;
Whatever body it receives,
    By that is it protected.

---

[1] Sc. the 'Golden Embryo' mentioned above.
[2] Or, 'to have Brahman as its source'.   [3] Or 'lord of life'.
[4] *See* pp. 314 ff.   [5] i.e. righteousness, unrighteousness and wisdom.

¶ 11. By delusions bred by touch, sight and imagination (*saṅ-kalpana*),[1]
By watering it with food and drink,
The self is made to grow, is born:
The embodied [self] in [different] states takes on
Forms in accordance with its [former] works,
    Each in its order due.

¶ 12. Many the forms both gross and subtle
That the embodied [self] clothes with [2] its own attributes,—
With attributes [derived] from works
And attributes [derived] from self:
But He is seen to be another,—the cause of this conjunction.

¶ 13. Endless and beginningless is God:
In the midst of chaos He
All things doth emanate,—how manifold his forms!—
The One Encompasser of all:
By knowing Him a man is from every fetter freed.

¶ 14. *Śiva*, the Benign, is God:
Maker of what becomes (*bhāva*) and what does not become:
Affection (*bhāva*) can lay hold of Him,[3] 'Homeless'[4] is his name:
Maker of [all] creation (*sarga*), [maker of its] parts:
Whoso should know Him, the body casts aside!

VI

¶ 1. 'Inherent Nature', some sages say,
'Time', others,—both deluded!
No, it is the majesty of God in the world [made manifest]
That turns and sets in motion Brahman's [awful] wheel!

¶ 2. For from all eternity this whole universe
Doth He encompass:
He knows, He the architect of time,
Possessed of attributes, omniscient:

By Him are works (*karma*) commanded,
[By Him do works] evolve,—
[Works] we think of [as diffused among the elements,]
Among earth and water, fire, wind and space.

---

    [1] Or, 'touch, sight, imagination and delusion'.
    [2] Or, 'chooses as'.
    [3] Or, 'He can be grasped in [the process of] becoming': or, 'He can be grasped by the mind.'
    [4] Lit. 'without nest'.

¶ 3. His work accomplished He takes his rest,
Then once again conjoins (*yoga*) Himself
With principle after principle (*tattva*),[1]—
With one, with two, with three, or eight,[2]
With time, and the subtile attributes (*guṇa*) of self.

¶ 4. [All] works does He initiate,
[And works] are never free from quality (*guṇa*):
All modes of being (*bhāva*) He directs.
When once these cease to be, the work once done must perish.
When works have perished, He goes on:
Other than essence is He,
[Other than any 'thing' even as it really is.]

¶ 5. He is the Beginning, the efficient cause of the conjoining,[3]
Seen as beyond the three times—partless too:
Of old did we worship Him, this God adorable,
Become becoming, in his thought subsisting, omniform!

¶ 6. Higher and other is He than [world-]tree, time and forms:
From Him the world evolves, fully diversified:
Righteousness He brings, evil repels, Master of good fortune,
Immortal, self-subsistent,[4] of all the home and ground (*dhāma*);
    So must He be known.

¶ 7. Of lords supreme Great Lord,
Of gods the highest God,
Of kings the highest King—utterly beyond!
So should we know Him,—God,
Lord of the worlds, adorable!

¶ 8. There is naught He needs to do, he works not with any tool:
Like unto Him is none, none greater [than He] is known:
Manifold is his exalted power, [as manifold] revealed:
His works of power and wisdom inhere in his very nature
    (*svābhāvika*).

¶ 9. No one in the [whole] world is his master,
No one his ruler; no outward sign (*liṅga*) has He:
He is the Cause, Lord of the senses' lord.[5]
No one begat Him, no one is his lord.

¶ 10. Like a spider the One God
Involves Himself in threads

---

[1] Or, 'with the essence of essence'.
[2] The figures refer to the categories of the Sāṁkhya system.
[3] i.e. of *puruṣa* ('person', spirit) and *prakṛti* (Nature).
[4] Or, 'subsisting in selves'.
[5] i.e. the individual self: or, 'of the masters of tools (*karaṇa*)'.

Of primal Nature (*pradhāna*) born
From out his very essence (*svabhāva*):
May He grant us entry into Brahman!

¶ 11. The One God, in all contingent beings hidden,
Pervading all, of all beings the Inmost Self,
Of [all] works (*karma*) the overseer, in Him all beings dwell,
Witness, observer, absolute, alone (*kevala*),
    Devoid of attributes!

¶ 12. This One holds sway among the inactive many,
    Makes the one seed manifold;
Wise men who see Him in their selves subsistent,[1]
Taste everlasting joy (*sukha*),—no others.

¶ 13. Eternal among eternals, conscious (*cetana*) among the
    conscious,
The One among the many, he disposes over desires:
He is the Cause, He can be comprehended
In theory (*sāṁkhya*) as in spiritual exercise (*yoga*);
Knowing this God a man is from every fetter freed.

¶ 14. There the sun shines not, nor moon, nor stars;
These lightnings shine not there, let alone this fire:
All things shine with the shining of this light,
This whole universe reflects his radiance![2]

¶ 15. The One [great] swan in the middle of this world
Is the same as the fire in ocean['s depths] deep hidden:
By knowing Him indeed a man surpasses death;
No other path is there on which to go.

¶ 16. Maker of all is He, all-knowing, source of selves,[3]
He knows, He the architect of time,
Possessed of [all] attributes, omniscient:
Lord of primeval Nature, [Lord of all] knowers of the field,[4]
Lord of the constituents of Nature (*guṇa*),
Cause of the round of birth and death (*saṁsāra*),
[Cause of] deliverance,
[Cause of our] sojourn here and of [our] imprisonment.

¶ 17. Being all this,[5] He is immortal, subsistent as the Lord,
Wise, present everywhere, protector of this world:
For all eternity He rules this moving world,
There is no other cause [like Him] in sovereignty!

---

[1] Or, 'as self-subsistent'.   [2] Cf. p. 181.
[3] Or, 'of Himself': or, 'having Self as source'.   [4] See pp. 303–6.
[5] Or, 'consisting of That (i.e. Brahman)'.

¶ 18. Of old did he raise up (*vidhā-*) Brahmā,
[Of old] entrust him with the Vedas:
On liberation bent I fly to his sheltering care,—
[The care] of the God who illumines self and soul (*ātmabuddhi*).[1]

¶ 19. No parts has He, no part in action,
Tranquil, unblemished and unflecked,
The highest bridge to immortality,
Like a fire whose fuel is spent.

¶ 20. When men shall roll up space
As though it were a piece of leather,
Then will there be an end of suffering
For him who knew not God![2]

¶ 21. By much austerity and by the grace of God
Did the wise Śvetāśvatara make Brahman rightly known
To those who had gone furthest on the ascetic path,—
Vessel of purity supreme, to the company of seers well pleasing.

¶ 22. This highest mystery of the Veda's end
Was propounded in an earlier age;
Let it not be told to an unquiet man,
Or to one who is neither son nor pupil.

¶ 23. To the great-souled man who loyally
And greatly loves (*bhakti*) [his] God,
Who loves his spiritual master even as his God,
The matter of this discourse will shine with clearest light,—
    With clearest light will shine.

[1] Or, 'who illumines his own intellect'. Var. 'who has the grace of making himself known'. Many other translations are possible.
[2] Or, 'apart from knowing God'.

Maitri Upanishad

I

[The teacher speaks]

¶ 1. 'The building up [of the sacrificial fire] by the ancients was really a sacrifice to Brahman. Therefore the sacrificial priest should meditate on the Self when he builds up these fires. So in very truth is the sacrifice fulfilled completely and entire.'

'To whom should one's meditation be directed?'

'To Him who is called the breath of life (*prāṇa*).'

There is a story about this:

¶ 2. Once there was a king called Brihadratha. He appointed his son [ruler] over his kingdom, and, meditating on the impermanence of the body, he retired to the forest in a spirit of dispassion [towards the things of this world]. There he stood, mortifying himself exceedingly, gazing up at the sun, his arms held aloft. After a thousand days had elapsed the Master Śākāyanya, who had knowledge of the Self, approached him like a smokeless fire, burning in his glory (*tejas*).

'Arise, arise; choose [whatever] boon [thou wilt],' he said to the king.

[The king] did obeisance to him and said: 'Master, I have no knowledge of the Self, [but] thou knowest the truth (*tattva*) [about it], or so we have heard. [I pray thee,] tell us about it.'

'Such things did happen in times gone by. This is a most difficult question, son of Ikshvāku: choose thou some other boon,' said Śākāyanya.' [But] the king [bowing] his head to the other's feet till it touched them, intoned this dirge:

¶ 3. 'Master, foul-smelling, insubstantial, is this body, a compact mass of skin and bones, sinews, marrow, flesh and semen, blood, mucus, tears and rheum, urine and faeces, bile and phlegm: what point is there in satisfying one's desires in that? Assailed is this body by desire and anger, greed and delusion, fear, depression and envy, separation from what one wants and close association with what one does not want, hunger and thirst, old age and death, disease, sorrow and the like: what point is there in satisfying one's desires in that?

¶ 4. 'We see this whole [world] decay: gnats, flies and other [insects], the grass and trees,—they come to be only to be dissolved.

'But why speak of these? There are other [beings] superior [far to these], great warriors and now and then a world-conqueror (*cakravartin*)—men like Sudyumna, Bhūridyumna, Indra-dyumna, Kuvalayāśva, Yauvanāśva, Vadhryāśva, Aśvapati, Śaśabindu, Hariścandra, Ambarīsha, Nanaktu, Saryāti, Yayāti, Anaranya, Ukshasena and the rest: then there are kings like Marutta and Bharata, to name only the first. With a crowd of relatives looking on they said goodbye to rank and riches (*mahatīṁ śriyam*) and passed on from this world to the next.

'But why speak of these? There are others higher yet. [And what happened to them? For] we [all] know about the suppression of the Gandharvas,[1] the demons, sprites, ogres, hordes of ghosts, goblins, divine serpents, ghouls and the like.

'But why speak of these? Among other things [we see] the drying up of mighty oceans, the crumbling to ruin of lofty peaks, the unfixing of the pole star, the cutting of the ropes [that restrain] the wind, the engulfing of the earth, the fall of the gods from their [high] estate: of such is the round of coming to be and passing away (*saṁsāra*). What point is there in satisfying one's desires in that? For once a man has tasted of them he is seen to come back to earth ever and again.

'Save [me from it], I pray thee: in this round of existence I am like a frog in a well without issue (*andha*). Master, thou art our [only] way,[2] thou art our [only] way!'

II

¶ 1. And the Master Śākayanya was well pleased with the king and said to him:

'Brihadratha, great king, banner of Ikshvāku's race, right soon wilt thou come to know the Self, thy goal achieved, and by the name of "Marut, (the wind)", [henceforth] shalt thou be known. This, assuredly, is thine own (*te*) Self.'

'But, Master, which?'

To him [the Master] said:

¶ 2. '"He who, without causing the breath (*ucchvāsa*) to stop, rises aloft, changing yet changeless, [he who] dispels the darkness, —he is the Self." So said the Master Maitri; and he continued: "He who, serenity itself, rises aloft from this body, reaches the highest light, and appears in his own form,—he is the Self."[3] So he said. This is the immortal, [this] the free from fear: this is Brahman!

¶ 3. 'This in truth, O king, is the wisdom of Brahman, the wisdom of all the Upanishads, told to me by the Master Maitri; and I [in turn] will tell it to thee.

---

[1] A type of semi-divine being.   [2] i.e. 'refuge'.   [3] Cf. p. 124.

'[Once there lived ascetics called] Vālakhilyas: they had
destroyed evil [in themselves], they were gloriously effulgent,
chaste. So have we heard. Then they said to Kratu Prajāpati:
'"Master, this body is like a cart,—unconscious (*acetana*).
Now, what kind of suprasensuous being is it that has the power
(*mahiman*) to set it up in such a way that it really appears to be
conscious? Who is it that impels it [into action]? If, Master, thou
knowest this, then tell us."

'To them [the Master] said:

¶ 4. '"This have we heard. He who stands on high, seemingly
chaste though surrounded by the 'constituents' of Nature,—he is
the pure, the purified, the void, the tranquil: [he is] not the
breath of life (*a-prāṇa*), not the self (selfless): infinite [is he],
indefectible (*akshaya*), stable (*sthira*), eternal, unborn, on himself
[alone] dependent. [So] he abides in his own magnificence
(*mahiman*). By him is this body set up so that it really appears to
be conscious: he it is who impels it [into action]."

'They said: "Master, how can this body be set up in such a
way that it really appears to be conscious by one who has
neither basis nor goal (*aniṣṭha*)? Or how can such a one impel it
[into action]?"

'To them he said:

¶ 5. '"Here [in the body] this subtle, impalpable, invisible one
known as 'Person', begins to move, or rather a fraction of
himself does so, though there was no awareness (*buddhi*) [of him]
beforehand, just as when a sleeper awakes, there is no awareness
of the awakening beforehand.

'"Assuredly, this part of him is pure consciousness, reflecting
the Person himself; [1] [it is] the 'knower of the field' [2] whose
subtle body is made up of [3] conception (*samkalpa*), will (*adhyavasāya*), and self-consciousness (*abhimāna*), Prajāpati under the
name of 'common to all men' (*viśva*). By consciousness this body
is set up so that it really appears to be conscious [itself]: he it is
who impels it [into action]."

'They said: "Master, if this body is set up in such a way that
it really appears to be conscious, by one who appears to have
neither basis nor goal (*aniṣṭha*), how can it be he who impels it
[into action]?"

'To them he said:

¶ 6. '"In the beginning Prajāpati stood one [and alone]. As One
he found no pleasure. By meditating on [him]self he emanated
many creatures.

'"He looked at them: [they were] unawake and lifeless
(*a-prāṇa*) like a stone, standing erect like a pillar. This gave him
no pleasure; and he bethought himself, 'Suppose I were to enter

---

[1] Or, 'to be found in every person'.   [2] *See* p. 303.
[3] Or, 'who has the marks of'.

into them in order to wake them up.' [So] making [him]self [light] as the wind he [tried to] enter in. Being [but] One he could not. So he divided [him]self into five parts: as such he is called 'in-breath' (*prāṇa*), 'out-breath' (*apāna*), 'concentrated breath' *samāna*), 'upper breath' (*udāna*) and 'diffused breath' (*vyāna*). . . . [A gloss on the functions of the 'breaths' is omitted.] . . .

'"Though he had divided [him]self into five parts, [he remained] hidden in the secret place [of the heart],—he who consists of mind, whose body is the breath of life, whose form is light, whose idea [1] is the Real (*satya*, 'Truth'), whose self is space.

'"Still he had not accomplished his purpose, and so from the inmost [recesses] of the heart he thought [to himself]: 'Would that I could enjoy things [other than myself]!' Then he pierced open these apertures [in the body], and, rising up and out [of it], he [started to] enjoy the objects of sense with these five reins [of the senses]. These organs of external perception are his reins; the 'organs of action' are the steeds; the body is the chariot, the mind the charioteer. The [three 'constituents'] of Nature are his [three-stranded] whip, and it is he who wields it.

'"This body whirls round and round like a potter's wheel [driven on] by the potter, set up so that it appears to be conscious. He it is who impels it [into action].

¶ 7. '"This self, so the seers inform us, wanders around on earth in body after body,[2] apparently unaffected by the fruits of [its] works, be they white or black. Because he is unmanifest, subtile, invisible, impalpable, and possesses nothing (*nirmama*), he must surely be impermanent (*anavastha*) and a worker (*kartṛ*) in what is not Being (*asat*); and yet he is in no sense a worker [nor does he do anything] (*a-kartṛ*): he is permanent [and abiding] (*avastha*). He is indeed the pure, the stable, the unmoved, the unaffected (*alepya*), unflurried, free from desire, standing still (*avasthita*) like a spectator, self-subsistent. [Yet] in so far as he is a recipient of pious works (*ṛtabhuj*), he conceals [him]self behind a veil [woven from] the [three] 'constituents' of Nature (*guṇa*),[3] abiding the same the while (*avasthita*),—abiding the same the while."

III

¶ 1. 'They said: "Master, if the pre-eminence (*mahiman*) of this self is such as you describe it, there is surely another, different one. Who is this, [also] known as 'self', who [really] is unaffected by the fruits of [his] works, be they white or black, and who must [ever again] enter the wombs of good and evil [women]

---

[1] Or, 'will' (*saṅkalpa*).   [2] Or, 'in [all] bodies'.
          [3] Or, 'attributes'.

thus ascending or descending [in the order of existence], wandering around at the mercy of [all manner of] dualities (*dvandva*)?"
¶ 2. '[He said:] "There is indeed another, different [self]: it is
known as the 'elemental' [or 'individual'] self (*bhūtātman*)
which [really] is affected by the fruits of [his own] works, be they
white or black, and who must [ever again] enter into the wombs
of good or evil [women], thus ascending or descending [in the
order of existence], wandering around at the mercy of [all manner
of] dualities.

'"Let us define it further. The five 'subtle elements' (*tan-mā-
tra*) are classified as *bhūtas*, '[individual contingent] beings', and
the five gross elements (*mahābhūta*) are classified under the same
head. The combination of the two is called the body. Now, when
we speak [of a self as being] 'within the body', we most certainly
mean this '[elemental or] individual self' (*bhūtātman*). Now this
[self itself] has [another] *immortal* self which is [unaffected by the
body] 'like a drop of water on a lotus petal'. That [other] one,
however, is subject to the 'constituents' of Nature.

'"Because it is subjected [to them], it becomes confused; and
because it is confused, it does not see [that] the Lord (*prabhu*)
God (*bhagavan*) who indwells the self [1] [is the sole] cause of
agency. Swept away by the currents of Nature's constituents and
made turbid by them, unstable, fickle, mutilated, full of desire,
restless (*vyagra*), it becomes conscious of itself as a separate
individual.[2] Thinking, 'This am I, this is mine', it of its own
accord (*ātmanā*) binds [it]self like a bird [entangled] in a net.
Accordingly, overcome by the fruits of [its own] works, it must
[ever again] enter into the wombs of good and evil [women], thus
ascending or descending [in the order of existence], wandering
around at the mercy of [all manner of] dualities."

'"Which one is this?" [they asked him].

'To them he replied:
¶ 3. '"Now, it has been said elsewhere: The agent is this self-
same individual self [working] through the faculties (*karaṇa*); [3]
he who causes agency [in the agent himself, however,] is the
Person within.[4] It is just like a lump of iron, when subject to [the
heat of] fire: beaten [into shape] by workmen (*kartṛ*, 'agents'), it
becomes diversified. Just so this individual self, subject to that
Person within, and beaten [into shape] by the constituents of
Nature, becomes diversified. The manner (*rūpa*) of this diversifi-
cation is as follows: this [individual self] is transmuted into a
mass of [subsidiary] beings [divided into] four categories (*jāla*)
and fourteen species in eighty-four different ways.

---

[1] The 'immortal' or the 'individual' self ?
[2] Lit. 'comes to self-conceit' (*abhimānatva*).
[3] 'Through the faculties' may equally be taken with the next phrase.
[4] i.e. 'God'.

'"The constituents of Nature [of which the body is formed], however, are [themselves] set in motion by the Person like a potter's wheel by a potter.[1] [But to return to the simile of the lump of iron:] when the lump of iron is beaten [into shape], the fire is not affected; so too that Person [within] is not affected: but the individual self *is* affected because it is inextricably mixed up [with Nature's constituents].

¶ 4. '"Now, it has also been said elsewhere: The body owes its existence to sexual intercourse; it grows up in the [dark] hell [of the womb]. Then it issues forth through the passage [the normal function of which is] passing water. Its frame is of bone coated with flesh and buttressed up with skin. It is filled right up with faeces and urine, bile, phlegm, marrow, fat, grease and many other cankers,[2]—just like a treasure-house filled with treasure!

¶ 5. '"[This] too has been said elsewhere:

'"[The following qualities] belong to [the constituent of Nature called] 'Darkness': mental confusion, fear, depression, sleepiness and fatigue, intoxication,[3] old age, sorrow, hunger and thirst, wretchedness, anger, atheism, ignorance, jealousy, cruelty, stupidity, shamelessness, shapelessness (*nirākṛtitva*), conceit, lack of equanimity.

'"[The following] belong to [the constituent of Nature called] 'Passion': inward craving, cloying love, passion, greed, wishing others ill (*hiṁsā*), sexual pleasure (*rati*), hatred, secretiveness, envy, desire, instability, fickleness, distraction, ambition, acquisitiveness, favouritism, reliance on worldly wealth, aversion to objects repellent to the senses and attachment to [objects] attractive [to them], churlish speech and gluttony.

'"The individual self is replete with these and subject to them. Therefore it takes on many a different form,—yes, it takes them on."'

IV

¶ 1. 'Then those chaste [Vālakhilyas], full of amazement, approached [him] together and said: "Master, to thee be homage; teach us [further]. Thou art our [only] way;[4] there is no other. By what method can the individual self attain to union (*sāyojya*) with the Self once it is rid of this [body]?"'

'To them [the Master] said:

¶ 2. '"Now, [this too has been said elsewhere: There can be no reversal of any deed once it has been performed any more than the [direction of] the waves [can be reversed] in a great river. The

---

[1] This seems to be an interpolation from II. 6.
[2] Lit. 'diseases'.   [3] Or, 'heedlessness'.
[4] i.e. 'refuge'.

approach of death cannot be warded off any more than the ocean tide.

'''[The individual self] is like a lame man [weighed down] by fetters made up of the fruits of good and evil deeds; like a prisoner, not his own master, bound; like one in the realm of death, beset by all manner of fear; like a man drunk with wine, intoxicated with the wine of delusion; like one possessed by an evil [spirit], driven haplessly this way and that; like one bitten by a great snake, bitten by the attractions of sense (viṣaya); like [one groping his way] in thick darkness, blinded by passion; like the [victim of] a juggler's tricks, subject to deception (māyā); like [a man in] a dream, seeing a false appearance; like the inside of a reed, empty of pith; like an actor, wearing the same costume for only a moment; like painted scenery, falsely attractive.

'''And so it has been said:

> The things of sound and touch and sense that man
> Aspires to, are rather worthless nothingness (anartha):
> Clinging to them the individual self
>   Forgets his highest destiny (pada).

¶ 3. '''Now, the individual self has it in his power to counteract all this, and this is the formula: study of the Veda and its exegesis; performance of one's own [caste] duty; the regular fulfilment [of one's duties] in [each of the four] stages of life [prescribed for the three higher castes or classes]; this is the principle (vrata) behind the individual code of caste duty (svadharma). [All] other [rules] are as chaff. The one leads upwards, the other down. This is the individual code of caste duty laid down in the Vedas. No one who transgresses this code can claim to be fulfilling [his duty in the four] stages of life.

'''Some say that the man who fails to fulfil [his duty in the four] stages of life is a [holy] ascetic. This is scarcely appropriate. [However,] no man who does not practise asceticism can make much progress towards knowledge of the Self or perfection in works.

'''For [Maitri] also said:

> By ascetic practice Goodness,[1]
> By Goodness mind is won,
> By mind the Self, which gotten,
> No more return [to earth].

¶ 4. ''''Brahman is!' So said one who was conversant with Brahman-wisdom (vidyā).

''''This is the gate [which leads] to Brahman!' So said one who, by mortifying himself, had destroyed evil [in himself].

[1] The highest of the 'constituents' of Nature: or, 'virtue'.

"'Oṁ, [this is] Brahman's greatness!' So said one, well trained (*su-yukta*), ceaselessly meditating.

"'Hence, by wisdom—by mortification of self—and by meditation—Brahman can be conceived of. Whoso knows this and reveres Brahman in this threefold way, he, surpassing Brahman,[1] will go [yet further], he [will surpass] the gods in the realm of divinity (*adhidaivatva*) and attain to a bliss (*sukha*), unchanging and unlimited, beyond [all] ill.

"'So when the charioteer [2] is freed from [all those encumbrances] that filled him and held him down, then does he attain to union (*sāyojya*) with the Self."

¶ 5. 'They then said: "Master, how well dost thou salute Him (*abhivādin*)! How well dost thou salute Him! We have stored up in our minds [all that thou hast said] just as thou didst say it. Here is another question: [we pray thee] answer it.

"'Fire, wind, the sun, time, the breath of life, food,—Brahmā, Rudra, Vishnu: some meditate on one, some on another. Which is the best? Tell us that."

'To them he replied:

¶ 6. "'These indeed are the most exalted forms (*tanu*) of Brahman all-highest, immortal, and incorporeal. To whichever [of these forms] one is attached in this world, in the world of that [particular form of Brahman] will he take his pleasure (*pratimud-*). So said he. For Brahman is, surely, the whole universe.

"'On these most exalted forms of His one should meditate and one should praise them; then discard them! In their company one moves higher and higher in [different] states of being (*loka*). Then at the universal dissolution he comes to the Unity of the Person,—yes, of the Person."'

V

¶ 1. 'Now [we come to] Kutsyāyana's hymn of praise:

> Thou art Brahmā, Thou Vishnu,
> Thou Rudra, Thou Prajāpati:
> Thou Agni, Varuna, Vāyu,
> Thou Indra, Thou the Moon:
> Thou food, Thou Yama, Thou the Earth,
> Thou All, Thou the Unfallen (*acyuta*)!
>
> For thine own sake, for Nature's sake
> The many subsist in Thee:
> O Lord of All, all hail to Thee,

---

[1] Meaning probably 'the Veda'.   [2] *See* II. 6.

> O Self of All, all works (*karma*) enacting!
> Savouring all, all life art Thou,
> Lord of all sport (*krīḍā*) and [all] delight (*rati*)!
>
> All hail to Thee, thy Self at peace,
> All hail to Thee, most hidden mystery,
> Unthinkable, incommensurable,
> Without beginning, without end!

¶ 2. 'In the beginning this [world] was just [the "constituent" of] Darkness, one: and that must have been within the All-Highest. Stirred into motion by the All-Highest it lost its uniformity (*viśamatvam prayāti*). The form [that emerged therefrom] is [the "constituent"] Passion. Passion, again, when stirred into motion, lost its uniformity. That [produced] the form of [the "constituent"] Goodness. Goodness, again, when stirred into motion, flowed forth as savour (*rasa*, "essence"). This part which is pure consciousness, reflecting the [All-Highest] Person [Himself],[1] is the "knower of the field";[2] and its subtle body is made up of[3] conception, will and self-consciousness: it is Prajāpati under the name of "common to all men". These forms have previously been mentioned.[4]

'Now, you students of sacred knowledge (*brahmacārin*), that part of Him which is appropriated to Darkness is none other than Rudra; that part of Him which is appropriated to Passion is none other than Brahmā; while that part of Him which is appropriated to Goodness is none other than Vishnu. So this One became a Trinity (*tridhā*); he came to be eightfold, elevenfold, twelvefold, in numberless forms; and because He "came to be" (*ud-bhūta*), He [Himself became] a contingent being (*bhūta*), entered into contingent beings, and moves [among them]. He became the king of [all] contingent beings. Hence He is the Self both within and without,—both within and without.'

VI

¶ 1. '[The All-Highest Self] sustains [him]self in two modes,—as this breath of life (in the microcosm) and as that sun up there (in the macrocosm). Likewise, he has these two paths,—an inner one and an outer one; both return [to their point of departure] in a day and a night. The sun up there is [his] external self, the breath of life [down here] is [his] internal (innermost) self. Hence the way (*gati*) of the internal self is analogous to the way of the external self. For this too did [Maitri] say:

'"Every man who has [right] knowledge, who has rid himself of

---

[1] Or, 'to be found in every person'.   [2] *See* p. 303.
[3] Or, 'it has the marks of'.   [4] *See* II. 5.

evil, who keeps an eye upon his eye [and the other senses], who
has purified his mind, whose goal and ground (*niṣṭhā*) is That
(Brahman), and whose eyes are turned inward,—[that man is]
He (the Self)."

'The way of the external self is analogous to the way of the
internal self. For this too did [Maitri] say:

'"The golden Person in the sun who surveys this [world] from
his golden throne (*avastha*), he it is who dwells within the lotus
of the heart, consuming food."

¶ 2. 'Now, he who dwells within the lotus of the heart, consuming food, is none other than that invisible solar fire that
dwells in heaven, known as time, devouring all contingent beings
as its food.'

'What is the lotus, and what is it made of?'

'That lotus is none other than space. The four points of the
compass and the four intermediate points make up its leaves.

'These two, the breath of life and the sun, go to meet each other:
they should be revered with the syllable "Oṁ", with ejaculatory
prayers (*vyāhṛti*), and with the Sāvitrī prayer.

¶ 3. 'There are two forms of Brahman,—the formed and the
unformed. The formed is unreal (*a-satya*), the unformed is real:
that is Brahman, that is light, and light is the sun. [The syllable]
Oṁ came to be the self of this [sun]. It (the sun) divided [it]self
threefold; so too Oṁ is [made up] of three elements ($A + U + M$).
By these is the whole universe woven, warp and woof, within
Him (the Highest Self).[1] For this too did [Maitri] say:

'"Meditate on the sun as Oṁ, integrating [your]self the while."

¶ 4. ... [four lines omitted] ... 'For this too did [Maitri] said:

'"The three-footed Brahman has its roots above; [2] its boughs
are space, wind, fire, water, earth and much besides. This
Brahman has the name of 'the Lone (*eka*) Fig tree'. Its is that
glory (*tejas*) which is in the sun up there, and [Its] this [glory] of
the syllable Oṁ. Hence should one revere It with [this syllable]
Oṁ unceasingly, It (the sun) alone can awaken it (the syllable
Oṁ?)."

'For this too did [Maitri] say:

> "Surely this syllable is holy,
>   Surely this syllable is all-high (*para*),
> Whoso shall know this syllable,
> What he desires is his!"

¶ 5. 'Now [this] too has been said elsewhere:
[The syllable] Oṁ (i.e. $A + U + M$) is the sound-form of this
[Self].
Female, male and neuter: this is his sex[-form].

---

[1] Reading *asminn iti* for *asmīti*.   [2] Cf. pp. 181, 309.

Fire, wind and sun: this is his light[-form].

Brahmā, Rudra and Vishnu: this is his [form of] sovereignty.

The householder's fire, the fire for the ancestors and the fire for the gods: this is his mouth[-form].

Rig-Veda, Yajur-Veda and Sāma-Veda: this is his knowledge [-form] (*vijñāna*).

Bhūr, bhuvas, suvar: this is his [form of] world conditions.

Past, present and future: this is his time[-form].

Breath, fire and sun: this is his heat[-form].

Food, water and the moon: this is his growth[-form].

Intellect (*buddhi*), mind and the ego: this is his thought[-form].

In-breath, out-breath and diffused breath: this is his breath [-form].

By saying 'Oṁ' [all] these are praised, honoured and acquired. For this too did [Maitri] say:

'"This, Satyakāma, is the higher and the lower Brahman,— this syllable Oṁ."'

[Section 6 and most of section 7 are omitted.]

¶ 7. . . . 'This too did [Maitri] say:

'"Where knowledge (*vijñāna*) is of a dual nature (as between subject and object), then the self hears, sees, smells, tastes and feels: it knows everything. [But] where knowledge is not of a dual nature, it transcends cause, effect and action (*karma*) [of any kind], [it is] beyond speech, nothing can be likened to it, one cannot tell of it."'

"What is it then?"

"Impossible to say."'

[Section 8 (which is substantially the same as VII. 7) and section 9 are omitted.]

¶ 10. 'Now there is something else that should be known. [One line omitted] . . . The conscious Person (i.e. spirit) resides within material Nature (*pradhāna*): he is the eater (*bhoktṛ*) and eats (*bhuj-*) the food [supplied] by material Nature (*prakṛti*). For the individual self is food for him, material Nature being its maker (*kartṛ*).[1] This means that the three constituents of Nature are what is eaten [and experienced], while the eater [and experiencer] is the Person who resides within it.

[The remainder of section 10 is omitted.]

¶ 11. 'Food is indeed the highest form of the Self: for the breath of life is made up of food. Now, if one does not eat, one cannot think, hear, feel, see, speak, smell or taste, and so one loses one's vital breaths (i.e. dies). So [Maitri] said: "If one does eat, one has an ample supply of the breath of life and is able to think, hear, feel, speak, taste, smell and see." For thus too did he say:

---

[1] Or, 'the agent on its behalf'.

"From food indeed do creatures come to birth,
Whatever [creatures] dwell on earth.
Then again by food they live,
And again pass into it in the end." [1]

¶ 12. 'Now [this] too has been said elsewhere: All these beings
busily set out every day in their eager desire to get food. The sun
[itself] obtains food through its rays, and through this [food] it
gives out heat. Refreshed by food these living creatures (*prāṇa*)
digest it, and it is by [absorbing] food that fire blazes forth.
Because he craved for food Brahman [2] fashioned this universe.
Hence one should revere the Self as food. Thus too did [Maitri]
say:

"From food do creatures come to birth,
Once born by food they grow:
Eaten it eats [all] beings,
Hence it is known as food (*an-na*, eatable)." [3]

¶ 13. 'Now, [this] too has been said elsewhere: The form of the
Lord Vishnu known as "supporter of all" is nothing less than
food. The breath of life is the sap (*rasa*, essence) of food; mind, of
life; the understanding (*vijñāna*), of mind; bliss, of the understanding. The man who knows this will come to possess food, the
breath of life, mind, understanding and bliss; knowing this, he
will eat the food of as many beings as eat food here [on earth],
for he will indwell them:

Food overcomes(?) decay,
Is full of charm, they say:
Food is the breath of life in beasts;
Food is the foremost, food the healer:
Such is the tradition handed down.

¶ 14. 'Now, [this] too has been said elsewhere: Food is the
origin (*yoni*) of this whole universe. The origin of food is time, and
of time the sun. The form of time is the year characterized by the
twelve [months] and made up from seconds and other units of
time.... [Several lines are omitted]. ... For thus too did [Maitri]
say:

"However many divisions of time there be,
Through all of them he moves [, the sun]."

'Who reveres Brahman as time, from him time (i.e. death)
withdraws to a very great distance. For thus too did [Maitri] say:

---

[1] *See* p. 138.   [2] Or, 'Brahmā'.   [3] *See* p. 138.

> "From Time do creatures, flowing, issue,
> From Time they grow and prosper,
> In Time they reach their home [in death]:
> Time is formless, [Time] has form!"

¶ 15. 'There are, certainly, two forms of Brahman,—time and the timeless. That which existed before the sun is the timeless; it cannot be divided into parts. That which begins with the sun, however, is time. And the form of this [time] which has parts is the year. From the year [all] these creatures are born; through the year, once born, they grow, in the year they find their home [in death].[1] So it is that the year is Prajāpati, time, food, the nest of Brahman, and the Self. For thus too did [Maitri] say:

> "All beings Time digests [2]
>   In the Great Self (mahātman).
> In whom or what is Time digested?
>   Who knows this, knows the Veda."

¶ 16. 'This [form of time] is embodied; [it is] the royal ocean in which all creatures [have their being]. In it stands this [sun] called Savitri (the Begetter) from which the moon, stars, planets, the year and other [measurements of time] are generated. From these the whole universe [proceeds]; and whatever there is of good and evil here in [this] world [proceeds] from them [too]. So it is that Brahman has the sun as its self (= body?).[3] One should revere the sun as being synonymous with time. Some say, "Brahman is the sun". For thus too did [Maitri] say:

> "Offerer, recipient, oblation, sacred formula,
>   Sacrifice, Vishnu, Prajāpati,
> The Lord is everyone who exists, the Witness
>   Who shines in the circle [of the sun] up there."

¶ 17. 'In the beginning this [world] was Brahman, the One unbounded,—unbounded to the east, unbounded to the south, unbounded to the west, unbounded to the north, [unbounded] above and below, unbounded in every direction. East and west, north and south, do not enter into his [mode of] conception, nor yet do across, above and below.

'Inconceivable is this All-Highest Self, uncircumscribed, unborn, beyond all logic and discursive thought, unthinkable! Space is his self (= body?); and He, the One, alone remains awake when all things fall to ruin. Out of this space he causes all that consists of thought alone to awaken. By this He thinks [into existence] this [material world] and into Him it disappears.[4]

---

[1] The word used of the sun setting.   [2] Lit. 'cooks'.
[3] Or, 'Brahman is the self of the sun'.
[4] A word used of the sun setting.

'His is that gleaming form that gives heat in the sun up there, [his] the glow of the smokeless fire in its many shimmering forms, [his] too that fire in the stomach which digests food. For thus too did [Maitri] say:

'"He who is in the fire here, He who is in the heart [within], and He who is in the sun up there, He is One. And he who knows this comes to the oneness of the One."'

¶ 18. 'The practical method [for coming to this oneness consists in]: breath-control, withdrawal [of the senses from their objects], meditation (*dhyāna*), concentration (*dhāraṇā*), analytic discrimination (*tarka*), and "enstasy" (*samādhi*): this is known as the sixfold Yoga. [It is] by this [Yoga that]:

> When a seer beholds the Maker, Lord,
> The Person golden-hued, whose womb is Brahman,[1]
> He knows: transcending (*vihāya*) good and evil,
> He makes all one in That which never changes.

'For thus too did [Maitri] say:

> "As on a burning mountain beasts and birds
>   Make not their home,
> So in men who Brahman know, no imperfection
>   Can find a resting-place."

¶ 19. 'Now, [this] too has been said elsewhere: When a wise man has withdrawn the mind from what is external, and breath [-control] (*prāṇa*) has caused the objects of sense to disappear,[2] then let him stand [mentally] still, forming no conceptions.

'Since the empirical self (*jīva*) called the 'breath of life' (*prāṇa*) arose here [on this earth] from what is other than the breath of life (*a-prāṇa*), so should this empirical self (*prāṇa*) concentrate his [controlled] breathing on [the so-called] fourth state [which is beyond the waking state, dream and dreamless sleep].[3]

> What is not thought in the midst of thought abiding,
> Unthinkable, the highest mystery—
> There fix thy thought, [there] that subtle body (*liṅga*)
> Which has nothing to support it.

¶ 20. 'Now, [this] too has been said elsewhere: There is a higher [form of] concentration than this. By pressing the tip of the tongue against the palate, and by stopping voice, mind and breath, one may see Brahman by discriminating [the eternal from the contingent] (*tarka*). When of one's own accord (*ātmanā*) one sees the Self which is more minute than the minute shining forth

---

[1] Or, 'womb (origin) of Brahman'. But see *Bhagavad-Gītā*, XIV. iii.
[2] Lit. 'made them lie down'.
[3] p. 201.

because the [discursive] mind has been laid to rest (*kṣaya*),[1] then, having seen [this] Self of one's own accord, one becomes selfless (*nirātman*); and because of this selflessness [such a man] must be regarded as being beyond the categories of number and of cause [and effect] (*asāṁkhyo 'yoniḥ*), [which is] the mark of spiritual freedom (*mokṣa*). This is the highest mystery. For thus too did [Maitri] say:

> "By stilling (*prasāda*) thought one kills
> Both good and evil deeds;
> Self-stilled, abiding in the Self,
> One wins unalterable happiness (*sukha*)."

¶ 21. 'Now, [this] too has been said elsewhere: There is a channel called *Sushumnā*, leading upward, conveying the breath of life and piercing through into the palate. By means of this [channel] being integrated (*yukta*) with the breath, [the syllable] Oṁ and the mind, [the individual self] ascends aloft. By turning the tip of the tongue back against the palate and by integrating (*saṁyuj-*) [the experience of] the senses, wide expanse (*mahiman*) looks down on wide expanse. Then he moves towards selflessness; and because of this selflessness he experiences neither pleasure (*sukha*) nor pain: he attains to absolute isolation (*kevalatva*). For thus too did [Maitri] say:

> "Let another stop and still the breath
> That has been checked before, and then,
> Crossing the further shore (*pāra*), at last
> By the boundless (*a-pāra*) integrate it in the head."

¶ 22. 'Now, [this] too has been said elsewhere: There are two Brahmans to be meditated on,—[that which is] sound and the soundless. Now, the soundless one can be revealed by [the one that is] sound. In this case the sound is Oṁ. Ascending by this one ends up in the soundless. So [Maitri] said: "This is the Way, this the Immortal, this is union (*sāyujyatva*), this is the cessation [of becoming] (*nirvṛtatva*)."

'So too, just as a spider, climbing upwards on a thread, wins through to unencumbered space, so too does the man of meditation, climbing upwards on [the thread of the syllable] Oṁ, win through to self-dependence (*svātantrya*).

'Other students of [Brahman as] sound [put it] differently. By closing their ears with their thumbs they hear the sound of the space within the heart. Seven similes are used to illustrate this: it is like [the sound of] rivers, or a bell, or a brazen [vessel], or a wheel, or the croaking of frogs, or rain, or as one speaks in a

---

[1] Lit. 'destroyed'.

windless place. Transcending [all] distinguishing marks they find their home [1] in the highest, soundless, unmanifest Brahman. There they have no separate characteristics (*dharma*), no separate marks to distinguish one from another like the various pollens that [the bee] transmutes into honey (p. 109). For thus too did [Maitri] say:

> "Two Brahmans there are which must be known,
> > Brahman as sound, and [Brahman] beyond (*para*);
> Once deeply versed in Brahman as sound,
> > A man goes on to Brahman beyond."

¶ 23. 'Now, [this] too has been said elsewhere: [Brahman as] sound is the syllable Oṁ. Its summit is silent (*śānta*), soundless, free from fear and sorrow, blissful, well content, stable, motion-less, immortal, unfailing, enduring: Vishnu is Its name, meaning that It is above and beyond everything. Both should be revered. For thus too did [Maitri] say:

> "The higher and the lower God
> > Whose name is Oṁ,
> Soundless and void of contingency (*śūnyabhūta*) [2]
> > Fix Him firmly in thy head!"

¶ 24. 'Now, [this] too has been said elsewhere: The body is a bow, Oṁ the arrow, the mind its tip, darkness the target. Pierce the darkness, and thou wilt come to That which is not shrouded in darkness. Pierce That [again], and thou wilt see as it were a wheel of sparks, throbbing, of the colour of the sun, mighty in power and vigour (*ūrjasvat*),—Brahman beyond the darkness, shining in the sun up there, [shining] in the moon and lightning. And seeing Him, thou wilt draw nigh to immortality. For thus too did [Maitri] say:

> "If one's meditation on the highest truth (*tattva*)
> > Is vitiated by other goals besides,
> Then one's understanding (*vijñāna*) of the Undifferentiated
> > Becomes lost in difference.

> But once all things of mind dissolve, [one reaches]
> > The joy (*sukha*) which sees the Self [alone]: [3]
> That is Brahman, the immortal, pure!
> That is the Way! [4] That the [ideal] world!"

¶ 25. 'Now, [this] too has been said elsewhere: When a man's senses are withdrawn as [they are] when one is drowsy, when his

---

[1] Or, 'disappear', a word used of the setting of the sun.
[2] Or, 'having become empty.'
[3] Or, 'whose witness is the Self'.   [4] Or, 'goal'.

thought is crystal clear as in sleep, when, constrained by nothing, he sees in the vacuum (*bila*) of sense the shining Guide whose name is Oṁ who knows not sleep or age or death or sorrow, then does he too become a [1] shining guide whose name is Oṁ who knows not sleep or age or death or sorrow. For thus too did [Maitri] say:

> "Because one integrates (*yuj-*) the breath (*prāṇa*),
> [The syllable] Oṁ and all things manifold,
> Or because they are [themselves already] integrated,
> [This spiritual exercise] is known as *Yoga*,—integration.

>> Oneness of breath and mind
>>   And [all] the senses,
> Abandonment of all emotive states (*bhāva*),—
>   This is called *Yoga*,—integration."'

¶ 26. 'Now, [this] too has been said elsewhere: Just as a fowler catches water-fowl in a net and offers them in sacrifice in the fire of his stomach, so does [the Yogin] catch hold of the senses (*prāṇa*) with [the syllable] Oṁ and offer them in sacrifice to that Fire which knows no ill.

'Again, [it is like] a heated cauldron; for just as butter bursts into flame when the cauldron comes into contact with [burning] grass or wood, so too does that [entity] called 'other than the breath of life' (*a-prāṇa*) burst into flame when it comes into contact with the breath of life.[2] What bursts into flame is a form of Brahman, the highest step [3] of Vishnu, the "rudrahood" of Rudra. Dividing [it]self into innumerable parts, It fills [all] these worlds. For thus too did [Maitri] say:

> "As sparks from fire,
>   As rays from the sun,
> So too do the breath of life and every other [being]
>   Issue from It in order due."'

[Section 27 is omitted.]

¶ 28. 'Now, [this] too has been said elsewhere: Passing beyond the elements, the senses and their objects, then seizing the bow whose string is the life of a wandering friar and whose arch is steadfastness, [armed] with an arrow made of unpretentiousness, let a man strike down the primeval doorkeeper of Brahman.[4] [This doorkeeper] is the lord of self-conceit; his crown is confusion, his earrings are craving and envy, his staff is sluggishness, drunkenness and wickedness. Seizing his bow whose string is anger and whose arch is greed, he slays these creatures with the

---

[1] Or, 'the'.   [2] Or, 'breaths (senses)'.
[3] Or, 'place, stage'. *See* p. 4.   [4] i.e. the ego.

arrow of desire. Let [this man] slay him, and then let him [embark] on the boat of Oṁ and cross to the farther side of the space within the heart; then, as [this] space within the heart gradually reveals itself, let him enter the hall of Brahman as a miner in search of precious metals enters a mine. Then let him rip open the fourfold sheath of Brahman [1] with [the knife of] his spiritual director's teaching. Then will he stand [revealed] in his own magnificence (*mahiman*) as pure and purified, void and tranquil, other than the breath of life (*a-prāṇa*) and selfless, infinite and indefectible (*akṣaya*), stable and eternal, unborn and self-dependent. Then, seeing [himself] abiding in his own magnificence, he will look down on the wheel of the round of birth and death (*saṁsāra*) as upon a rolling [chariot-]wheel. For thus too did [Maitri] say:

> "If for six months an embodied soul (*dehin*)
> Is integrated and [from *saṁsāra*] always freed (*mukta*),
> Then will he know *Yoga*,—integration,
> The perfect, supreme and infinite mystery.

> The embodied soul, with fuel still burning,
> Transfixed by Passion and Darkness' [darts],
> Attached to sons and wife and home,
> Can never win [this integration],—never!'"

¶ 29. So spake Śākāyanya from the depths of his heart. Then he bowed to [Brihadratha and said]: 'By this Brahman-wisdom, O king, [these] sons of Prajāpati climbed the path of Brahman. By the practice of Yoga a man obtains contentment, ability to bear with [all] dualities, and tranquillity.'

This most secret mystery should not be told to one who is not a son or a pupil or to one who is unquiet, but it may be given to one who is solely devoted (*bhakta*) [to it] and who possesses all the virtues (*guṇa*).

¶ 30. 'Oṁ: let a man be clean and in a clean place; let him be firm in virtue (*sattva*); let him study Being, speak of Being, meditate on Being, sacrifice to Being. Then, relapsed into Brahman which [Itself] is Being and longs for the real (*satya*), [behold!] he is another! And his reward is this: his fetters are cut away, he has no [idle] hopes, fears others as little as he fears himself, desires nothing; he has stridden on to a joy (*sukha*) unlimited that can never pass away: [therein] he abiding stands.

'To be rid of desire is most certainly like the most precious sample from the choicest treasure. For the man who is compounded of every [kind of] desire, who has the marks of will

[1] *See* pp. 137–40.

(*adhyavasāya*), conception (*saṁkalpa*) and [individual] self-consciousness (*abhimāna*), is bound. The man who is the opposite of this is free (*mukta*).

'On this subject [there are] some [who] say: As a result of the differentiation of Nature [difference in] quality [arises, and this] leads to the enslavement of the self by the will. For once the will is destroyed—[and the will itself] is an imperfection (*doṣa*),—[then there is] freedom (*mokṣa*).

'For by the mind one sees, by the mind one hears. Desire, conception, doubt, faith, infidelity, tenacity (*dhṛti*) and the lack of it, modesty, thought (*dhī*) and fear,—all this indeed is mind.

'Swept away by the currents of Nature's constituents, made turbid by them, unstable, fickle, mutilated, full of longing, restless, a man reaches [the stage of individual] self-consciousness. "This I am, this is mine," he thinks, and so of his own accord (*ātmanā*) he binds [him]self as a bird [entangled] in a net. Hence the man who has the marks of will, conception and [individual] self-consciousness is bound: the man who is the opposite of this is free (*mukta*). Therefore let a man remain without will, without conceptions, without [individual] self-consciousness: this is the sign of [his spiritual] liberation (*mokṣa*). This is the path [that leads] to Brahman here; this is the hole in the door through which one will reach the farther shore beyond the darkness. For herein all desires are concentrated (*samāhita*). On this point there is the following quotation:

> When the five senses (*jñāna*) and the mind
>   Are stilled,
> When intellect (*buddhi*) is motionless,
> That, they say, is the highest Way.'[1]

So spake Śākāyanya from the depths of his heart. Then he bowed to [Brihadratha]. Marut [that is, Brihadratha], paying him due honour, his aim achieved, departed by the northern way, for here [on earth] there is no way [of reaching Brahman] by devious paths. This is the [sole] path to Brahman here. Breaking through the door of the sun, he ascended on high. On this point there is the following quotation:

> Unending are the rays of him
> Who, like a lamp, indwells the heart,—
> White, black and brown,
> Yellow, blue, light red.
>
> One of them stands on high:
> This splits apart the circle of the sun,
> Strides right beyond the world of Brahmā;
> Thereby men tread the highest Way.[1]

[1] Or, 'goal'.

A hundred other rays has he
　　Established too on high:
By them men journey to the abodes
　　Of the [various] kinds of gods.

Many and manifold are his rays,
　　Giving a feeble light below;
Helpless the man who by their influence
Wanders on earth to exhaust [the residue of his] works (*karma*).

Hence [our] blessed Lord (*bhagavat*), the sun up there, is the cause of emanation, of heaven and of final emancipation (*apavarga*).

¶ 31. 'What is the essence (*ātmaka*) of these senses [that makes] them burst into activity? And who is it that makes it his business to restrain them?' So has it been asked.

The answer is: 'They are of the essence of the self (*ātman*), for [it is] the self [who] makes it his business to restrain them. There are nymphs (i.e. objects of sense) to be recognized and [the senses] known as "rays": with [these] five rays [the self] consumes objects of sense.'

'Which self?'

'He who has been described as the "pure and purified, void and tranquil"[1] and by similar epithets. He is to be comprehended by his own characteristic marks (*liṅga*).'

Some say that the characteristic mark of Him who has no characteristic mark is like the heat which inheres (*āviṣṭa*) in fire or the extremely faint (*śiva*) taste in water. Others say that [this mark] is speech, hearing, sight, mind, and breath; others, intellect (*buddhi*), perdurance (*dhṛti*), memory and wisdom (*prajñā*). Now, these are [the characteristic marks] of Him just as sprouts are of seed, or as smoke, light and sparks are of fire. On this point there is the following quotation:

As sparks from fire,
　　As rays from the sun,
So too does the breath of life and every other [being]
　　Issue from It in order due.

¶ 32. From This indeed do all living things (*prāṇa*), all worlds, all the Vedas, all the gods and all contingent beings issue forth, [though it abides ever] in [it]self. Its secret name (*upaniṣad*) is the 'Real of the real'.

Now, just as clouds of smoke issue separately from a fire laid with damp wood, so too this [whole world] is breathed forth from that great Being (*bhūta*),—the Rig-Veda, the Yajur-Veda, the

---

[1] *See* ¶ 28, p. 236.

Sāma-Veda, the Atharva-Veda, [the hymns of the] Angirases, the collections of stories, the ancient tales, wisdom, the secret doctrines, verses, aphorisms, commentaries and commentaries on commentaries.[1]

All these beings are its own.

[Section 33 and part of section 34 are omitted.]

¶ 34. As fire whose fuel's exhausted
     Is extinguished at its source,
     So thought for lack of thinking-matter (vṛtti)
     Is extinguished at its source.

     [The thought] of a mind in search of [only what is]
         real
     Is extinguished at its source;
     [The thoughts] of one confused by the senses' objects
     Are false,—obedient to the tyranny of works!

     For the round of birth and death is thought [out by
         oneself];
     Go to, then, cleanse [thy thoughts]:
     As is thy thought, so dost thou become;
     This is an everlasting mystery.

     For by quietening down (prasāda) his thoughts a man
     Destroys [all] actions (karma), fair or foul;
     With self serene, in self abiding,
     He attains the all-highest joy (sukha).

     If as firmly as a creature's thought is fixed
     On what lays open to the senses,
     If it were thus on Brahman [fixed],
     Who would be left from bondage not set free?

     Two sorts of mind there are, they say,
        One pure, and one impure:
     Impure—by mingling with desire,—
     Of desire quite emptied—pure.

     When, by making mind all motionless,
        Unclinging, undistracted,
     A man attains to mindlessness,
     Then is that the highest state (pada).

     Confine the mind within the heart
        Until it is destroyed:
     This is both wisdom and release;
     All else is bookish wordiness!

[1] See p. 46.

His mind clean washed of stain through enstasy,
In Self absorbed,—how great the joy of such!
    Language cannot describe it,
Oneself must grasp it with an inward faculty!

Water in water, fire in fire,
Sky in sky,—how should one discern it?
Let the mind thus disappear,
For so a man is freed (*parimuc-*)!

The mind itself in man is the cause
    Of bondage and release;
Attached to objects it brings bondage to itself;
Absence of object—that is called release!

[The last two lines of section 34 are omitted.]

¶ 35. Homage to the fire that dwells on earth, mindful of the
world! On this worshipper the world bestow!
    Homage to the wind that dwells in the atmosphere, mindful of
the world! On this worshipper the world bestow!
    Homage to the sun that dwells in heaven, mindful of the
world! On this worshipper the world bestow!
    Homage to Brahman that dwells in all, mindful of all! On this
worshipper all bestow!

The face of Truth (*satya*) is hidden
By the golden vessel [of the sun];
Reveal it [to me], Pūshan, [that I may come]
To Vishnu, whose law is Truth (*satyadharma*).

The Person who is in the sun up there, I indeed am He!

He whose law is Truth (i.e. Vishnu) is the very 'sun-ness' of the
sun. That is the sexless,[1]—pure and personal (*puruṣam*, neut.).
    It is only a fraction of the glory (*tejas*) that pervades the sky
that [shines forth] in the eye and fire as it [shines] in the middle of
the sun. This is Brahman, this the immortal, this the splendour
(*bharga*), this He whose law is Truth.
    It is only a fraction of the glory that pervades the sky that is
immortal in the middle of the sun,—for the moon (*soma*) too and
[all] living beings (*prāṇa*) are no more than its sprouts. This is
Brahman, this the immortal, this the splendour, this He whose
law is Truth.
    It is only a fraction of the glory that pervades the sky that
shines as the Yajur-Veda in the middle of the sun: Oṁ—water—
light—[sweet] savour—the immortal—Brahman—*bhūr*—*bhuvas*
—*suvar*—Oṁ!

―――――――――――
[1] Or, 'without characteristics'.

A swan, eight-footed,[1] pure,
Three strands possessing,[2] subtile, changeless,
To good and evil blind (? *dvidharmo 'ndam*), in glory
    flaming,
The All: who sees him [thus], he sees [indeed].

It is only a fraction of the glory that pervades the sky that,
rising up in the middle of the sun, becomes two rays.[3] This is He
who knows as One together (*savit*), He whose law is Truth, this
the Yajur-Veda, this ascetic practice,[4] this fire, this wind, this the
breath of life, this the waters, this the moon, this the brightly
pure, this the immortal, this the realm of Brahman, this the ocean
of light. In this indeed sacrificial priests dissolve like salt; for this
is Brahman's Unity: for therein are all desires compressed (*samāhita*). On this point there is this quotation:

As a candle stirred by a gentle breeze throbs [faintly],
So [too] does He who permeates the gods.
Who knows this, knows the One together, knows duality,
[Goes to] the One Abode (*dhāma*) from here, partaking of
    its essence (*ātmaka*).

Those too who ever and again rise up like drops of spray,
Like lightning's brilliance from the thundercloud in highest
    heaven,
May be likened to the matted hair of [fire] whose trail is
    black,
For they too perforce are grounded in the glory (*yaśas*) of
    the light.
[Sections 36–7 are omitted.]

¶ 38. He who offers the daily fire-sacrifice, cuts through the net
of greed. Hence, cutting out confusion, he no longer approves
of anger, meditating on [its close connection with] desire. Then,
ripping open the fourfold sheath of Brahman [5] [he goes on to] the
highest [realms of] space. There, indeed, he pierces the circles of
the sun, the moon, fire, and the 'constituent' of Goodness.
[Passing on] from there he, [now] pure [himself], beholds that
highest of all homes (*dhāma*) called Vishnu, who dwells within
the 'constituent' of Goodness, unmoved, immortal, unfailing,
permanent, united in will (*kāma*) with what is Real and [in
knowing] with omniscience, dependent on himself [alone], [pure]
Consciousness (*caitanya*), abiding in his own magnificence
(*mahiman*). On this point there is this quotation:

---

[1] i.e. the eight points of the compass'.
[2] i.e. the three 'constituents' of Nature.
[3] i.e. duality.   [4] Or, 'heat'.   [5] *See* pp. 137–40.

In the middle of the sun the moon is set,
  In the middle of the moon the fire;
In the middle of the fire is Goodness set,
In the middle of Goodness [God] unfallen and unfailing
  (*acyuta*)!

After meditating upon Him as being more minute than the
minute, as measuring no more than a span or the length of a
thumb within the body, he will then reach the all-highest state
(*paramatā*), in which all desires are compressed and concentrated
(*samāhita*). On this point there is the following quotation:

No greater than the thumb or a span within the body,
Twofold or threefold shining like a torch,
That is Brahman, praised as such,
[That] the Great God!—He entered [all] the worlds!
Oṁ. Homage to Brahman: [to Brahman] homage!

VII

[Sections 1 to 6: the first half of each section, which enumerates
different metres, hymns, chants, seasons, 'vital breaths', planets,
gods, etc., as being manifestations of the highest principle, is in
all cases omitted.]
¶ 1. . . . .
Unthinkable [is He], unformed, profound, concealed, faultless,
compact, impenetrably deep, devoid of attributes and beyond the
'constituents' of Nature (*nirguṇa*), pure, resplendent, the
experiencer of Nature's constituents (*guṇabhuj*), awe[-inspiring],
immutable, Yoga's Lord, omniscient, most generous (*magha*),
incommensurable, beginningless and endless, bountiful, unborn,
wise (*dhimat*), indescribable, all things emanating, the Self of all,
all things experiencing, Lord of all, more inward than what is
[most] inward in all things.
¶ 2. . . . .
Beginningless and endless [is He], uncircumscribed, unlimited, not to be used by others, dependent on himself [alone],
sexless,[1] unformed, endless in power, ordainer (*dhātṛ*),[2] resplendent.
¶ 3. . . . .
[He is] the highest of all homes (*dhāma*) called Vishnu, at
peace, soundless, without fear or sorrow, contented bliss, stable,
unmoved, immortal, unfailing, permanent.

---

[1] Or, 'without characteristics'.   [2] Or, 'creator'.

¶ 4. . . . .
Pure within and purified [is He], void, tranquil, other than the breath of life,[1] selfless, unending.

¶ 5. . . . .
[He is] called Oṁ, effulgent, unsleeping, ageless, deathless, unsorrowing Guide.

¶ 6. . . . .
[He is] the wise (*prājña*), prop [of the universe] (*vidharaṇa*), indwelling all, imperishable, pure, purified, resplendent, long-suffering, at peace.

¶ 7. For He indeed is the Self within the heart, more minute [than the minute], kindled like fire, possessing every form. His food is all this universe. On Him are these creatures woven.

He is the Self remote from evil, ageless, deathless, knowing neither sorrow nor doubt, untrammelled, conceiving of the Real, desiring the Real. He is the Lord Supreme, He the King of [all] contingent beings, He their protector, He the dam that holds apart.

For He is assuredly the Self, the Lord, Śambhu,[2] Bhava,[2] Rudra,[2] Prajāpati, all things emanating, the Golden Embryo,[3] Truth, the Breath of Life, the [exalted] Swan,[4] Ruler (*śāstṛ*),[5] unfailing and unfallen (*acyuta*), Vishnu, Nārāyaṇa.[6]

He who is in the fire down here, He who is in the heart within, and He who is in the sun up there,—He indeed is One.

To Thee who art [all] this, possessing every form, dwelling in true space, all hail!

[Sections 8–9, attacking false teachers, are omitted.]

¶ 10. The gods and the demons (*asura*), in their desire [to know] the Self, approached Brahmā. Greeting him respectfully, they said: 'Master, we wish [to know] the Self; [we pray thee,] tell us.'

[Brahmā,] after pondering the matter for a long time, thought to himself: 'These demons are [in search] of a self that is quite different from the real one.[7] And so [it is that] they were taught a very different doctrine. Deluded, they live out their lives in accordance with their attachments, destroying the raft [of salvation] and approving what is false. They see the false as true, as [one who watches] a juggler's tricks.'

Hence, what is set down in the Vedas, that [alone] is true. In accordance with what the Vedas say, wise men live out their lives. Therefore a Brāhman should not study what is not in the Vedas. This should be his aim.[8]

¶ 11. The all-highest glory (*tejas*) is of the same essence (*svarūpa*)

---

[1] Or, 'not possessing breath'.
[2] A name of Śiva.
[3] *See* p. 10.
[4] *See* VI. 35, p. 241.
[5] Or, 'teacher'.
[6] An incarnation of Vishnu.
[7] Reading *anyat[am]ātmāno*.
[8] Or, 'This would profit him'.

as that which is hidden within the [spiritual] firmament [of the heart]; and this has been revealed in three ways,—in fire, in the sun and in the breath of life.

Again, the syllable Oṁ is of the same essence as that which is hidden within the [spiritual] firmament [of the heart]. By [uttering] this [syllable] that [essence] wells up from the depths, rises aloft and breathes: it is a perpetual support for meditation on Brahman. When stirred into activity that [essence] can be likened to heat emitting light, or to the stirring up of smoke. In the [spiritual] firmament [of the heart it was] as one branch only; rising up it develops branch upon branch. It is as if one were to throw salt into water, or it is like heat in melted butter, or like the wide-ranging [thought] of a thinker.

On this point there is this quotation:

'Why is it said to be like lightning?' 'Because at the very moment of being released upwards it lights up the whole body in a flash. This is why one should revere this uncircumscribed glory by [uttering the syllable] Oṁ.'

The 'person' native to the eye
In the right eye situated
Is Indra; in the left eye his spouse
   Has made her home.

The meeting of the two
Is in the hollow of the heart:
In it a clot of blood
[Brings] vigour (*tejas*) to them both.

There is a channel rising from the heart
Right up to the eye where it is fixed;
This is a passage for them both,
Though one, in two divided.

The mind impels the body's fire,
The fire stirs up the wind:
Wind moving in the chest
Gives out a pleasing sound.

Stirred into action in the heart by [the heart's] ethereal fire
It's smaller than the small; in the throat it's double small;
On the tongue's tip triple small, this know;
When out it comes, it is the alphabet, they say!

Seeing death [the wise man] sees [it] not,
   Nor sickness nor yet sorrow;
But seeing All, he sees [it], and attains
   To All in every way.

He who sees with the [waking] eye, and he who roves in
    dream,
He who [dreamless] sleeps, and he who transcends the
    dreamless,—
These are the four states (*bheda*) of [mortal man]:
    Of these the greatest is the fourth.
In the three [first] a quarter of Brahman moves,
    Three quarters in the last.

For experiencing what is true and false
Twofold is the Great Self's nature,
Yes, twofold is the Great Self's nature.

The Bhagavad-Gītā

The Bhagavad-Gītā

I

Dhritarāshtra said:
§ 1. On the field of justice, the Kuru-field,
My men and the sons of Pāndu too
Stand massed together, intent on war.
What, Sanjaya, did they do?

Sanjaya said:
§ 2. Then did Duryodhana, the king,
Surveying the host of Pāndu's sons
Drawn up in ranks, approach
His teacher (Drona) saying:

§ 3. 'Teacher, behold this mighty host
Of Pāndu's sons
Drawn up by the son of Drupada,
Thine own disciple, wise and skilled.

§ 4. Here are men, brave and mighty archers,
Equals of Bhīma and Arjuna in [the art of] war,—
Yuyudhāna, Virāta,
And Drupada, the mighty charioteer,

§ 5. Dhrishtaketu, Cekitāna,
And Kāshī's valiant king,
Kurujit, Kuntibhoja,
And the Shibi's king, foremost of fighting men,

§ 6. High-mettled Yudhāmanyu
And valiant Uttamaujas,
Subhadrā's son and the sons of Draudapī,—
All of them mighty charioteers.

§ 7. Listen too, thou best of Brāhmans,
To [the list of] those outstanding on our side,
Leaders of my army.
Of these I speak to thee that thou mayst know.

§ 8. Thyself, Bhīshma, and Karna too,
And Kripa, victor in the fight,
Ashvatthāman and Vikarna,
And Somadatta's son as well.

§ 9. Many another hero too
Will risk his life for me.
Various are their arms and weapons,
And all of them are skilled at war.

§ 10. Imperfect are those our forces
    Which Bhīshma guards,
But perfect these their forces
    Under [great] Bhīma's care.

§ 11. So stand firm in all your ranks
Each in his appointed place;
Guard Bhīshma above all others,
    Every one of you!'

§ 12. [And] (Bhīshma,) the aged grandsire of the Kuru clan,
    To give him cheer,
Cried out with a loud cry like lion's roar
And undaunted blew his conch.

§ 13. Then conches, cymbals, drums,
    Tabors and kettledrums,
Burst into sudden sound;
Tumultuous was the din.

§ 14. Then too did (Krishna,) Madhu's son and Pāndu's [third-]
    born (Arjuna,)
Standing erect on their great chariot
    Yoked to [snow-]white steeds,
Their godly conches loudly blow.

§ 15. [The conch called] Panchajanya did Krishna blow,
[The conch called] Devadatta Arjuna;
The mighty conch [called] Paundra
Blew Bhīma of dreadful deeds.

§ 16. [The conch called] Anantavijaya
Blew Kuntī's son, Yudhishthira, the king:
Sughosha and Manipushpaka
[Blew] Nakula and Sahadeva.

§ 17. And Kāshī's king, archer supreme,
And Shikandin, the great charioteer,
Dhrishtadyumna, Virāta too,
And unconquered Sātyaki,

§ 18. Drupada and the sons of Draupadī,
And Subhadrā's strong-armed son,
    Blew each his conch
[Resounding] from every side.

§ 19. At the din [they made] the hearts
Of Dhristarāshtra's sons were rent:
    And heaven and earth it made
    Tumultuously resound.

§ 20. Then (Arjuna,) whose banner is an ape,
    Gazed upon the serried ranks
Of Dhritarāshtra's sons. The clash of arms
Began. He lifted up his bow.

§ 21.   To Krishna then
    These words he spake:
'Halt thou my chariot [here]
Between the armies twain,

§ 22. That I may see these men drawn up,
    Spoiling for the fight,
    [That I may see] with whom I must do battle
In this enterprise of war.

§ 23. I see them [now], intent on strife,
    Assembled here;
All eager they to please by waging war
[Old] Dhritarāshtra's baleful son.'

§ 24. Thus Arjuna: and Krishna,
    Hearkening to his words,
Brought that splendid chariot to a halt
    Between the armies twain.

§ 25. And there in front of them Bhīshma and Drona stood
    And all the [assembled] kings;
And Krishna said: 'Arjuna, behold
    These Kurus gathered [here].'

§ 26.   And Arjuna beheld
    Fathers, grandsires,
Venerable teachers, uncles, brothers, sons,
    Grandsons and comrades,

§ 27. Fathers-in-law and friends
Standing there in either host.
And the son of Kuntī, seeing them,
All his kinsmen thus arrayed,

§ 28. Was filled with deep compassion
And, desponding, spake these words:
'Krishna, when these mine own folk I see
Standing [before me], spoiling for the fight,

§ 29. My limbs give way [beneath me],
My mouth dries up, and trembling
Takes hold upon my frame:
My body's hairs stand up [in dread].

§ 30. [My bow,] Gāndīva, slips from my hand,
My very skin is all ablaze;
I cannot stand, my mind
Seems to wander [all distraught].

§ 31. And portents too I see
Boding naught but ill.
Should I strike down in battle mine own folk,
    No good therein see I.

§ 32. Krishna, I hanker not for victory,
Nor for the kingdom, nor yet for things of pleasure.
What use to us a kingdom, friend,
What use enjoyment or life [itself]?

§ 33. Those for whose sake we covet
Kingdom, delights and things of pleasure,
Here stand they, arrayed for battle,
Surrendering both wealth and life.

§ 34. They are our venerable teachers, fathers, sons,
They too our grandsires, uncles,
Fathers-in-law, grandsons,
Brothers-in-law, kinsmen all;

§ 35. These would I nowise slay
Though they slay [me], my friend,
Not for dominion over the three [wide] worlds,
How much less for [this paltry] earth.

§ 36. And should we slaughter Dhritarāshtra's sons,
Krishna, what sweetness then is ours?
Evil, and only evil, would come to dwell with us,
Should we slay them, hate us as they may.

§ 37. Therefore have we no right to kill
The sons of Dhritarāshtra, our own kinsmen [as they are].
Should we lay low our own folk, Krishna,
How could we find any joy?

§ 38. And even if, bereft of sense by greed,
    They cannot see
That to ruin a family is wickedness (doṣa)
And to break one's word [1] a crime,

----
[1] Or, 'injury to a friend'.

§ 39. How should we not be wise enough
To turn aside from this evil thing?
For the annihilation of a family
We know full well is wickedness.

§ 40. Annihilate a family, and with it
Collapse the eternal laws that rule the family.
Once law's destroyed, then lawlessness
Overwhelms all [we know as] family.

§ 41. With lawlessness triumphant, Krishna,
The family's [chaste] women are debauched;
From debauchery of the women [too]
Confusion of caste is born.

§ 42. Yes, [caste-]confusion leads to hell—
[The hell prepared] for those who wreck
The family and for the family [so wrecked].
So too their ancestors fall down [to hell],
Cheated of their offerings of food and drink.

§ 43. These evil ways of men who wreck the family,
[These evil ways] that bring on caste-confusion,
[These are the ways] that bring caste-law to naught
    And the eternal family laws.

§ 44. A sure abode in hell there is
For men who bring to naught
The laws that rule the family:
So, Krishna, have we heard.

§ 45. Ah, ah: so are we [really] bent
On committing a monstrous evil deed?
Coveting the sweet joys of sovereignty,
[Look at us,] all poised to slaughter our own folk!

§ 46. O let the sons of Dhritarāshtra, arms in hand,
Slay me in battle, though I,
Unarmed myself, will offer no defence;
Therein were greater happiness for me!'

§ 47. So saying Arjuna sat down
Upon the chariot-seat [though] battle [had begun],
Let slip his bow and arrows,
His mind distraught with grief.

II

Sanjaya said:
§ 1. To him thus in compassion plunged,
His eyes distraught and filled with tears,
[To him] desponding Krishna spake
  These words.

The Blessed Lord said:
§ 2. Whence comes this faintness on thee?
  [Now] at this crisis-hour?
This ill beseems a noble, wins none a heavenly state,
But brings dishonour, Arjuna.

§ 3. Play not the eunuch, son of Prithā,
  For this ill beseems thee:
Give up this vile faint-heartedness,
Arise, O scorcher of the foe.

Arjuna said:
§ 4. Krishna, how can I in battle
With Bhīshma and Drona fight,
Raining on them my arrows?
For they are worthy of respect.

§ 5. For better were it here on earth to eat a beggar's food
Than to slay preceptors of great dignity.
Were I to slay here my preceptors, ambitious though they may be,
Then should I be partaking of blood-sullied food.

§ 6. Besides we do not know which is the better part,
Whether that we should win the victory or that they should
  conquer us.
There facing us stand Dhritarāshtra's sons:
Should we kill them, ourselves would scarce desire to live.

§ 7. My very being (*svabhāva*) is assailed by compassion's harmful
  taint.
With mind perplexed concerning right and wrong (*dharma*) [I
  turn [to thee and ask:
Which is the better course? Tell me, and [let thy words be]
  definite and clear;
For I am thy disciple: teach me, for all my trust's in thee.

§ 8. I cannot see what could dispel
My grief, [this] parching of the senses,—
Not though on earth I were to win an empire,—
Unrivalled, prosperous,—or lordship over the gods themselves.

Sanjaya said:
§ 9. So speaking Arjuna, scorcher of the foe,
    To Krishna said:
    'I will not fight':
And having spoken held his peace.

§ 10. And Krishna faintly smiled
Between the armies twain,
And spake these words to Arjuna
In his [deep] despondency.

    The Blessed Lord said:
§ 11. Thou sorrowest for men who do not need thy sorrow,
And speakest words that [in part] are wise.[1]
    Wise men know no sorrow
    For the living or the dead.

§ 12. Never was there a time when I was not,
Nor thou, nor yet these lords of men;
Nor will there be a time when we shall cease to be,—
    All of us hereafter.

§ 13. Just as in this body the embodied soul
Must pass through childhood, youth and age,
So too [at death] will he take another body up:
In this a thoughtful man is not perplexed.

§ 14. But contacts with the world outside
Give rise to heat and cold, pleasure and pain:
They come and go, impermanent;
Arjuna, put up with them!

§ 15. For wise men there are,
The same in pleasure as in pain
Whom these [contacts] leave undaunted:
Such are conformed to immortality.

§ 16. Of what is not there is no becoming;
Of what *is* there is no ceasing to be:
For the boundary-line between the two
Is seen by men who see things as they really are.

§ 17. Indestructible [alone] is That,—know this,—
By Which this whole [universe] was spun.[2]
No one at all can bring destruction
On This which passes not away.

---

[1] Var. 'Thou dost not speak as a wise man would'.
[2] Or, 'pervaded'.

§ 18. Finite, they say, are these [our] bodies
[Indwelt] by an [1] eternal embodied soul,—
[A soul] indestructible, incommensurable.[2]
   Fight then, O scion of Bharata!

§ 19. Who thinks that he [3] can be a slayer,
Who thinks that he is slain,
Both these have no [right] knowledge:
   He slays not, is not slain.

§ 20. Never is he born nor dies;
Never did he come to be, nor will he ever come to be again:
Unborn, eternal, everlasting he—primeval:
He is not slain when the body is slain.[4]

§ 21. If a man knows him as indestructible,
Eternal, unborn, never to pass away,
How and whom can he cause to be slain
   Or slay?

§ 22. As a man casts off his worn-out clothes
And takes on other new ones [in their place],
So does the embodied soul cast off his worn-out bodies
   And enters others new.

§ 23. He cannot be cut by sword,
   Nor burnt by fire;
The waters cannot wet him,
Nor the wind dry him up.

§ 24. Uncuttable, unburnable,
   Unwettable, undryable
Is he,—eternal, roving everywhere,
Firm-set, unmoving, everlasting.

§ 25. Unmanifest, unthinkable,
Unchanging is he called:
So realize that he is thus
And put away thy useless grief.

§ 26. And even if thou thinkst that he
Is constantly [re-]born and constantly [re-]dies,
Even so, [my] strong-armed [friend],
Thou lamentest him in vain.

§ 27. For sure is the death of all that comes to birth,
Sure the birth of all that dies.
So in a matter that no one can prevent
Thou hast no cause to grieve.

[1] Or, 'the'.   [2] Or, 'unfathomable'.
[3] i.e. the embodied soul.   [4] Cf. p. 174.

§ 28. Unmanifest are the beginnings of contingent beings,
    Manifest their middle course,
Unmanifest again their ends:
What cause for mourning here?

§ 29. By a rare privilege [1] may someone behold him,
And by a rare privilege indeed may another tell of him,
And by a rare privilege may such another hear [2] him,
Yet even having heard there's none that knows him.

§ 30. Never can this embodied soul be slain
In the body of anyone [at all].
And so for no contingent being
Hast thou any cause for sorrow.

§ 31. Likewise consider thine own (caste-)duty (*dharma*),
Then too hast thou no cause to quail;
For better than a fight prescribed by duty
Is nothing for a man of the princely class.

§ 32. Happy the warriors indeed
Who become involved in war,—
[A war] like this presented by pure chance
And opening the gates of paradise!

§ 33. But if thou wilt not wage this war
    Prescribed by thy (caste-)duty,
Then, by casting off both honour and (caste-)duty,
Thou wilt bring evil [3] on thyself.

§ 34. Yes, this thy dishonour will become a byword
In the mouths of men in ages yet to come;
And dishonour in a man well-trained to honour
[Is an ill] surpassing death.

§ 35. 'From fear he fled the battlefield,'—
So will they think, the mighty charioteers.
Greatly esteemed by them before,
Thou wilt bring upon thyself contempt.

§ 36. Many a word that is better left unsaid
Will such men say as wish thee ill,
    Disputing thy competence.
What could cause thee greater pain than this?

§ 37. If thou art slain, thou winnest paradise;
And if thou gain the victory, thine the earth to enjoy.
    Arise, then, son of Kuntī,
    Resolved to fight the fight.

[1] Or, 'As a marvel'.   [2] Or, 'hear of'.   [3] Or, 'incur guilt'.

§ 38. [First learn to] treat pleasure and pain as things equivalent,
Then profit and loss, victory and defeat;
    Then gird thyself for battle.
Thus wilt thou bring no evil on thyself.[1]

§ 39. This wisdom (*buddhi*) has been revealed to thee in theory
    (*sāmkhya*);
Listen now to how it should be practised (*yoga*):
If by this wisdom thou art exercised (*yukta*),
Thou wilt put off the bondage inherent in [all] works (*karma*).

§ 40. Herein no effort goes to seed,
Nor is there any slipping back:
Even a little of this discipline (*dharma*)
Saves from the monstrous terror [of rebirth].

§ 41. The essence of the soul (*buddhi*) is will (*vyavasāya*),
    If it is single here [on earth]:
But many-branched and infinite
    Are the souls of men devoid of will.

§ 42-4. The essence of the soul is will,—
[The soul] of men who cling to pleasure and to power,
Their minds seduced by [flowery words],
Are not equipped for enstasy (*samādhi*).

Such men give vent to flowery words,
    The fools,
Delighting in the Veda's lore,
Saying there is naught else.

Desire their essence, paradise their goal,—
[Their words] tell of [re-]birth as fruit of works,
Expatiate about the niceties of ritual
By which pleasure and power can be achieved.

§ 45. [All nature is made up of] three 'constituents' (*guṇa*):
These are the Veda's goal. Have done with them:
Have done with [all] dualities (*dvandva*), stand ever firm on
    Goodness; [2]
Think not of gain or keeping the thing gained, but be thyself.

§ 46. As much use as there is in a water-tank
Flooded with water on every side,
So much is there in all the Vedas
For the Brāhman who discerns.

---

[1] Or, 'incur [no] guilt'.   [2] Or, 'courage' or 'truth'.

§ 47. Work alone is thy proper business,
Never the fruits [it may produce];
Let not your motive be the fruit of work,
Nor your attachment to [mere] worklessness (*akarma*).

§ 48. Stand fast in Yoga, surrendering attachment;
In success and failure be the same,
And then get busy with thy works.
Yoga means 'sameness' and 'indifference' (*samatva*).

§ 49. For lower far is the [path of] active work [for its own sake]
Than the Yoga of the soul (*buddhi*).
    Seek refuge in the soul!
[How] pitiful are they whose motive is the fruit [of works]!

§ 50. Whoso is integrated by [the Yoga of] the soul
Discards both good and evil works:
Brace thyself (*yuj-*) then for [this] Yoga!
Yoga is skill in [performing] works.

§ 51. For those wise men who are integrated by [the Yoga of] the
    soul,
Who have renounced the fruit that's born of works,
These will be freed from the bondage of [re-]birth
And fare on to that region that knows no ill.

§ 52. When thy soul shall pass beyond
Delusion's turbid quicksands,
Then wilt thou learn disgust
For what has been heard [ere now] [1]
And for what may yet be heard.

§ 53. When once thy soul, by Scripture (*śruti*) once bewildered,
    Stands motionless and still,
    Immovable in enstasy,
Then shalt thou win [the prize which is] Yoga, [integration].

Arjuna said:
§ 54. [Tell me,] Krishna, what is the mark of the man of steady
    (*sthita*) wisdom,
    The man immersed in enstasy?
How does he speak,—this man of steadied thought?
    How sit? How walk?

The Blessed Lord said:
§ 55. When a man puts from him all desires
    That prey upon the mind,
Himself (*ātmanā*) contented in the self alone,
Then is he called a man of steady wisdom.

----

[1] Meaning the Veda.

§ 56. Whose mind is undismayed [though beset] by [many a]
   sorrow,
Who for pleasure has no further longing,
From whom [all] passion (*rāga*), fear, and wrath have fled,
Such a man is called a sage of steadied thought.

§ 57. Who has no love (*abhisneha*) for any thing,
Who rejoices not at whatever good befalls him,
Nor hates the bad that comes his way,
Firm-stablished is the wisdom of such a man.

§ 58. And when he draws in on every side
His senses from their proper objects,
   As a tortoise might its limbs,
Firm-stablished is the wisdom of such a man.

§ 59. For the embodied soul who eats no more
   Objects of sense must disappear,—
Save only the [recollected] flavour,—and that too
Must vanish at the vision of the Highest.

§ 60. And yet however much
   A wise man strive,
The senses' tearing violence
May seduce his mind by force.

§ 61. [Then] let him sit, curbing them all,—
   Integrated (*yukta*)—intent on Me:
For firm-stablished is that man's wisdom
   Whose senses are subdued.

§ 62. Let a man [but] think of the things of sense,—
   Attachment to them is born:
From attachment springs desire,
From desire is anger born.

§ 63. From anger comes bewilderment,
From that the wandering of the mind (*smṛti*),
From this the destruction of the soul: [1]
With soul destroyed the man is lost.

§ 64. But he who roves among the things of sense,
His senses subdued to self, from hate and passion free,
   And is self-possessed [himself],
Is not far off from calm serenity (*prasāda*).

---

[1] *Buddhi:* or 'intellect'.

§ 65. And from him thus becalmed
All sorrows flee away:
For once his thoughts are calmed, then soon
Will his soul (*buddhi*) stand firmly [in its ground].

§ 66. No soul (*buddhi*) has he who knows not integration
(*ayukta*);
In him there's no development (*bhāvanā*):
For the undeveloped there is no peace.
Whence should there be joy (*sukha*) to a peaceless man?

§ 67. Hither and thither the senses rove,
And when the mind is attuned to them,
It sweeps away [whatever of] wisdom a man may possess,
    As the wind a ship at sea.

§ 68. And so, whose senses are withheld
From the objects proper to them,
    Wherever they may be,
Firm-stablished is the wisdom of such a man.

§ 69. In what for all [other] folk is night,
Therein the man of self-restraint is [wide-]awake.
What time all [other] folk are awake,
That time is night for the sage who sees.

§ 70. As the waters flow in to the sea,
Full filled, unmoving in its depths,
So too do all desires flow into the [heart of] man:
And such a man wins peace,—not the desirer of desires.

§ 71. The man who puts off all desires
And roams around from longing freed,
Who does not even think, 'This I am,' or 'This is mine,'
    Draws near to peace.

§ 72. This is the fixed, still state (*sthiti*) of Brahman;
He who wins through to this is nevermore perplexed.
Standing therein at the time of death
To the Nirvāna that is Brahman too [1] he goes!

III

Arjuna said:
§ 1. If, Krishna, thou think'st that wisdom (*buddhi*)
Is a loftier [course] than [the mere doing of] deeds,
Then why dost thou command me
    To do a hideous deed?

[1] Or, 'the Nirvāna of Brahman'.

§ 2. Thou dost confuse my intellect, or so it seems,
   With strangely muddled words:
So tell me with authority the one [simple way]
Whereby I may attain the better part.

   The Blessed Lord said:
§ 3. Of old did I proclaim the twofold law (*niṣṭhā*)
[That] in this world [holds sway],—
For the men of theory (*sāṁkhyas*) wisdom's Yoga,
For men of action (*yogin*) the Yoga of works (*karma*).

§ 4. Not by leaving works undone
Does a man win freedom from the [bond of] work,
   Nor by renunciation alone
Can he win perfection['s prize].

§ 5. Not for a moment can a man
Stand still and do no work;
For every man is powerless and forced to work
By the 'constituents' born of Nature.

§ 6. Whoso controls his limbs through which he acts
But sits remembering in his mind
Sense-objects, deludes himself:
   He's called a hypocrite.

§ 7. How much more excellent he all unattached,
Who with his mind controls [those] limbs,
And through those limbs [themselves] by which he acts
Embarks on the Yogic exercise (*yoga*) of works!

§ 8. Do thou the work that is prescribed for thee,
For to work is better than to do no work at all;
For he who does not work will not succeed
Even in keeping his body in good repair.

§ 9. This world is bound by bonds of work
Save where that work is done for sacrifice.
Work to this end, then, Arjuna,
From [all] attachment freed.

§ 10. Of old the Lord of Creatures (Prajāpati) said,
Emitting creation (*prajā*) and with it sacrifice:
'By this shall ye prolong your lineage,
Let this be to you the cow that yields
The milk of all that ye desire.

§ 11. With this shall ye sustain the gods,
So that the gods may sustain you [in return]:
Sustaining one another [thus]
Ye shall achieve the highest good.

§ 12. For, so sustained by sacrifice, the gods
Will give you the food of your desire.
Whoso enjoys their gift, yet gives nothing [in return],
  Is a thief, no more nor less.'

§ 13. Good men who eat of the leavings of the sacrifice
  Are freed from every taint;
But evil are they, and evil do they eat
Who cook [their food] for their own [selfish] sakes.

§ 14. From food [all] contingent beings are born,
    And food from rain;
  And rain derives from sacrifice,
  And sacrifice from works (*karma*).

§ 15. From Brahman [1] work arises, know thou this,
And Brahman from the Imperishable [2] is born;
Therefore is Brahman, penetrating everywhere,
  Firm-stablished on the sacrifice.

§ 16. So was the wheel in motion set;
And whoso fails to match his turning [with the turning of the
    wheel],
Living an evil life, the senses his pleasure-ground,
  Lives out his life in vain.

§ 17. Nay, let a man take pleasure in self alone,
In self his satisfaction find,
In self alone content:
[Let him do this, for then]
There is naught he needs to do.

§ 18. In works done and works undone
On earth what interest has he?
What interest in all contingent beings?
On none of them does he depend.

§ 19. And so, detached, perform unceasingly
The works that must be done
For the man detached who labours on (*karma*),
  To the Highest must win through.

§ 20. For only by working on (*karma*) did Janaka
And his like attain perfection.
Or if again for the welfare [3] of the world thou carest,
  Then shouldst thou work [and act].

---

[1] Meaning 'manifest Nature'.   [2] Or, 'the syllable Oṁ'.
[3] Or 'control'.

§ 21. [For] whatever the noblest does,
That too will others do:
The standard that he sets
All the world will follow.

§ 22. In the three worlds there's nothing
    That I must do at all,
Nor anything unattained which I have not attained;
Yet work [is the element] in which I move.

§ 23. For were I not tirelessly
To busy myself with works,
Then would men everywhere
Follow in my footsteps.

§ 24. If I were not to do my work,
These worlds would fall to ruin,
And I should be a worker of confusion,
Destroying these [my] creatures.

§ 25. As witless [fools] perform their works
    Attached to the work [they do],
So, unattached, should the wise man do,
Longing to bring about the welfare of the world.

§ 26. Let not the wise man split the mind (buddhi)
Of witless men attached to work:
Let him encourage [1] all [manner of] works,
[Himself,] though busy, controlled and integrated (yukta).

§ 27. It is Nature's [three] 'constituents'
That do all works wherever [works are done];
[But] he whose self is by the ego fooled,
    Thinks, 'It is I who do.'

§ 28. But he who knows how 'constituents' and works
Are parcelled into categories, seeing things as they are,
Thinks thus: 'Constituents on constituents act,'
[And so thinking] remains detached.

§ 29. By the constituents of Nature fooled
Are men attached to the constituents' works:
Such men, dull-witted, only know in part.
Let not the knower of the whole
Upset [the knower of the part].

§ 30. Cast all thy works on Me,
Thy mind in self withdrawn (adhyātmacetas);
Have neither hope, nor thought that 'This is mine':
Cast off this fever! Fight!

[1] Or, 'cause them to enjoy'.

§ 31. Whoso shall practise constantly
This my doctrine, firm in faith,
    Not envying, [not cavilling,]
He too shall find release from [the bondage that is] work.

§ 32. But whoso refuses to perform my doctrine,
    Envious [yet, and cavilling],
Of every [form of] wisdom fooled,
Is lost, the witless [dunce]! Be sure of that.

§ 33. As is a man's own nature,
So must he act, however wise he be.
All beings follow Nature:
What can repression do?

§ 34. In all the senses passion and hate
Are seated, [turned] to their proper objects:
Let none fall victim to their power,
For these are brigands on his road.

§ 35. Better one's own duty (*dharma*) [to perform], though void
    of merit,
    Than to do another's well:
Better to die within [the sphere of] one's own duty:
    Perilous is the duty of other men.

    Arjuna said:
§ 36. By what impelled does [mortal] man
    Do evil,
    Unwilling though he be?
He's driven to it by force, or so it seems to me.

    The Blessed Lord said:
§ 37. Desire it is: Anger it is:
Arising from the 'constituent' of Passion,—
All-devouring, fount of wickedness:
Know this to be thine enemy on earth.

§ 38. As fire is swathed in smoke,
As mirror [fouled] by dust,
As embryo all covered up by the membrane-envelope,
So is this [world] obscured by this.

§ 39. This the wise man's eternal foe;
By this is wisdom overcast:
Whatever form it will it takes,[1]—
    A fire insatiate!

                    [1] Or, 'in the form of desire'.

§ 40. Senses, mind and soul (*buddhi*), they say,
   Are the places where it lurks;
Through these it fences wisdom in,
Leading astray the embodied soul.

§ 41. Therefore restrain
   The senses first:
   Strike down this evil thing!—
Destroyer [alike] of what we learn from holy books
And what we learn from life.

§ 42. Exalted are the senses, or so they say;
   Higher than they the mind;
Yet higher than the mind is soul (*buddhi*):
What is beyond the soul is he.[1]

§ 43. Know him who is yet higher than the soul;
And of thyself (*ātmanā*) [2] make firm [this] self.
   Vanquish the enemy, Arjuna!
[Swift is he] to change his form,[3]
And hard is he to conquer!

IV

The Blessed Lord said:
§ 1. This changeless way of life (*yoga*) did I
To Vivasvat [once] proclaim;
To Manu Vivasvat told it,
And Manu to Ikshvāku passed it on.

§ 2. Thus was the tradition from one to another handed on,
   The Royal Seers came to know it;
[But] in the long course of time
   The way of life (*yoga*) on earth was lost.

§ 3. This is the same primeval way of life (*yoga*)
   That I preach to thee today;
For thou art loyal, devoted (*bhakta*), and my comrade,
   And this is the highest mystery.

   Arjuna said:
§ 4.   Later thy birth,
   Earlier Vivasvat's:
How should I understand thy words,
That in the beginning thou didst proclaim it?

---

[1] i.e. the 'self'. Some have referred it to desire.
[2] Or, 'by means of the self'.
[3] Or, 'in the form of desire'.

The Blessed Lord said:
§ 5. Many a birth have I passed through,
And [many a birth] hast thou:
   I know them all,
   Thou knowest not.

§ 6. Unborn am I, changeless is my Self;
Of [all] contingent beings I am the Lord!
Yet by my creative energy (*māyā*) I consort
With Nature—which is mine—and come to be [in time].

§ 7. For whenever the law of righteousness (*dharma*)
Withers away, and lawlessness (*adharma*)
   Raises its head,
Then do I generate Myself on earth.

§ 8. For the protection of the good,
For the destruction of evildoers,
For the setting up of righteousness,
I come into being, age after age.

§ 9. Who knows my godly birth and mode of operation (*karma*)
   Thus as they really are,
He, his body left behind, is never born again:
   He comes to Me.

§ 10. Many are they who, passion, fear and anger spent,
Inhere in Me, making Me their sanctuary:
Made pure by wisdom and hard penances,[1]
They come [to share in] the manner of my being.

§ 11. In whatsoever way [devoted] men approach Me,
In that same way do I return their love (*bhaj-*).
Whatever their occupation and wherever they may be,
   Men follow the path I trace.

§ 12. Desiring success in their (ritual) acts (*karma*),
   Men worship here the gods;
For swiftly in the world of men
Comes success, engendered by the act [itself].

§ 13. The four-caste system did I generate
With categories of 'constituents' and works;
Of this I am the doer, know thou this:—
And yet I am the Changeless One
Who does not do [or act].

[1] Or, 'by the hard penances of wisdom'.

§ 14. Works can never affect Me.
I have no yearning for their fruits.
Whoso should know that this is how I am
Escapes the bondage [forged] by works.

§ 15. This knowing, the ancients too did work,
Though seeking [all the while] release [from temporal life]:
    So do thou work [and act]
As the ancients did in the days of old.

§ 16. What is work? What worklessness?
Herein even sages are perplexed.
So shall I preach to thee concerning work;
And once thou hast understood my words,
From ill thou'lt win release.

§ 17. For a man must understand
[The nature] of work, of work ill-done,
    And worklessness, [all three]:
Profound, [hard to unravel,] are the ways of work!

§ 18. The man who sees worklessness in work [itself],
        And work in worklessness,
    Is wise among his fellows,
Integrated (yukta), performing every work.

§ 19. When all a man's emprises
Have neither motive nor desire [for fruit],—
His works burnt up in wisdom's fire,—
Then wise men call him learned.

§ 20. When he's cast off [all] attachment to the fruit of works,
    Ever content, on none dependent,
Though he embark on work [himself],
In fact he does no work at all.

§ 21. Nothing hoping, his thought and mind (ātman) restrained,
    Giving up all possessions,
He only does such work
As is needed for the body's maintenance,
    And so avoids defilement.

§ 22. Content to take whatever chance may bring his way,
Surmounting all dualities (dvandva), knowing no envy,
The same in failure and success,
Though working [still], he is not bound.

§ 23. Attachments gone, deliverance won,
His thoughts are fixed on wisdom:

He works for sacrifice [alone],
And all the work [he ever did]
Entirely melts away.

§ 24. The offering is Brahman, Brahman the sacrificial ghee
Offered by Brahman in Brahman's fire:
Who fixes all his thought (*samādhi*) on this sacrificial rite (*karma*)
[Indwelt by] Brahman, to Brahman must he go.

§ 25. Some Yogins offer sacrifice
To the gods as their sole object,
In the fire of Brahman others
Offer sacrifice as sacrifice
[Which has merit in itself].

§ 26. Yet others offer the senses,—hearing and the rest,—
    In the fires of self-restraint;
Others the senses' proper objects,—sounds and the like,—
    In the fires of the senses.

§ 27. And others offer up all works of sense,
All works of vital breath,
In the fire of the practice (*yoga*) of self-control
    By wisdom kindled.

§ 28. Some offer up their wealth, some their hard penances,
Some spiritual exercise (*yoga*), and some again
Make study and knowledge [of Scripture] their sacrifice,—
Religious men whose vows are strict.

§ 29. Some offer the inward breath in the outward,
Likewise the outward in the inward,
    Checking the flow of both,
    On breath control intent.

§ 30. Others restrict their food
And offer up breaths in breaths.
All these know the [meaning of] sacrifice,
For by sacrifice all their defilements are made away.

§ 31. Eating the leavings of the sacrifice,
The food of immortality,
    They come to eternal Brahman.
This world is not for him who performs no sacrifice,—
    Much less another [world].

§ 32. So, many and various are the sacrifices
Spread out athwart the mouth of Brahman.
They spring from work, all of them; be sure of this,
[For] once thou knowest this, thy deliverance is sure.

§ 33. Better than the sacrifice of wealth
    Is the sacrifice of wisdom.
    All works without exception
In wisdom find their consummation.

§ 34. Learn to know this by humble reverence [of the wise],
    By questioning, by service,
[For] the wise who see things as they really are
    Will teach thee wisdom.

§ 35. Once thou hast known this, wilt thou never again
Be perplexed [as now thou art]:
By [knowing] this thou wilt behold [all] beings
In [thy]self,—yes, everyone of them,—and then in Me.

§ 36. Nay, though thou wert the very worst
    Among all evil-doers,
[Yet, once thou hast mounted] wisdom's bark,
Thou wilt surmount all this tortuous [stream of life].

§ 37. As a kindled fire
    Reduces its fuel to ashes,
So does the fire of wisdom
Reduce all work to ashes.

§ 38. Nothing on earth resembles wisdom
In its power to cleanse [and purify];
And thus in time a man may find himself
Within [him]self,—a man perfected in spiritual exercise (*yoga*).

§ 39. A man of faith, intent on wisdom,
His senses [all] restrained, will wisdom win;
And, wisdom won, he'll come right soon
    To perfect [1] peace.

§ 40. The man, unwise, devoid of faith,
Doubting at heart (*ātman*), must perish:
No part in this world has the man of doubt,
Nor in the next, nor yet in happiness.

§ 41. Let a man in spiritual exercise (*yoga*) all works renounce,
Let him by wisdom his doubts dispel,
    Let him be himself (*ātmavat*) and then
[Whatever] his works [may be], they will never bind him [more].

§ 42. And so, [take up] the sword of wisdom, cut
This doubt of thine, unwisdom's child,
    Still lurking in thy heart:
Prepare for action [2] [now], stand up!

---

[1] Lit. 'highest'.   [2] Or, 'resort to Yoga'.

V

Arjuna said:
§ 1. 'Renounce [all] works:' [such is the course] thou recommendest:
And then again [thou sayest]: 'Perform them (*yoga*).'
Which is the better of these two?
Tell me this in clear, decisive [words].

The Blessed Lord said:
§ 2. Renouncing works,—performing them (*yoga*),—
Both lead to the highest good;
But of the two to engage in (*yoga*) works
Is more excellent than to renounce them.

§ 3. This is the mark of the man
Whose renunciation is abiding:
He hates not, nor desires,
For, surmounting all dualities (*nirdvandva*), how easily
He wins release from bondage!

§ 4. 'There must be a difference between theory (*sāṁkhya*) and practice (*yoga*),'
So say the simple-minded, not the wise.
Apply thyself to only one, whole-heartedly,
And win the fruit of both.

§ 5. [True,] the men of theory attain a [high] estate,
But that [same state] achieves the man of practice too;
For theory and practice are all one:
Who sees [that this is true], he sees [indeed].

§ 6. Hard to attain is [true] renunciation
Without practising [some] Yogic exercise (*yoga*):
The sage well-versed in Yogic exercise and integrated (*yoga-yukta*)
Right soon to Brahman goes.

§ 7. Well-versed in Yogic exercise, his self made clean,
With mind (*ātman*) and sense subdued,
His self become the [very] self of every being,
Though working yet, he suffers no defilement.

§ 8. 'Lo, nothing do I do':
So thinks the integrated (*yukta*) man
Who knows things as they really are,—
Seeing the while and hearing, touching, smelling,
Eating, walking, sleeping, breathing,

§ 9. Talking, emitting, grasping,
Opening and shutting the eyes:
'The senses are busied with their proper objects:
[What has that to do with me?'
This is the way] he thinks.

§ 10. And on he works, though he's [long] renounced attachment,
   Ascribing his works to Brahman; [1]
   Yet evil cannot touch him,
As water [cannot touch] the petal of a lotus.

§ 11. With body, mind and soul (*buddhi*), and senses too,—
[With these] alone and isolated [from the self],—
   Do Yogins practise work
Renouncing [all] attachment for the cleansing of the self.

§ 12. The integrated man, renouncing the fruit of works,
   Gains an abiding peace:
The man not integrated, whose works are prompted by desire,
Holds fast to fruits and thus remains enslaved.

§ 13. [And so,] all works renouncing with his mind,
   Quietly he sits in full control
Within [this] body,[2] city of nine gates:
He neither works nor makes another work.

§ 14. Nor agency nor worldly works
Does [the body's] lord engender,[3]
Nor yet the bond that work to fruit conjoins;
It is Nature (*svabhāva*) that initiates the action.

§ 15. The good and evil works of anyone at all
He takes not on,—that all-pervading lord.[4]
By ignorance is wisdom overspread;
   Thereby are creatures fooled.

§ 16. But some there are whose ignorance of self
   By wisdom is destroyed:
Their wisdom, like the sun,
Sheds [a ray of] light on That All-highest.

§ 17. Souls (*buddhi*) bent on That, selves bent on That,
With That their aim and That their aspiration,
They stride [along the path] from which there's no return,
   [All] taints by wisdom washed away.

[1] Or, 'casting his works on God (*brahman*)'.
[2] Reading *dehe*.
[3] Or, 'The Lord of the world does not engender agency or work'.
[4] Or, 'Lord'.

§ 18. [These] wise ones see the selfsame thing (*sama*)
In a Brāhman, wise and courteous,
    As in a cow or elephant
Nay, as in a dog or outcaste.

§ 19. While yet in this world, [the world of] emanation [and
    decay,]
They've conquered, for their minds are stilled in That which
    ever is the same (*sāmya*):
For devoid of imperfection and ever the same (*sama*) is Brahman;
    Therefore in Brahman [stilled] they stand.

§ 20. Winning some pleasant thing [the sage] will not rejoice,
Nor shrink disquietened when the unpleasant comes his way;
Steadfast and stilled his soul (*buddhi*), [all] unconfused,
He will know Brahman, in Brahman [stilled] he'll stand.

§ 21. His self detached from contacts with the outside world,
    In self he finds his joy (*sukha*);
His self in Brahman integrated by spiritual exercise (*brahma-
    yogayuktātmā*)
    He finds imperishable joy.

§ 22. For the pleasures men derive from contacts
Assuredly give rise to pain,
    Having a beginning and an end.
    In these the wise take no delight.

§ 23. Let a man, remaining in this world,
And before he is released from the body ['s bondage]
Stand fast against the onset of anger and desire;
    Only so in joy will he be integrated.

§ 24. His joy within, his bliss within,
    His light within, that Yogin
    Becomes Brahman and draws nigh
To Nirvāna that is Brahman too.[1]

§ 25. Nirvāna that is Brahman is the lot
Of seers in whom [all] taint of imperfection is destroyed;
Their doubts dispelled, [all] self-controlled,
They take their pleasure in the weal
Of all contingent beings.

§ 26. Around these holy men whose thoughts are fast controlled,
    Estranged from anger and desire,
    Knowing [at last] the self,
Nirvāna that is Brahman fares.

---

[1] Or, 'the Nirvāna of Brahman'.

§ 27. [All] contacts with things outside he puts aside,
    Fixing his gaze between the eyebrows;
Inward and outward breaths he makes the same
    As they pass up and down the nostrils;

§ 28. With sense and mind and soul (*buddhi*) restrained,
    The sage on deliverance intent,
Who has forever banished fear, anger and desire
    Is truly liberated.

§ 29. [Then] does he learn to know Me, who alone enjoy
The sacrifice and fierce austerities, great Lord
Of all the worlds, friend of all contingent beings,
[And knowing Me] he reaches peace.

VI

The Blessed Lord said:
§ 1. The man who does the work that is his to do,
    Yet covets not its fruits,—
He [it is who] at once renounces and yet works on (*yogin*),
Not he who builds no sacrificial fire and does no work.

§ 2. What men call renunciation
Is practice (*yoga*) too; this must thou know.
For without renouncing [all] set purpose (*saṁkalpa*)
None can engage in spiritual exercise (*yogin*).

§ 3. For the sage who would climb [the heights of] spiritual
    exercise (*yoga*),
    Works are said to be the means;
But for that same sage who has reached that peak
They say quiescence is the means.

§ 4. For when a man knows no attachment
To objects of sense or to the deeds [he does],
When all set purpose he's renounced,
Then has he climbed [the heights of] spiritual exercise (*yoga*),
    Or so they say.

§ 5. Raise self by self,
Let not the self droop down;
For self's friend is self indeed,
So too is self self's enemy.

§ 6. Self is friend to the self of him
Whose self is by the self subdued;
But for the man bereft of self
Self will act as an enemy indeed.

§ 7. The higher self of the self-subdued
Who quietness knows, is rapt in enstasy,[1]—
In cold as in heat, in pleasure as in pain,
    Likewise in honour or disgrace.

§ 8. With self content in wisdom learnt
From holy books and wisdom learnt from life,
With sense subdued, unmoving in the heights,
The Yogin [stands]: 'Integrated', so he's called;
Alike to him are clods of earth, stones, gold.

§ 9. Outstanding he whose soul (*buddhi*)
Views in the self-same way
Friends, comrades, enemies, those indifferent,
Neutrals, the men he hates and those who are his kin,—
    The good and the evil too.

§ 10. Let the Yogin ever integrate [him]self
Standing in a place apart,
Alone, his thoughts and self restrained,
Devoid of [earthly] hope, nothing possessing.

§ 11. Let him for himself set up
A steady seat in a clean place,
Neither too high nor yet too low,
With cloth or hides or grass bestrewn.

§ 12. There let him sit and make his mind a single point;
Let him restrain the motions of his thought and senses,
    And engage in spiritual exercise (*yoga*)
        To purify the self.

§ 13. Remaining still, let him keep body, head and neck
    In a straight line, unmoving;
Let him fix his gaze on the tip of his own nose,
    Not looking round about him.

§ 14. [There] let him sit, his self all stilled,
His fear all gone, firm in his vow of chastity,
His mind controlled, his thoughts on Me,
    Integrated, [yet] intent on Me.

§ 15. Thus let the Yogin ever integrate [him]self,
    His mind restrained;
Then will he approach that peace
Which has Nirvāna as its end
And which subsists in Me.

[1] Or, 'The self . . . is supremely rapt in enstasy'.

§ 16. Yoga is not for him who eats too much,
Nor yet for him who does not eat at all,
Nor for him who is all too prone to sleep,
Nor yet for him who [always] stays awake.

§ 17. [Rather] is Yoga [made] for him
Who knows the mean (*yukta*) in food and recreation,
Who knows the mean in all his deeds and gestures,
Who knows the mean in sleeping as in waking:
[This is the Yoga] that slaughters pain.

§ 18. When thought, held well in check,
    Sinks into the self alone,
Then is a man from longing freed, though all desires assail him:
    They call him 'integrated'.

§ 19. As a lamp might stand in a windless place,
Unflickering,—this likeness have we heard
Of such Yogins who control their thought
And practice the integration of the self.

§ 20. When thought by Yogic exercise is checked
    And comes to rest,
And when by self one sees the self in self
    And finds content therein,

§ 21. That is the utmost joy which transcends [all things of]
    sense,
    And which soul (*buddhi*) [alone] can grasp.
When he knows this and [knowing it] stands still,
Departing not an inch from the Reality [he sees],

§ 22. He wins a prize beyond all others,—
        Or so he thinks.
    Therein he [firmly] stands,
Unmoved by any suffering, however grievous it may be.

§ 23. This he should know is what is meant by 'Yoga',—
    The unlinking of the link with suffering and pain.
This is the Yoga which must be brought about (*yuj-*)
With firm resolve and mind all undismayed.

§ 24. Let him all desires renounce whose origin
Lies in the will (*samkalpa*), all of them without remainder;
Let him restrain in every way
By mind alone the senses' busy throng:

§ 25. His soul (*buddhi*) held fast in steadfastness,
Little by little he'll come to rest;
    Stilling the mind in self,
He must think of nothing at all.

§ 26. Whenever the fickle mind
Unsteady roves around,
From thence he'll bring it back
And subject it to the self.

§ 27. For upon this man of Yoga whose mind is stilled
     The highest joy descends:
[All] passion laid to rest, free from [all] stain,
     Brahman he becomes.

§ 28. [And] thus [all] flaws transcending,
The man of Yoga, constant in integrating self,
With ease attains the highest joy,
     Brahman's [saving] touch.

§ 29. With self by Yoga integrated, [now] he sees
     The self in all beings standing,
        All beings in the self:
     The same in everything he sees.

§ 30. Who sees Me everywhere,
     Who sees the All in Me,
     For him I am not lost,
     Nor is he lost for Me.

§ 31. Who loves and worships (*bhaj-*) Me, embracing unity,
     As abiding in all beings,
        In whatever state he be,
That man of Yoga abides in Me.

§ 32. By analogy with self who sees
     The same [essence] everywhere
        In pleasure as in pain,
He among Yogins is supreme, or so men think.

   Arjuna said:
§ 33. So fickle [is my mind] that I cannot descry
     The still, firm-stablished state
Of this Yoga thou hast preached
As 'being the same [in everything]'.

§ 34. For fickle is the mind,
Impetuous, exceeding strong:
How difficult to curb it!
As easy to curb the wind, I'd say.

   The Blessed Lord said:
§ 35. Herein there is no doubt,
Hard is the mind to curb and fickle;
But by untiring effort and by transcending passion
     It can be held in check.

§ 36. Hard to come by is this self-control (*yoga*)
By one whose self is not restrained; this [too] I think;
But the man who strives, [all] self-controlled,
Can win it if he but use [the appropriate] means.

Arjuna said:
§ 37. [Suppose] a man of faith should strive in vain,
His restless mind from Yoga weaned,—
He fails to win the perfect prize [proffered] by Yoga,—
  What path does he tread then? [1]

§ 38. Does he, both objects unachieved, come crashing down
  And perish like a riven cloud,
    His firm foundation gone,
    Bemused on Brahman's path?

§ 39. Krishna, this doubt thou canst dispel for me
  So that none of it remains,
  For there seems to be no other
Who can dispel this doubt [of mine].

The Blessed Lord said:
§ 40. Not in this world nor in the next
Is such a man destroyed or lost:
No doer of fair works will tread
An evil path, my friend, no, none whatever.

§ 41. The worlds of doers of good works he'll win,
  And dwell there endless years;
And then will he be born again, this man who failed in Yoga,
In the house of pious men by fortune blest.

§ 42. Or else he will be born in a family
Of real Yogins possessed of insight;
But such a birth as this on earth
  Is yet harder to win.

§ 43. There is he united with the soul (*buddhi*)
As it had matured in his former body;
And once again he [girds his loins,]
Struggling for [Yoga's] highest prize.

§ 44. By [the force of] that same struggle he'd waged in former
  times
He's swept away though helpless [of himself];
For even he who does no more
Than wish to know what Yoga is,
Transcends that 'Brahman' which is [no more than] wordy rites.

---

[1] Or, 'What goal does he reach?'.

§ 45. But cleansed of taint, that man of Yoga
    Strives on with utmost zeal,
Through many, many births [at last] perfected;
    And then the highest path he treads.[1]

§ 46. Higher than the [mere] ascetic is the Yogin held to be,
    Yes, higher than the man of wisdom,
    Higher than the man of works:
    Be, then, a Yogin, Arjuna!

§ 47. But of all the men of Yoga
The man of faith who loves and honours (*bhaj-*) Me,
    His inmost self absorbed in Me,
He is the most fully integrated: this do I believe.

VII

    The Blessed Lord said:
§ 1. Attach thy mind to Me:
Engaged in Yogic exercise, put thy trust in Me:
[This doing] listen how thou mayest come to know Me
    In my entirety, all doubt dispelled.

§ 2. This wisdom derived from sacred writ
And the wisdom of experience
I shall proclaim to thee, leaving nothing unsaid.
This knowing, never again will any other thing
    That needs to be known remain.

§ 3. Among thousands of men but one, maybe,
    Will strive for self-perfection;
And even among these [athletes] who have won perfection['s
    crown]
But one, maybe, will come to know Me as I really am.

§ 4. Eightfold divided is my Nature,—thus:
Earth, water, fire and air,
Space, mind, and also soul (*buddhi*),
    The ego [last].

§ 5. This is the lower: but other than this
I have a higher Nature; this too must thou know.
[And this is] Nature seen as life
By which this universe (*jagat*) is kept in being.

§ 6. From these [2] [two Natures] all beings take their origin;
    Be very sure of this.
    Of the whole [wide] universe
The origin and the dissolution too am I.

---

[1] Or, 'reaches the highest goal'.   [2] Or, 'this'.

§ 7. Higher than I
  There's nothing whatsoever:
On Me the universe (*sarvam*) is strung
Like clustered pearls upon a thread.

§ 8. In water I am the flavour,
In sun and moon the light,
In all the Vedas Oṁ [the sacred syllable],
In space I'm sound: in man [his] manliness am I.

§ 9. Pure fragrance in the earth am I,
  Flame's onset in the fire;
[And] life [am I] in all contingent beings,
In ascetics [their] fierce austerity.

§ 10. Know that I am the eternal seed
  Of all contingent beings:
Reason in the rational,
Glory in the glorious am I.

§ 11. Power in the powerful I,—
[Such power] as knows nor passion nor desire:
Desire am I in contingent beings,
[But such desire as is] not at war with right (*dharma*).

§ 12. Know too that all states of being, whether they be
Of [Nature's constituent] Goodness, Passion or Darkness,
  Proceed from Me;
But I am not in them, they are in Me.

§ 13. By these three states of being
Inhering in the 'constituents'
  This whole universe is led astray,
  And does not understand
That I am far beyond them:
I neither change nor pass away.

§ 14. For [all] this is my creative power (*māyā*),
  Divine, hard to transcend.
Whoso shall put his trust in Me alone,
Shall pass beyond this [my] uncanny power (*māyā*).

§ 15. Doers of evil, deluded, base,
Put not their trust in Me;
Their minds seduced by this uncanny power,
They cleave to a devilish form of life (*bhāva*).

§ 16. Fourfold are the doers of good
Who love and worship (*bhaj-*) Me,—
The afflicted, the man who seeks for wisdom,
The man who strives for gain, and the man who wisdom knows.

§ 17. Of these the man of wisdom, ever integrated,
Who loves and worships (*bhakti*) One alone, excels:
To such a man I am exceeding dear,
    And he is dear to Me.

§ 18. All these are noble and exalted,
But the man of wisdom is my very self, so must I hold.
His self [already] integrated, he puts his trust in Me,
    The [one] All-Highest Way.[1]

§ 19. At the end of many a birth
The man of wisdom resigns himself to Me,
[Knowing that Krishna,] Vasudeva's son, is All:
A man so great of soul (*mahātman*) is exceeding hard to find.

§ 20. [All] wisdom swept away by manifold desires,
Men put their trust in other gods,
Relying on diverse rules and precepts:
For their own nature forces them thereto.

§ 21. Whatever form, [whatever god,] a devotee
    With faith desires to honour,
That very faith do I confirm in him,
Making it unswerving and secure.

§ 22. Firm stablished (*yukta*) in that faith,
He seeks to reverence that [god],
And thence he gains all he desires,
Though it is I who am the true dispenser.

§ 23. But finite is the reward (*phala*)
    Of such men of little wit:
Whoso worships the gods, to the gods will [surely] go,
[But] whoso loves and worships (*bhakta*) Me,
        To Me will come indeed.

§ 24. Fools think I am the Unmanifest
In manifest form displayed:
They know nothing of my higher state,
    The Unchangeable, All-Highest.

§ 25. Because my creative power (*yoga-māyā*) conceals Me,
    I am not revealed to all:
This world, deluded, knows Me not,—
[Me,] the Unborn and Changeless.

---

[1] Or, 'goal', or 'refuge'.

§ 26. All beings past and present,
   And yet to come
   I know:
But none there is that knoweth Me.

§ 27. By dualities (*dvandva*) are men confused, and these arise
   From desire and hate;
Thereby are all contingent beings
Bewildered the moment they are born.

§ 28. But some there are for whom [all] ill is ended,—
   Doers of what is good and pure:
Released [at last] from the confusion of duality,
Steadfast in their vows, they love and worship (*bhaj-*) Me.

§ 29. Whoso shall strive to win release from age and death,
   Putting his trust in Me,
Will come to know That Brahman in Its wholeness,
What appertains to self [1] and the whole [mystery] of works.

§ 30. Whoso shall know Me and all that appertains
To contingent being, to the divine and to the sacrifice,
Will come to know Me at the time of passing on,
For integrated their thought will be.

VIII

Arjuna said:
§ 1. What is That Brahman? What that which appertains to self?
[And] what, O best of men, are works (*karma*)?
What is that called which appertains to contingent beings?
   What that which appertains to the divine? [1]

§ 2. Who and in what manner is he
Who appertains to the sacrifice here in this body?
And how, at the time of passing on,
Mayst thou be known by men of self-restraint?

The Blessed Lord said:
§ 3. The Imperishable [2] is Brahman, the All-Highest,
Nature (*svabhāva*), they say, is what appertains to self:
Creative force (*visarga*) is known as 'works' (*karma*),
For it gives rise to the [separate] natures of contingent beings.

---

[1] Most translators have 'overself' and the like, contrary to Upanishadic
usage.
[2] Or, 'the sacred syllable Oṁ'.

§ 4. To contingent beings a perishable nature appertains,
  To the divine [pure] spirit (*puruṣa*);
But it is I myself who appertain to the sacrifice
Here in this body, O best of men who bodies bear.

§ 5. Whoso at the hour of death,
Abandoning his mortal frame,
Bears Me in mind and passes on,
Accedes to my Divinity (*mad-bhāva*): have no doubt of that.

§ 6. Whatever state (*bhāva*) a man may bear in mind
When the time comes at last to cast the mortal frame aside,
  Even to that state does he accede,
For ever does that state of being make him grow into itself
  (*tad-bhāva-bhāvita*).

§ 7. Then muse upon Me always,
  And go to war;
For if thou fixest mind and soul (*buddhi*) on Me,
  To Me shalt thou most surely come.

§ 8. Let a man's thoughts be integrated with the discipline (*yoga*)
Of constant striving: let them not stray to anything else [at all];
So by meditating on the divine All-Highest Person,
[That man to that All-Highest] goes.

§ 9. For [He it is who is called] the Ancient Seer,
Governor [of all things, yet] smaller than the small,
Ordainer [1] of all, in form unthinkable,
Sun-coloured beyond the darkness. Let a man meditate on Him
  [as such].

§ 10. With mind unmoving when his turn comes to die,
Steadied (*yukta*) by loyal love (*bhakti*) and Yogic power,
Forcing the breath between the eyebrows duly,
[So will such a man] draw nigh to the divine All-Highest Person.

§ 11. The imperishable state [2] of which the Vedic scholars speak,
Which sages enter, [all their] passion spent,
For love of which men lead a life of chastity,
[That state] will I proclaim to thee in brief.

§ 12. Let a man close up all [the body's] gates,
  Stem his mind within his heart,
  Fix his breath within his head,
Engrossed in Yogic concentration.

---

[1] Or, 'creator' or 'supporter'.   [2] Or, 'word'.

§ 13. Let him utter [the word] Oṁ, Brahman in one syllable,
  Keeping Me in mind;
Then when his time is come to leave aside the body,
  He'll tread the highest Way.[1]

§ 14. How easily am I won by him
Who bears Me in mind unceasingly,
Thinking of nothing else at all,—
  A Yogin integrated ever.

§ 15. Coming right nigh to Me, these great of soul,
  Are never born again.
For rebirth is full of suffering, knows nothing that abides:
[Free from it now] they attain the all-highest prize (saṁsiddhi).

§ 16. The worlds right up to Brahmā's realm
[Dissolve and] evolve again;
But he who comes right nigh to Me
Shall never be born again.

§ 17. For a thousand ages lasts
  One day of Brahmā,
And for a thousand ages one such night:
This knowing, men will know [what is meant by] day and night.

§ 18. At the day's dawning all things manifest
Spring forth from the Unmanifest;
And then at nightfall they dissolve again
In [that same mystery] surnamed 'Unmanifest'.

§ 19. Yea, this whole host of beings
Comes ever anew to be; at fall of night
It dissolves away all helpless;
At dawn of day it rises up [again].

§ 20. But beyond that there is [yet] another mode of being,—
Beyond the Unmanifest another Unmanifest, eternal:
This is He who passes not away
When all contingent beings pass away.

§ 21. Unmanifest surnamed 'Imperishable':—
This, men say, is the All-Highest Way,[2]
And this once won, there is no more returning:
This is my all-highest home.[3]

---

[1] Or, 'Go to the highest goal or refuge'.
[2] Or, 'goal' or 'refuge'.
[3] dhāma: or, 'law' or 'light'.

§ 22. That is [indeed] the highest Person (Spirit);
By love and worship (*bhakti*) is He won, and nowise else.[1]
In Him do all contingent beings subsist;
　　By Him this universe was spun.[2]

§ 23. Some to return, some never to return,
Yogins set forth when they pass on;
The times [and seasons of them all]
　　I shall [now] declare.

§ 24. Fire, light, day, the moon's light fortnight,
The six months of the sun's northern course,—
Dying in these to Brahman do they go,
　　The men who Brahman know.

§ 25. Smoke, night, the moon's dark fortnight,
The six months of the sun's southern course,—
[Dying] in these, a Yogin wins the light of the moon,
　　And back he comes again.

§ 26. These courses—light and dark—are deemed
To be unchanging [laws] on earth.
One leads to [the place of] no return,
By the other one returns again.

§ 27. Knowing these courses twain
　　No Yogin is bemused.
　　So, Arjuna, ever be
　　In Yoga integrated.

§ 28. For knowledge of the Veda, for sacrifice, for grim
　　austerities,
For gifts of alms a meed of merit is laid down;
All this the Yogin leaves behind who knows this [secret teaching;]
[And knowing it] he draws right nigh to the highest primal state
　　(*sthāna*).

IX

The Blessed Lord said:
§ 1. But most secret and mysterious
Is the teaching I will [now] reveal,—
[A teaching] based on Holy Writ, consonant with experience:
To thee [will I proclaim it,] for in thee there is no envy;
And knowing it, thou shalt be freed from ill.

---

[1] Or, 'not confounding any other with Him'.
[2] Or, 'pervaded'.

§ 2. Science of kings, mystery of kings
Is this,—distilling the purest essence,
To the understanding evident, with righteousness enhanced,
How easy to carry out! [Yet] it abides forever.

§ 3. Men who put no faith
In this law of righteousness (*dharma*),
Fail to reach Me and must return
To the road of recurring death.

§ 4. By Me, Unmanifest in form,
This whole universe was spun: [1]
In Me subsist all beings,
I do not subsist in them.

§ 5. And [yet] contingent beings do not subsist in Me,—
Behold my sovereign power (*yoga*)!
My Self sustains [all] beings, it does not subsist in them;
    It causes them to be.

§ 6. As in [wide] space subsists the mighty wind,
    Blowing [at will] ever and everywhere,
So too do all contingent beings
Subsist in Me: so must thou understand.

§ 7. All contingent beings pass
Into material Nature which is Mine
When an aeon comes to an end; and then again
When another aeon starts, I emanate them forth.

§ 8. Firm-fixed in my material Nature
    Ever again I emanate
This whole mighty host of beings,
Powerless themselves,—from Nature comes the power.

§ 9. These works of mine
Bind Me not nor limit Me:
As one indifferent I sit
Among these works, detached. [2]

§ 10. [A world of] moving and unmoving things
Material Nature brings to birth, while I look on and supervise:
This is the cause and this the means
    By which the world revolves.

§ 11. For that a human form I have assumed
    Fools scorn Me,
Knowing nothing of my higher nature (*bhāva*),—
Great Lord of [all] contingent beings.

---

[1] Or, 'pervaded'.   [2] Or, 'detached from these works'.

§ 12. Vain their hopes and vain their deeds,
Vain their 'gnosis', void their wit;
A monstrous, devilish nature they embrace
   Which leads them [far] astray.

§ 13. But great-souled men take up their stand
   In a nature [all] divine;
And so, with minds intent on naught but Me,
They love and worship (*bhaj-*) Me,
Knowing Me to be the Beginning of all that is,
As Him who cannot pass away.

§ 14. Me do they ever glorify,
[For Me] they strive, full firm their vows;
To Me they bow down, devoted in their love (*bhakti*),
And integrated ever [in themselves], they pay me worship (*upās-*).

§ 15. Others again with wisdom's sacrifice
Make sacrifice to Me and worship Me
As One and yet as Manifold,
With face turned every way, in many a guise.

§ 16. I am the rite, the sacrifice,
The offering for the dead, the healing herb;
I am the sacred formula, the sacred butter am I,
I am the fire, and I the oblation [offered in the fire].

§ 17. I am the father of this world,
Mother, ordainer,[1] grandsire, [all] that need be known;
Vessel of purity [am I, the sacred syllable] Oṁ;
   And the three Vedas am I too.

§ 18. [I am] the Way,[2] sustainer, Lord and witness,
[True] home and refuge, friend,—
Origin and dissolution and the stable state between,—
A treasure-house, the seed that passes not away.

§ 19. It is I who pour out heat, hold back
   The rain and send it forth;
Death am I and deathlessness,
What is not and that which IS.

§ 20. Trusting in the three Vedas, the Soma-drinkers, purged of
   ritual fault (*pāpa*),
Worship Me with sacrifice, seeking to go to paradise:
These win through to the pure world of the lord of the gods
And taste in heaven the gods' celestial joys.

---

[1] Or, 'creator' or 'sustainer'.   [2] Or, 'goal'.

§ 21. [But] once they have [to the full] enjoyed the broad
    expanse of paradise,
Their merit exhausted, they come back to the world of men.
And so it is that those who stick fast to the three Vedas [only]
Receive [a reward] that comes and goes; for it is desire that they
    desire.

§ 22. For those men who meditate upon Me, no other [thought
    in mind],
    Who do me honour, ever persevere,
    I bring attainment
    And possession of what has been attained.

§ 23. [Yet] even those who worship other gods with love (*bhakta*)
And sacrifice to them, full filled with faith,
    Do really worship Me,
Though the rite differ from the norm.

§ 24. For it is I who of all acts of sacrifice
    Am Recipient and Lord,
But they do not know Me as I really am,
And so they fall [back into the world of men].

§ 25. To the gods go the gods' devotees,
To the ancestors their votaries,
To disembodied spirits the worshippers of these,
But those who sacrifice to Me shall come to Me.

§ 26. Be it a leaf, or flower, or fruit, or water
That a zealous soul may offer with love's devotion (*bhakti*),
    That do I [willingly] accept,
For it was love (*bhakti*) that made the offering.

§ 27. Whatever thou dost, whatever thou eatest,
Whatever thou dost offer up in sacrifice or give away in alms,
    Whatever penance thou mayst perform,
    Offer it up to me.

§ 28. So from [those] bonds which works [of their very nature
    forge],
Whose fruits are fair or foul, thou shalt be freed:
Thy self [now] integrated by renunciation and spiritual exercise
    (*yoga*),
    Free, thou shalt draw nigh to Me.

§ 29. In all contingent beings the same [1] am I;
None do I hate and none do I fondly love (*priya*);
But those who commune (*bhaj-*) with me in love's devotion
    (*bhakti*)
    [Abide] in Me, and I in them.

                            [1] Or, 'indifferent'.

§ 30. However evil a man's livelihood may be,
Let him but worship Me with love (*bhaj-*) and serve (*bhaj-*) no
    other,
Then shall he be reckoned among the good indeed,
    For his resolve is right.

§ 31. Right soon will his self be filled with righteousness (*dhar-
    mātmā*)
    And win eternal rest (*śānti*).
    Arjuna, of this be sure:
None who pays me worship of loyalty and love (*bhakta*) is ever
    lost.

§ 32. For whosoever makes Me his haven,
    Base-born though he may be,
Yes, women too, and artisans, even serfs,—
Theirs it is to tread the highest Way.[1]

§ 33. How much more, then, Brāhmans, pure and good,
And royal seers who know devoted love (*bhakta*).
Since thy lot has fallen in this world, impermanent and joyless,
    Commune with Me in love (*bhaj-*)!

§ 34. On Me thy mind, for Me thy loving service (*bhakta*),
For Me thy sacrifice, and to Me be thy prostrations:
Let [thine own] self be integrated, and then
Shalt thou come to Me, thy striving bent on Me.

X

The Blessed Lord said:
§ 1. [Now] once again, my strong-armed [friend],
    Give ear to my all-highest word
Which I shall speak to thee [alone],
For therein is thy delight [2] and thy welfare is my wish.

§ 2. None knows from whence I came,[3]—
Nor gods' celestial hosts nor mighty seers:
For I am the Beginning of the gods [themselves]
As of the mighty seers and all in every way.

§ 3. Whoso shall know Me as Unborn, Beginningless,
    Great Lord of [all] the worlds,
Shall never know delusion among men,
    From every evil freed.

---

[1] Or, 'goal'.   [2] Or, 'For thou art [beloved of Me]'.
[3] Lit. 'my origin'. Var. 'lordly power'.

§ 4. Intellect (*buddhi*), wisdom, freedom from delusion,
Long-suffering, truth, restraint, tranquillity,
Pleasure and pain, coming-to-be and passing away,[1]
    Fear and fearlessness as well,

§ 5. Refusal to do harm, equanimity (*samatā*), content,
Austerity, open-handedness, fame and infamy,—
Such are the dispositions (*bhāvā*) of contingent beings,
And from Me in all their diversity they arise.

§ 6. The seven mighty seers of old,
    Likewise the Manus four,[2]
Sharing in my mode of being,[3] were born [the children] of [my] mind;
From them [arose] these creatures in the world.

§ 7. Whoso should know my far-flung power and how I use it (*yoga*):[4]
[Whoso should know these] as they really are,
Is [truly] integrated (*yujyate*); and this his integration (*yoga*)
Can never be undone. Herein there is no doubt.

§ 8. The source of all am I;
    From Me all things proceed:
This knowing, wise men commune with (*bhaj-*) Me,
    Full filled with warm affection.[5]

§ 9. On Me their thoughts, their life they'd sacrifice for Me;
[And so] enlightening one another
And telling my story constantly,
They take their pleasure and delight.

§ 10. And since these men are ever integrated
And commune with (*bhaj-*) Me in love (*prīti*),
I give them an integrated soul [6]
By which they may draw nigh to Me.

§ 11. Out of compassion for these same men
[All] darkness born of ignorance I dispel
    With wisdom's shining lamp;
[Yet all the while] I still abide in the [true] nature of my Self.[7]

Arjuna said:

---

[1] Or, 'exaltation and depression'.
[2] Or, 'The seven mighty seers, the four ancients, and the Manus too'.
[3] Or, 'originating from Me'.
[4] Or, 'creative power'.
[5] *Bhāva*: Or, 'with [the right] disposition' or 'perseverance'.
[6] *Buddhiyoga*, cf. II. 49. Or 'discipline of mind'.
[7] Or, 'abiding in their selves', but this forces the Sanskrit.

§ 12–13. All-Highest Brahman, highest home (*dhāma*),
All-highest vessel of Purity art Thou.
    All seers agree that Thou
Art the Person, eternal and divine,

Primeval God, unborn and all-pervading Lord.
    So too Nārada, the godly seer,
Asita, Devala and Vyāsa [have declared];
And Thou Thyself dost tell me so.

§ 14. All this Thou tellest me is true;
    So, Krishna, I believe,
For, Blessed Lord, nor gods nor demons
Acknowledge [this] manifest [world] as thine.[1]

§ 15. By Thy Self Thou thyself dost know
Thy Self, O Thou, the All-Highest Person,
[Thou that] bestowest being on contingent beings,
    [Thou] the Lord of [all] contingent beings,
[Thou] God of gods and Lord of [all] the world.

§ 16. Tell me, I pray Thee, leaving naught unsaid,
Of the fair and far-flung powers [that centre] on thy Self,[2]
    By which Thou dost pervade these worlds,
      Standing [unchanged the while].

§ 17. How am I to know Thee, Thou master of Yogic power,
    Though I think upon Thee always?
And in what several modes of being
Should I think about Thee, Blessed Lord?

§ 18. Tell me again in detail full
Of thy far-flung power and how thou usest it (*yoga*); [3]
For as I listen to thy undying words,
    I cannot have enough.

    The Blessed Lord said:
§ 19. Lo, I shall tell thee
Of the fair and far-flung powers [that centre] on my Self,[2]—
Those of them, at least, that are fundamental,
    For of the details [4] there is no end.

§ 20. I am the Self established
In the heart of all contingent beings;
I am the beginning, the middle, and the end
    Of all contingent beings too.

---

[1] Or, 'know thy manifestation'.
[2] Reading *vibhūtīr ātmanaḥ subhāḥ*.
[3] Or, 'creative power'.   [4] Or 'extent'.

§ 21. Among the Ādityas Vishnu am I,
Among lights the radiant sun,
Among the Maruts Marīci am I,
Among stars I am the moon.

§ 22. Of the Vedas the Sāma Veda am I,
    Indra among the gods;
Among the senses I am mind,
Amongst contingent beings thought.

§ 23. Among the Rudras Śiva am I,
Among sprites and monsters the Lord of Wealth (Kuvera),
Of the Vasus I am Fire,
Among the mountains I am Meru.

§ 24. Of household priests know that I
    Am the chief, Brihaspati,
Among warlords I am Skanda, [god of war,]
Among lakes I am the Ocean.

§ 25. Bhrigu I am among the mighty seers,
Among utterances the single syllable [Oṁ],
Among sacrifices I am the sacrifice of muttered prayer,
Among things immovable the Himalayas,

§ 26. Among all trees the holy fig tree,
Nārada among the celestial seers,
Citraratha among the heavenly minstrels,
Among perfected beings Kapila, the silent sage.

§ 27. Among horses know that I
Am Uccaihśravas, (Indra's steed,) from nectar born,
Among princely elephants [Indra's called] Airāvata:
    Among men I am the King.

§ 28. Of weapons I am the thunderbolt,
Of cows the milch-cow of desires.
I am Kandarpa, [god of love,] generating seed:
Among serpents I am Vāsuki, [the serpent king].

§ 29. Of Nāga-serpents Ananta am I,
    Of water-dwellers Varuna;
Of the ancestors I am Aryaman,
Among those who subdue I am Yama, [the god of death].

§ 30. Among demons Prahlāda am I,
Among those who reckon Time;
Among beasts I am [the lion], the king of beasts,
And among birds Garuda, [Vishnu's bird].

§ 31. Among those who purify I am the Wind,
Rāma I am among men-at-arms;
Among water-monsters I am the crocodile,[1]
Among rivers [the Ganges, surnamed] Jāhnavī.

§ 32. Among emanations the beginning and the end
      And the middle too am I;
Among sciences I am the science concerned with Self,
Of those who speak I am [their very] speech.

§ 33. Among the letters of the alphabet I am 'A',
Among grammatical compounds the *dvandva*.
In very truth I am imperishable Time,
I the ordainer [2] with face turned every way.

§ 34. I am Death that snatches all away,
And the origin of creatures yet to be.
Among feminine nouns [3] I am fame, fortune, speech,
Memory, intelligence, steadfastness, long-suffering.[4]

§ 35. Among chants the Great Chant am I,
      Among metres the Gāyatrī,
Among months I am [the first,] Mārgashīrsha,
Among seasons flower-bearing [spring].

§ 36. I am the dicing of tricksters,
      Glory of the glorious;
Victory and firm resolve am I.
      And the courage of the brave.[5]

§ 37. Among Vrishni clansmen I am [Krishna,] Vasudeva's son,
      Among Pāndu's sons I am Arjuna;
      Among sages I am Vyāsa,
Among psalmists the psalmist, Ushanas.

§ 38. Of those who subdue the rod of chastisement am I,
And the statecraft of those who seek the upper hand;
The very silence of hidden, secret things am I,
      And the wisdom of the wise.

§ 39. What is the seed of all
Contingent beings, that too am I:
No being there is, whether moving or unmoving,
      That could exist apart from Me.

---

[1] Or, 'shark' or 'dolphin'.   [2] Or, 'creator'.
[3] Lit. 'women'.   [4] All these nouns are feminine in Sanskrit.
[5] Or, 'goodness of the good'.

§ 40. Of [these] my far-flung powers divine
    There is no end;
As much as I have said concerning them
    Must serve as an example.

§ 41. Whatever being shows wide power,
    Prosperity or strength,
    Be sure that this derives
From [but] a fragment of my glory.

§ 42. But where's the use for thee
    To know so much?
This whole universe I hold apart [supporting it]
With [but] a fragment [of Myself], yet I abide [unchanging].

XI

Arjuna said:
§ 1. Out of thy gracious favour to me Thou
Hast uttered the all-highest mystery
Called 'what appertains to Self',[1]
And by that word [of thine] banished is my perplexity.

§ 2. For I have heard of the coming-to-be
And passing away of contingent beings;
[This hast Thou told me] in detail full,
As well as the majesty of [thine own] Self which passes not away.

§ 3. Even as Thou hast described [thy] Self to be,
    So must it be, O Lord Most High;
[But] fain would I *see* the [bodily] form
Of Thee as Lord, All-Highest Person.

§ 4. If, Lord, Thou thinkest that I can
Thus see Thee, then show Thou forth,
Lord of creative power (*yoga*),
[This] Self that passes not away.

The Blessed Lord said:
§ 5. Son of Prithā, behold my forms
In their hundreds and their thousands;
How various are they, how divine,
How many-hued and multiform!

§ 6. Ādityas, Rudras, Vasus, the Aśvins twain,
    The Maruts too—behold them!
Marvels never seen before, —how many!
    Arjuna, behold them!

[1] *See* note on VII. 29, p. 282.

§ 7. Do thou today this whole universe behold
Centred here in One, with all that it contains
Of moving and unmoving things;
    [Behold] it in my body,
And whatsoever else thou fain wouldst see.

§ 8. But never canst thou see Me
With this thy [natural] eye.
A celestial eye I'll give thee:
Behold my creative power (*yoga*) [1] as Lord!

Sanjaya said:
§ 9. So saying Hari,[2]
The great Lord of Yogic power,
Revealed to the son of Prithā
His all-highest sovereign form,—

§ 10. [A form] with many a mouth and eye
And countless marvellous aspects;
Many [indeed] were its divine adornments,
Many the celestial weapons raised on high.

§ 11. Garlands and robes celestial He wore,
Fragrance divine was his anointing:
[Behold] this God whose every [mark] spells wonder,
    The infinite, facing every way!

§ 12. If in [bright] heaven together should arise
The shining brilliance of a thousand suns,
    Then would that [perhaps] resemble
The brilliance of that God so great of Self.

§ 13. Then did the son of Pāndu see
The whole [wide] universe in One converged,
There in the body of the God of gods,
Yet divided out in multiplicity.

§ 14. Then filled with amazement Arjuna,
His hair on end, hands joined in reverent greeting,
Bowing his head before the God,
    [These words] spake out:

Arjuna said:
§ 15. O God, the gods in thy body I behold,
And all the hosts of every kind of being;
Brahmā, the Lord, [I see], throned on the lotus-flower,
Celestial serpents and all the [ancient] seers.

---

[1] Var. 'form'.   [2] A name of Vishnu-Krishna.

§ 16. Arms, bellies, mouths and eyes all manifold—
So do I see Thee wherever I may look,—infinite thy form.
End, middle or beginning in Thee I cannot see,
O Monarch Universal, [manifest] in every form.

§ 17. Thine the crown, the mace, the discus,—
A mass of glory shining on all sides,
So do I see Thee,—yet how hard art Thou to see,—for on every
    side,
There's brilliant light of blazing fire and sun. O, who should
    comprehend it? [1]

§ 18. Thou art the Imperishable, [thou] wisdom's highest goal,
Thou, of this universe the last prop and resting-place,
Thou the changeless, [thou] the guardian of eternal law (*dharma*),
Thou art the eternal Person; [at last] I understand!

§ 19. Beginning, middle, end Thou knowest not,—how infinite
    thy strength!
How numberless thine arms,—thine eyes the sun and moon!
So do I see Thee,—thy mouth a flaming fire
Burning up this whole [universe] with its blazing glory.

§ 20. For by Thee alone is this space between heaven and earth
Pervaded,—all points of the compass [by Thee pervaded too];
Gazing on this, thy marvellous, frightening form,
The three worlds shudder, All-Highest Self (*mahātman*)!

§ 21. Lo, the hosts of gods are entering into Thee:
Some, terror-struck, extol Thee, hands together pressed;
Great seers and men perfected in serried ranks
Cry out, 'All hail,' and praise Thee with copious hymns of
    praise.

§ 22.   Rudras, Ādityas, Vasus, Sādhyas,
All-gods, Aśvins, Maruts and [the ancestors] who quaff the
    steam,
Minstrels divine, sprites, demons and the host, of perfected
    saints,
    Gaze upon Thee, all utterly amazed.

§ 23.   Gazing upon thy mighty form
With its myriad mouths, eyes, arms, thighs, feet,
    Bellies, and sharp, gruesome tusks,
The worlds [all] shudder [in affright],—how much more I!

---

[1] Lit. 'immeasurable', or 'incomprehensible'.

§ 24. Ablaze with many coloured [flames] Thou touch'st the sky,
Thy mouths wide open, gaping, thine eyes distended, blazing;
I see Thee, and my inmost self is shaken:
I cannot bear it, I find no peace, O Vishnu!

§ 25. I see thy mouths with jagged, ghastly tusks
Reminding [me] of Time's [devouring] fire:
I cannot find my bearings, I see no refuge;
Have mercy, God of gods, Home of the universe!

§ 26. Lo, all these sons of Dhritarāshtra
Accompanied by a host of kings,
Bhīshma, Drona and [Karna,] son of the charioteer,
And those foremost in battle of our party too,

§ 27. Rush [blindly] into thy [gaping] mouths
That with their horrid tusks strike [them] with terror.
    Some stick in the gaps between thy teeth,
See them!—their heads to powder ground!

§ 28. As many swelling, seething streams
Rush headlong into the [one great] sea,
So do these heroes of this world of men
    Enter thy blazing mouths.

§ 29. As moths, in bursting, hurtling haste
Rush into a lighted blaze to their destruction,
So do the worlds, well-trained in hasty violence,[1]
Pour into thy mouths to their own undoing.

§ 30. On every side thou lickest, lickest up,—devouring,—
Worlds, universes, everything—with burning mouths;
Vishnu! thy dreadful rays of light fill the whole universe
With flames of glory, scorching [everywhere].

§ 31. Tell me, who art Thou, thy form so cruel?
Homage to Thee, Thou best of gods, have mercy!
Fain would I know Thee as Thou art in the beginning,
For what Thou workest (*pravṛitti*) I do not understand.

    The Blessed Lord said:
§ 32. Time am I, wreaker of the world's destruction,
Matured,—[grimly] resolved (*pravṛtta*) here to swallow up the
    worlds.
Do what thou wilt, all these warriors shall cease to be,
    Drawn up [there] in their opposing ranks.

    [1] This is the same phrase in Sanskrit as that translated as 'in bursting,
hurtling haste' two lines above.

§ 33. And so arise, win glory,
Conquer thine enemies and enjoy a prosperous kingdom!
Long since have these men in truth been slain by Me,
    Thine it is to be the mere occasion.

§ 34. Bhīshma, Drona, Jayadratha,
Karna and all the other men of war
Are [as good as] slain by Me. Slay them then—why falter?
Fight! [for] thou shalt conquer thine enemies in battle.

    Sanjaya said:
§ 35. Hearing these words of Krishna, [Arjuna,]
Wearer of the crown, hands joined in veneration, trembling,
Bowed down again to Krishna and spake again
With stammering voice, as terrified he did obeisance.

    Arjuna said:
§ 36. Full just it is that in praise of Thee
The world should find its pleasure and its joy,
That monsters by terror [tamed] should scatter in all directions,
And that all who've won perfection should do Thee homage.

§ 37. For why should they not revere Thee, great as is thy Self,
More to be prized art Thou than Brahmā,[1] [Thou] the first
    Creator,
Gods' Lord, the world's [abiding] home, unending.
Thou art the Imperishable, Being, Not-Being and what surpasses
    both.[2]

§ 38. Thou art the Primal God, Primeval Person,
Thou of this universe the last prop and resting-place,
Thou the knower and what is to be known, [Thou our] final home
    (dhāma),
O Thou whose forms are infinite, by whom the whole [universe]
    was spun.[3]

§ 39. Thou art [the wind-god] Vāyu, Yama [the god of death],
The god of fire (Agni) and water (Varuna) and the moon:
Prajāpati art Thou, and the primordial Ancestor:
All hail, all hail to Thee, [all hail] a thousandfold,
    And yet again, All hail, all hail!

§ 40. All hail [to Thee] when I stand before Thee,
[All hail] when I stand behind Thee,
All hail to Thee wherever I may be,

    [1] Or, 'Brahman'. The whole phrase could mean 'Most reverend creator
of Brahmā (or Brahman)'.
    [2] Or, 'that All-Highest' with some MSS.
    [3] Or, 'pervaded'.

[All hail to Thee], Thou All!
How infinite thy strength, how limitless thy prowess!
All dost Thou bring to consummation,[1] hence art Thou All.

§ 41. How rashly have I called Thee comrade, for so I thought of Thee,
[How rashly said,] 'Hey Krishna, Hey Yādava, Hey comrade!'
Little did I know of this thy majesty,
Distraught was I, . . . or was it that I loved Thee?

§ 42. Sometimes in jest I showed Thee disrespect
As we played or rested or sat or ate at table,
Sometimes together, sometimes in sight of others:
I crave thy pardon, O Lord, unfathomable, unfallen.

§ 43. Thou art the father of the moving and unmoving world,
Thou its venerable teacher, most highly prized;
None is there like Thee,—how could there be a greater?—
In these three worlds, O matchless is thy power.

§ 44. And so I bow to Thee, prostrate my body,
Crave grace of Thee, [my] Lord adorable;
Bear with me, I pray Thee, as father [bears] with son,
Or friend with friend, or lover with the one he loves.

§ 45. Things never seen before I've seen, and ecstatic is my joy;
Yet fear and trembling possess my mind.
Show me, then, God, that [same human] form [I knew],
Have mercy, Lord of gods, Home of the universe!

§ 46. Fain would I see Thee with [thy familiar] crown and mace,
Discus in hand, just as Thou used to be;
Take up again thy four-armed form,
O Thousand-armed, to whom every form belongs.

The Blessed Lord said:
§ 47. Because I desired to show thee favour, Arjuna,
By my Self's mysterious power (*ātmayoga*) I showed thee this my All-Highest form,—
Glorious, all-embracing, infinite, primeval,—
Which none has seen before save thee.

§ 48. Not by the Vedas, not by sacrifice,
Not by [much] study or the giving of alms,
Not by rituals or grim ascetic practice,
Can I be seen in such a form in the world of men:
To Thee alone have I revealed it.

---

[1] Or, 'comprisest'.

§ 49. Thou needst not tremble nor need thy spirit be perplexed,
Though thou hast seen this form of mine, awful, grim.
Banish all fear, be glad at heart: behold again
That same [familiar human] form [thou knewest].

Sanjaya said:
§ 50. Thus speaking did the son of Vasudeva
Show his [human] form to Arjuna again,
    Comforting him in his fear.
For once again the high-souled (*mahātman*) [Krishna]
Assumed the body of a friend.

Arjuna said:
§ 51. Now that I see [again] thy human form,
    Friendly and kind,
I have returned to my senses
And regained my normal state.

The Blessed Lord said:
§ 52. Right hard to see is this my form
    Which thou has seen:
This is the form the gods themselves
    Forever crave to see.

§ 53. Not by the Vedas or grim ascetic practice,
Not by the giving of alms or sacrifice
Can I be seen in such a form
    As thou didst see Me.

§ 54. But by worship of love (*bhakti*) addressed to Me alone
    Can I be known and seen
In such a form and as I really am:
[So can my lovers] enter into Me.

§ 55. Do works for Me, make Me thy highest goal,
Be loyal in love (*bhakta*) to Me,
Cast off [all other] attachments,
Have no hatred for any being at all:
For all who do thus shall come to Me.

XII

Arjuna said:
§ 1. Of those who are thus ever integrated
And serve Thee with loyal devotion (*bhakta*),
And those who [revere] the Imperishable Unmanifest,
Which are the most skilled in spiritual exercise (*yoga*)?

The Blessed Lord said:
§ 2. Those I deem to be the most integrated
    Who fix their thoughts on Me
And serve Me, ever integrated [in themselves],
    Filled with the highest faith.

§ 3. But those who serve the indeterminate,
    Imperishable Unmanifest,
Unthinkable, though coursing everywhere,
Sublime, aloof, unmoving, firm,

§ 4. Who hold in check the complex of their senses,
    In all things equal-minded,
In others' weal rejoicing,
Those too attain to Me.

§ 5. [But] greater is the toil of those
Whose thinking clings to the Unmanifest;
For difficult [indeed] it is for embodied men
To reach and tread the unmanifested Way.[1]

§ 6. But those who cast off all their works on Me,
    Solely intent on Me,
And meditate on Me in spiritual exercise (*yoga*),
Leaving no room for others, [and so really] do Me service,

§ 7. These will I lift up on high
Out of the ocean of recurring death,
    And that right soon,
For their thoughts are fixed on Me.

§ 8. On Me alone let thy mind dwell,
Stir up thy soul (*buddhi*) to enter Me;
    Thenceforth in very truth (*eva*)
In Me thou'lt find thy home.

§ 9. But if thou art unable in all steadfastness
    To concentrate thy thoughts on Me,
        Then seek to win Me
        By effort unremitting.

§ 10. And if for such effort thou lack'st the strength,
Then work and act for Me, make this thy goal;
For even if thou workest only for my sake,
    Thou shalt receive the prize.

---

[1] Or, 'goal'.

§ 11. And then again if even this exceeds thy powers,
   Gird up thy loins,[1] renounce
The fruit of all thy works
   With self restrained.

§ 12. For better is wisdom than [mere] effort,
   Better than wisdom meditation;
And better than meditation to renounce the fruits of works:
Renunciation leads straightway to peace.

§ 13. Let a man feel hatred for no contingent being,
   Let him be friendly, compassionate,
Let him be done with thoughts of 'I' and 'mine',
The same in pleasure as in pain, long-suffering,

§ 14. Content and ever integrated,
His self restrained, his purpose firm,
Let his mind and soul (*buddhi*) be steeped in Me,
Let him worship Me with love (*bhakta*):
   Then will I love him [in return].

§ 15. That man I love from whom the people do not shrink,
   And who does not shrink from them,
Who's free from exaltation, fear,
   Impatience and excitement.

§ 16. I love the man who has no expectation,
Is pure and skilled, indifferent,
Who has no worries, and gives up
All [selfish] enterprise, wrapt up in (*bhakta*) Me.

§ 17. I love the man who hates not, nor exults,
   Who mourns not nor desires,
Who puts away both pleasant and unpleasant things,
   Who's loyal, devoted and devout (*bhaktimat*).

§ 18–19. I love the man who is the same
To friend and foe, [the same]
Whether he be respected or despised,
The same in heat and cold, in pleasure as in pain,

Who's put away attachment and remains
Unmoved by praise or blame, who's taciturn,
Contented with whatever comes his way, of steady mind,
Homeless, [but] loyal, devoted and devout.

§ 20. But as for those who reverence these deathless [words]
Of righteousness (*dharmya*) which I have just now spoken,
Putting their faith [in them], making Me their goal,
My loving devotees (*bhakta*)—these do I love exceedingly.

[1] Reading *udyogam* with some MSS. for *mad-yogam*.

XIII

Arjuna said:
§ 0.[1] What is Nature? What the 'person'?
What the 'field', and what its knower?
 This, Krishna, would I know.
What too is knowledge? What that which should be known?

The Blessed Lord said:
§ 1.   This body
 Is called the 'field',
And he who knows it is the 'knower of the field',
Or so it has been said by men who know it.

§ 2. Know that I am the 'knower of the field'
 In every field;
Knowledge of [this] field and [this] knower of the field
 I deem to be [true] knowledge.

§ 3. What the field is and what it is like,
What are its changes and which derives from which,
And who He is [the knower of the field,] and what his powers [2]
 Hear now from Me in brief.

§ 4. In many ways has it been sung by seers,
In varied hymns, each in its separate way,
In aphoristic verses concerning Brahman,
 Well reasoned and conclusive.

§ 5. Gross elements, the ego,
 Intellect (*buddhi*), the Unmanifest,
  The eleven senses
And the five sense-objects on which the senses thrive,

§ 6. Desire, hate, pleasure, pain,
Sensus communis,[3] thought and constancy,—
These, in briefest span, are called the 'field'
 Together with its changes.

§ 7. To shun conceit and tricky ways,
To wish none harm, to be long-suffering and upright,
To reverence one's preceptor, purity,
Steadfastness, self-restraint,

§ 8. Detachment from the things of sense,
And selflessness most certainly,
Insight into birth, death, old age, disease and pain,—
And what constitutes their worthlessness,

 [1] Most MSS. omit this verse.
 [2] Var. 'nature'.   [3] Uncertain.

§ 9. To be detached and not to cling
To sons, wives, houses and the like,
A constant equal-mindedness
Whatever happens, pleasing or unpleasing,

§ 10. Unswerving loyalty and love (*bhakti*) for Me
With spiritual exercise (*yoga*) on no other bent,
To dwell apart in desert places,
To take no pleasure in the company of men,

§ 11. Constant devotion to the wisdom appertaining to self,
To see where knowledge of reality must lead,
[All] this is 'knowledge',—or so it has been said.
Ignorance is what is otherwise than this.

§ 12. [And now] shall I tell thee that which should be known:
Once a man knows it, he attains to immortality.
All-Highest [1] Brahman is It called,—beginningless,—
Call it not 'Being', [call it] not 'Not-Being'.

§ 13. Hands and feet It has on every side,
On every side eyes, heads, mouths and ears;
In the world all things encompassing
      [Changeless] It abides.

§ 14. Devoid of all the senses,
It yet sheds light on [2] all their qualities,
[From all] detached, and yet supporting all;
Free from Nature's constituents,[3] It yet experiences them.

§ 15. Within all beings, yet without them;
Unmoved, It moves in very truth;
So subtle It is you cannot comprehend It;
Far off It stands, and yet how near It is!

§ 16. Undivided, in beings It abides
      Seeming divided:
This is That which should be known,—
[The One] who upholds, devours and generates [all] beings.

§ 17.   Light of lights,
'Beyond the darkness' It is called;
[True] knowledge, what should be known, accessible to knowledge,
      Abiding in the heart of all.

[1] Var. 'dependent on Me', 'suffused in Me'.
[2] Or, 'has the semblance of'.   [3] Or, 'qualities'.

§ 18.   And so in brief I have explained
The 'field' and 'knowledge' and 'that which should be known';
The man who loves and worships (*bhakta*) Me, on knowing this,
Becomes fit [to share in] my own mode of being.

§ 19. 'Person' and 'Nature': [what are these?]
Both are beginningless, this know.
And know that change and quality [1]
    Arise from Nature.

§ 20. Nature, they say, is [itself] the cause
Of cause,[2] effect and agency,
While 'person' is said to be the cause
In the experience of pleasure and of pain.

§ 21. For [this] 'person' is lodged in Nature,
Experiencing its 'constituents';
Because he attaches himself to these,
He comes to birth in good and evil wombs.

§ 22. [And yet another One there is who,] surveying and approving,
Supports and [Himself] experiences [the constituents of Nature],
The Mighty Lord: 'All-Highest Self' some call Him,
'All-highest Person' in this body.

§ 23. Who 'person' knows and Nature
And Nature's constituents to be such,
Whatever his station be in life,
    He is not born again.

§ 24. By meditation some themselves
    See self in self,
Others by putting sound reason into practice (*sāṁkhyayoga*),
Yet others by the exercise (*yoga*) of works (*karma*).

§ 25. But some, not knowing thus,
Hear it from others and revere it;
And even these, taking their stand on Scripture,[3]
    Pass beyond death indeed.

§ 26. Whatever being comes to be,
Be it motionless or moving,
[Derives its being] from the union
Of 'field' and 'Knower of the field': this know.

       [1] Or, 'the constituents of Nature'.   [2] Reading *kāraṇa*.
       [3] Or, 'what they hear'.

§ 27. The same in all contingent beings,
   Abiding [without change], the All-Highest Lord,
When all things fall to ruin, [Himself] knows no destruction:
   Who sees Him, sees [indeed].

§ 28. For seeing Him the same, the Lord,
   Established everywhere,
He cannot of himself to [him]self [1] do hurt;
Hence he treads on the highest Way.[2]

§ 29. Nature it is which in every way
   Does works [and acts];
No agent is the self: who sees it thus,
   He sees indeed.

§ 30. When once a man can see that [all] the diversity
Of contingent beings abides in One [alone],
   And from That alone they radiate,
   Then to Brahman he attains.

§ 31. Because this All-Highest Self knows no beginning,
No quality,[3] it passes not away;
Though abiding in [many a] body,
He does not act nor is He defiled.

§ 32. Just as the ether, roving everywhere,
Knows no defilement, so subtle [is its essence],
So does this Self, though everywhere abiding
And embodied, know no defilement.

§ 33. As the one sun lights up
   This whole universe,
So does the 'Knower of the field'
   Illumine [this] whole 'field'.

§ 34. Whoso with wisdom's eye discerns the difference
Between 'field' and 'Knower of the field',
And knows deliverance from beings in their material (*prakṛti*)
   form,
      Treads on the highest Way.[4]

XIV

The Blessed Lord said:
§ 1. [And now] again I shall proclaim
The highest wisdom, best of doctrines (*jñāna*);
On knowing this all sages, when they passed on hence,
   Attained the highest prize.

[1] Or, 'the Self'.   [2] Or, 'goal'.
[3] Or, 'constituent of Nature'.
[4] Or, 'goes to the highest goal'. This alternative will no longer be noted.

§ 2. With this wisdom as their bulwark
They reached a rank [in the order of existence] equivalent to
    (*sādharmya*) my own;
And even when [the universe is once again] engendered, they are
    not born [again],
And when [again] it is dissolved, they know no trepidation.

§ 3. Great Brahman is to Me a womb,
    In it I plant the seed:
From this derives the origin
    Of all contingent beings.

§ 4. In whatever womb whatever form
    Arises and grows together,
Of [all] those [forms] great Brahman is the womb,
    I the father, giver of the seed.

§ 5. Goodness—Passion—Darkness:
These are the 'constituents' from Nature sprung.
    They bind the embodied soul
In the body, though [the soul itself is] changeless.

§ 6. Among these Goodness, being immaculate,
    Knowing no sickness, dispenses light,
[And yet] it binds by [causing the soul] to cling
    To wisdom and to joy (*sukha*).

§ 7. Passion is instinct with desire: this know.
From craving and attachment it wells up:
    It binds the embodied soul
    By [causing it] to cling to works.

§ 8. From ignorance is Darkness born: mark this well.
    All embodied souls it leads astray.
With fecklessness and sloth and sleepiness
        It binds.

§ 9. Goodness causes a man to cling to joy,
    Passion to works;
But Darkness, stifling wisdom,
    Attaches to fecklessness.

§ 10. Once Passion and Darkness it dominates,
    Goodness comes to grow; [1]
    So Passion and Darkness
When they dominate the other two.

[1] Reading *vardhate*.

§ 11. When at all this body's gates
    Wisdom's light arises,
        Then must thou know
That Goodness has increased.

§ 12. When Passion's waxing strong,
        These [states] arise:
Greed, [purposeful] activity, committing oneself to works,
        Ambition and disquiet.

§ 13. When Darkness is surging up,
        These [states] arise:
Unlighted darkness, unwillingness to act,
        Delusion, fecklessness.

§ 14. But when an embodied soul comes face to face with the
        body's dissolution,
        And Goodness [then] prevails,
Then will he reach the spotless worlds
    Of those who know the highest.

§ 15. [Another] goes to his demise when Passion [predominates];
He will be born among such men as cling to works:
And as to him who dies when Darkness [has the upper hand],
    He will be born in wombs of deluded fools.

§ 16. Of works well done, they say,
The fruits belong to Goodness, being without spot:
    Pain is the fruit of Passion,
        Ignorance of Darkness.

§ 17. From Goodness wisdom springs,
        From Passion greed,
From Darkness delusion, fecklessness,
        And ignorance—how not?

§ 18. Upward is the path of those who abide in Goodness,
    In the middle stand the men of Passion.
Stuck in the modes of the vilest constituent,
    The men of Darkness go below.

§ 19. When the watching [self] sees that there is no agent
        Other than [these] constituents,
And knows what is beyond them,
    Then will he come [to share]
In that mode of being which is Mine.

§ 20. Transcending these three constituents
   Which give the body its existence,[1]
From birth and death, old age and pain delivered,
   The embodied soul wins immortality.

   Arjuna said:
§ 21. What signs, Lord, mark him out,—
[This man] who has transcended the three constituents?
How does he behave? And how does he step out beyond
   These three constituents?

   The Blessed Lord said:
§ 22. Radiance—activity—yes, delusion too—
When they arise, he hates them not;
And when [in turn] they cease,
He pines not after them.

§ 23. Indifferent he sits,
   By the 'constituents' unruffled:
'So the constituents are busy,' thus he thinks:
   Firm-based is he, unquivering,

§ 24. The same in pleasure as in pain, and self-assured,
The same when faced with clods of earth or stones or gold;
For him, the wise, are friend and foe of equal weight,
Equal the praise or blame [with which men cover him];

§ 25. Equal [his mind] in honour and disgrace,
Equal to ally and to enemy,
He renounces every [busy] enterprise:
'He has transcended the "constituents"': so must men say.

§ 26. And as to those who do Me honour with spiritual exercise
   (yoga)
   In loyalty and love (bhakti) undeviating,
   Passed [clean] beyond these 'constituents',
   To becoming Brahman they're conformed.

§ 27. For I am the base supporting Brahman,—
Immortal [Brahman] Which knows no change,—
[Supporting too] the eternal law of righteousness (dharma)
   And absolute beatitude (sukha).

XV

   The Blessed Lord said:
§ 1. With roots above and boughs beneath,
They say, the undying fig tree [stands]:
Its leaves are the [Vedic] hymns:
   Who knows it, knows the Veda.

                    [1] Or, 'arising from the body'.

§ 2. Below, above, its branches straggle out,
Well nourished by the constituents; sense-objects are its twigs.
Below, its roots proliferate
Inseparably linked with works in the world of men.

§ 3. No form of it can here be comprehended,
No end and no beginning, no sure abiding-place:
This fig tree with its roots so fatly nourished—
[Take] the stout axe of detachment and cut it down!

§ 4. And then search out that [high] estate [1]
To which, when once men go, they come not back again.
I fly for succour to that Primeval Person
'From whom flowed forth primordial creativity (*pravṛtti*).'

§ 5. Not proud, not fooled, [all] taint of attachment crushed,
Ever abiding in what concerns the self, desire suppressed,
Released from [all] dualities made known in pleasure as in pain,
The undeluded march ahead to that state [2] which knows no
    change.

§ 6. That [state] is not illumined
    By sun or moon or fire:
Once men go thither, they come not back again,
For that is my all-highest home (*dhāma*).

§ 7. In the world of living things a [minute] part of Me,
Eternal [still], becomes a living [self],
Drawing to itself the five senses and the mind
    Which have their roots in Nature.

§ 8. When [this] sovereign [self] takes on a body
    And when he rises up therefrom,
He takes them [with him], moving on,
As the wind [wafts] scents away from their proper home.

§ 9. Ear, eye, touch, taste and smell
    He turns to due account,—
        So too the mind;
[With these] he moves among the things of sense.

§ 10. Whether he rise up [from the body] or remain therein,
Or whether, through contact with the constituents, he tastes
    experience,
        Fools do not perceive him;
But whoso possesses wisdom's eye sees him [indeed].

---

[1] Or, 'place, region'. Var. *para*, 'the highest'.
[2] Or, 'place, region'.

§ 11. And Yogins, fighting the [spirit's] fight,
See him established in the self;
Not so those men whose self is unperfected,—
However much they strive, witless, they see him not.

§ 12. The splendour centred in the sun
Which bathes the whole world in light,
[The splendour] in the moon and fire,—
Know that it [all] derives from Me.

§ 13. [Thus] too I penetrate the earth and so sustain
    [All] beings with my strength;
Becoming [the moon-plant] Soma, the very sap [of life],
    I cause all healing herbs to grow.

§ 14. Becoming the digestive fire, I dwell
    In the body of all that breathes;
Conjoined with the inward and outward breaths,
    I digest the fourfold food.

§ 15. I make my dwelling in the hearts of all:
From Me stem memory, wisdom, refuting [doubt].[1]
Through all the Vedas it is I that should be known,
For the Maker of the Veda's end [2] am I, and I the Vedas know.

§ 16. In this world there are these two 'persons',—
    Perishable the one, Imperishable the other:
The perishable is all contingent beings,
The Imperishable they call 'the sublime, aloof' (*kūṭastha*).

§ 17. But there is [yet] another Person, the [All-]Sublime (*uttama*),
    Surnamed 'All-Highest Self':
The three worlds he enters and pervades,
Sustaining them,—the Lord who passes not away.

§ 18. Since I transcend the perishable,
And am more exalted than the Imperishable itself,
So am I extolled in common as in Vedic speech
    As 'the Person [All-]Sublime'.

§ 19. Whoever knows Me, unconfused,
    As 'the Person [All-]Sublime',
Knows all and [knowing all] communes with (*bhaj-*) Me
    With all his being (*bhāva*), all his love (*bhāva*).

§ 20. And so have I [at last] revealed
    This most mysterious doctrine:
Let a man but understand it, for then he'll be
A man who [truly] understands, his [life's] work done.

---

[1] Uncertain.   [2] *Vedānta*, i.e. the Upanishads.

XVI

The Blessed Lord said:
§ 1. Fearless and pure in heart,
  Steadfast in the exercise (*yoga*) of wisdom,
Restrained and open-handed, performing sacrifice,
Intent on studying Holy Writ, ascetic and upright,

§ 2. None hurting, truthful, from anger free,
Renouncing [all], at peace, averse to calumny,
Compassionate to [all] existent beings, free from nagging greed,
Gentle, modest, never fickle,

§ 3. Ardent, patient, enduring, pure,
  Not treacherous nor arrogant,—
Such is the man who's born [to inherit]
  A godly destiny.

§ 4. A hypocrite, proud of himself and arrogant,
Angry, harsh and ignorant
Is the man who's born [to inherit]
  A devilish destiny.

§ 5. A godly destiny means deliverance,
A devilish one enslavement; this is the usual view.
But fret not, Arjuna, for thou art born
  To a godly destiny.

§ 6. Two orders of contingent beings in this world there are:
    The godly and the devilish.
Of the godly I have discoursed enough,
Now listen to my words about the devilish.

§ 7. Of creative action (*pravṛtti*) and its cessation (*nivṛtti*)
  The devilish folk know nothing;
In them thou'lt find no purity nor yet
  Seemly behaviour or truthfulness.

§ 8. 'The world's devoid of truth,' they say,
'It has no ground, no ruling Lord;
It has not come to be by mutual causal law;
Desire alone has caused it,[1] nothing else.'

§ 9. Fast holding to these views,
Lost souls (*ātman*) with feeble minds,
They embark on cruel and violent deeds,—malignant
  [In their lust] for the destruction of the world.

---

[1] Var. 'random, without any cause'.

§ 10. Insatiate desire's their starting-point,—
Maddened are they by hypocrisy and pride,[1]
Clutching at false conceptions, deluded as they are,
Plying their several trades: impure are their resolves.

§ 11. Unmeasured care is theirs
Right up to the time of death,
[For] they aim at nothing but to satisfy their lusts,
    Convinced that this is all.

§ 12. Bound by a hundred fetters [forged] by hope,
    Obsessed by anger and desire,
They seek to build up wealth unjustly
    To satisfy their lusts.

§ 13. 'This have I gained today,
This whim I'll satisfy;
This wealth is mine, and much more too
Will be mine as time goes on.

§ 14. He was an enemy of mine; I've killed him,
And many another too I'll kill.
I'm master [here], I take my pleasure [as I will];
I'm strong and happy and successful!

§ 15. I'm rich and of a good family.
Who else can match himself with me?
I'll sacrifice and I'll give alms:
[Why not?] I'll have a marvellous time!'
So speaks [the fool] deluded in his ignorance!

§ 16. [Their minds] unhinged by many a [foolish] fancy,
    Caught up in delusion's snare,
Obsessed [by one thought only]; 'I must satisfy my lusts,'—
    Into foul hell they fall.

§ 17. Puffed up with self-conceit, unbending,
Maddened by their pride in wealth,[2]
They offer sacrifices that are but sacrifice in name
And not in the way prescribed,—the hypocrites!

§ 18. Selfishness, force and pride,
Desire and anger—these do they rely on,
Envying and hating Me
Who dwell in their bodies as I dwell in all.

---

[1] Or, 'possessed of hypocrisy, pride and frenzy'.
[2] Or, 'filled with the madness and pride of wealth'.

§ 19. Birth after birth in this revolving round
These vilest among men, strangers to [all] good,
Obsessed with hate and cruel, I hurl
      Into devilish wombs,

§ 20. Caught up in devilish wombs,
Birth after birth deluded,
They never attain to Me:
And so they tread the lowest path.

§ 21. Desire—Anger—Greed:
This is the triple gate of hell,
      Destruction of the self:
Therefore avoid these three.

§ 22. When once a man is freed
From these three gates of darkness,
Then can he work for self's salvation (*śreyas*),
Thence tread the highest Way.

§ 23. Whoso forsakes the ordinance of Scripture
And lives at the whim of his own desires,
Wins not perfection, [finds] no comfort (*sukha*),
[Treads not] the highest Way.

§ 24. Therefore let Scripture be thy norm,
Determining what is right and wrong.
Once thou dost know what the ordinance of Scripture bids thee
      do,
Then shouldst thou here perform the works [therein prescribed].

XVII

Arjuna said:
§ 1. [And yet there are some] who forsake the ordinance of
      Scripture,
And offer sacrifice, full filled with faith.
      Krishna, where do they stand?
On Goodness, Passion or on Darkness?

The Blessed Lord said:
§ 2. Threefold is the faith of embodied souls;
[Each of the three] springs from [a man's own] nature.
[The first is] of Goodness, [the second] of Passion,
[The third] of Darkness. Listen to this.

§ 3. Faith is connatural to the soul (*sattva*)
      Of every man:
Man is instinct with faith:
As is his faith, so too must he be.

§ 4. To the gods do men of Goodness offer sacrifice,
To sprites and monsters men of Passion;
To ghosts and the assembled spirits of the dead
The others—men of Darkness—offer sacrifice.

§ 5-6. And this know too. Some men there are
Who, without regard to Scripture's words, savagely mortify
    [their flesh],
Buoyed up by hypocrisy and self-regard,
Yielding to the violence of passion and desire,

And so torment the mass of living things
Whose home their body is, the witless fools,—
And [with] them Me Myself within [that same] body hidden:
    How devilish their intentions!

§ 7. Threefold again is food,—
[Food] that agrees with each [different type of] man:
So too sacrifice, ascetic practice and the gift of alms.
Listen to the difference between them.

§ 8. Food that promotes a fuller life, strength, health,
Vitality (*sattva*),[1] pleasure and good-feeling,—
[Foods that are] savoury, rich in oil, and firm,
Heart-gladdening: these are agreeable to the man of Goodness.

§ 9. Foods that are pungent, sour, salty, stinging hot,
Sharp, rough and burning,—these are what
The man of Passion loves. And they it is that cause
    Pain, misery and sickness.

§ 10. Whatever's stale and tasteless,
    Rotten and decayed,—
Leavings, what's unfit for sacrifice,
Is food agreeable to the man of Darkness.

§ 11. The sacrifice approved by sacred ordinance
And offered up by men who would not taste its fruits,
Who concentrate their minds on this [alone]:
'In this sacrifice lies duty': [such sacrifice] belongs to Goodness.

§ 12. But the sacrifice that is offered up by men
    Who bear its fruits in mind,
    Or simply for vain display,
Know that [such sacrifice] belongs to Passion.

[1] Or, 'soul', 'mind', or 'courage'.

§ 13. The sacrifice in which no proper rite is followed, no food
    distributed,
No sacred words recited, no Brāhman's fees paid up,
No faith enshrined,—[such sacrifice]
    Men say belongs to Darkness.

§ 14. [Due] reverence of gods and Brāhmans,
    Preceptors and wise men,
Purity, uprightness, chastity, refusal to do harm,—
    This is [true] penance of the body.

§ 15. Words that do not cause disquiet,
[Words] truthful, kind and pleasing,
The constant practice too of sacred recitation,—
    This is the penance of the tongue.

§ 16. Serenity of mind and friendliness,
    Silence and self-restraint,
And the cleansing of one's affections (bhāva),—
    This is the penance of the mind.

§ 17. When men possessed of highest faith,
Integrated and indifferent to the fruits [of what they do],
    Do penance in this threefold wise,
Men speak of penance in Goodness' way.

§ 18. Some mortify themselves to win respect,
Honour and reverence, or from sheer hypocrisy:
    Here [on earth] this must be called
Penance in Passion's way,—fickle and unsure.

§ 19. Some mortify themselves following perverted theories,
    Torturing themselves,
    Or to destroy another:
This is called penance in Darkness' way.

§ 20. Alms given because to give alms is a sacred duty
To one from whom no favour is expected in return
At the [right] place and time and to a [fit] recipient,—
This is called alms given in Goodness' way.

§ 21. But [alms] given in expectation of favours in return,
Or for the sake of fruits [to be reaped] hereafter,
[Alms] given too against the grain,—
This is called alms given in Passion's way.

§ 22. Alms given at the wrong place and time
    To recipients unworthy
Without respect, contemptuously,—
This is called [alms given] in Darkness' way.

§ 23. Oṁ, THAT, IT IS: This has been handed down,—
    A threefold pointer to Brahman:
By It were allotted their proper place of old
    Brāhmans, Vedas and sacrifice.

§ 24. And so [all] acts of sacrifice, the giving of alms and penance
    Enjoined by [Vedic] ordinances
And ever again enacted by Brahman's devotees
Begin with the utterance of [the one word] Oṁ.

§ 25. THAT: [so saying,] do men who hanker for deliverance
Perform the various acts of sacrifice,
    Penance and the gift of alms,
Having no thought for the fruits [they bring].

§ 26. IT IS (*sat*): in this the meanings are conjoined
    Of 'Being' and of 'good':
So too the [same] word *sat* is appropriately used
    For works that call forth praise.

§ 27. In sacrifice, in penance, in the gift of alms
[The same word] *sat* is used, meaning 'steadfastness':
And works performed with these purposes in mind,
    [These] too are surnamed *sat*.

§ 28. Whatever offering is made in unbelief,
Whatever given, whatever act of penance undertaken,
Whatever done,—of that is said *asat*, 'it is not':
    For naught it is in this world and the next.

XVIII

    Arjuna said:
§ 1. Krishna, fain would I hear the truth
    Concerning renunciation,
    And apart from this
[The truth] of self-surrender.

    The Blessed Lord said:
§ 2. To give up works dictated by desire,
Wise men allow this to be renunciation;
Surrender of all the fruits [that accrue] to works
Discerning men call self-surrender.

§ 3. '[All] works must be surrendered, [for works themselves
    are] tainted with defect':
    So say some of the wise;
But others say that works of sacrifice, the gift of alms
And works of penance are not to be surrendered.

§ 4. Hear then mine own decision
In [this matter of] surrender:
Threefold is [the act of] self-surrender;
    So has it been declared.

§ 5. Works of sacrifice, the gift of alms and works of penance
Are not to be surrendered; these must most certainly be done;
It is sacrifice, alms-giving and ascetic practice
    That purify the wise.

§ 6. But even those works should be done [in a spirit of self-surrender],
For [all] attachment to what you do and [all] the fruits [of what you do]
    Must be surrendered.
This is my last decisive word.[1]

§ 7. For to renounce a work enjoined [by Scripture]
    Is inappropriate;
    Deludedly to give this up
Is [the way] of Darkness. This [too] has been declared.

§ 8. The man who gives up a deed simply because it causes pain
Or because he shrinks from bodily distress,
Commits an act of self-surrender that accords with Passion's way;
Assuredly he will not reap surrender's fruit.

§ 9. But if a work is done simply because it should be done
And is work enjoined [by Scripture],
And if [all] attachment, [all thought of] fruit is given up,
Then [that work is done] in Goodness' way, I deem.

§ 10. The self-surrendered man, suffused with Goodness, wise,
Whose [every] doubt is cut away,
Hates not his uncongenial work
Nor cleaves to the congenial.

§ 11. For one still in the body it is not possible
To surrender up all works without exception;
Rather it is he who surrenders up the *fruits* of works
Who deserves the name 'a self-surrendered man'.

§ 12. Unwanted—wanted—mixed:
    Threefold is the fruit of work,—
[This they experience] at death who have not surrendered [self],
But not at all such men who have renounced.

[1] Lit. 'thought'.

§ 13. In the system of the Sāṁkhyas
Five factors are laid down;
By these all works attain fruition.
  Learn them from Me.

§ 14. Material basis, agent,
Instruments of various kinds,
The vast variety of motions,
And fate, the fifth and last:

§ 15. These are the five factors
Of whatever work a man may undertake,
  Of body, speech or mind,
No matter whether right or wrong.

§ 16. Since this is so, the man who sees in self alone
The agent, does not see [at all].
Untrained is his intelligence,
And evil are his thoughts.

§ 17. A man who's reached a state where there is no sense of 'I',
Whose soul (*buddhi*) is undefiled,—
Were he to slaughter [all] these worlds,
Slays nothing. He is not bound.

§ 18. Knowledge—its object—knower:—
[These form] the threefold instrumental cause of action (*karma*).
Instrument—action—agent:
[Such is] action's threefold nexus.

§ 19. Knowledge—action—agent:—
[These too are] three in kind, distinguished by 'constituent'.
The theory of 'constituents' contains it [all]:
  Listen to the manner of these [three].

§ 20. That [kind of] knowledge by which one sees
One mode of being, changeless, undivided
In all contingent beings, divided [as they are],
Is Goodness' [knowledge]. Be sure of this.

§ 21. But that [kind of] knowledge which in all contingent beings
Discerns in separation all manner of modes of being,
    Different and distinct,—
This thou must know is knowledge [born] of Passion.

§ 22. But that [kind of knowledge] which sticks to one effect
As if it were all,—irrational,
Not bothering about the Real as the [true] object [of all
  knowledge],
This trifling [knowledge] is Darkness' own. So is it laid down.

§ 23. The work (*karma*) of obligation, from [all] attachment free,
Performed without passion, without hate,
  By one who hankers not for fruits,
  Is called [the work] of Goodness.

§ 24. The work in which much effort is expended
By one who seeks his own pleasure and desire
And ever thinks, 'It is I myself who do it,'
Such [work]'s assigned to Passion.

§ 25. The work embarked on by a man deluded
Who has no thought of consequence, nor cares at all
For the loss and hurt [he causes others] or for the human part
He plays himself, is called [a work] of Darkness.

§ 26. The agent who, from attachment freed,
    Steadfast and resolute,
Remains unchanged in failure or success,
And never speaks of 'I', is called [an agent] in Goodness' way.

§ 27. The agent who pursues the fruits of works,
Passionate, greedy, intent on doing harm, impure,
A prey to exultation as to grief,
Is widely known [to act] in Passion's way.

§ 28. The agent, inept (*ayukta*) and vulgar, stiff and proud,
    A cheat, low-spoken,[1] slothful,
Who's subject to depression, who procrastinates,
Is called [an agent] in Darkness' way.

§ 29. Divided threefold too are intellect (*buddhi*) and constancy
According to the constituents. Listen [to Me,
For I shall] tell it forth in all its many forms,
    Omitting nothing.

§ 30. The intellect that distinguishes between activity
And its cessation, between what should be done and what
    should not,
Between danger and security, bondage and release,
    Is [an intellect] in Goodness' way.

§ 31. The intellect by which lawful right (*dharma*) and lawless
    wrong,
What should be done and what should not
    Are untruly understood,
    Is [an intellect] in Passion's way.

---

[1] Or, 'dishonest'.

§ 32. The intellect which, by Darkness overcast,
Thinks right is wrong, law lawlessness,
    All things their opposite,[1]
Is [an intellect] in Darkness' way.

§ 33. The constancy by which a man holds fast
In check the works of mind and breath and sense,
    Unswerving in self-discipline (*yoga*),
Is constancy in Goodness' way.

§ 34. The constancy by which a man holds fast
[In balance] pleasure, self-interest and righteousness,
Yet clings to them, desirous of their fruits,
Is constancy in Passion's way.

§ 35. [The constancy] by which a fool
Will not let go sleep, fear or grief,
    Depression or exaltation,
Is constancy in Darkness' way.

§ 36. Threefold too is pleasure:
Arjuna, hear this now from Me.
[That pleasure] which a man enjoys after much effort spent,
Making an end thereby of suffering,

§ 37. Which at first seems more like poison
But in time transmutes itself into what seems to be
Ambrosia,—is called pleasure in Goodness' way,
For it springs from that serenity which comes from apperception
    of the self.[2]

§ 38. [That pleasure] which at first seems like ambrosia,
Arising when the senses meet the things of sense,
But in time transmutes itself into what seems to be
Poison, that pleasure, so it's said, is in Passion's way.

§ 39. [That pleasure] which at first
And in the sequel leads the self astray,
Which derives from sleep and sloth and fecklessness,
Has been condemned [3] as pleasure in Darkness' way.

§ 40. There is no existent thing in heaven or on earth
        Nor yet among the gods,
Which is or ever could be free
From these three constituents from Nature sprung.

[1] Or, 'all things contrary [to truth]'.
[2] *ātma-buddhi-prasāda:* Or, 'of one's own intellect (soul)' or 'of intellect and self'.
[3] Lit. 'declared'.

§ 41. To Brāhmans, princes, artisans and serfs
Works have been variously assigned
    By [these] constituents,
And they arise from the nature of things as they are (*svabhāva*).

§ 42. Calm, self-restraint, ascetic practice, purity,
    Long-suffering and uprightness,
Wisdom in theory as in practice, religious faith,—
[These] are the works of Brāhmans, inhering in their nature.

§ 43. High courage, ardour, endurance, skill,
In battle unwillingness to flee,
An open hand, a lordly mien,—
[These] are the works of princes, inhering in their nature [too].

§ 44. To till the fields, protect the kine and to engage in trade,—
[These] are the works of artisans, inhering in their nature;
But works whose very soul is service
Inhere in the very nature of the serf.

§ 45. By [doing] the work that is proper to him [and] rejoicing [in
    the doing],
    A man succeeds, perfects himself.
[Now] hear just how a man perfects himself
By [doing and] rejoicing in his proper work.

§ 46. By dedicating the work that is proper [to his caste]
To Him who is the source of all beings' activity (*pravṛtti*),
By whom this whole universe was spun,[1]
A man attains perfection and success.

§ 47. Better to do one's own [caste] duty, though devoid of merit,
    Than to do another's, however well performed.
By doing the works prescribed by his own nature
    A man meets with no defilement.

§ 48. Never should a man give up the works to which he's born,
    Defective though they be;
    For every enterprise is choked
    By defects, as fire by smoke.

§ 49. With soul (*buddhi*) detached from everything,
With self subdued, all longing gone,
Renounce: and so thou'lt find complete success,
Perfection, works transcended (*naiṣkarmya*).

---

[1] Or, 'pervaded'.

§ 50. Perfection found, now learn from Me
   How Brahman thou mayst reach.
This briefly [will I tell thee],
It is wisdom's highest bourn.

§ 51. Let a man be integrated by his soul (*buddhi*), now cleansed,
Let him restrain [him]self with constancy,
Abandon things of sense,—sound and all the rest,—
Passion and hate let him cast out;

§ 52. Let him live apart, eat lightly,
   Restrain speech, body, mind,
Let him practise meditation constantly,
Let him cultivate dispassion;

§ 53. Let him give up all thought of 'I', force, pride,
Desire and hatred and possessiveness,
Let him not think of anything as 'mine', at peace,—
[If he does this,] to becoming Brahman he's conformed.

§ 54. Brahman become, with self serene,
   He grieves not nor desires;
The same to all contingent beings,
He gains the highest love and loyalty (*bhakti*) to Me.

§ 55. By love and loyalty he comes to know Me as I really am,
   How great I am and who;
And once he knows Me as I am,
   He enters [Me] forthwith.

§ 56. Let him then do all manner of works,
   Putting his trust in Me;
For by my grace he will attain
To an eternal, changeless state (*pada*).

§ 57. Give up in thought to Me all that thou dost;
   Make Me thy goal:
Relying on the Yoga of the soul (*buddhi*),
   Think on Me constantly.

§ 58. Thinking on Me thou shalt surmount
   All dangers by my grace,
But if through selfishness thou wilt not listen,
   Then wilt thou [surely] perish.

§ 59. [But] if thou shouldst think, relying on thine ego,
   'I will not fight,'
Vain is thy resolution,
[For] Nature will constrain thee.

§ 60. Bound art thou by thine own works
Which spring from thine own nature;
[For] what, deluded, thou wouldst not do,
That wilt thou do perforce.

§ 61. In the region of the heart of all
Contingent beings dwells the Lord,
Twirling them hither and thither by his uncanny power (*māyā*)
[Like puppets] fixed in a machine.

§ 62. In Him alone seek refuge
With all thy being, all thy love (*bhāva*);
And by his grace shalt thou attain
An eternal state, the all-highest peace.

§ 63. Of all mysteries most mysterious
This wisdom have I told thee;
Ponder on it in all its amplitude,
Then do whatever thou wilt.

§ 64. And now again give ear to this my all-highest Word,
   Of all the most mysterious:
      'I love thee well.'
Therefore will I tell thee thy salvation (*hita*).

§ 65. Bear Me in mind, love Me and worship Me (*bhakta*),
Sacrifice, prostrate thyself to Me:
So shalt thou come to Me, I promise thee
Truly, for thou art dear to Me.

§ 66. Give up all things of law (*dharma*),
Turn to Me, thine only refuge,
[For] I will deliver thee
From all evils; have no care.

§ 67. Never must thou tell this [Word] to one
Whose life is not austere, to one devoid of love and loyalty
   (*bhakta*),
To one who refuses to obey,
Or one who envies Me.

§ 68. [But] whoever shall proclaim this all-highest mystery
   To my loving devotees (*bhakta*),
Showing the while the highest love and loyalty (*bhakti*) to Me,
   Shall come to Me in very truth.

§ 69. No one among men can render Me
More pleasing service than a man like this;
Nor shall any other man on earth
Be more beloved of Me than he.

§ 70. And whoso shall read this dialogue
Which I and thou have held concerning what is right (*dharmya*),
It will be as if he had offered Me a sacrifice
Of wisdom: so do I believe.

§ 71. And the man of faith, not cavilling,
Who listens [to this my Word],—
He too shall win deliverance, and attain
To the goodly worlds of those whose works are pure.

§ 72. Hast thou listened, Arjuna, [to these my words]
With mind on them alone intent?
And has the confusion [of thy mind]
That stemmed from ignorance, been dispelled?

Arjuna said:
§ 73. Destroyed is the confusion; and through thy grace
I have regained a proper way of thinking (*smṛti*):
    With doubts dispelled I stand
    Ready to do thy bidding.

Sanjaya said:
§ 74. So did I hear this wondrous dialogue
Of [Krishna,] Vasudeva's son
And the high-souled Arjuna,
[And as I listened,] I shuddered with delight.

§ 75. By Vyāsa's favour have I heard
    This highest mystery,
This Yoga from [great] Krishna, Yoga's Lord himself,
    As he in person told it.

§ 76. O king, as oft as I recall
This marvellous, holy dialogue
    Of Arjuna and Krishna
I thrill with joy, and thrill with joy again!

§ 77. And as often as I recall that form of Vishnu—
    Utterly marvellous—
    How great is my amazement!
I thrill with joy, and thrill with joy again!

§ 78. Wherever Krishna, the Lord of Yoga, is,
    Wherever Arjuna, Prithā's son,
There is good fortune, victory, success,
Sound policy assured. This do I believe.

GLOSSARY OF NAMES

Aditi, goddess of the infinite sky and mother of the Ādityas.
Ādityas, a group of celestial deities, of whom Varuna is the chief.
Agni, the fire god.
Angirases, a group of minor deities.
Aryaman, one of the Ādityas.
Asura, originally a class of deity connected chiefly with the sky
and contrasted with the *devas* ('gods'). By the time of the
Brāhmanas and Upanishads, however, the Asuras had
become demonized. In the Upanishads and Bhagavad-Gītā in
this edition the word is translated as 'demon' or 'devil'.
Aśvins, twin gods not unlike Castor and Pollux. Among other
things they are heavenly physicians.

Brahmā, the creator god.
Brihaspati, the high priest of the gods.

Gandharvas, a group of minor male deities connected with
marriage. Later they become the heavenly minstrels.

Indra, in the Rig-Vedic period, becomes the lord of the gods. He
seems to be both a storm god and the Aryan hero *par excellence*.
In later times his importance greatly diminished.

Manu, father of the human race.
Maruts, a group of storm gods closely associated with the
lightning.
Mātariśvan, in the earliest texts fire, later the wind.

Parjanya, god of the rain clouds.
Prajāpati, 'Lord of creatures', the creator god *par excellence*.
Pūshan, a god connected among other things with roads.

Rāma, hero of the second Sanskrit Epic, the *Rāmāyana*, regarded
by his devotees as an incarnation of Vishnu.
Rudra, originally a rather maleficent storm god of no great
importance, he is subsequently identified with Śiva and
worshipped by his devotees as the supreme deity.
Rudras, another name for the Maruts (q.v.).

327

Sādhyas, a class of inferior deities.

Śankara, the greatest of the monistic commentators on the Upanishads and Bhagavad-Gītā.

Savitri, the 'Stimulator' or 'Begetter'. A name of the sun god.

Skambha, the 'Support'. The first principle in two hymns of the Atharva-Veda (pp. 18–27); he later fades out, giving way to Brahman.

Soma, a plant from which an intoxicating fluid was made and which was extensively used in the sacrifice. Later identified with the moon.

Śunahśepa, a hero who was to have been sacrificed to Varuna but was reprieved by him.

Tvashtri, a creator god.

Varuna, a sky and water god, guardian of the cosmic law.

Vasus, a group of deities associated with Indra.

Vāyu, god of the wind.

Virāj, the first emanation from *Purusha*, Primal Man. Later it came to mean primal matter.

Vishnu, in the Rig-Veda he is Indra's comrade in arms. His distinctive act is that he paces out the universe. By the time of the Great Epic he was regarded by his worshippers as being the supreme deity who becomes incarnate from time to time. In the Bhagavad-Gītā Krishna appears as his incarnation.

Viśvakarman, the 'All-Maker'.

Yama, originally the first man; he becomes the ruler of the underworld and god of death.